NATURE AND SCIENTIFIC METHOD

**STUDIES IN PHILOSOPHY
AND THE HISTORY OF PHILOSOPHY**

General editor: Jude P. Dougherty

**Studies in Philosophy
and the History of Philosophy   Volume 22**

Nature and
Scientific Method

edited by Daniel O. Dahlstrom

THE CATHOLIC UNIVERSITY OF AMERICA PRESS
Washington, D.C.

Publication of this book has been funded in part by a gift to the
Associates of The Catholic University of America Press by
Msgr. Edward A. Synan.

Copyright © 1991
The Catholic University of America Press
All rights reserved
Printed in the United States of America

The paper used in this publication meets the minimum
requirements of American National Standards for Information
Science—Permanence of Paper for Printed Library materials,
ANSI Z39.48-1984.
 ∞

LIBRARY OF CONGRESS CATALOGING-IN-PUBLICATION DATA
Nature and scientific method / edited by Daniel O. Dahlstrom.
    p. cm. — (Studies in philosophy and the history of
philosophy ; v. 22)
   Includes bibliographical references.
    1. Science—Methodology.   2. Science—Philosophy.
3. Philosophy of nature.   I. Dahlstrom, Daniel O.
II. Series.
B21.S78 vol. 22
[Q175.3]
100 s—dc20   89-70817
[502.8]
ISBN 0-8132-0723-1 (alk. paper)

Contents

Introduction   vii

PART I: CONTEMPORARY ISSUES

1. ROM HARRÉ, Causality and Reality   3
2. PATRICK A. HEELAN, Hermeneutical Philosophy and the History of Science   23
3. ROBERT SOKOLOWSKI, Explaining   37
4. JUDE P. DOUGHERTY, Abstraction and Imagination in Human Understanding   51
5. FRANCIS J. COLLINGWOOD, Duhem's Interpretation of Aristotle on Mathematics in Science   63
6. NICHOLAS RESCHER, Baffling Phenomena   81
7. MARIO BUNGE, Basic Science Is Innocent; Applied Science and Technology Can Be Guilty   95

PART II: HISTORICAL STUDIES

8. R. F. HASSING, Thomas Aquinas on *Phys.* VII.1 and the Aristotelian Science of the Physical Continuum   109
9. JEAN DE GROOT, Philoponus on Separating the Three-Dimensional in Optics   157
10. JEAN DIETZ MOSS, Ludovico Carbone's Commentary on Aristotle's *De caelo*   175
11. RICHARD J. BLACKWELL, Foscarini's Defense of Copernicanism   199
12. EDITH SYLLA, Galileo and Probable Arguments   211
13. RICHARD H. KENNINGTON, Bacon's Critique of Ancient Philosophy in *New Organon* I   235

14. ANDREA CROCE BIRCH, The Problem of Method in
    Newton's Natural Philosophy   253
15. DANIEL O. DAHLSTROM, Kant's Metaphysics of Nature   271
16. EDWARD H. MADDEN, The Reidian Tradition: Growth
    of the Causal Concept   291

Publications of William A. Wallace, O.P.   309
Contributors   319
Index   323

Introduction

διὸ σκεπτέον πρῶτον τί ἐστιν ἡ φύσις
—Aristotle, *Metaphysics*, 995a18

I

The right method, the right "way after" (*methodos*) something, depends on what we are pursuing. "Hence we should first inquire what nature is," Aristotle concludes. The present volume is a collection of systematic and historical studies addressing the terms of this Aristotelian inference. In the first part of the volume, what we understand nature to be as well as its relation to how we understand nature are examined from contemporary realist and hermeneutical points of view, in the light of the use of models in contemporary physics, and in the face of baffling phenomena.

Rom Harré elaborates the structure of an inductive argument, based upon criteria of disclosability and manipulability, for a *policy realist* reading of scientific theories. Policy realism countenances the indefinite revisability of specific concepts together with the conservation of ontological categories determined by certain basic "affordances," that is, dispositions realized relative to some human practice. Harré concludes by suggesting how quantum field theory, as a physics of affordances, can be given a policy realist reading.

Patrick Heelan's original essay is a speculation on the contribution of methodological and existential hermeneutics to the history and philosophy of science. Likening historical research to the creation of a library's fundamental reference corpus, Heelan illustrates how a (never completely transparent) structure of presumptions grounds interpretation and how accordingly interpretation must be open-ended and holistic, poietic and prudential. In history and in science, Heelan concludes, stability, consensus, and confirmation are achievements, credited to a researcher's narrative act of making past phenomena present to us.

Robert Sokolowski challenges the thesis that the task of the philosopher consists in identifying certain ultimate names and statements (or objects and states of affairs) and reducing other statements (or states of affairs) to them, as is often undertaken in the sciences. Sokolowski argues that the philosophical task consists instead in recovering and clarifying the concrete activities of thinking and disclosing. He concludes by masterfully clarifying how, within the framework of these activities, names and explanations (and things and causes) have dynamically related, yet irreducible roles.

Through an interpretation of Aristotle's account of the role of imagination in knowing, *Jude Dougherty* argues for a realist interpretation of the models, both iconic and sentential, involved in the scientific knowledge of nature. Dougherty recounts the role played by Bohr's image of a liquid drop for the nucleus of an atom, in the imaginations of Lisa Meitner and Otto Frisch as they took the first steps toward the development of the theory of fission. This example illustrates, Dougherty concludes, the Aristotelian claim that thinking always has recourse to images and indeed images of real objects, even as it moves beyond images to some universality.

Francis J. Collingwood recounts how fundamental insights of Aristotle persist in Duhem's philosophy of science. Collingwood argues that Duhem's conception of the fundamental role of the quantification of sensory data, his appreciation of the resulting limitations of physical theory, and even his sometimes criticized reticence regarding conjecture represent a rigorous adherence to the texts of Aristotle. The aim of Collingwood's study is to indicate how Duhem foresaw the need to strip away all qualitative notions in elaborating a mathematics capable of handling physical experiments and collations.

Nicholas Rescher outlines the kinds of possible reaction to the sort of phenomena, prominent in the development of science and in the psychological domain, that are not simply novel or puzzling but cannot be accommodated within an accepted view of the natural order. After suggesting the advisability of accepting such phenomena as real, Rescher sketches features of the particular view of science entailed by this suggestion. Countenancing *baffling phenomena,* Rescher argues, underscores not only the historical, provisional, and indeed teleological character of science but also the possibility and utility of insisting on the separation of phenomena and theory.

Mario Bunge challenges the common nonsense of baldly placing moral blame for the threats of global ecological and nuclear disasters on the shoulders of scientists and technologists. While demonstrating the irreducibility to one another of basic science, applied science, and technology, Bunge concedes that the three domains often in fact overlap; for example, in contrast to technologists, both basic and applied scientists are essentially discoverers. In contrast to basic science, however, applied science and technology are not morally neutral; that is to say, they can be put to evil use. The applied scientist or technologist is morally blameworthy, Bunge concludes, only when participating in the design or planning of what is unambiguously evil.

II

Part II contains essays on specific conceptions of nature and scientific method in the history of science and philosophy, from Aristotle to early American philosophy. Aquinas's interpretation of the motor causality principle first presented in Aristotle's *Physics,* that is, that fundamental principle of premodern physics that everything moved is moved by another, is the subject of R. F. *Hassing*'s essay. Hassing demonstrates that the principle concerns the physical continuum, common to bodies as such in abstraction from any determinate natural form, but according to an Aristotelian conception of motion that cannot be adequately reconstructed in the familiar modern terms of velocity or momentum. In conclusion Hassing disputes the assumption that the motor causality principle is refuted by classical mechanics.

In the second essay *Jean de Groot* examines the physical basis for mathematical demonstration in Philoponus' reconciliation of geometrical optics with Aristotle's theory of light. In the course of rejecting the ancient supposition of visual rays emitted from the eye, Philoponus detaches consideration of the mathematical properties of visual rays from consideration of their physical properties. This move, however, raises questions about the ontological status of those mathematical properties, especially from the standpoint of Aristotle, who explicitly rules out even the theoretical separability of physical forms from matter. Focusing on Philoponus' *Corrolarium de Loco* as well as his commentaries on Aristotle's *Categories* and *Physics,* de Groot demonstrates how Philoponus conceived the separability of quantity on the basis of distinctions delivered by Aristotle himself.

The subject of *Jean Dietz Moss*'s essay is a manuscript she recently uncovered in Florence, containing a commentary on Aristotle's *de caelo* by Ludovico Carbone, an enigmatic figure whose apparent plagiarizing of lectures on logic, given at the Collegio Romano, provides a key piece of evidence for reconstructing Galileo's access to Aristotelian logic. In an attempt to strengthen the case for interrelationships among the Collegio Romano, Carbone, and Galileo, Moss compares Carbone's commentary with Galileo's "Physical Questions," MS 46.

Richard Blackwell addresses the historical significance of the *Letter* of Paolo Antonio Foscarini, placed on the Index by the Catholic church as part of its condemnation of Copernicanism and cited as evidence for the widespread acceptance of that doctrine deemed by the church "false and completely contrary to the divine Scriptures." Blackwell outlines the principles of interpretation advanced by Foscarini, a Carmelite priest and Galileo admirer, in his attempt to demonstrate the possibility of a Copernican reinterpretation of biblical passages and theological doctrines that seem to require geocentrism. Blackwell concludes that this attempt constituted the main document arguing for reconciliation of Copernicanism and Scripture in the hands of church officials prior to the condemnation.

The essay by *Edith Sylla* begins by tracing Averroist and probabilist ways of accommodating reason and revelation in the Middle Ages. This sketch is offered as a backdrop for appreciating the development of Galileo's views on the suitable mode of interpreting biblical statements in the light of probable arguments, relevant to those statements, that might be advanced by science in the future. In this way Sylla suggests the inadequacy of standard attempts to interpret the conceptions of scientific method among the parties to the Galileo affair largely in terms of some sort of disjunctive dilemma of hypothesis or certitude, that is, calculated conjecture to save the phenomena or demonstrative truth. Instead, Sylla argues that due consideration must be given to the rhetorical form of Galileo's writings and the status of the probable arguments they entail.

Bacon's unique and widely influential critique of ancient philosophy in the first part of *New Organon* is the basis for his new concept of method. Yet this critique has been largely neglected by students of Bacon, thus prompting the study by *Richard H. Kennington*. After carefully elaborating the sphere and rationale of the exclusion of final causes in Bacon's attempt to reform the ancient order of demonstration, Kennington attempts to clarify Bacon's rejection of natural species as the starting point of knowledge, in favor of an experimental interpretation of nature, aimed at disclosing the laws of bodies as collections of simple natures. In contrast to standard interpretations, Kennington aims to show the basic harmony of the ideals articulated by Bacon: a new way of contemplation and the mastery of nature.

Andrea Croce Birch examines the various senses of "analysis" and "synthesis" in Pappus' geometry and Newton's natural philosophy, as she attempts to develop the plausible rationale for Newton's controversial methodological remark "as in mathematics, so in natural philosophy." Birch argues that the remark is motivated as much by a concern for methodological differentiation as by a concern for methodological unity.

Daniel O. Dahlstrom examines Kant's demarcation of the first installment of his physics, the so-called metaphysics of nature, from the transcendental philosophy by means of the empirical concept of matter. Taking issue with several critics, Dahlstrom argues that for Kant, whereas transcendental principles are derived from the conditions of any possible experience, the system of metaphysical principles of nature is based upon the concept of objects in motion, a concept empirical in both content and instantiation. On this interpretation, the autonomy of transcendental philosophy and that of physics are respectively assured, though with the implication that the principles of physics are only conditionally necessary.

Edward H. Madden traces the growth of the causal concept in the Scottish and American realist tradition stemming from Thomas Reid. Madden demonstrates how Francis Wayland, the Scot appointed president of Brown University in 1827, amends Reid's views by acknowledging an efficient causality (power) other than agent causality. A serious lacuna in Wayland's analysis, clarification of the kinds of entities constituting causes and effects, is filled by James McCosh, the Scot appointed president of Princeton University in 1868, whose concept of powerful particulars also avoids Wayland's construal of power as an "unknowable ontological tie." Madden shows, in conclusion, that the concept of powerful particulars was meant by McCosh to encompass even the unobservable referents of theoretical terms, thus representing, within the antiskeptical tradition of Reid, a decisive rejection of Reid's own rigid inductivism.

III

The mark of *Rev. William A. Wallace, O.P.*, is evident at every turn in this volume. The essays by Heelan, Moss, and Blackwell build explicitly on his groundbreaking studies of Galileo and the Collegio Romano; in the essays by Harré, Sokolowski, Dougherty, and Rescher there is an unmistakable resonance with the spirit of Wallace's realist approach to the philosophy of science. The studies by DeGroot, Madden, and Collingwood reflect the Aristotelian and Thomistic core of Wallace's convictions and lifelong work, as do the essays by Wallace's own former students, Hassing and Birch. Even Bunge's ethical concern for distinguishing science, applied science, and technology reflects a lifelong penchant of Father Wallace, the former engineer who received a doctorate in theology for his *The Role of Demonstration in*

Moral Theology: A Study of Methodology in St. Thomas Aquinas. None of this is accidental, since the present volume is dedicated to William Wallace, who has taught us all lessons on the necessity of systematically and historically grappling with concepts of nature and of scientific method. Each essay in the present volume was composed in honor of William Wallace, in gratitude for his example and inspiration and in fond appreciation of this historian and philosopher, scholar and priest.

PART I
CONTEMPORARY ISSUES

1   Causality and Reality
ROM HARRÉ

In his monumental work, *Causality and Scientific Explanation*, Father Wallace made a convincing case for the claim that the sciences not only have always been framed within a metaphysics of real causality but would be unintelligible without that framing. In that book he traced in detail the transformations in the way causality has been understood that have attended the growth of science. Inspired by Father Wallace's example I want to address myself to the question of whether perhaps contemporary physics has expanded beyond the framework of classical causality. The first step will be to analyze the classical concept of causation into what I take to be its basic components. Then, in the second phase of the argument, I will try to show that at least part of the classical conception survives contemporary physics as an ineliminable element of its basic conceptual structure.

WEAK AND STRONG CAUSATION

The need to respond to Hume's critique of the commonsense notion of causation[1] (if we can say that there is such a thing) has led to what I shall distinguish as a *weak* and a *strong* understanding of causal production. The regularity or concomitance view, upon which Hume placed such great weight, has found expression in contemporary logic in the material conditional. Read according to this interpretation, "*If* event of type A occurs *then* event of type B will occur" is false only if an event of type A occurs without one of type B following it. This reading has been elaborated by crypto-Humeans such as the late J. L. Mackie into a theory of causation in which the idea of productive causality is replaced by that of necessary and sufficient conditions.[2] From the time of Hume there has been a strong tendency to take the

---

1. David Hume, *An Enquiry Concerning Human Understanding* (1777; reprint, Oxford: Clarendon Press, 1951).
2. J. L. Mackie, *The Cement of the Universe* (Oxford: Clarendon Press, 1974).

ontology of the world in which the causal relation occurs to be exhausted by the concept of "event." If there are, in the end, nothing but events, then in the end what must be causal is of course an event. How an event can be productive or generative seems quite mysterious. But it is easy to see how it can figure as the fulfillment of a necessary and sufficient condition.

The transition to a truly post-Humean conception of causation that at the same time mirrors some important aspects of pre-Humean views is initiated by a shift in ontology, admitting both material beings as samples of extended substances and substantial particulars as the basic particulars of the world. In this ontology events are taken to be changes in the properties of relatively enduring things and so are materially dependent on a grounding in individual substances. The poles, so to say, of the conception of an event are creations and annihilations of things. But in transferring the "*if/then*" form to a discourse relative to this ontology, a radical reinterpretation is required. Instead of recording concomitances between instances of types of events, conditional propositions are now taken to be ascriptions of dispositions and tendencies to the relevant material particulars the assumption of whose existence is part of the implicit content of the proposition. "*If* ignition *then* explosion" must now be filled out to read something like "*If* this dynamite is ignited *then* it will explode." Causation as the manifestation of the dispositions of powerful particulars is the *weak* post-Humean concept.

But the ascription of dispositions to material particulars opens up a further range of scientific questions. Why does this or that particular "have" the disposition? The natural sciences have made enormous progress by looking for answers to this question in terms of the *constitutive* properties of the substances in question, taken in physical (and logical) isolation from one another and independently of spatiotemporal location. Thus the dispositional properties arise from the constituent properties within a certain environment of circumambient conditions. The metaphor of "arise" has to be looked at closely but I rely on commonsense understanding for the moment, if I may. As the bearers of dispositions and tendencies the enduring material particulars then play the role of the causal mechanisms underlying the productive process succinctly described in the original conditional proposition. This original conditional proposition "heads" the conceptual structure, so to speak.

The natural sciences have used both micro- and macrostructural accounts of the constitutive properties that ground dispositions. Each leads to a characteristic explanatory regress. However, the overwhelming majority of such accounts has been microstructural. Despite the numerical preponderance of microstructure over macrostructure as the cited grounding, the technique of referring constitutive properties of individual substances to larger wholes of which they are themselves microstructural and macrostructural explanatory formats is profound because it leads one away from the prescriptions of the "chemical" model, in particular from the idea that substances are fully constituted in isolation from one another.

The *strong* concept of causation then arises by adding a grounding to the dispositions of particulars in terms of their constitutive properties. Causal mechanisms are simply interacting assemblages of powerful particulars. When stimulated by an event (the cause in the old ontology) they behave in such a way as to transform themselves so that an event of the effect type can be observed, detected, or inferred to occur. The general format admits of a great variety of instantiations. The triggering event may be a mixing of a chemical, the completing of a circuit, the capture of a neutron rendering a subatomic nucleus unstable, and so on. How much of this basic layout is preserved in the conceptual structure of the deepest reaches of contemporary physics?

Assessing the significance of post-Humean developments and their complementary pre-Humean revivals for the concept of causality depends, I believe, on how the current debates about realism are resolved. The theory of a class of phenomena is usually presented in a discourse whose terms are purported to denote real beings, occupants of spatiotemporal tracts, the constituents of the mechanisms of causal production adverted to in the preceding analysis of causation. In some cases the powerful particulars whose dispositions are realized in the observed patterns of phenomena are not perceptible. In many more, even when they are, their constituent structures, micro- or macro-, are beyond the reach of observation. Should the explanatory and predictive success of such a theory be taken as grounds for accepting its *denotata* as beings of the same ontological status as the phenomena recorded in the concomitance reading of the conditional statements describing manifest causal processes? This is the classical formulation of the question that defines at least one aspect of the problematics of scientific realism. My next step will be to identify some varieties of realism and to lay out the case for preferring one of them.

TWO VARIETIES OF REALISM

At the first sight it would seem to be uncontroversial that whatever the outcome of the debates concerning its merits, realism should be defined in terms of truth and falsity. This assumption has directed much of the recent debate. The most overt expression of that assumption has been in the principle of bivalence. According to this principle the theoretical propositions of a science are true or false by virtue of the way the world is, regardless of whether we, as scientists, are able to decide the matter for any given theoretical proposition.

However, there are profound objections to this way of presenting scientific realism. They turn on how the preceding formulation can have any actual application to any of the sciences as they are practiced by human beings, in particular whether it can be applied uniformly to all the propositions of a theory. Of course there are logicists who treat all the propositions of a theory on a par, roughly as premises. They will have no qualms about "gross" bivalence. But by the same token they are the most vulnerable to skeptical doubts about the viability of the deductive model as the structure of scientific theories in general. There are at least two main reasons why such applicability is in doubt.

a. It is a point of logic (the paradox of Clavius) that for any given experimental or observational data base there are always, in principle, an infinity of theories that will explain that data base in the sense of serving as a set of premises from which, with initial conditions added, it can be recovered by deduction. One member of the set of possible theories no doubt is actually true, but the selection of the correct one can never finally be made. This is particularly clear for the class of theories that are typical of fundamental physics.

b. Though experimental science attains the kind of results permitting the testable attribution of dispositional properties to beings (whether observable or unobservable) on the basis of the effects to which they are alleged to contribute, we may be unable even in principle to ascribe occurrent properties to such beings. However, for reasons of conceptual convenience we sometimes assign pseudo-occurrent properties to an unobservable being whose dispositions we believe we have seen manifested in some piece of equipment. We speak of the "entropy" of a system without supposing that there are two thermodynamic beings, entropy *and* energy. We may sometimes assign pseudopredicates to terms purporting to denote such beings, though we may have no way in which these pseudo- or dummy predicates can be interpreted even as fictional properties. In the terms of the preceding analysis, though we may come to know the causal powers of such beings, for example, the symptoms they induce, we may be unable to check empirically hypotheses about how those powers are grounded. Even the use of an apparently innocuous term like *being* may be too richly loaded with metaphysics since it does have an air of individuality, of spatiotemporal continuity, and so on, that is unjustified in many contexts. These remarks are particularly apposite in the case of our attempts to make sense of the theories of fundamental physics.

A resolution of some of these difficulties is possible, but it will not emerge before I have first outlined an alternative characterization of realism, inaugurated as far as I know by Robert Boyle and recently reintroduced independently by Ian Hacking and further elaborated in different ways by Joseph Margolis and by me.[3] I shall call this stance "policy realism." It identifies adherence to realism with the adoption of a certain policy in the way one reads theories. The policy realist does not read theories as putatively true or false descriptions of some element of reality, hidden or manifest, but as sets of directions for manipulating observable and unobservable material things that will bring previously unobserved beings, perhaps even some once thought to be unobservable in principle, to the "light of day." He will not be disappointed if the things he finds turn out not to have been correctly described by the theory that served him as his guide. It is a comfort to policy realists to observe that this is how scientists, when uncontaminated by "philosophy," usually read theories, their own, their colleagues', and their rivals'.

I feel impelled to reject truth realism in its universalistic "gross" bivalence form because the arguments against it strike me as strong enough to encourage one to seek some alternative. However, to construct an argument to recommend policy realism as a preliminary classification of the kinds of beings denoted by the nominative terms of scientific theories is needed. For the purposes of this argument one can classify according to the manner in which a putative being is related to human or other sentient observers, remembering that all such observers are embodied in the material world. There is something particularly misleading about presenting the complex *material* practice of performing experiments as if it could be condensed into the process by which a conjunction of singular propositions is generated. Practices are not propositions and much mischief has been done by treating the empirical basis of science in that way.

In Realm 1 are beings that can be observed and studied by observers using their unaided senses. I shall not undertake a defense of a realist

3. Robert Boyle, *The Origin of Forms and Qualities* (Oxford, 1666); Ian Hacking, *Representing and Intervening* (Cambridge: Cambridge University Press, 1983); Joseph Margolis, *Pragmatism Without Foundations* (Oxford: Basil Blackwell, 1986).

theory of perception here. Suffice it to remark that I believe this has been more or less successfully achieved by James J. Gibson.[4]

In Realm 2 are all those beings that are currently taken to be unobservable by reason of technical limitations in our equipment but that are of the same ontological status and often of the same natural kind as some of the beings in Realm 1. Viruses were Realm 2 beings in 1900, and the planets of the stars in the Milky Way are Realm 2 beings now. Finally Realm 3 comprises all those putative or courtesy "beings" that for a diversity of reasons we are fairly sure will never become observable, let alone observed, no matter what technical advances there are. I shall not further analyze the notion of "observation" in this paper, relying instead on the commonsense understanding of the cluster of practices in which scientists and others are engaged. But I do need the distinction between using an instrument to observe something, say a binding site on a virus particle, and using an instrument to detect something, say the radiation from a distant X-ray source.

The argument for policy realism for Realms 1 and 2 runs as follows:

i. There are some cases in which theory has anticipated our experience of Realm 1 beings in the sense that (a) they were identified experimentally; (b) that description actually served as a guide in the carrying out of the material project of searching the world for an exemplar (if a kind is in question) or a sample (if a substance has been proposed) or a particular (if it is singular being), the identifying description of which was adumbrated in theory. Call the successful outcome of such a search a "disclosure."

ii. It is historically contingent whether a given class of beings lies in Realm 1 or Realm 2, since the boundary between these realms can shift with technical innovations.

iii. We should, then, read theories whose *denotata* are in Realm 2 as if they referred to something as guides or prescriptions for research programs designed to establish unambiguous physical links between embodied scientists and instances of the beings in question.

Realms 1 and 2 are linked together by the common role of the disclosure relation as a physical interaction between the beings to which scientists can refer using their theories and those scientists themselves.

But to extend this argument to Realm 3 we need another kind of relation between scientists and material reality, because the beings of Realm 3 can never be manifested. I draw on Boyle and Hacking for

---

4. James J. Gibson, *Ecological Optics* (Ithaca, N.Y.: Cornell University Press, 1983).

a sketch of another relation that sometimes obtains between people and the world, namely manipulation.

In defending the corpuscularian conception of matter Robert Boyle proposed the following line of argument. Analyzing the manipulations we make of material things and substances, for instance, in performing those chemical operations that lead to changes in the forms and qualities of the reagents, we can see that these are essentially mechanical interventions. Mechanical acts have only mechanical effects, so they must have just those kinds of effects on any objects we are manipulating, whether the targets of our actions are observable or unobservable, whichever realm they are in.

Unobservable mechanical changes brought about by such interventions, in their turn, are manifested as changes in the forms and qualities of observable material things. How does this demonstrate the reality of corpuscles? We are able to bring about changes via a manipulation of unobservable entities through our mechanical interventions in nature, and these interventions and changes are of the same kind as those where we can easily observe the whole chain of events. Ian Hacking has proposed a very similar line of argument. In typically epigrammatic style he has remarked, "If you can spray them (e.g., protons) then they are real." Our theories tell us how to manipulate those beings that lie in Realms 2 and 3. We know we have been successful when we get the expected manifestations in Realm 1 *in both bases*. We already have a justified policy-realist reading for Realm 2 theories, and now via the common *manipulation* relation we have tied Realm 2 into Realm 3 ontologically.

The overall structure of the whole argument then looks like this: Realism is justified for Realm 1 theories by observational criteria; Realm 1 and 2 are tied together by the common role of "disclosures" and differ only contingently in their historical boundary vis-à-vis the possibilities of disclosure. Realm 2 and Realm 3 are tied together by the common role of "manipulations" and differ only contingently vis-à-vis the possibility of successful intervention in the unobserved.

The last step in the argument is to link all this to an account of how meaning is acquired by terms that are used to refer to unobserved beings. This will help to build up a set of indicators by which we can pick out those theories that are promising candidates for successful acts of disclosure if they seem to involve Realm 1 and 2 types of beings, and for successful acts of manipulation if they seem to involve Realm 2 and Realm 3 beings. This is an *inductive* argument, since we have good evidence that promising theories are both successful disclosure-wise and as regards manipulation for Realm 1. Realm 1 and Realm 2 type theories differ only contingently and not in ways relevant to disclosure, so we have inductive support for applying the same reasoning to justifying a policy-realist reading of Realm 2 theories. By parity of reasoning the tie of Realm 1 to Realm 2, including as it does both disclosure and manipulative success, supports via the manipulative component an induction to Realm 3 type theories. We have created an inductive argument for policy realism without committing ourselves to the unqualified, universalistically applied bivalence principle.

But we have yet to give an account of the characteristics of a theory that would make it "promising" for a policy-realist reading. I shall call this characteristic "plausibility." A full account of what makes a theory plausible is beyond the scope of this paper. I need only that feature of the processes of theory construction that is immediately relevant to the support for the two-stage inductive argument for policy realism. Don Schon, in an insufficiently noticed work, offered a general account of the genesis of theoretical concepts, commensurate with the "models and analogies" account popularized by Stephen Toulmin, Mary Hesse, Max Black, and others.[5] For the more general catachretic process Schon coined the phrase "displacement of concepts." A theory comes into being when a concept well entrenched in one context, say "selection" in the discourse of farmers, is displaced to a new context in talk about nature in general. The power and the intelligibility of the concept in its new context depend on our implicit grasp of the context from which it was displaced. Model building and analogizing, and so on, are special cases of Schonian displacement. It is not hard to see how the displacement relation can be used to identify plausible theories. The intension (or connotation) of a concept can be analyzed hierarchically. Aristotle's intensional hierarchy of essence, property, and accident can be modernized to a threefold structure: ontological category (the most resistant to revision), natural kind, and finally definite description (the least resistant).

A displaced concept will a fortiori suffer some revision. "Domestic selection," for example, is of the same ontological category as "natural selection," but the concept of "natural selection" does not include the root idea of intentional decisions by a selector. However, it is the conservation of ontological category and sometimes of natural kind that endows a displaced (theoretical) concept with its power to guide real world searches, since it specifies the kind of being for which we should

---

5. Donald A. Schon, *The Displacement of Concepts* (London: Tavistock, 1963); Stephen E. Toulmin, *Philosophy of Science* (London: Hutchinson, 1953); Mary B. Hesse, *The Structure of Scientific Inference* (London: Macmillan, 1981); Max Black, *Models and Metaphors* (Ithaca, N.Y.: Cornell, 1963).

search and so the nature of the search procedure itself. Shall we look in Africa, or through a telescope, or use a bolometer or buy some time on the big accelerator at CERN? J. L. Aronson's notion of "common ontology" deploys essentially the same scheme in his treatment of some classical problems of philosophy of science, such as reduction.[6] A theory is plausible for policy realism if its concepts are displacements that preserve certain kind or category characteristics. Which kind must be preserved can be understood only relative to the possibility of setting up research programs, that is, relative to a policy-realist reading. Thus the virus theory of disease is plausible for a policy-realist reading since the concept of "virus" is such that viruses are a subcategory of organisms, and organisms are occupants of spatiotemporal tracts; that is, they are a subsubcategory of material things. Thus we know what it would be like to find a virus. But it does not take much reflection to realize that we have no idea at all what it would be like to find a quark, a field potential, or an intermediate vector boson, in the mundane sense of "find." I shall argue that the ontological status of these Realm 3 beings, as delivered to us by their displacement history, is such that it is their manipulability not their demonstrability that is at issue in a policy-realist reading of, say, quantum field theory.

REVISABILITY, DISCLOSURE, AND MANIPULATION

What does the indefinite revisability argument against a general use of the bivalence principle to characterize realism show, in the light of the two-step inductive argument in favor of policy realism? Discussions with J. L. Aronson have convinced me that the bivalence principle does have an important part still to play, and that notions like "verisimilitude," "scientific progress" as "getting close to the truth" can, in a limited but very important way, be retained. In simple policy realism, instead of defining scientific progress as getting closer to the truth, it is conceived in terms of having a more comprehensive and better authenticated "museum" or "collection" of specimens of the ontological categories and natural kinds described by theory, and by having a better "tested" and more reliable and extensive repertoire of material practices. Using "truth" to characterize these "collections" seemed a tendentious move since, to continue the metaphor, the staff of the museum are forever reclassifying the exhibits, weeding out forgeries, and so on. But in museums there are some superordinate

---

6. Jerrold L. Aronson, *A Realist Philosophy of Science* (London: Macmillan, 1986).

categorizations that do not change. No matter how many Dutch masters turn out to be van Megerens they are all still *paintings*. This is where the thrust of Aronson's reminder is to be felt.

Historical examples show that the evolution of a theory family such as the theory of organic evolution, the theory of natural selection, or the quantum field theory in which all intermediate vector bosons are generically photonic, under the joint pressures of theoretical invention and empirical discovery, preserves the underlying source model, or as Aronson puts it, the common ontology. Revisability is indefinite, not infinite. Successful disclosures fix the ontological category of kinds of beings in conceptual displacements from Realm 1 and Realm 2. Successful manipulations fix the high-level categories for Realm 2 to Realm 3 displacements. Given this it seems that we can say that there are truth claims that scientists can make that are immune from the standard revisability argument upon which skepticism and ultimately antirealism usually rest. These are the ontological claims that can be made after successful disclosures or successful manipulations.

But how do successful disclosures and manipulations fix ontological level truth claims? The induction from Realm 1 to Realm 2 depends on the way ontological kinds are preserved in the displacement of concepts. An organism and a microorganism are both *things* (they exhibit stable dispositions). Fixing the ontological kind also fixes the mode of search (for example, exploring space and time) and criteria for having found an exemplar germane to research projects in this or that domain. In general one cannot find that which does not exist *in the way that is presupposed in the mode of search*. The Realm 2 to Realm 3 induction depends on similar considerations, with manipulation conditions playing the same role for this leg of the argument that search modes did in the first leg. The empirical principle is similar, too. One cannot manipulate beings of one ontological category with techniques appropriate to those of another.

In this way a revisability hierarchy appears quite naturally that orders the propositions of a theory taxonomically. We are often wrong about the detailed specifications of the beings whose existence is confirmed for us by either disclosures or manipulations. (The skeptic needs the confirmed cases of his thrust, since he bases his case on the thought that no matter how robust our empirical knowledge may seem it is nevertheless revisable.) But once this kind of existential confirmation or disconfirmation through experiment has occurred then the ontology is stabilized *at the level of the ontological category that has been instantiated in the mode of search that led to the disclosure or in the method of manipulation that succeeded*. Retrospectively then we can say that there is a qualified bivalence aspect to, or element in, policy realism. Prior to all empirical investigations we can say that the ontological propositions of a theory family are true or false by virtue of the way the world is, whether or not we now know it, and we can mean something useful by that remark. This narrower version of bivalence does have application in the natural sciences, unlike the generic version, which has proved so vulnerable to a very simple skeptical application of the revisability argument.

A careful reading of Hume shows that his skepticism regarding the efficacy of strict reason in natural science took two forms. The one that has attracted more attention has been his "scope" skepticism, the attack on induction as a technique of reason that would lead us inexorably from the particular to the general, from today to the whole scope of past, present, and future. One must always remind oneself that Hume never doubted that induction was a vital human practice. From the point of view of the philosophy of physics his "depth" skepticism is of equal importance. His attack on the use of concepts of "power" and "causal efficacy," seen in the context of the debates in eighteenth-century philosophy of physics, is an intervention in a dispute about the proper ontological foundations for physical theory: material atoms or real forces. Hume was an antirealist.

My dispute is with the Humean skepticism of the second kind, the kind of skepticism that has been revived in recent years by van Fraasen with his "critical empiricism" and by Laudan with his "problem-solving." Neither is prepared to admit the inductive arguments sketched previously. Both reject the conclusion that theory anticipates experience in the pragmatic way of the policy realist position. Both these authors seem to accept the reasonableness—but I hope not the rationality!—of induction. Their concerns arise from doubts about the legitimacy of the use of theory to plumb the depths. My argument is inductive, from cases in which plausibility demonstrably facilitates programs of material search to the claim that it is reasonable to depend on it in cases yet to be investigated. On the general principle that you cannot have your cake and eat it, once induction is admitted as a reasonable procedure anywhere in our intellectual life then the fact that my philosophical arguments to depth antiskepticism are inductive cannot be raised as a defect in them.

But the problem of the status of the "platform" of these inductions remains. Why does a disclosure of a material thing, in physical interaction with an embodied scientist, count as evidence for a robust ontological claim? Whatever happens subsequently, science will never go back on the claim that the nucleus of Halley's comet is a black *thing* about the size of the island of Jersey. There are several possibilities. It might be that the being disclosed is functioning as a meaning-giving sample for the concept of "thing." But at this late stage of the history of the world that is implausible. Something close to this though may be right. "If *this* is not a thing I do not know what is (I'll be a monkey's uncle)!" The being in question is of a type that is or once was criterial for the concept. But, as traditional skepticism has insisted, even that is an induction and may prove to have been mistaken (compare A. J. Ayer's pen that could have turned into a pig). But this is the wrong kind of skepticism to move a philosopher of science. This is the "neurotic" kind immune to any considerations of reason, such as the chemical analysis of the material of Ayer's lively pen. It seems to me that the only other route to a denial of the truth of the ontological statements made on the basis of the disclosures of science is to turn to traditional grand metaphysical theories, such as Berkeleyan idealism. That level to debate is one into which I shall not enter.

DISPOSITIONS, AFFORDANCES, AND UR-STUFF

The discussion of the proper form in which to express dispositional concepts was sparked off in recent times by the extensive use that Gilbert Ryle[7] made of such concepts in his attempts to analyze psychological concepts in such a way as to demonstrate the implausibility of Cartesian mentalism. For the most part Ryle was content to express dispositional attributions in simple conditional propositions. This left open the question of how one could justify the attribution of a disposition to a quiescent being, to a being that had not up till the moment of asking ever manifested the behavior referred to by the consequence clause in the dispositional conditional. Armstrong, so far as I know, was the first to point out that the epistemological demands for the use of dispositional concepts had an ontological consequence, though he did not express it that way. There must be some occurrent state that fits or readies the being in question to exhibit the behavior in question when the conditions are right, that is, when the antecedent clause is instantiated. This thought has led to the proposal of a generic form for dispositional attributions that conjoins a conditional with a categorical clause as follows:

If C then D in virtue of N

where N is a placeholder for an account of the relevant occurrent

---

7. Gilbert Ryle, *The Concept of Mind* (London: Hutchinson, 1949); David Armstrong, *A Materialist Theory of the Mind* (London: Routledge and Kegan Paul, 1968).

properties of the being that has the disposition, and relevance in this context is determined by some (usually scientific) theory.

Reflection on real cases leads one to notice that which of its many dispositions any being displays both momentarily and in the course of its life history will depend on the circumambient conditions that elicit it. There are very few dispositions that are elicited by every possible environmental circumstance, and it takes a nice touch with philosophical analysis to show that this case differs from that of occurrent properties. Dispositionalists are inclined to be rather demanding as to which occurrent properties they will be willing to take nondispositionally, those not to be treated as displays of permanently activatable dispositions. In the case of many dispositions the most important variable is human practice.

J. J. Gibson has given us the word *affordance* for dispositions that are realized relative to some human practice. A floor appears to us as solid; that is, among other things we see it as affording walking. Indeed, the very concept of "solidity' is largely exhausted by human relative affordances. Something of the same idea can be found in the writings of Edmund Husserl. He pointed out that we do not see a pair of scissors only as two crossed pieces of steel but as an instrument or tool for cutting, and it is in that guise that it "appresents" itself to us. In philosophy of science there has been a widespread neglect of the significance of experiments. Most philosophers influenced by logicist ways of dealing with philosophical problems have forgotten the experiments as a material practice and concentrated only on the role that descriptive propositions taken from the results play in logical moves consequential on the *reading* of the experiment. But experiments are human actions and incorporate human perceptibility demands. Human choice and the exigencies of human technology determine which of its indefinitely extensive range of dispositions and powers a tract of physical reality will display to human investigators. This suggests that the properties investigated in scientific research are affordances.

POLICY REALISM IN THE PHILOSOPHY OF PHYSICS

In contemplating the literature of modern physics one author stands out for his philosophical profundity, namely Niels Bohr.[8] The obscurity of his writings and the delphic character of his verbal pronouncements are sometimes cited as evidence of an alleged confusion of

---

8. Niels Bohr, *Atomic Physics and Human Knowledge* (New York: Wiley, 1958).

mind. I think not. It seems to me that there is profound kinship between Bohr's philosophy of physics and Kant's system of critical philosophy as presented in the *Critique of Pure Reason* (first edition) and in *The Metaphysical Foundations of Natural Science*.[9]

Kant:

(i) noumena produce an undifferentiated flux of experience

(ii) categories applied as schematisms synthesize the flux into ordered structures that appear in our experience as phenomena

Bohr:

(i) Ur-stuff from a human point of view is undifferentiated

(ii) the concepts of classical physics, realized as apparatus, acting on the Ur-stuff, engender that which we experience as experimental phenomena

According to Kant the phenomena we experience must therefore exemplify certain a priori categories such as causality and substance (the doctrine of the synthetic a priori). According to Bohr the results of experiments must always be expressed in the conceptual system of classical physics (one possible reading of his correspondence principle).

If this is right there are no more phenomena in the absence of apparatus for Bohr than there were for Kant prior to the syntheses. It is this Kantianism that challenges the fundamental principle of experimentation in classical physics: that the apparatus is transparent, that there is an unambiguous causal relation between a preexisting state of the world and the state of the apparatus that, in suitable circumstances, is taken as its measure. If contemporary physics were like classical physics we could ask meaningfully whether the state of some experimental apparatus were or were not a faithful representation or measure of some state of the world, the independent classical phenomenon. But for Bohr there is no such thing as the independent phenomenon. Wave equations do not describe evolving physical systems that exist and change independently of the apparatus built to investigate them. There are no such systems. The phenomena we induce in nature are the product of an interaction specific to this or that kind of experimental equipment. There is electron-inducing equipment that produces tracks *described* as the trajectories of electrons, but the tracks are the product of the apparatus.

9. Immanuel Kant, *Critique of Pure Reason*, trans. N. Kemp Smith (1787; reprint, London: Macmillan, 1952); *Metaphysical Foundations of Natural Science*, trans. J. Ellington (1786; reprint, Indianapolis: Bobbs Merrill, 1970).

What can we say about the Ur-stuff of the world? We cannot say what it would be like if there were no apparatus interacting with it. So it enters physics as a pure surd. But can we say on the basis of experiments that "it" has this or that disposition? Has "it" a disposition to appear electronwise in this class of equipment and mesonwise in that? But dispositions that are strictly relative to human practices are affordances. More carefully put, then, it follows from the Bohr position that what can be known about the world as Ur-stuff is what it can or does afford. It is as if our knowledge of ice were confined to whether it seemed to us walkable or not. Its thickness would lie outside the boundaries of attributes ascribable to it on the basis of what we could do.

The difference between ascribing simple dispositions and ascribing affordances expresses something like a Newtonian as against a Kantian conception of physics. For Newton, once one had a clear idea of the dispositions of observable material things—their impenetrability, mobility, inertia, and so on—one was then entitled to build up a conceptual picture of the unobserved real stuff of the world by, as Newton said, "esteeming" these to be the universal properties of matter. No mention is made of the conditions under which these dispositions are manifest, and none need be made because Newton, like Boyle, thought of these as "cosmickal" dispositions, that is, true of all material beings independent of time, place, and conditions. But on Bohr's Kantian-style view we can say only that the Ur-stuff affords spin-up electrons, polarized photons, and so on. These are phenomena, brought into being through the use of apparatus. We are not justified in ascribing to the Ur-stuff dispositions to appear in such ways.

Policy realism (even with the heavily qualified addition of the ontological level bivalence principle) as applied to fundamental physics must be worked out in terms of a search for beings (entities, processes, and substances) that are afforded by the Ur-stuff. It follows that a noncancellable contribution from the apparatus must be taken into account both conceptually and ontologically when the results of a search program, motivated by the "guide" interpretation of theoretical terms, are assessed.

CAN QUANTUM FIELD THEORY BE "READ" REALISTICALLY?

It is usually instructive to tackle a fairly new scientific specialty as philosophical example. Quantum field theory has many interesting aspects, not least the ontological ambiguity that attaches, at first sight, to its leading concepts. Is it a keyhole through which we can catch a glimpse of the causal mechanisms that engender the interactions among subatomic particles? Or is it just another clever piece of auxiliary mathematics, like the Hilbert space representation of quantum mechanics?

The theory is made intelligible through the concept of "intermediate vector particle." The field by means of which one electron acts upon another is replaced by an exchange of virtual particles. The electromagnetic interaction is pictured as an exchange of virtual photons. Picturing of interactions is systematized by the use of Feynman diagrams, which resemble photographs of the tracks scored out in suitable media by real particles. Included in these "pictures" are the notional tracks of virtual particles. What is the source of the specification of particles of this strange status? A quantum mechanical description of an interaction between "two particles" eventuates in an algebraic expansion that is read as a set of amplitude terms. Each amplitude term expresses one mode of interaction, and the set is ordered in the familiar quantum mechanical way by the probability of that mode's being experimentally realized. Each amplitude term can be "parsed" in such a way as to yield (for a two particle interaction, say an electromagnetic interaction between two electrons) three "parts." The meaning of two of these is readily fixed as referring to the two electrons that are interacting; the third "part" is the field term. What makes quantum field theory interesting is that the meaning for the third term is created within the same ontology as the meanings of the two "electron" terms. In the example we are discussing it is called the *photon propagator.* Algebraically the "spare" term looks like a photon expression; at least it is markedly photonic. Read in that framework it now appears in corpuscularian guise, comfortably represented by a wavy line in the relevant Feynman diagram. It is now entered into the ontology as an intermediate vector particle (IVP). For each interaction type there are indefinitely many such diagrams, and of course correspondingly indefinitely many IVPs. How seriously should we take all this picturing? According to Feynman not seriously at all.

But much has happened since Feynman drew his first diagram. An experimental program motivated by a corpuscularian reading of the physics, just as in the preceding brief sketch, has been markedly successful. The significance of the program can be seen only if the pattern of reasoning underlying it is brought out clearly. Let us start by reflecting on the electromagnetic interaction as presented in quantum field theory. How did we know how to read the "spare" term? It looked like a photonic term as it would appear in the physics of, say, the propagation of light. Taken naively we now seem to have made room

Causality and Reality 19

for at least two species of the genus *photon*. There is the manifest species and now there is the virtual species as well. But is not this slipping from realizing that we have two species of a generic concept to thinking that we must therefore have two species of a generic being? It looks as if taking the virtual member of the pair seriously as a kind of physical reality is a simple example of the fallacy of reification. There matters might have rested but for the extension of the quantum field theoretical program to other kinds of interaction, particularly the weak (neutrino-electron) and the strong (neutron-proton) interactions.

The meaning of the third "part" of the amplitude term is created within the same ontology as the meanings of the other parts. But no virtual photon can ever be manifested experimentally. Then how is the semantics that is expressed in the Feynman diagram to be controlled? It would be a mistake to see this control as stemming from some deeply held ontological prejudice or metaphysical theory in favor of a corpuscularian picture of the universe. It seems clear that it is the exigencies of experimentation that fix the picture, the material practices through which high-energy physics is carried on, that is, by recording *tracks* and *clicks*. This fact about our equipment, that that is what it can do, is reflected in the iconic conventions of the Feynman diagram. We could equally well point to photonic talk as to trackish diagrams.

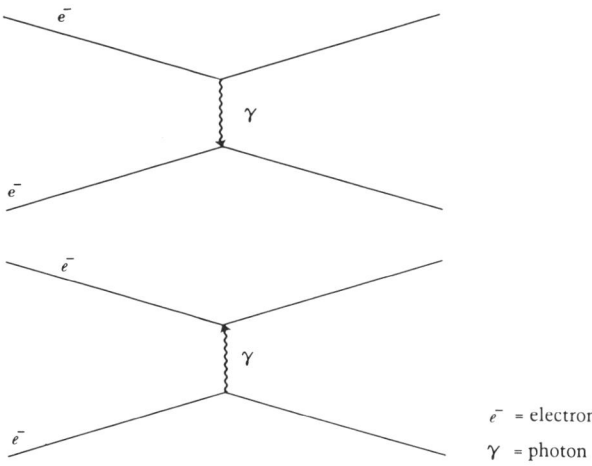

$\bar{e}$ = electron
γ = photon

Since it is the apparatus that determines that nature shall be displayed as tracks and clicks, and not any other way, the iconic conventions of the Feynman diagram and the readiness among physicists to use photonic talk underline the fact that quantum field theory is a physics of affordances.

Properties such as energy and momentum are assigned to IVPs through conservation principles provided that the "exchange" picture is made sufficiently sophisticated. Since each diagram represents a possible state of affairs, the two diagrams in the subjoined figure must be superimposed. They are equally likely. Furthermore since each amplitude term has its own diagram in which more and more complex modes of exchange are pictured and since there are an indefinite number of amplitude terms in the algebraic expansion and so an indefinite number of such diagrams for each interaction type, say electron-electron, the number of IVPs invoked in the total set of possibilities, each with its probability weighting, is not sharp. One way of thinking about quantum mechanics would have all these exchange modes somehow *there*, only one of which can be realized in any one experimental moment. This seems a bad convention for understanding the physics of the electromagnetic interaction, or any other for that matter. A better way of looking at the matter is to say that none of these alternatives is real, waiting in the wings to be called on stage by being coupled with an operator representing an observable. Instead each represents a real world state that the Ur-stuff affords in interaction with the apparatus that realizes electron affordances as ionizing tracks. This interpretation is notional since there is no way in which any further step toward realizing IVPs as tracks or clicks could be achieved. Why then do we not consign them to the role of a heuristic model and take quantum field theory as a sophisticated piece of auxiliary mathematics?

The answer is quite clear once we turn our attention to the role played by these concepts in some typical patterns of practical reasoning. I have already pointed out that adopting photonic talk leads one to see that "photon" is a genus of which there are two species, real and virtual. In the case of the electromagnetic interaction the photonic talk is controlled by the empirically determined properties of the real species. Under the genus "photon" we take in only beings that are represented in physics by expressions something like ih/q. But when the quantum field theory is extended to other interactions the analogy relation between the real and the virtual species is reversed. In the case of the weak interaction the characteristics of the IVP (the $W+$ and $W-$ particles) were given through the mathematical analysis, which was itself modeled on that successfully achieved for the electromagnetic interaction. But there was not yet an experimentally real species of W particle. The success of the IVP, the virtual species in maintaining the structure of the mathematical analysis, suggested that it would be reasonable to "work backward," so to say, to try to find a free W particle. The strength of this pattern of reasoning seems to me to be dependent on taking the affordance line. It is not that quantum field theory depicts that loose in the universe, so to say, there are W particles and we can find them, but that taking them to be as specified suggests that apparatus that would realize W particles as affordances of the Ur-stuff could be constructed. What should the Ur-stuff afford that would make us say such a thing? It will have to afford a certain pattern of tracks. In the neutral-current events that are explicated by the quantum field theory treatment of the weak interaction, we have once again a genus, the W particle, and two species. The virtual species is presented in the Feynman diagram and the real species would be presented in a certain result of a track-seeking experiment at CERN. Photonic talk—for these are yet another variety of photon—if one goes by the form of their algebraic representation, is controlled in this case by the virtual species, the reverse of the direction of control we saw in the electromagnetic case. Thus "W particle talk" is a way of talking about certain particulate affordances of the Ur-stuff available to people because of the apparatus at CERN.

What inclines us to say that W particles are real? Or, as physicists are inclined to say, that they have been discovered? It is not that they have been disclosed to view in the way that bacteria or the stars of the Milky Way have been. Instead we know that by imposing fields on the apparatus it is possible to transform the topography of the tracks in just the way that in similar circumstances we transform the topography of the tracks of charged particles of other sizes and charges right up to pieces of cork hanging on strings and oil drops in a Millikan apparatus. There is a common principle of manipulation and even a common technique that applies across the Realm 1 and Realm 2 to Realm 3 boundary. We know what is the ontological kind of W particles because we know what is the kind of all those other genera of "particles" that we can manipulate in similar ways. But are the W beings "particles"? Yes and no. We have learned by now to be rather cautious in taking affordances for independent states of the universe. Yes, W particles are particles, since they make tracks. But they are the tracks they have made because that is the kind of apparatus we have set up. We have "squeezed" the Ur-stuff into track-making entities, and why not call them "particles"? After all, their remote ancestor in the ontological induction was the charged cork ball in the old-fashioned electroscope.

2   Hermeneutical Philosophy and the History of Science
PATRICK A. HEELAN

This essay is dedicated to William Wallace, a great natural philosopher but, above all, a great source historian in the history of science and a wise interpreter of those sources. I wish I could have presented to him on this occasion a small work, a miniature, of his specialty, such as a document, say, from the Jesuit archives explaining the anomalous minute in the Galilean file of the Holy Office for 26 February 1616. But it is not my trade to search out such documents nor my good fortune to know more than the average curious reader about this minute. The essay I shall contribute is a speculative piece about hermeneutical method in the history and philosophy of science. The essay develops thoughts inspired, on the one hand, by Husserl and Heidegger and on the other by the exquisite fragments from the past recovered by historians among whom we have the privilege of having known one of the greatest in our time.

HERMENEUTICS: METHODOLOGICAL AND
EXISTENTIAL HERMENEUTICS

The nature of the link between scientific theory and scientific phenomena is suggested by the view of the early Heidegger that all human knowledge is hermeneutical.[1] Hermeneutics (or—what is the same thing—interpretation) may be taken either as a *method of inquiry,* or as *the way of being (or Being) characteristic of human life.* The former is the art or science of interpreting explicit language or symbols and is some-

---

1. See Martin Heidegger, *Being and Time* (New York: Seabury Press, 1962), also Paul Ricoeur, *Hermeneutics and the Human Sciences,* trans. J. B. Thompson (Cambridge: Cambridge University Press, 1981), and Patrick Heelan, "Perception as a Hermeneutical Act," *Review of Metaphysics* 37 (1983): 61–75. Hermeneutics also enters into C. S. Peirce's analysis of "Thirdness": that something—a *sign*—is taken to stand for something—an *object*—by an *interpretant,* the act of interpretation by a community of interpreters. See Peirce (1931–58), vol. 1, 1.300–1.353, esp. 1.338; also 2.228–2.308; for the interpretative character of perception, see 5.182–5.184.

times called *methodological hermeneutics*. The latter, often called, by contrast, *existential hermeneutics*, defines what being human is. The human way of being-in-the-world means that every act of human understanding is mediated by human life and culture, by a cultural role. Hermeneutics in this double sense is, of course, both a new method and a new starting point for philosophy.

To the contrary, the classical tradition of metaphysics and epistemology assumed the existence of a privileged realistic standpoint, absolute, universal, or transcendental, that was not a function of human life: I call this classical tradition *Demiurgic*. In this tradition, all knowledge that was truly "science" claimed to have such a viewpoint. At first, philosophy claimed this viewpoint, then Christian theology, then modern science. Both modern science and modern philosophy inherit the principle of the Demiurgic viewpoint from the classical Hellenistic tradition.

It is a presupposition of hermeneutical phenomenology, however (and of this study), that the essence of being human is being-in-the-world, that is, being oriented hermeneutically to a social and historical world that we understand to the extent that we negotiate a path within it. In keeping with this viewpoint, I take scientific knowledge to be just a form of worldly truth—though admittedly in our culture a particularly important one—fashioned by a historical human community that gives it temporal and local expression. We humans belong among worldly things, to the domain of *res* or *reality*. To this domain also belong the worldly things we know, among them scientific phenomena. The general claim that all natural and naturalizable human knowledge, scientific, philosophical, and theological, is historically, culturally, and geographically situated does not imply that such inquiry is in the end sterile but only that all truth for humans is *poietic*. As such it is worldly, that is, intrinsically conditioned by the historical world we inhabit, or it is conditioned by the power of the historical human imagination to envision other possible worlds and to discover invariants at their center.

THE HERMENEUTICAL CIRCLE:
METHODOLOGICAL HERMENEUTICS

There is a certain reciprocity characteristic of all hermeneutical activity, whether methodological or existential: this is the so-called hermeneutical circle.[2]

---

2. See Heidegger's *Being and Time*, 188–95; also Hans-Georg Gadamer, *Truth and Method*, trans. G. Barden and J. Cumming (New York: Seabury Press, 1975). For an

First, consider methodological hermeneutics, that is, interpretation as a method of inquiry, and consider the stages through which such an inquiry passes. For an example, I take Wallace's work on MS 27, 46, and 71 of Galileo's early Latin manuscripts.[3] The interpreter also comes upon a text in the course of historical inquiry. Wallace's inquiry is focused on the continuities between medieval Aristotelianism and Galileo's "new science." The same texts that drew Wallace's attention are pertinent to many other kinds of inquiry also, such as the history of education or the influence of the Jesuits on the new science. But in Wallace's case, his focus of interest emerged naturally, as it were, out of an interest in the philosophy of science and a respect for the scholastic achievements of the premodern period.

The interpreter must have some initial background interest in the text, for otherwise, why should he or she be concerned with it? The pursuit of this interest brings a focus to the chase, it provides it with a definite structure antecedent to all found answers, and it provides a criterion for success in terms of which both the chase and the quarry will be evaluated. This structure of interests against the background of unquestioned knowledge is what Hans-Georg Gadamer calls "the prejudice-structure" of the interpreter. The use of the word *prejudice* in this sense does not fit comfortably with common English usage; the sense would be better captured, perhaps, by the term "structure of presumptions." Such a structure of presumptions, says Gadamer, is not a bad thing; to the contrary, it is necessary for any inquiry and a good thing if open to criticism and revision.[4] The structure of interests that focuses the inquiry may narrow or change in the course of the inquiry itself, but the priority of what Gadamer calls "prejudice structure" to scholarly goal will always remain.

The question of continuity between Aristotle and the "new science" turned out to depend on determining that the sources of MS 21 and 46 were Aristotelian and on showing that they were contemporaneous with the writing of MS 71 on motion. By studying textbooks of the period in a Paris library, Wallace showed the dependency of MS 21 on the lecture notes of Jesuits of the Collegio Romano belonging to the period around 1590. Other studies had already shown that MS

---

excellent summary, see Gadamer's essays in John M. Connolly and Thomas Keutner (eds.), *Hermeneutics versus Science? Three German Views* (Notre Dame, Ind.: University of Notre Dame Press, 1988), and pp. 30–36 of the introduction by the editors.

3. See, for example, W. Wallace, "Reinterpreting Galileo on the Basis of His Latin Manuscripts," 3–28 in W. Wallace (ed.), *Reinterpreting Galileo* (Washington, D.C.: Catholic University of America Press, 1986). The Galileo references are to the National Edition, Antonio Favaro (ed.), *Le Opere di Galileo Galilei*, 20 vols. (Florence: G. Barbera, 1890–1909).

4. See Gadamer, *Truth and Method*, 235–74.

46 was also derivative from the lectures of certain Jesuits teaching at the Collegio Romano at the same period. By bringing all three manuscripts together, Wallace was able to provide convincing evidence that Galileo continued a medieval tradition, originally centered in Paris and Oxford, of interpreting Aristotle in a way that favored mathematics in the natural sciences. The mathematical interpretation of Aristotle opposed the then dominant Averroist tradition of Padua and other scholastic centers.

The key theses of the mathematical interpretation of Aristotle that flourished in Paris, Oxford, and then in the late sixteenth century were for a while taught at the Collegio Romano, were that mathematics could be descriptive of the natural world and that mathematics was to be favored (according to the prescriptions of the *Posterior Analytics*) in giving demonstrations in the natural sciences.

There were also other interests motivating Galilean studies. An important one centered on human intellectual and political liberation, and it was in competition with these Enlightenment interests that Wallace's work had most significance. Carried forward by the image of the Copernican revolution, these Enlightenment interpretations wanted to assess, and to magnify, the revolutionary differences between medieval science and the new and modern science of Galileo. The modern era burst into flower in the age of Galileo, Descartes, Bacon, and Locke; it saw itself as a new beginning, an *Instauratio,* a people newly liberated from the tyranny of mind and body exercised by the authorities of the medieval world. This movement of the Enlightenment culminated in the nineteenth century with the positivist account of modern science that endowed the origins of science with a mythic stature, making Galileo its hero in the warfare against superstition and tyranny. Here, by contrast with Wallace, the stress was on discontinuity with the past.

These two approaches to the texts of Galileo were complemented by yet a third. Alexandre Koyré wanted to trace the "origins" of the *mathematical ideal* of contemporary science, as exemplified by the mathematical physics of the Göttingen school of the first two decades of this century, to Galileo and his contemporaries but particularly to Galileo. Such an ideal as it presents itself in the contemporary practice of science seemed to him to be Platonic, rather than Aristotelian, in character and grounded in the thinking of the ancient atomists whom Aristotle so strongly opposed.[5] Koyré's "origins" owed much to Edmund Husserl.

5. See A. Koyré, *Galilean Studies* (Atlantic Highlands, N.J.: Humanities Press, 1978), 74 and passim.

Despite the fact that all three interpretations are evidentially grounded, all three fall under some "suspicion" in relation to the "prejudice-structure" of their research programs. Each must be assessed by subjecting its "prejudice-structure" to critical awareness and assessing the extent to which this may have undercut the multiply coded truth by limiting the inquiry. In the example I have chosen to illustrate the structure of historical inquiry, Wallace's results confirm contemporary reassessments of the Enlightenment as a movement of political and intellectual liberation in which scientific, political, and theological models were used with little regard to distinctions among them. However, the aim of this paper is not so much to pursue the implications of this very significant piece of scholarship as to use it as a takeoff point for some reflections on historical method.

I want then to present an account, on the speculative side, of prejudice-dominated hermeneutical research. I want to organize the account around the image of a library. A library has many stacks, each furnished with many shelves. Among them will be one stack of special importance to the inquiry because in it will be collected during the course of the inquiry the fundamental reference corpus (of books and other things) with respect to which all answers in a particular inquiry will be given.

Imagine now the installation of a great library like that of the monastery in *The Name of the Rose* but initially with empty stacks. Let these be called by the names of towns and countries. MS 27, MS 46, and MS 71 from the National Edition will be placed in the stack of the fundamental reference corpus. In addition all and only such works will be placed in this stack as will be judged to be relevant to the inquiry into the three manuscripts. The process of inquiry can then be monitored by the expansion of books and other resources in the fundamental reference corpus and in the development of subsidiary resources organized in different stacks so as to provide answers to questions of possible relevance to the inquiry. These bodies of documents and other relevant material when duly gathered will constitute the locus for interpretative evidence. All questions will be answered with reference to what these resources can on interpretation be made to say or do.

If our interest coincides with those of the Enlightenment, that is, if it is in our interest to claim a rupture with the past, we shall call its fundamental corpus *Gallia,* and its subsidiary corpora by the names of French cities, *Lutetia, Lugdunum,* and so on. Then Gallia will be filled with books and other works relevant to the theme of intellectual rupture and liberation. In such a research program, the principal topic would generate a multitude of subsidiary studies, on the "natural" origins of political power as well, perhaps, as on such topics as Eucharistic debates and scientific disputes on the vacuum. The project of assembling or reassembling the relevant sources into bodies of texts and other materials suitable for an inquiry will have as its outcome two bodies of resources, a fundamental corpus for the major questions and a multitude of subsidiary corpora. It is evident that the contents of each resource is open (that is, never absolutely complete) and that the number of subsidiary resources is in principle endless.

Wallace's concern centered on the three Latin Manuscripts, particularly on MS 27, for his purpose was to investigate the sources for continuity between Galileo's new mathematical science of nature and medieval science. We shall call its fundamental corpus *Italia*, and take as the names of its subsidiary corpora the names of Italian cities, *Roma*, *Padua*, and so on. I shall not detail how the scholarly chase was pursued—I am not a historian—how imagination led the way, what strategies were tried, and what good fortune unexpectedly offered. The eventual outcome, however, was that his "Italia" came to be populated with a *finite* set of books and other works, the names of which are listed, with an occasional addition or subtraction, in Wallace's scholarly writings.[6]

Besides Galileo's early notebooks, there is in Wallace's fundamental corpus Raymond Fredette's doctoral dissertation at the University of Montreal, Villoslada's *Storia del Collegio Romano* (Rome, 1954), Sommervogel's *Bibliographie de la Compagnie de Jesus* (Brussels and Paris, 1890–1932), L. Carbone's *Additamenta ad commentaria D. Francisci Toleti in Logicam Aristotelis* (Venice, 1597), P. Vallius' *Logica* (Lyons, 1622), and particular manuscripts in the *Staatsbibliothek*, Bamberg. There is also a list of secondary sources, containing the names of Finocchiaro, Moss, Shea, Crombie, Cosentino, Lohr, and others, each containing references to original primary sources in addition perhaps to those already listed. We do not know how many subsidiary questions, each

---

6. The following provide a sample of William Wallace's scholarly writings on this topic: *Galileo's Early Notebooks* (Notre Dame, Ind.: University of Notre Dame Press, 1977), *Prelude to Galileo: Medieval and Sixteenth Century Sources of Galileo's Thought* (Dordrecht and Boston: Reidel, 1981), *Galileo and His Sources: The Heritage of the Collegio Romano in Galileo's Science* (Princeton: Princeton University Press, 1984), "Galileo's Concept of Science: Recent Manuscript Evidence," 15–40, in G. V. Coyne et al. (eds.), *The Galileo Affair: A Meeting of Faith and Science* (Vatican City: Specula Vaticana, 1985), "Reinterpreting Galileo on the Basis of His Latin Manuscripts," 3–28, in W. Wallace (ed.), *Reinterpreting Galileo* (Washington, D.C.: Catholic University of America Press, 1986), and "Galileo's Sources: Manuscripts or Printed Works?" in S. Wagonheim and G. Tyson (eds.), *Print and Culture in the Renaissance* (Newark, Del.: University of Delaware Press, 1986).

with its own corpus, were developed during the course of this inquiry. The number, however, must have been finite, and each corpus must have been likewise finite in size.

Koyré's concern was with a certain conception of the "origins of modern science," which was much influenced by Edmund Husserl, about which I shall say more later. Let us call his fundamental corpus *Germania*, and its subsidiary corpora by the names of German cities, *Colonia, Augustodunum*, and so forth. He gathered into his fundamental corpus the works of Plato and the ancient Greek atomists and those writers of the late Renaissance, such as Nicholas of Cusa, Giordano Bruno, and Kepler, who broke (for whatever reason) with the finite and qualitative Cosmos of the medievals to pursue infinite worlds and (mostly hermetic) mathematical strategies.

I have stressed the central role of the fundamental reference corpus for it is needed to give specification to the aim of the inquiry as this becomes publicly articulated during the course of the inquiry. The strategy of inquiry is twofold: to compile (1) a fundamental reference corpus (2) that is capable of sustaining a good, coherent, and acceptable interpretation responsive to the goals of the inquiry. A good, coherent, and acceptable interpretation is always relative to a fundamental reference corpus constructed in the way described, and it is one capable of answering all relevant questions of the interpreting community in a satisfactory way in terms of the community's home language.[7] This answer needs some commentary.

First, it is evident that the hermeneutical process is never unique nor methodologically deterministic, for there are more ways than one of constructing an amplified reference corpus in relation to a given text, reflecting different possible traditions of inquiry, interpretational interests, home languages, or judicious choices. Hermeneutics is open-ended, which is a kind of indeterminacy. Not only is hermeneutics open-ended: it is nonunivocal and dialectical, for different interpretations may rest on significantly different, that is, noninterchangeable, fundamental reference corpora, since each corpus has been constructed to fulfill a different interest. The meaning of a single text then turns out to be not single but multiple, each meaning associated group-theoretically with its fundamental reference corpus, but since these are noninterchangeable, they generate noncommuting transformation groups that leave the text but not its meanings on the analogy

---

7. By the "home language" of a community, I mean the discourse it has received from its traditions, by which it articulates its world and gives meaning to its life and projects. See G. Nicholson, *Seeing and Reading* (Atlantic Highlands, N.J.: Humanities Press, 1984), 15.

of quantum mechanics intact; the different meanings then are "complementary" meanings of the same text.[8]

Second, it is also evident that the reference corpus is not just a collection of already fully interpreted exhibits but that in assembling a corpus some of its parts may acquire new or revised meanings. Interpretation, in other words, is *holistic*.

Third, it is also evident that any construction of a reference corpus must be made judiciously; that is, the selection of the additional texts, relevant artifacts, or other works must be such as to tell an ever more "satisfying" and "plausible" story shaped by the goals of the interrogation. Good judgment or *phronesis*—and the debate that every judgment call can provoke—is also of the essence of the interpretative method.

Fourth, the metaphor of the library tends to overemphasize the literary character of hermeneutics at the expense of those physical, technological, and other realistic methods of research that are necessary to provide the reports and studies that end up in "Italia." Nonliterary or existential hermeneutics will be discussed later.

The process of interpretation involves a back and forth movement between, on the one hand, a holistic meaning emerging from a reference corpus constructed around the original text and, on the other, the progressively more detailed story relevant to our interests that the corpus is made to tell as it grows and as it is refined. The process of refining or "tuning" the corpus by additions and subtractions continues until a more or less single story that is plausible and satisfies the goals of the inquiry can be told to our community in our home language. At that point, the fundamental reference corpus, while remaining open-ended, has a certain architectonic fullness; it has—or better, ought to have—the kind of completeness demanded of evidence in a court of law.

The fundamental reference corpus has reached an architectonic fullness when three considerations are fulfilled: (1) the interrogation of the text is satisfactorily "tuned" by the reference corpus; that is, the reference corpus provides a sufficient background context of history, science, culture, and so on, to give a fine enough point to the question for interpretation; (2) the reference corpus comprises a sufficient evidentiary base in which interpretations can be tested and verified; and (3) a sufficiently determinate reading can be given of the

---

8. See Patrick Heelan, *Space-Perception and the Philosophy of Science* (Berkeley and Los Angeles: University of California Press, 1983), and "Natural Science as a Hermeneutic of Instrumentation," *Philosophy of Science*, 50 (1983): 181–204.

text against the background of the reference corpus, one capable of providing unambiguous and defensible answers that are satisfying and plausible to any interpreter sharing the same home language and the same interrogatory goals.

The process just described of constructing a reference corpus by judicious selection and rejection is a species of "tuning" to the original text in order to make it speak to the point of the inquiry. Without such a "tuning," the ability of the original text to respond to the questions raised by a research program would be incomplete, indefinite, and incoherent. Since the selectivity involved in "tuning" the corpus to the text is a creative poietic activity, the hermeneutical circle or the hermeneutical process of "discovering" truth in symbols is then artistic in character as well as interpretative.

IS HERMENEUTICAL METHOD SCIENTIFIC?

The process so described is creative, poietic, open-ended, and holistic, but is it science? Surely, one might say, what a text means is what the author (or authorizing authority) of the text intended, this is surely the only research project that can be called "scientific," everything else being just as surely invention!

To discover the author's intentions is certainly a worthwhile research goal, though it is not the only scientific goal of significance. But even research into the author's intentions is fraught with special problems: the author is dead; the author's society is dead; the author's home language is dead; to express the dead author's intentions in a way that makes sense to us today involves bridging the historical and cultural interval that separates us and finding a way to interpret the author's life, culture, and home language in terms of our life, culture, and home language. Moreover, it may turn out that the author had many and confused intentions. Only if one believes in a perennial store of uninterpreted wisdom, a Demiurgic access to the way things were and really are, a philosophical and scientific language that speaks for all peoples, times, and places, does it make sense to regard the author's intentions as a single scientific research goal with a unique definite answer. These are not the suppositions of this speculative essay.

That a text or an inscription can make sense to us in some other way than by being the carrier of the author's intentions seems obvious; however, that such queries can be resolved "scientifically" by the hermeneutic method just described is on the surface not so sure. "Scientific knowledge" has always—perhaps, mistakenly—been associated with universal timeless theoretical knowledge. Scientific knowledge, however, is more correctly explanatory knowledge; that is, it seeks to understand phenomena from a third-person standpoint in terms of the process of their coming to appear in the human life world.[9]

THE HERMENEUTICAL CIRCLE: EXISTENTIAL HERMENEUTICS

Existential hermeneutics is the mode of being human, of playing human roles, of being-in-the-world. Humans first experience themselves as involved practically in the world. They deal with things in the course of a variety of praxes to accomplish human ends. People are involved with tools such as hammers, or instruments such as word processors, things that carry them forward toward the fulfilment of the purpose they are presently attempting to fulfill.

Things first appear, then, not as in themselves but as instruments of human life and action. To pause to reflect on the things we use, to stop to analyze what they may be in themselves, tends to remove these things from the context of human life and action in order that they may be looked at as if they had a fixed, permanent, and possibly exclusive set of properties in themselves. To borrow an example from Heidegger, a hammer known is a hammer used in the praxis of hammering; once it is on the shelf it is just a resource, for hammering or for some other use. Thus, it is action or praxis that displays or uncovers what a thing is but at the expense of covering up what it might also or otherwise be. The "truth," in the Heideggerian sense, is that things show themselves to be a human resource.[10] For us to designate them in some other way by some alleged set of permanent and essential properties independent of human interests is to distort the "truth" of things.

The hammer shows itself to be a hammer within the praxis of hammering, and as long as the hammer does its job, it borrows its existential nature from the human action. What a hammer is, then, is to be arrived at by a hermeneutics of human action. The hammer hides itself in successful praxis and shows itself only when praxis breaks

---

9. A *first-person standpoint* is one from which the phenomenon can be described; in contrast, a *third-person standpoint* is one from which the conditions of possibility of the phenomenon can be studied. The former is descriptive; the latter is explanatory.

10. Truth, for Heidegger, is *aletheia*, the simultaneous revealing and hiding of practical knowledge; things revealed as a human resource are his "ready-to-hand," as opposed to things defined by fixed concepts, which are his "present-at-hand"; see his *Being and Time.*

down, as when the hammer turns out to be defective. Thus, when it breaks in use, the disruption of the purposeful activity can help us to limn out the kind of thing a hammer ought structurally to be. Every worldly object, like the hammer, borrows its existential sense from a human praxis. It is in this way that the being of worldly things is existentially hermeneutic: they borrow what they are from human life.

Although Heidegger can be, and often is, interpreted as rejecting Husserl's concern with essences, invariants, and theories, on the grounds that such distract one from the centrality and ambiguity of human life and praxis, it is clear that human life and praxis were also important to the Husserl of the *Crisis*. It is clear that although Husserl regarded theory as central to scientific and to all developed knowledge, theory for him was not the permanent and unchanging reflection of an alienated being but an "idealization" of which the reality was the life world. Even in his last years and while still wistful about theory as the transcendental structure of all historical life worlds, Husserl had begun to leave the transcendental interests of phenomenology behind in favor of genetic constitution based on human praxes and history and a phenomenology of the life world.

As I have pointed out elsewhere,[11] one finds in the *Crisis* two quite different senses for "idealization," both, however, dependent on Göttingen science, one, the algebraic, taking theory to be the (transcendental) limit of infinitely perfectible measurement, and the other, the geometric, taking theory to be the ideal but historical essence of perceptual objects defined by human life and action. It is the latter that makes contact with Heidegger and compensates for a significant limitation of Heidegger's viewpoint, just as Heidegger's hermeneutics compensates for a significant limitation of Husserl's phenomenology. Both are important for the study of scientific inquiry.

Concern for the existential hermeneutic viewpoint common to both Heidegger and the later Husserl does not invalidate the further question that Husserl alone asked: what are the *theoretical* conditions of possibility of those worldly objects that show themselves again and again in perception? Husserl connected them with invariants of noetic-noematic structures and took his inspiration from the transformation theory of geometry—and then of physics—that were essential to the Göttingen approach to science during the golden years when Husserl was a professor there.

---

11. P. Heelan, "Husserl's Later Philosophy of Science," *Philosophy of Science* 54 (1987): 368–90.

By the *theoretical* conditions of possibility of perceptual objects Husserl meant the structure of perception that enables perceptual objects to show themselves again and again the way they do in the life world. The notion of theory so implied is closer to the notion of explanation, for it is an account from a third-person standpoint of the process by which the phenomenon comes to appear as it does. This notion of theory is different from the notion of *conceptual idealization* (whether reached by a convergent mathematical process or by a generalizing and abstractive process), for, unlike the explanatory notion of theory, idealization implies the first-person standpoint.

Theory as conceptual idealization from the first-person standpoint was the kind of theory that Heidegger objected to as destructive of the hermeneutical perspective. This for him was the abstractive, alienating move that converted things as ingredients of human praxis (what he called the "ready-to-hand") to museum pieces forever fixed in their categorial representations (what he called the "present-at-hand").[12] The former retain the dramatic ambiguity they have as actors in human life, at once showing themselves and hiding from view, opening up and at the same time covering up, and so sharing the mysterious quality of human life.

HISTORICAL METHOD

The work of Edmund Husserl suggests that historical method begins by transforming what we know about the past into *historical phenomena* accompanied by a historical narrative. A historical phenomenon is one that is present-to-us (a part of our contemporary world) but as-past (as being part of the tradition that, either in the present or after its recovery by the present, influences our life and culture); it is then a phenomenon that (at least, after its recovery) is present-to-us-as-past.[13] It is like a familiar object, an airplane, receding into

---

12. Within the context of Heidegger's work as interpreted, say, by Kockelmans, theory is taken to mean "taking a second look at the things that we encounter in our world and, particularly, in conceiving and projecting them as being *merely* there," through processes of abstraction, idealization, and formalization; Joseph Kockelmans, "On the Hermeneutic Dimensions of the Natural Sciences," *Études Phénoménologiques*, no. 2 (1986): 51, 78. Such a process reducing things to present-at-hand is not, of course, unique to modern science or modern technology but is, in Heidegger's view, the characteristic feature of modern culture and attributable to modern science and technology. Whatever is the justice of this observation about our propensity to specify things theoretically in one sense of the term *theory*, I am concerned with the sense of theory as theory actually functions in the doing of science.

13. This is Husserl's view of history; see David Carr, *Time, Narrative, and History* (Bloomington, Ind.: Indiana University Press, 1986), 3–4.

the distant skies. Just as the profile we see of the airplane is a distant receding profile of a familiar object, so the now-present profile of the past historical phenomenon is a distant presently receding profile of that historical phenomenon.

An important thesis of Husserl's is that historical phenomena are in the present; thus they do not preexist contemporary life and culture in a fixed and immutable way. Historical interpretation supposes, of course, the preexistence of the fundamental reference corpus of historical relics and exhibits, but these are not historical phenomena understood in relation to human life and culture; they are merely a potential semiotic field to be transformed by interpretation. The transformation into history is an existential hermeneutic transformation of the material relics of the past (with its texts, monuments, works of art, and so forth) into a "living" phenomenon coming to us from the past. It is the work of the *historian as the maker of history* to compose the historical narrative that makes the past to "live" for us: to make its presence felt like an airplane receding into the distant skies. In this way we learn about our past so as to live with it. The historian as the maker of history is then a performer whose function is a narrative performance aimed to bring alive for a community the past-in-the-present; such a living sharing is an existential hermeneutic.

That the historical hermeneutical method, though creative and poietic, can nevertheless yield stable, communicable, consensual, and evidentially grounded results may be surprising, but it is no more surprising than that laboratory praxis, also creative and poietic, can yield stable, communicable, consensual, and evidentially grounded results in the physics laboratory. Neither preexists human life and scientific culture in an immutable way; each derives its determinations from its own existential hermeneutical praxis, one from narrative history and the other from laboratory praxis.

Returning to classical philosophy (and, until recently, its offspring, analytic philosophy of science and history), in contrast with the hermeneutical viewpoint expressed earlier, classical philosophy adopts the standpoint of a universal, uninvolved, Demiurgic representing Mind. The world as knowable by such a Demiurgic Mind is knowable only in and through surrogate mirror images of reality, namely, theoretical models—"ideas" in the classical sense—or surrogate material fields such as a uniquely specified fundamental reference corpus that is presumed closed. What the hermeneutical viewpoint adds to the classical viewpoint is the awareness that neither the theories under which we represent to ourselves the historical world nor the resources such as the fundamental reference corpus that we construct for the purpose of making the historical world "live" for us are themselves the objects of historical knowledge. These last are the references to which both refer, and they are not immutable beings frozen in the forever past but historical phenomena that appear to us as poietic constructions of human culture like the *Concorde* receding into the skies.

3 Explaining

ROBERT SOKOLOWSKI

The theme of this essay is the difference between the simple and the complex in speech and in disclosure. I claim that the task of philosophy is not to get at the simple but to illuminate the simple and the complex in their relation to one another and thus to bring out what it is to be simple and what it is to be complex.

I

There is a difference between simply naming something and articulating it in some way. It is one thing just to say "illness," and another to say "Illness is a burden," "An illness is not as bad as a moral collapse," or some of the many other things we say when we speak about illnesses. The name just presents the thing all at once; the articulation brings out something definite in or about it.

Furthermore, names are a part of articulations, whereas articulations do not seem to be part of names: "Illness" is part of "Illness is a burden," but "Illness is a burden" does not seem to be part of "illness." Names therefore seem more elementary than predications, relations, and other forms of assertion. It might also seem that what is named is more elementary than what is achieved in articulation: that, for example, illness as a simple thing is more elementary than illness's being a burden.

Since this seems to be the case, we might be tempted to look for the most elementary names of all and to look for the most elementary nameable things. We might be tempted to try to find atomic names and atomic things. If we could find such names and things, we could, it seems, get a kind of control over all the articulations that can be made with and upon them. We would have some sort of key to something.

But this expectation is misguided. It presupposes that names and the nameable have a priority in being over articulations and the articulated, and that we can get to what is prior just as we can get to the bricks out of which a house is made. But in fact names and articulations are equally primary. There are names only because there are articulations, and there are articulations only because there are names. Furthermore, there are simple nameables only because there are articulated patterns, and there are articulated wholes only because there are things that can be simply named. The things that *are* move back and forth between being simple and being articulated; being is not to be identified just with the simple. The philosophical task is not to show how articulations can be melted down into names and the named; the philosophical task is not to get down to some sort of element or base; the philosophical task is to think both names and articulations in their reciprocities. It is to think them in their distinctions from one another, because they *are* only in these distinctions.

If there is a difference between names and articulations, there is another difference between asserting something and explaining what we have asserted. Correlatively, there is a similar difference between what is stated (a state of affairs) and that which explains a state of affairs (its causes).

In the case of assertions and explanations, we deal entirely with articulations. We go from one statement to another, from one state of affairs to another. We go from a fact to its explanation. There is no temptation to melt the articulation down into its elementary names and their elementary nameable things. But there is another kind of reduction we may be tempted to make.

We may be inclined to want to reduce all statements into two kinds of ultimate, atomic propositions: (1) to statements that are atomic because they merely register or report an immediately experienced simple fact and (2) to statements that are atomic because they are self-evident and true by virtue of the terms used in them. We will call the first group *protocol statements* and the second group *self-evident statements*. Protocol and self-evident statements together seem to be the rock-bottom basis for argumentation, just as simple names seem to be the rock-bottom basis for assertions.

And once again, over on the side of things as opposed to the side of argumentation, we might be inclined to reduce all states of affairs to two kinds of ultimate, atomic arrangements: (1) to simple factual arrangements and (2) to essential relationships that hold, necessarily, among various kinds and features of things.

We might then be inclined to think that the task of philosophy is to find out which statements are protocol statements and which are self-evident, or at least that philosophy should provide a technique or a criterion for identifying such statements. It seems that if it could do this, philosophy would provide us with a way of controlling argumentation and making it work well. It would also provide us, it might seem, with a more secure access to what is real: to the plain facts presented in protocol statements and to the ultimate, essential relationships disclosed by self-evident statements, the relationships that provide the unquestionable context for particular facts and individual experiences.

But once again, the task of philosophy is not to work its way to such ultimate building blocks but to think assertion and explanation in their reciprocities: to think both what is the case and the reasons why things are as they are, and to think these two in their distinction from one another, since both facts and causes *are,* as such, only by being distinguished from one another. The philosophical task is to clarify a fact as fact, a cause as cause, and an assertion as such, an explanation as such. This philosophical task can be accomplished only by positioning a fact against its causes and the causes against what they explain; and by positioning an assertion against its explanation and the explanation against what it explains.

We have distinguished the following elements:

1. Atomic names and basic statements
2. Atomic objects (nameables) and basic states of affairs

Within the level of articulations, we have distinguished:

3. Protocol statements and explanations (at the extreme, self-evident explanations)
4. Plain, "protocol" facts and causal states of affairs (at the extreme, self-evident or essential causes)

And we claim that philosophy should not be drawn off into the artificial abstraction of atomic names and atomic statements or atomic objects and atomic states of affairs; that it also should not be drawn off into the artificial abstraction of protocol statements and self-evident statements, or simple facts and ultimate explanations. Instead, philosophy is to recover and clarify the concrete activity of thinking and disclosing, an activity in which names, assertions, and explanations, as well as things, states of affairs, and causes, all play a part, and in which no one of these could subsist without the others.

II

In order to be as concrete as possible, let us work with the larger whole. Instead of beginning with the relationship between names and assertions, let us work with argumentation or discourse and examine first the difference between assertion and explanation.

In the simplest type of speech, one statement of fact just follows another in a continuous display, the speaker leading and the interlocutor following or joining in: "He got very angry then." "And what did she do?" "She left the room. He went to the telephone and called his office." It may be necessary to repeat a statement if the speaker wants to emphasize something or if he has not been heard correctly, but such repetition is not an explanation of what he wanted to say; it is just a pause in the concatenating display.

But sometimes it is necessary to explain. What was said arrests the conversation in a new way. We no longer simply concatenate, and the speech does not simply pause to repeat; what was said becomes not just said again but said as a target. Instead of moving on to say more about yesterday's meeting, the conversation becomes riveted on something that was said about yesterday's meeting: the "that" becomes an occasion for a "why?" This "that" is not left behind as we go on to others: it becomes what we ask about, what we delve into, what we are called upon to explain. One statement, one fact, becomes highlighted, identified as questionable, arresting as an issue.

When such an arrest occurs, there are two different ways in which the target can be explained. (1) In one, the truth of an articulation is established by saying something other than what was said in the questionable statement, "Why did he get angry at that moment?" "For several days before, he had felt offended by what they were doing; this was the last straw." This outburst of anger is explained by all those other irritations. (2) But in another way of explaining, a fact is explained by bringing out more fully what the fact itself is, so that the questionability of the fact evaporates. This is not merely to repeat the fact but to bring out more clearly what it is: "Why did he get angry when he was being mocked?" "Well, he was being humiliated, and before his friends and family. People get angry when that happens. That's what anger is. Don't you see that?"

This second form of explanation, bringing out more fully what the thing is, is an appeal to self-evidencing. It does not explain through an other but through the same. However, it is an explanation; something more has to be said, even though the more is not other. It does not just repeat what was said before; rather, it turns what was said before—"He got angry when Steve mocked him"—into a theme to be dwelt upon and thus explained.

When we explain something by giving a cause that is other to the fact to be explained, it is obvious that we are doing more than we did when we stated the fact. The otherness makes the more to be palpable. When we explain by appealing to self-evidences, however, it might appear that we are not explaining, not doing anything more, but only repeating what had been said. Indeed, in silly answers this may be the case ("Why did the Redskins play fewer games in 1969 than they did this year?" "Because the season was shorter then"). But not all "redundant" answers are trivial; there are times when it is necessary to bring out more fully what is there before us, to bring it out in its own necessities and on its own terms in such a way that those who do not comprehend may be helped to comprehend.

Such clarification is more situated, more rhetorical, more tailored to an audience than is the explanation through a cause other than what is explained, a cause that is more independent of the circumstances of the speech ("The plant has turned toward the left because the source of light lies in that direction"). However, the appeal to an external cause, although it seems more objective, is really derivative; it presupposes the explanations in which what is going on is displayed on its own terms for what it is in itself. And although situated, such a clarification through self-evidencing is still objective. It brings out what the thing or the fact truly is, not merely how it happens to seem to someone.

The point is that things and facts very often have to be brought out for what they are in themselves. It is not the case that the only causes we are ignorant of are the hidden causes, those not already visible in what is being questioned. When we look for a cause that is other to what we want to explain, we usually know that we are ignorant and that we should inquire. But often the very thing before us is not present in the way it should be; it may be only vaguely presented and its internal, axiomatic necessities, those that should show up on its face, may be obscured. Such ignorance is often called a failure in the conceptual understanding of what is going on; often it issues in the vague, inauthentic use of words that are merely associated with the phenomenon and do not name or register it. How we can *not* know what is plain to see is a perplexing philosophical issue.

And so sometimes a question that we ask is a call not for more other information but for a clearer view of what is already there. Such questions into self-evidences can be of two kinds. In some cases they are real calls for help. The questioner does not understand what is going on and needs a clarification. His inability to understand may be formulated as a request for an external cause of what is happening, but in fact there is no external explanation for what he wants. There is only a more vivid and precise display of the occurrence. In other cases the questioner is not at a loss but simply contemplates questioningly. He does not ask the reason why humiliated people become angry but contemplates and hence questions anger as the response to insult. He is involved in a different kind of questioning: not a helpless kind but one well in control. Knowing what anger is, he sets out as both questioner and respondent to bring out what it is ever more completely. He probes the axioms of anger.

But let us stay for a while with the case of the questioner who needs help to understand what is going on. Even here there are two ways in which the questioner can be answered.

a. In one case the respondent will know that anyone who understood what is going on would not ask a question like that. The questioner shows that he thinks there are two distinct things here, the insult and the anger, whereas there really is only one: insult/anger go together as one, not as a two whose being together needs a cause. The intelligibility and the unity of the reply come out of the necessities of the thing itself. The questioner is ignorant of the unity in what to him seems like two things, and the respondent's task is to bring out this unity.[1]

b. In another case, the source of the fact is not the thing itself but some agreement or convention made by someone. The fact itself is the kind of thing that comes to be by agreement. "Why did he stop running after he crossed home plate?" "That's what the rules are. There is nowhere else to go after you have crossed home plate." This response clarifies what is going on, and it does so by appealing to a kind of external cause, one that informs the procedure and makes it to be what it is (a crossing of home plate), but the fact is what it is not simply in and by itself (as anger, the roots and branches of a tree, the future, and heat all are) but because someone said it should be so.

This gives us two kinds of self-evidences: (a) those that bring out the essence of a thing and (b) those that stipulate what a thing will be.

---

1. A good example of a merely apparent "one" that is really an accidental unity of two distinct things can be found in Elie Kedouri, *Nationalism* (London: Hutchinson, 1960), 89. Kedouri observes that nationalism is sometimes identified as a politics of the Right, sometimes as a politics of the Left. In either case, he says, "this conjunction . . . is a fortuitous accident." To state this in the terms we have been using, if one were to probe the being of an entity called "right-wing (or left-wing) nationalism," one would not come to any axioms for this thing as a whole. Nationalism may in fact be right-wing or left-wing, but it is not essentially so.

The first kind lies in the nature of the thing; the second lies in convention. Each, furthermore, has its own sort of ignorance. If I do not know why the football game has been stopped and the Raiders have been penalized ten yards, someone can simply tell me what the rules are and why they are being applied now. My informant may go on to explain why these rules make sense in the full context of the game, but ultimately he will have informed me that the rules have been decided in a certain way and that this is now happening as it is because of those rules. This activity is one of those rules in action, one of those conventions being applied.

But if I say I do not know why people who have been insulted feel resentment or why we anticipate the future and remember and forget what is past, it makes no sense for my informant to appeal to a decision made by someone to explain why these things are so. I do not need an informant; I need someone to clarify things for me. I do not, furthermore, need someone to clarify just the meanings of words, because no one clarifies "merely" the meaning of words: one clarifies the things that are meant by the words. In this case one would clarify insult and resentment; or the future, the past, memory, and anticipation; or law and reason; or religion and politics; or whatever is especially questionable at the moment. Someone has to show me that these things just are and have to be the way they are and that we could not imagine them otherwise.

Conventions, rules, and decisions are somehow "inside" the activities that illustrate them: the Raiders' losing ten yards *is* the penalty for clipping. And yet the conventions, rules, and decisions have their original being somehow "outside" their illustrations and applications: their origin is the agreement that establishes them as rules. But the order of insult-resentment and the order of time do not originate anywhere else apart from this exchange and that remembering. The same ordering may occur in other instances, but it does not have an origin or a cause apart from its being in its instances. It was never chosen to be as it is; it does not exist by virtue of having been decided. Therefore, there is nothing "else" or "other" to appeal to in explaining these forms and relationships. They are to be explained only by being more fully brought out.

Furthermore, we are not upset with someone who does not know why the game has been interrupted or why, say, this man is speaking for such a long time in the Senate ("He's carrying on a filibuster, which means . . ."). It is quite normal for people not to know such things: to see the bodily manifestation of the rule but not to know the rule itself. It does not diminish their humanity not to know this sort of thing.

And the remedy is straightforward. It is simply to tell them what the rule is and perhaps to tell why it was formulated as it was. But we do get upset with someone who says or shows he does not know the ordering of the natural kinds and necessary forms that are common and prominent in the life we live. He should know these things just by having grown up. And we are exasperated in searching for a remedy. If he does not know these things already, what can we appeal to in making them clear to him? There is nothing other to them that explains why they are as they are.

Sometimes stories are told that seem to try to explain why things are as they are. Such stories are legends, myths, and fables. We can, for example, imagine someone's reciting a legend along these lines:

> Human beings at one time were so constituted that each man lived entirely in the present. He had no future and no past. Some men were stronger than others, and the stronger asserted themselves by destroying the weaker when they came in contact with them. The weaker were simply annihilated, the stronger went on as though nothing had happened. The gods were distressed at this injustice, so they changed men into time-filled beings, in order to make them more equal to one another. At any moment a man would have lived through only part of his life and would have to wait for the rest. This change made men more subdued; no matter how strong a man might be at one time, he could not tell how he would compare with others in the future, so he was careful to make friends with others even while he was the stronger, so that he would not have to fear others if he became weak. Furthermore, besides concealing the future from man, the gods allowed him to remember his past, so that he would strive to be a friend to himself, since he had to live in the present with his past self. Thus time was given by the gods as a way of generating justice and friendship among men.

A story like this seems to try to explain a natural ordering—in this case, the form of time—as though it were the outcome of a decision. It seems to try to treat a natural kind as though it were a convention. But in fact such a story only appears to be an explanation through something other than what it strives to explain; in fact it has a much more contemplative purpose. It makes us think about time. We know that the events did not occur as the story says they did, but we still like to hear stories such as this. We like them precisely because we know they are not true, because we realize that they are telling us something distinct from what they explicitly state. We know the story is false; we also know that any other story like it would be false; and therefore we come to appreciate that the things being discussed just are in their relationships: nothing has made them to be the way they are, and nothing could explain them except the shape or form that they have themselves. By the recognized falsity of the story, we are thrown back on the things themselves, on time or wrath, forgiveness or generosity, war or death, in their internal ordering. The stories help us sense the self-evidencing, as such, of the things themselves.

III

Let us look back at the various forms of explanation we have discussed. We have distinguished:

1. Explanations through an other, through a cause that is external to that which is to be explained: "This car was crushed by that explosion."

2. Explanations through a decision, rule, or convention: "He left the plate and stopped batting because he had three strikes, and when you have three strikes, you're out." Such explanations work through an other, through an agreement distinct from what is going on here and now, but this cause is both external and internal to the fact being explained, since the rule, although formulated by others at another time, constitutes the fact and makes it be what it is.

3. Explanations through the same as what is to be explained, not through an other; explanations done by clarifying the internal ordering of the explicandum itself: "Insult provokes resentment; that is the way it is." This kind can be subdivided as follows:

    a. Clarifications made for someone who does not grasp the internal ordering of the thing.

    b. Clarifications made out of contemplative enjoyment of the ordering itself.

4. Explanations through legend, myth, fable, and stories, which seem to go outside the thing in explaining it and seem to appeal to a decision or convention that establishes the thing as it is, but which really amount to a contemplative enjoyment of the thing itself as an issue or as a perplexity.

The third kind of explanation, the most elusive and problematic of the four, suffers from neglect in our current cultural and philosophical climate. This sort of explanation presumes that something like "natural kinds" exists, that there is something like an internal ordering or a definition or form in things, something that makes a thing to be and to show up as it is. This sort of explanation works within what was once called the formal cause. But the ruling opinion in our time resists acknowledging a form or nature in things, and for at least three reasons.

First, the explanations that have been so successful in the natural sciences, in biology, chemistry, and physics, make us inclined to explain things in terms of the elements and forces that make them up. The "definition" of an animal or a plant or even a human mental activity, such as perception or recognition, would generally be held to designate only an apparent unity and ordering, only an epiphenomenon. The "truth" of the thing in question, we are inclined to say, is the sum of "its" gravitational, subatomic, electromagnetic, neurological, and other elements and forces. Natural kinds seem to be dissolved into the stuff or particles and forces of which they are made.

Second, we generally turn to evolutionary and historicist explanations for the current appearances of things. We tend to see the forms of living things as the outcome of evolutionary pressures, opportunities, and accidents; we tend to see human forms as the provisional outcome of the historical process; and we may see everything as the current state of an evolving universe. Once again, natural kinds dissolve, this time into temporary organizations that are to be explained by what went before them, as well as by what they are made of, but not in terms of what they themselves are.

Third, another reason why we are inclined to dismiss natural kinds is that they would impede the control we think we can and should have over nature and its processes. Natural kinds and essential necessities would get in the way of the enterprise of mastering nature. If things are thought to be reducible to their elements, and if they are considered to be the outcome of the evolutionary process, we feel free to rearrange their elements in some other way. Our arrangement would be no less natural than the one that has evolved apart from our intervention, by chance, and the new arrangement will probably prove to be more useful for our purposes than the one that nature gave us. And in our enterprise of mastering nature, we hope to be able to control not only the things outside us but even our own organisms and our neurological and mental life. We hope to do this by discovering the appropriate elements that make them up and the formulas that govern their combination.

The analysis we have presented in this essay runs, of course, counter to this prevailing opinion. We recognize a form in things. And we do not limit forms merely to organic and animal species; indeed the plant and animal species may be the weakest examples of natural kinds, since they are relatively modest variations on the forms of "Plant" or "Animal" as such. But there are more definitive natural kinds and formal orderings to be found in such things as time, the future and the past, imagination, pictures, numbers, political society, poetry, choices, generosity and greed, and other things that can be named as one. It is true that what is named as one may in some cases turn out not to be one; it may turn out to be an accidental or coincidental unity, not a substantial one. In such cases no axioms or self-evident essentials will surface in the thing. The attempt to clarify what the thing is in itself will result in showing that the thing is not "one" in itself, but this discovery too is an achievement, and it may be of considerable importance if the thing in question is a factor in some major public controversy or policy. But the fact that some things that seem to be one do fall apart into many, and exhibit no axiomatic necessity when they are analyzed, does not mean that there are no substantial unities at all. Indeed the possibility of recognizing something as only seeming to be one implies that we can tell the difference between a merely apparent and a true substantial unity.

And besides natural kinds, there are also things that are one by convention, such as a home run, a penalty for clipping, or a presidential inauguration, and things that are one by virtue of having been made, such as my car, the Air and Space Museum, Park Avenue, and the Chesapeake Bay Bridge. Such things are not accidental conglomerates; they each are one and not many, but they are one by virtue of an anticipation (there has to have been an "idea" of each of them before it could come to be). But they do have their axioms and their internal necessities, and they do reward our investigation by presenting a form to our curiosity, even though the form was first apprehended in someone's design, not in a thing.

If we are dealing with a true form, with a nameable something that yields self-evidences upon analysis, we should be able to say things about it that are necessarily true. We should be able to clarify the thing in itself. But the best example of such clarification is not necessarily the production of a few essential statements, such as "Resentment is the response to insult" or "The past can be relived in memory." Rather, the best example will lie in an extended discourse in which the essentials of the thing are both shown and stated, an extended discourse in which the gist of the thing can be recognized. Someone who denies there is anything essential in things would have to assert that there is really no difference between a scatterbrained, loose, associative account of a topic and an account in which the thing is effectively presented. He would have to say there is no difference between a speech in which the speaker never gets to the point and one in which the point is clearly made. No one can really deny that such differences exist.

IV

We have discussed the relation between statements and explanations, between facts and causes. Let us now turn back to the contrast between names and articulations and between the named and the articulated. In both these pairs, each member is what it is only as positioned against the other. The object named is named only to be articulated, and the articulated is there only to be absorbed back into what is named. The named is latently articulated; the explicitly articulated relapses into the sense of what is named.

If I name an object ("Pennsylvania Avenue") I bring it into focus as the first step in unpacking it. I unpack it by saying of it something simply factual, or something proper, or something essential: "Pennsylvania Avenue is being resurfaced"; "Pennsylvania Avenue is *the* national avenue"; "Pennsylvania Avenue is a thoroughfare." In such statements, what the predicate expresses is not merely attached to the avenue; the predicate expresses the avenue in one of its ways of being and being manifested. The object is and is presented in its features. And a thing is named in preparation for its being registered or reported as being or being manifested in its features. Naming prepares for articulation.

But an articulation is not stated continuously. As a statement it is episodic. Once it has been made, what has been articulated settles back into the object as part of the object's sense, part of the object's recognized way of being able to be manifested. Once I have registered that Pennsylvania Avenue is being resurfaced, I behave toward the avenue in an appropriate way. I may avoid it for a few days; then I may drive on it with the expectation that the surface will be smoother than it was the last time I was on it. I may also say certain things about it that are implied by its being resurfaced. I have a lasting conviction that it is being, or has been, resurfaced, but this conviction is not simply an attribute of my own psyche and my own nervous system. It is the way Pennsylvania Avenue "seems" to me, whether as bodily present, or as remembered, imagined, or talked about in its absence. All the articulations are folded back into what is named; they either may be restated again or may serve as unstated premises for other articulations that depend on them. They become part of its recognized sense.

Furthermore, it is not just the features of the object that become folded into what is named when the object is named; the internal causes of those features' belonging to the object are also folded into it. "John insulted Helen and she shouted angrily at him": from that point on Helen will have been the one who answered John in a flash of anger, but she also will have been an instance of the link between insult and resentment. She will have illustrated the form, the internal ordering of anger as such, and we will be able to contemplate anger by thinking about what she did (as, on a much larger scale, Homer contemplated wrath by thinking about what Achilles did). Not only protocol statements or simple facts become absorbed into Helen; the self-evident forms that create the space for protocols and that clarify what the protocols are become absorbed into her as well.

Whenever we name anything, we appreciate that what we name has all these dimensions latent within it. If the thing we name is familiar to us, its factual and essential sediments are also familiar: we can say a lot about the history of our old house, for example, or our old car. And we appreciate a difference between our car's having been repainted three years ago and its being able to traverse distances; we appreciate the difference between the factual and the axiomatic. If the thing we name is new to us, we may understand its kind, with all the concomitant essentials, while not knowing much about its particular history and features ("Here's a parka that you've never seen before"), or we may not even know at all what the axioms of the thing are ("Look at this"; "What is it?"). But even if we do not know "what it is," we do anticipate being able to unpack it both for what it is and for what it happens to be. We expect it to have some "what" and some "thats". As nameable it promises articulations and explanations, unless of course it merely appears to come forward as one, unless it is just an accidental unity. The nameable always presents itself with the aura of facts and causes, the aura of statement and explanation.

If we do penetrate to the axioms of the thing, if we go beyond this poem and its features to the form of poetry as such, we come to relationships that present themselves as necessary. But these relationships can be possessed in two different ways. They can be recognized as self-evidencing; because of our thinking, we may appreciate that they could not be other than they are. We may have an insight into their necessity; we may enjoy what Husserl calls an eidetic intuition. Or we may hold them rather as strong opinions. We may sense vaguely that they are more than mere factual attributes of the thing, we may appreciate that somehow they are necessary, but we may not have thought about them long enough and well enough to grasp their necessity. In some cases we may be content to turn to the legend that explains them instead of to an analysis. There is nothing wrong with leaving many necessities in the form of opinion; we cannot push every issue to its final definition.² But the possibility of an axiomatic analysis is always there, and we always sense the difference between just moving on to more features of what we name and moving into its necessities.

In our normal involvement with things, we move from the thing to its features and to its causes; then we move back to the thing again. We look through the forms of being nameable, being articulated, and being explained. But in our philosophical reflection we look at what we normally look through: we look at the forms of presentation through which we identify things. We examine, as we have in this essay, the form of being nameable, the form of being articulated, and the form of being explained. In turning our attention to this aspect, we do not leave the being of things; instead we recover the larger context and the more concrete whole.³

---

2. See Yves R. Simon, *The Tradition of Natural Law,* ed. Vukan Kuic (New York: Fordham University Press, 1965), 72: "In philosophy, also, complete rigor requires that every concept be analyzed into its components up to the level of the indefinables. One reason why philosophy rarely exists in a perfectly rigorous and scientific condition is that the complete analysis of a philosophical term is an operation involving such strain that few people can stand it. A philosopher who cares to have any readers must generally stop short of the indefinables, just when he has reached a level where the reader experiences a feeling of sufficient clarity. If intellectual training is sound, this feeling is dependable, and if it is unsound, not much can be done anyway."

3. There is an interesting parallel between retrospective and prospective explanations and pseudoexplanations.

(1) Retrospectively, we explain a phenomenon (a) by giving the cause that precedes it ("This car was damaged by that explosion") and is other to it. However (b) sometimes we give what seems to be an antecedent cause but really is an elaboration of the form of the phenomenon in question; this occurs when we tell a legend that clarifies the nature of the thing being discussed.

(2) Prospectively, we can explain a phenomenon (a) by giving the *purpose* for which it is done ("Dick is shoveling the snow so that Jane can go shopping"). There is a definite otherness between the event and its purpose, just as there is a definite otherness between a phenomenon and the cause that precedes it. However we also can explain an event prospectively (b) by giving the *end* that is maturating within it, the end by which the event is defined: a child's faltering steps are "walking" in its incipient stages, and adolescence is definable as incipient adulthood. Now we may give a pseudoexplanation by treating the end as if it were a purpose. We may speak as if the purpose of toddling were walking, as if the purpose of adolescence were maturity, as if toddling and adolescence were chosen in view of walking and maturity, as if the latter were distinctly other to the former. But although a purpose is other to that which is chosen for it, an end is really immanent in its event. The final cause is a version of the formal cause. To treat the end as a purpose is like treating a form as the outcome of a choice. (I am grateful to Francis Slade for his remarks about the difference between purpose and end.)

4   Abstraction and Imagination in Human Understanding
JUDE P. DOUGHERTY

I

Niels Bohr perhaps without realizing that he was paraphrasing Aristotle once said that he could not understand any thing unless he could make a model of it. The role of models, especially iconic models, in thinking is the subject of this paper. I present it as a commentary on Aristotle's *De Anima* III, where in discussing the nature of thinking Aristotle affirmed the indispensable role of imagination. His time-transcending analysis is important for a number of reasons:

1. In drawing distinctions between perception, judgment, imagination, and memory, it contributes to an understanding of the complex processes of abstraction and induction.

2. It anchors in the natural structure the focus of thought.

3. It enables us to understand the roles that models play in theory construction.

4. It not only conforms to actual practice in science as it does to everyday knowing but pertains equally to experienced and inferred entities.

One of the problems encountered in contemporary philosophy of science is the need to give a proper account of the role of models. Are they mere conceptual schema, invented to handle a mass of data conveniently, or are they forced upon us in some way by the reality under consideration? The first alternative is favored by various forms of positivism; the second is the realist position.

The central issue between realism and positivism in the philosophy of science is the status of conceptual schema. Most of what we know in contemporary physics is known by inference. The entire submicroscopic realm is one that has been inferred as a result of attempts to explain phenomena that have been encountered directly or indirectly.

Molecules, atoms, electrons, protons, neutrons, mesons, and their activity are inferred. In talking about them we form conceptual schema that the positivist, heir to centuries-old nominalism, treats as convenient ways of handling complex data. On the positivist's account, the conceptual schema of "atom" is a mere convenience. The data are real enough—they are given in measurements of one sort or another—but to posit a nonexperienced source is to make an unwarranted intellectual leap. To interpret those data as flowing from a structure independent of the mind is to go beyond what is given in experience. Contrary to this scenario offered by the contemporary heirs of Henri Poincaré and Ernest Mach such as Hilary Putnam and Larry Laudan, I will argue that Aristotle's account of mind and imagination provides us with the basis for a realistic interpretation of our scientific knowledge of nature. Aristotle's account of the role of imagination in thinking not only is consistent with his doctrine of abstraction but enables us to understand how the mind bridges the gap between the experienced effect and the inferred cause.

At the root of the positivist's account of science is a confidence in Hume's notion of causality. Science, on Hume's principles, is reduced to description and prediction. But contemporary philosophy of science has a difficult time holding on to a Humean conception of causality. No physicist is content with merely describing sequence. The inquisitive mind looks for explanations. Structures are inferred. The difference in kind among natural structures is said to account for difference in phenomena. In attempts at explanation, structures are usually given visual representation; data are usually expressed in equations and linked to an imagined structure. Although much of what we know about atomic phenomena can be expressed mathematically, that knowledge lacks explanatory power unless it is linked to a mechanism thought to be responsible for that which is measured. The inferred mechanism is presented diagrammatically, schematically, or pictorially by means of a model. Modeling requires images. Commonly recognized are two types of models, iconic and sentential. A picture or a diagram is an iconic model; an equation, like other statements, is a sentential representation of something judged to be the case. Not everything we know can be expressed sententially. That we also think by means of pictures and diagrams is something Aristotle recognized when he described thinking as consisting of both imagination and judgment.

II

For the purpose of illustration as we reflect on *De Anima* III, permit me to relate an episode in the history of science that I take to be a rich source of relevant material. In late December 1938, Lise Meitner and her nephew Otto Frisch, one a theoretical chemist, the other a physicist, walked in the woods near Göteborg, Sweden. The problem before them was one created by the German physicists Otto Hahn and Fritz Strassman, namely, the seeming formation of barium from uranium. That the nucleus of the uranium atom could be split was at that time unthinkable. Attempting to understand the reports of Hahn and Strassman, Meitner and her nephew allowed their imagination full play. In the conversation that took place between them, Meitner and Frisch recalled that Bohr had once suggested that the nucleus of an atom resembled a liquid drop. If a drop could divide itself into smaller drops by elongating until a constricted neck formed in the middle and then could tear itself apart into two drops, perhaps something like this could happen to the uranium nucleus. Strong forces would resist, just as surface tension resists such a breakup in a drop of water. But nuclei are electrically charged and this might diminish the effect of the surface tension. Lise Meitner began to make some calculations on the back of a letter and on some scraps of paper. Frisch followed her calculations. Yes, the charge of a uranium nucleus might be a "wobbly uncertain drop, ready to divide itself at the slightest provocation, such as the impact of a neutron." When the two drops parted they would fly apart with tremendous energy, an energy calculated by Meitner to be approximately 200 million electron-volts.

Lise Meitner remembered at this point how to compute the masses of nuclei from the so-called packing fraction. If the uranium nucleus divided, the two particles formed would be lighter than the original nucleus by about one-fifth of the mass of the proton. With some quick arithmetic, she multiplied the lost one-fifth of mass by the speed of light squared. It came out almost exactly at 200 million electron volts. The lost one-fifth would supply exactly the 200 million electron-volts of energy with which the drop would tear apart. The importance of their insight was not lost on them. "So here was the source of all that energy," said Frisch. It is reported that the two looked at each other with incredulity, and then again with triumph.

Within a few days they had submitted their speculations to Niels Bohr, who was about to embark for the United States. In a paper reporting their discovery for the British journal *Nature,* they described the division of the nucleus as *fission*. The source of the term itself is interesting. As they were writing the paper, Frisch had asked a young biologist what he and his confreres called the splitting of a cell. "Fission," he replied, and Frisch had the word he needed. Ruth Moore, from whom this account is taken, writes, "the process was simply, accurately and perceptively named for all time."[1]

Next came the task of testing their theory by experimentation. Among the first tests were those of the Roman scientist Enrico Fermi, now established in Manhattan, who on meeting Bohr's ship learned of the Meitner-Frisch theory. Within days the word was out: within less than a month four major laboratories in the United States had experimentally confirmed the Meitner-Frisch explanation by bombarding nuclei with neutrons and measuring the mass lost and the energy produced. In Aristotelian language the next step in the thinking process, "supposition," had taken place. "Supposition," or what was thought to be the case, was affirmed of reality.

I will come back to this story as my commentary unfolds, but permit me to quickly call attention to a number of its Aristotelian facets. First, Meitner and Frisch were clearly searching for an explanation of something that begged to be understood. They were looking for the mechanism responsible for the phenomena reported by their German colleagues. Though the data they were attempting to explain seemed implausible they nevertheless accepted those data on the authority of Hahn and Strassman. Meitner and Frisch, as well as the scientific world on both sides of the Atlantic, believed the Hahn-Strassman report to be accurate. Acceptance of the work of others is normal procedure in the sciences. Most theoretical physics is based on the authoritative reports of colleagues.

Aristotle would understand the instance of explaining as a search for a cause. There is no doubt that Meitner and Frisch were looking for a cause. Their search led them to an imagined source. Note also the role of analogy or metaphor. The source of the energy released was imagined to be something like a drop of water, elongating and dividing. The nucleus was conceived in visual terms as a fluid. Clearly the mind was proceeding by analogy from something better known to something less known. The familiar was serving as a model for the unfamiliar. The mechanism responsible for the phenomena was understood by means of an iconic model. The mind was not satisfied by a mere mathematical description of the phenomena reported. Not surprisingly the value of the Meitner-Frisch explanation was recog-

---

1. Niels Bohr, *The Man, His Science and the World They Changed* (Cambridge, Mass.: M.I.T. Press, 1985).

nized universally. But was the explanation correct? If it were, it could not simply be checked by repeating the experiment that gave rise to it in the first place, though laboratories in Europe and North America were eager to do so. For Aristotle, explanations are different than mere reports. An explanation has to satisfy by linking a causal mechanism to the phenomenon observed and initially reported as raw data. Meitner, Frisch, Bohr, Fermi, and the many others who quickly saw the implications of the explanation began to integrate that knowledge with other things they knew. The plausible explanation became the accepted one as all that was known about the nature of uranium and its various isotopes cohered. Every attempt at interpretation was tested with every possible real or imagined experiment. The Meitner-Frisch explanation was dependent upon previous success in the construction of a model for the uranium atom. That model was initially constructed in an attempt to explain the cause of certain phenomena associated with the sensorially distinguishable and describable element uranium. Now that model was employed to explain something never intended, namely its break up into barium and krypton.

There are points I wish to emphasize: (1) the implicit philosophical realism evident in the thought of Meitner and Frisch, (2) the fact that their model actually provided a plausible mechanism for the phenomena observed. By means of the model, properties were associated with their structural cause. The Meitner-Frisch mode of procedure followed what I take to be an Aristotelian description of scientific method. In understanding the mind renders intelligible the activity or properties encountered by means of the imagined source. To provide a reasonable source is the function of the model. It is not simply a question of before and after, since the source is never directly experienced. There is a linking of behavior to that which is thought to behave by means of a plausible mechanism that can only be thought by means of a model. I stress, it is not simply a question of sequence, contiguity in place, continuity in time, and a habit of associating those events designated cause and effect; rather the mind is led to affirmation, because the inferred cause is seen to be responsible for the phenomena in question. The cause must be presented to the mind by means of an image, not just any image but one rendering a plausible mechanism. The mind immediately rules out a multiplicity of images in favor of likely candidates. As mere logical possibility gives ground to real possibility, images are quickly discarded. The closer one comes to a true explanation the fewer the images that can be entertained. Finally only one imaged source is regarded as plausible and is given the status of genuine cause. The imagined structure can be said to be instantiated. I am using the term *structure* here not as a synonym for substantial form but as a quality consequent upon extension, a quality reflective of form but not identical with form itself, nor with essence.

III

The Meitner-Frisch story will lend itself to further exploitation as we discuss Aristotle's theory of mind and imagination. As you can see, it is my contention that Aristotle's analysis pertains to unseen reality as much as to the world of immediate experience. The knowledge we have of the structures of the submicroscopic is by inference, yet the mental mechanisms by which we attain and hold that knowledge are not much different from the knowledge we have of the world of sense experience. Lest you think that I have drifted too far from my texts, let me return to *De Anima* III, where Aristotle describes our knowledge of the sensible particular. At 427a he says, "Thinking both speculative and practical is regarded as a form of perceiving; for in the one as well as in the other the soul discriminates and is cognizant of something which is."[2] Indeed the ancients go so far as to identify thinking and perceiving: But Aristotle is quick to point out that thinking, both speculative and practical, is different from perceiving. Thought is found only where there is a discourse of reasoning. Focusing his discourse on imagination, Aristotle distinguishes it from either perceiving or discursive thinking, though it is not found without sensation, or judgment without it.[3]

Clearly, for Aristotle, thinking is in part imagination, in part judgment. Imagination is distinguished from sensation or perceiving in another respect. Sensations are always true; imaginations can be false. Imagination is deliberative in human beings and can unify several images, some of which may not be united apart from the mind. In this fashion imagination plays a role in explaining falsehood. Images can be true and false of objects just as we sometimes make false perceptual reports. It is possible to instantiate as real that which is merely imaginable. Imagining lies within our own power—we can exercise it wherever we wish—but the forming of questions is not free. Imagination is a movement resulting from an actual exercise of a power by the knowing subject. It is not thrust upon it by an object independent of the mind, as would occur in perception. Imagination or phantasia (*phaos*: light), says Aristotle, provides light. It is not possible to see

2. 427a, 17–23.
3. 427b, 15–17.

without light.⁴ But the light of imagination is not the light provided by *nous*; imaginations remain in the organs of sense and resemble sensations.

Mind is to be understood as a capacity; it is a capacity to think and to judge. Though the mind may become each set of its possible objects, its condition is still one of potentiality. Thinking is not merely passive. Thinking can take place in the presence of objects both real and imagined. "To the thinking soul images serve as if they were contents of perception."⁵ Although the soul never thinks without an image it can go beyond the merely sensed. But it always thinks the forms in the images. No one can learn or understand anything in the absence of sense. When the mind is actively aware of anything, it is necessarily aware of it along with an image; for images are like sensuous contents except they contain no matter.⁶ In another passage Aristotle says, "When one exerts the intellect, although the object may not be quantitative, one envisages it as quantitative." This seeming contradiction produced by saying that images "contain no matter" yet are "quantitative" can easily be resolved.

Having established that images are essential to thought, Aristotle distinguishes between two different ways images function in cognitive acts. These parallel two different attitudes one can hold toward pictures. A figure in a drawing may be thought to be a likeness or contemplated simply as a picture. An image may be taken in its own right or taken as about something else, as a likeness.⁷ Some part of the soul is said to interpret an image in a certain way when we have a case of thinking. When the image occurs in its own right it seems to occur as a theoretical concept. When it occurs qua about something else, it appears as a likeness or memory state and is laden with its quantitative aspects.

Images and thoughts Aristotle acknowledges are difficult to distinguish. If an image can serve simply as an image of a triangle, then it can also function in general thought about triangles. The "image in its own right" exemplifies a set of properties that it presents. A thought is like an image in the sense that the properties by virtue of which the image exemplifies the thought are those that tell us what it is to be. The image exemplifies form. Or we can say the mind thinks the forms in the images.⁸ Although the image is particular, thoughts are sharable and intersubjective. A single universal is derived from a multiplicity

4. 429a, 3–4.
5. 421a, 14–15.
6. 432a, 5–9.
7. 451a, 1–2.
8. 431b, 2.

of experiences. Those experiences may not be confined to a single person but may be the result of collaborative efforts.

Aristotle holds that we must be capable of developing the internal structures that subserve thought but must be careful not to make inferences from internal structures to the nature of the world. The consistency within itself or the integrity of an image does not say anything about a nature that it may be taken to represent. To justify its adequacy one must make a claim based on demonstration, which is shared and public. Put another way, meaning is a matter of public agreement. The actual deployment of mental devices such as representational structures is a necessary condition not only for any functionally complete intellectual act but for communication.

A difficult question is the relation of imagination to abstraction. Whether Aristotle held a doctrine in which he distinguished between active and passive mind is debated by scholars on the basis of available texts. Given a comprehensive grasp of Aristotle's theory of knowledge and his theory of being, it is difficult to believe that he did not distinguish between active and passive mind. True, there is only one process of coming to know, but the awareness of commonality and the mental expression of it seem to be distinguishable acts. Controlled knowing of the sort that takes place in the sciences is analogous to what takes place at an earlier stage of knowing. I have in mind the deliberate focusing on commonality that occurs in controlled or scientific induction and the deliberate creation of images in order to understand that commonality and difference. It can be argued that controlled induction and model formation are but systematic attempts to do what the mind does naturally at a prior stage in coming to know. It is through the process of induction that the soul is "led to" or "brought to" the universal as present in the particular. When one of a number of logically indiscriminate particulars becomes the focus of interest, the earliest universal is present in the soul.[9] In the flux of the particulars the soul is gradually able to perceive the first constant and unchanging universal. The plurality of individuals is required to focus the mind's vision gradually on that universal that is present in all individuals but is finally perceived as such by the mind in one particular instance. This is the intuition (*nous*) that apprehends the commonality of the nature under consideration and is the originative source of scientific knowledge.

Of course, what one makes of these texts is the result of the epistemology and to some extent the ontology one brings to them. Con-

---

9. *Posterior Analytics*, II, 19 (100a, 10–14).

temporary debates bring to mind ancient disputes. The terminology is sometimes new, but the age-old problem of universals haunts present discussion. This problem is sometimes framed in its contemporary setting as the problem of the relation of language to reality. W. Quine, for example, has argued that the referent of a term is not determinately fixed and consequently reference is inscrutable in the sense that we can have no sure knowledge of the referent of our speech.[10] Hilary Putnam holds that even an ideal theory, that is, one that is compatible with all possible observations and satisfies all theoretical and operational requirements, can employ different models. Since multiple models can satisfy all epistemic conditions, there is no nonarbitrary way of selecting one of them as the unique model representative of the posited structure. If there are alternative possible models of a theory, how can we know which approximates reality? Putnam maintains that reference cannot be fixed by the mind's affirming a reality represented by the intentional model, since that would require the unintelligible notion of our minds' having access to reality that is unmediated by the theory whose reference is in question. Putnam also rejects the view that reference is determined by a causal relation between a structure independent of the mind and the language user, since such a view would presuppose realism.[11]

In another text, Putnam seems to be saying that the only reality to which we have access is "reality as it appears to us."[12] Putnam is, of course, not alone in maintaining such a position. Idealists, such as Nicholas Rescher, maintain almost the same thing. The realist will counter that Putnam's position is flawed by the fallacy of equivocation. In one sense to say that some item is mind-independent is to say that the item exists independently of the existence of any human mind. In another sense, to say that some item is mind-dependent is to say that it cannot be apprehended by the human mind in a way that is unmediated by some schema. The fact that some item is not mind-independent in the latter sense does not entail that it is not mind-independent in the former sense, and it is the former sense that is at issue in the realist conception of truth.

Niels Bohr recognized that theoretical concepts that are devoid of any perceptual content are problematic. He called them *idealizations,* but I think that in the mathematical sense there is no such thing as a

10. W. V. Quine, *Ontological Relativity and Other Essays* (New York: Columbia University Press, 1969), 29–39.
11. *Realism and Reason: Philosophical Papers,* vol. 3 (Cambridge: Cambridge University Press, 1983), chap. 1, "Models and Reality."
12. Ibid., 207.

straight line or a triangle in reality. If theoretical concepts are to have any genuine explanatory force, they cannot lose all connection with ordinary sense perception. Once science goes beyond the critical level where its concepts lose all connection with ordinary perceptual experience, it can no longer be regarded as providing a description of an actual mechanism. It should be noted that, in line with Bohr's description of scientific practice, Aristotelian realism does not require that true statements be regarded as conveying mental pictures that completely depict the inherent properties of the object in itself. Science is always open-ended. There is always more to be known, always better representation to be attained. But the mind in achieving this is not moving from the false to the true but from the less precise to the more precise. The progressive character of scientific inquiry is connected with its communal nature.

In this context, P. F. Strawson's contemporary defense of an Aristotelian realism is worth recalling. In Strawson's language the possibility of descriptive identification and reidentification of particulars implies not only a spatiotemporal world of external objects but intersubjective communication.[13] Material objects are ontologically basic from the point of view of particular identification. They are the particulars that can be identified and reidentified without reference to particulars of a different sort. Basic particulars must be publicly observable objects of a sort that different observers can literally see, or hear, or touch. Other sorts of particulars are not basic in this respect.

IV

To bring to a conclusion some of these observations: As Etienne Gilson once wrote, "Being is neither intuited by a sensibility nor understood by an intellect; it is known by a *man*. An organic chain of mental operations links the sense perception of what is known as being to the abstraction and to the judgment through which man knows it as being."[14] We started with the axiom, there is no intellection without accompanying sensation. But to recognize that principle is not to instantiate every image that accompanies thought. Some images are involuntary, spontaneously arising in the presence of their object; others are well crafted, well designed, themselves the product of much thought, created to represent as closely as conceivable the real. In the

---

13. P. F. Strawson, *Individuals: An Essay in Descriptive Metaphysics* (London: Methuen, 1959), 38f.

14. *Being and Some Philosophers*, 2d ed. (Toronto: Pontifical Institute of Medieval Studies, 1952), 206.

sciences we call them models. A model is an idealized or postulated representation of an unobservable entity or process. Elements employed in their representation are analogous to entities at least partially understood from elsewhere. Associated with the model is a theory indicating how the model may be expected to behave and so permitting specific predictions to be made. The crafting of a model is not arbitrary. In their initial vagueness and generality it is thrust upon us and held by us in a sensuous way by the imagination. But the intellect is not satisfied with vagueness. It wants precision even in the images it employs in judging and reasoning. If the images do not come, if they are not immediately evoked, that may be evidence that the source of the phenomena indirectly grasped as statistical reports has not been truly identified. We do not yet know what to make of our finding. This does not militate against the Aristotelian position. It simply means that not all that is encountered is understood. We may for the time being have masses of data that require interpretation. Sometimes the mathematics may lag behind the data, sometimes the postulated mechanism behind the statistically expressed correlation. The basic thrust of the scientific enterprise is to render intelligible that which does not explain itself. The continuity between prescientific and scientific knowledge was assumed in Aristotle's account of knowing. In our own day, the globally distributed character of independent reports, the similar profferring of tentative explanations, the employment of common images to represent indicate that the mind is not fabricating but discovering.

One often reads that scientific reports of nature supersede each other with remarkable frequency, that the reports to which we now subscribe have falsified previous reports taken to be true, and that we have reason to suspect that our present way of looking at things will give way to others. This is taken as evidence of the arbitrariness and unreliability of the conceptual schemes we currently employ. But the history of science discloses no such thing. In every period there have been false starts, but where explanations have been recognized as substantiated, they remain sometimes as vague accounts that have been rendered more precise by the refinement of data or the rigor of explanation. Enhancement is not falsification. The advancement of our knowledge of nature does not refute Aristotle's description of the cognitive process but reinforces it. Explanatory notions such as "cell," "bacterium," "virus," "molecule," "atom," "circulatory system," and "nerve fiber" were first theoretical entities before they became objects of direct or indirect perception.

As Aristotle knew well, the study of knowing cannot be divorced from the study of being. Man does not first know knowledge; he first knows things. Aristotle's fundamental questions remain: Does the thing exist? What is it? What are its properties? Why does it have these properties? It is impossible to answer any of these questions in everyday knowing without the employment of images; in the sciences of nature, without the employment of iconic models.

5   Duhem's Interpretation of Aristotle on Mathematics in Science
FRANCIS J. COLLINGWOOD

Science goes on as the curiosity of man sends him observing and cataloguing in myriad fields. Each new day and week sees more revelations as the incredibly sophisticated worlds of things and their activities yield to experiment and thought. Attempts to say what it all means and to understand how all the sorts of fields, and atomic and subatomic particles, co-relate, pass for philosophies of science. Said philosophies are concerned with methodology as well as with content. Each such philosophy tends to mirror the development of the physical sciences at the time of its writing. I wish to call attention to a philosophy of physics written by Pierre Duhem, who had the double qualification of being not only an excellent teacher and contributor to the field of thermodynamics but also a very accomplished historian of science. The first qualification means that he was well acquainted with the field he analyzed and conversant with allied sciences; the second means that he knew of a great number of historical attempts to develop physics and astronomy, with the varying degrees of success achieved. Thus his theory about the purpose and the proper procedures of physical science represents the best that one could expect to find at the turn of the last century. I believe that it well illustrates the thesis that there are perennial aspects to physical philosophy; that in seeking to make the world of inanimate matter intelligible, man continues to do the same sort of thing. He attempts to make new discoveries become a continuation of current beliefs. He attempts to make the world intelligible by quantifying the data that research turns up and by stating the laws of nature. In this way he systematizes his apprehensions of nature so as to understand it better. The explicit part of the systematizing of experience is of ancient origin. However, it has changed little in its aim of setting up clear-cut classifications of things and of making reductive explanations of complex things in terms of their components. Concentrating on the results of this activity is elaborating a theory about how nature works; it is making a philosophy of nature.

The first philosophy of nature that attempted to go beyond mere claims and untestable hypotheses was elaborated by Aristotle. It provided several very valuable notions in the attempt to understand material reality. It is found in the second book of his *Physics* as presuppositions about the role of causes in events and as a belief in the orderly repetitive sequencing of natural processes. There are other analyses of nature in other places in his writings, but nowhere is his philosophy of nature completely elaborated as a single coherent system. Aristotle also set down some fundamental truths about an empirical approach to constructing physical science. These also have to be gathered from various works. Duhem's writings show that he was quite conversant with this theory about doing science for he incorporated most of it into his attempt to explain what science is all about. However, Aristotle was a better theorist than he was a practitioner. His own attempts to investigate physical problems led him into unjustified assumptions and erroneous conclusions. Unfortunately for the progress of science and mankind, he had many followers in the succeeding centuries who followed his erroneous science and neglected his excellent methodology, which insisted upon the need to rely on actual experience as the warrant for doing science. Duhem gave a somewhat elaborate version of Aristotle's philosophy of science while he was developing what might be called a philosophy of scientific methodology. Thus Aristotle's philosophy of nature, as the presuppositions that underlie all physical science, as well as his theory of empirical knowing, is in Duhem's philosophy of science.

Duhem is noteworthy for both the rigor of his thinking and the clarity of his ideas as a physicist in the forefront of his field. He should have had a professorship in Paris, but pettiness forbade this.[1] He wrote with such conviction and expertise about the nature of physical science that it seems worthwhile to me to see how enduring is his analysis in a world that has seen so many revolutionary discoveries in physics and astronomy since his death in 1916. It is because I see a continuous thread of theory running from the pre-Socratics through Plato and Aristotle and Duhem (among others) into the present scientific enterprises that I brashly call this enduring viewpoint of science a perennial one. In what follows, I will elaborate, on my own, implications and

---

1. Stanley L. Jaki, *Uneasy Genius: The Life and Work of Pierre Duhem* (Boston: Martinus Nijhoff Publishers, 1984). In this work Jaki gives a heavily documented account of Duhem's life and of all his writings. See pp. 27–53 for the vengeance executed against Duhem by a prestigious author in the field of thermodynamics whose prized hypothesis was totally discredited in Duhem's doctoral dissertation.

consequences of Aristotle's well-known teachings, in order to give a fuller presentation of his philosophy, which he often stated so concisely. I do this in order to round out the fine Aristotelian influence that made Duhem's account of how to proceed in science so good.

The material causes that have preoccupied much of physical speculation and research have changed in kind from time to time and are still far from certain. However, that there is a reality underlying appearances is a perennial belief. Parmenides and Democritus, each in his own way, discounted the credibility of man's senses in reporting about our physical surrounds. Plato too saw sensation as fallacious. In a striking declaration, in the beginning of the *Timaeus*, he holds that any account of the physical universe will be a mere saving of the appearances of things by resorting to probabilities. Aristotle also believed that things may have parts that are qualitatively different from the composite whole. These are substrates underlying appearances. But he parts company with his predecessors on the issue of the reliability of the senses in reporting the appearance of physical substances. He holds that man's only access to the realm of nature lies in the ability of our external senses to replicate the appearances of things in our sensory consciousness. The sense in act becomes the sensible in act.[2] Rephrased, what we sense is the appearances of physical things: that is, things are for the senses what they appear to be. If there were some way of getting at the appearances of things other than by sensing, a check on them could be carried out. Certainly, in Aristotle's time, no such alternative knower existed. Consequently, then, as now, we must depend upon our senses, and the instruments that extend them, for the facts of nature. The human direct senses are usually fairly reliable for they cannot be made to detect what is not there, by imagination, or by intellect, or by memory, without our deliberately intending to do so. Apart from defects in the sensory organ, which might lead to a false identification of what is present, Aristotle saw no impediment to the senses acting naturally and detecting the colors, sounds, tastes, and so on, that are given in sensation. Viewpoints may obtrude, so that we have a bias when we are observing, as in wanting to see circular motion in a planetary revolution. This sort of false seeing would be an error of judgment in Aristotle's way of analyzing consciousness. By contrast, the sense, identifying with the quality of the sensible present to it, is specified by the actual determinate aspects of the sensible and thus obtains a reliable replica of how the quality exists in fact.

Aristotle repeatedly stated his theory that our senses have as their

2. *De Anima*, III, 2, 425b, 25.

proper function the correct reporting of the appearances of things, qua sensed. The sensed sensible has only an introspective existence. No one has successfully located one nor given a physical description of one; nor has any aspect of memory or imagination, or their contents, been successfully described physically or physiologically to date. As the sensed appearance of things it exists only in sensory consciousness. In short, introspective awareness is the first step in science, for it alone replicates for us, in our consciousness where we can work with it, that which exists in nature. So our being able to speak of sense data with a fair amount of agreement, even though no one has ever experienced one objectively, so as to describe it or to measure it, implies a uniformity of human sensation to that degree. What can be located in the public realm is the physical thing itself and the language or other signs referring to it. What the sense is receiving, or has received, from physical sources is privy to the sentient being that is conscious of it. Consequently, since no generalization as such, nor any science as such, nor any other sort of explanation as such is given in nature, all of these will be the result of human activity. Man in doing science will always be doing the same thing: using his perceived sense data in making up classifications, looking for the underlying factors and the encompassing principles, and trying to capture the whole of reality in his language or other conventional device. This is how he makes matter intelligible to himself.

Because neither language nor any other purely conventional device can replicate the actual features of matter, there will be a lack of fit between the thing under investigation and its description: words are abstract; things are infinitely detailed. The indispensable generalizations, which enable us to encompass all gravitational phenomena, as being attraction of mass for mass, for example, are incurably abstract. So are the common nouns that we use to typify things and to describe them. Both are instruments of understanding, and neither replicates things for any faculty, including understanding. This sort of reading of what is in nature is not at all the same as the feature by feature, detail by detail replication of physical things by a sense. However, they are complementary in human cognition as a whole. The dichotomy between what is sensed and how it is understood is a reason for Aristotle's concluding that mind cannot be classed as one of the human senses. "Most of all the senses make us know and bring to light many differences between things . . . we do not regard any of the senses as wisdom; yet surely these give the most authoritative knowledge of particulars."[3]

3. *Metaphysics* I, 1, 980a, 27, and 981b, 10.

In my view, this dichotomy is also a reason for relying on quantitative analysis of data to construct science. Quantity, as a component of every physical thing, can be known with an ever-increasing accuracy that approaches the exactness of stated physical laws. I will complete my brief review of what Aristotle held, at least implicitly, and that Duhem held explicitly. Science begins with careful observations. It is constructed in the human mind and is often tested for its value on the observational level. After looking at things through the senses the mind turns to its own devices, such as definitions, causal dependencies, other relationships, compositions, and geneses, and so on. With these it works out a theory about what appears to exist and what appears to be going on. Then it refers to the real world to determine whether it has saved the appearances. Science is a mental artifact that enables us to understand reality as it appears and to manipulate it. It enables us to predict some futures with reasonable accuracy in terms of what most probably will occur. All this is done with conventional nonreplicating symbols. Only our senses, with sometimes the aid of instruments, put us in actual contact with matter in a cognitive manner. More often today, as Duhem points out, our senses enter into science only to read the findings of the instruments, a sensory effort totally directed by and meaningful only to the mind.[4]

Aristotle relied on the endless repetitions of appearances to assure himself that although change is a constant occurrence in nature, nevertheless there are repeated similarities there also. Thus regularly any olive seed that sprouted begat an olive seedling, which grew to maturity and yielded a harvest of olives. The constant continuation of living species through reproduction manifested both regularity and causal dependence as reliable bases for correct prediction of events in the realm of appearances. I like to call this assurance of the connectedness of things the uniformity of nature. It is a main plank in Aristotle's philosophy of nature. He argues for it in *Physics* II as a generalization based upon observations open to anyone. It is a powerful belief supporting the elaboration of universals based upon repetitions. It supports the whole of astronomy and of particle physics, which constantly extrapolate, from a limited range of experience, to infer that similar or identical properties exist beyond the range of hands-on testing.

For Aristotle, the discerning of often repeated dependencies triggered the grasping of the dependency relationship by astute observers. Thus that a certain treatment always cures a certain kind of fever

---

4. Pierre Duhem, *The Aim and Structure of Physical Theory*, trans. Philip P. Wiener (Princeton, N.J.: Princeton University Press, 1954), pt. 2, chap. 4.

gives the medical person assurance of what to prescribe.[5] The need to have seed for the propagation of animal and vegetative life confirms the relationship of these two in the mind of the man of science. Repetition is characteristic of nature. The reassurance engendered by repetition of the same experiences led to an understanding that could be verbalized in a general way. According to Aristotle, just as the essential characteristics of a human being are manifested in the appearances and activities of each one, and so of any one, so also in more complex matters each instance will be typical. As he put it, the universal is present in the particular, although the mind may fail to see it.[6] Presumably we need many similar experiences, and these are the particulars, in order to attract our attention. But as far as his theory goes any one olive will have whatever it takes to be an olive and so will have the essence of olive and be a suitable locus for intuiting the universal. For the fabulous E. Rutherford a few instances of alpha particles' being repelled straight back to their source of emission led to the intuition that the atom had a positively charged very tiny nucleus, which reversed the positively charged alphas in their tracks. In mathematical matters one may intuit the essence of a straight line, or of a sphere, in the first experience of them but be lacking the proper language to express what seems so obvious. When these intuitions are stated as axioms, and understood, there seems to be a uniformity of mind that binds most persons to assent to the axioms. But this clarity is never found in physics.[7]

Outside the realms of mathematics and of commonsense awareness of things, the discovery and positing of general truths of nature require concentration to find the regularly recurring causal dependencies. Quite often this involves many people working on the same task, and experimental tampering with nature as well. Duhem was well aware of this. He wrote brilliant reports of his own research, giving credit to everyone who in any way assisted in his progress. He also made painstaking studies of the onset and development of particular notions in astronomy and chemistry and physics. He believed in the gradual progression of budding hypotheses into confirmed laws. There are no self-evident truths springing from the tedious labor of research. But it is all worthwhile, and sometimes the result of the calculating and pondering will be some quite fruitful generalization about the facts. Consider, for example, the mind-shattering results of

---

5. *Metaphysics* I, 981a, 5.
6. *The Posterior Analytics*, II, 19, 100a, 5.
7. Duhem dwells on this point, that physics is laborious and fraught with difficulties that are not found in mathematics. Cf. Duhem, *Aim*, II, 7.

research into blackbody radiation. An iron rod heated to a high temperature emits various colors of light, but no satisfactory formula expressed this correctly until Max Planck thought of treating the energy involved as if it existed in small chunks, even though the light was thought of as being waves. This is expressed in the abstract formula $E = h\nu$. This is read, the energy of a wave or particle is the product of its frequency multiplied by Planck's constant h. This formula signaled the start of quantum physics. It related the energy of a particle to frequencies, which differ from one another by definite discrete intervals. A whole host of phenomena related to the wave interpretation of radiated energy are adequately expressed in this formula. This is an example of the economy of thought that Duhem saw as the primary aim of physical theory. Had Duhem adopted this new way of doing energetics, as his way of developing thermodynamics was called, no doubt his brilliant mind would have contributed greatly to the advances in physics and chemistry that followed Planck's breakthrough. But Duhem was abiding by what he took to be the most prudent way to proceed in science, by refusing to grant status to tenuous hypotheses before they received solid evidence in their favor.

Since Aristotle's time experience has taught us to beware of taking anomalous instances as completely typical of olives or whatever. We have also learned that although general propositions often contain a valuable point of view, they may lead us to think that we know what we do not know. Aristotle's own error, in limiting his version of gravitational attraction to the center of the earth, proved to be a stumbling block to his followers for centuries. Nevertheless, in a realist approach to science, it is necessary to take observations into account in order to declare a general proposition.

General propositions are the basis of that part of Aristotle's logic that seeks to use demonstration as a method of drawing out implications. For example, man's being rational implies that he can laugh at the silly irrational experiences he may have. Rationality is the middle term, linking "being human" and "being able to laugh." Demonstrations do not abound in the Aristotelian writings. Middle terms were not easy to find in complex matters. However, the use of mathematics in the development of scientific knowledge was known to him. In his analysis of sensory apprehension Aristotle noted that the properties of size and shape, and of being in motion or at rest, are true of every physical object. Although, according to Aristotle, the quantitative and qualitative aspects of matter are inseparable, in reality they are separable in consciousness. Quantity can be considered in itself, as spatial displacement, without any mention of the qualitative aspects of things.

Of course, the qualities do locate the quantities for our senses in actual experience. However, since every visible object is a quantity, that fact is a basis for an analysis of the quantitative aspects of all bodies. Even though our judgments can be deceived in these matters, Aristotle aimed his study of physics at spatial magnitudes and motion and time. Mathematics, a science of quantity in its own right, would be an excellent instrument to assist in this endeavor. Thus he described optics and astronomy as physical branches of mathematics. He depicted them as studying mathematical lines qua physical: that is, treating physical lines as approximations to the purely ideal mathematical lines, which have extension in one direction only.

It was the investigation of such almost perfectly straight lines of sunlight, casting perfectly even-edged shadows, that played a role in Newton's belief that light was a stream of corpuscles. Light waves would, he thought, bend and show a ragged edge. Closer analysis would have shown diffraction of the light at the edges and challenged the corpuscular theory. The claims that light is a wave and that light is a particle were being put forth in Duhem's science of energetics, and he said that there is no crucial experiment that can decide the issue. Since light has never been made to show its face, the hypotheses involved are unevidenced. Consequently any hypothesis that saves the appearances is not preferable to any other similarly successful hypothesis. They are equally simply learned guesses. Today we must accept that light acts like a wave at times and also acts at times like particles, photons.

Scientific knowledge is attained when we become acquainted with the principles, conditions, and simplest elements of the objects of inquiry; such is the stipulation in the opening lines of *Physics* I. There follows a theory about the underlying substrates of physical things. In *Physics* II nature as the domain of self-perfecting activities of living things is discussed. It is in this book that the basic principles of Aristotle's philosophy of nature are to be found. The actual study of living things, other than man, is found in the biological writings. That is perhaps why the second book of the *Physics* only sets down the causes of physical things and the principles of analysis of nature as goal-oriented and contains no further discussion of living things.

The science of nature is concerned with spatial magnitudes and motion and time, we are told in the beginning of *Physics* III. It is in the subsequent part of this book that the problematic that was the chief interest of Aristotelian cosmologists is to be found. But also it is here that Aristotle departs from his stated best procedure for obtaining true science. He indulges in speculation based on insufficient observation and in some cases on no empirical information at all. His followers took this tack, ignoring, as he did, his own excellent analysis of how to proceed in setting up physical science. This must have scandalized Duhem, for, in his own theory of science, he insists on sticking to the methods that are aimed at preventing the intrusion of any unjustified principles and of any unevidenced claims. As a historian of science Duhem thoroughly analyzed the physical doctrines of many of his predecessors in science. His *Le Système du Monde* is a ten-volume history of cosmological research covering the period from Plato to Copernicus. In it Duhem saw a turning point in the direction that cosmological speculation was taking with the condemnation of errors in the teachings of the Aristotelians, by the bishop of Paris, Etienne Tempier, in 1277. At stake was the belief in the unlimited power of the Christian God conflicting with the interpretations about motion and place and infinity, and so on, that Aristotle had discussed in *Physics* III.

From the start of the fourteenth century the grandiose edifice of peripatetic physics was doomed to destruction. Christian faith had undermined all its essential principles . . . astronomy had rejected its consequences. The ancient monument was about to disappear; modern science was about to replace it.[8]

This terse statement is accompanied by a scolding of those who had claimed that the medieval period was barren of meaningful discussions of science. Duhem shows beyond dispute that the period was alive with speculation and controversy. The ten volumes are witness to how widespread was the interest in science in the medieval universities. Another text is more explicit on the clash between Christian belief and Aristotelian science.

But Christian orthodoxy grew angry with the numerous fetters Peripatetic philosophy and Averroism imposed in the name of logic upon divine omnipotence; it decided to break the fetters. In 1277, at the request of Pope John I, Etienne Tempier, bishop of Paris, convened an assembly of doctors of the Sorbonne, and other wise men. Without exception these theologians condemned every proposition that refused God the power to accomplish an act, under the pretext that the act was in contradiction with the Physics of Aristotle and Averroes. . . . In any case, even those who contested the validity of the condemnation did not dare uphold that the Assembly of 1277 formulated something nonsensical; they were constrained to admit, in contradiction to Aristotle's opinion, that one can attribute a movement to the universe as a whole without speaking words that signify nothing.[9]

8. Pierre Duhem, *Medieval Cosmology: Theories of Infinity, Place, Time, Void, and the Plurality of Worlds,* ed. and trans. Roger Ariew (Chicago and London: University of Chicago Press, 1985), paperback 1987. This is an abridged English translation of *Le Système du Monde.* Cf. p. 3.

9. Op. cit., 180.

Duhem saw Christian doctrine about the omnipotence of God as the factor that liberated medieval speculators from the errors of Aristotle. But it did not liberate them from relying on introspection. It did not reawaken in them the Stagirite's analysis of the direct senses as the only reliable testers of scientific claims. That liberation was long in coming.

What he saw in medieval science undoubtedly made Duhem aware of the sterility of speculation without recourse to actual experience of the physical world. It is with the qualities and the quantities that our senses make present to us that we are to begin our investigations of physical phenomena. Also the reduction to absurdity, a logical procedure, so favored by the medieval scholar, must be replaced by a mathematics that enables the physicist to calculate results. The aim of investigation remains the same as Aristotle had said. We need general propositions, based on repeated experiences of regularly recurring events, which enable us to understand those experiences in one sure intelligible grasp. What can be accomplished then is the achieving of the desired economy of thought, as the multiple, with its vagaries, gives way to the essential, as stated by the mind.

Duhem, because of his adherence to safe procedures, has been singled out for criticism as being opposed to progress in science.[10] I will elaborate upon my version of what Aristotle was claiming, as a basis for defending Duhem against that charge. When I take Aristotle literally, he says that the transition from sensory experience to the universal is a sort of induction and that the universal is a generalization based upon repeated experiences of a connection between events. What I take to be essential here is the relation between the events that are named as parts of the general proposition. The relatedness is given in sensory experience; the mind declares the relation. There are irregularities in the appearances, but these will not deter the physicist, for experience has taught him how to read the data. That the relation holds in all instances that have been experienced is the basis for proclaiming a physical law. One may be so sure of the truth of the generalization that he believes that he sees the necessity of the relation, that things could not be otherwise. But nothing in experience has given any reason to claim a knowledge about substrates underlying the bases for the proclaimed law. Whoever wants to introduce such factors must draw them from imagination and endow them with physical properties. For Duhem this is a waste of time, in trying to explain

---

10. Duhem, *Aim*. The foreword, written by de Broglie, criticizes Duhem for his antipathy to pictorial models.

what is fairly evident by what is obscure. Thus today's talk about gravitons, as the carriers of the gravitational force, would be interesting speculation; searching for them, without a clue as to their reality, would appear to be a poor use of time. It would be abandoning the empirical approach in order to chase chimeras.

Duhem was slow to embrace some new theories. His Aristotelianism led him to make the obtaining, and collating, of general propositions a paramount goal of scientific thinking. Duhem reasoned along this line of thought that the finer features of the objects being correlated by the law are not immediately relevant to the statement of the law, nor to its use. Similarly, what might be theorized about the smaller parts of the objects being analyzed, or about hidden processes, and the like, is not relevant as far as the statement of the law is concerned. Only when the smaller parts can be clearly discerned and the hidden processes brought to light can the lawlike behavior and predictable consequences be declared assuredly. However, prior to this, any guess that saves the appearances presents a mere possibility; no established law of physics need give way to this.

Duhem had great scorn for the controversies in which the learned medieval Aristotelians had engaged. They had departed from Aristotle's theory of science with its stress on experience. This was bad Aristotelianism! Only in the abandoning of eccentrics and epicycles in astronomy and in the destruction of Aristotle's dynamics with the creation of a new one did they appeal to observation. The attack by Tempier on Aristotelianism resulted not in a wholesale return to observation and discovery but rather to exploration of new possibilities in thought. That the new tack in thinking and discussing bore its own kind of fruit is evidenced by the invention of the infinitesimal calculus. Duhem tells us this in *Le Système du Monde*,[11] and he also makes clear that it is not discussion, nor novelty, that he deplores. It is the pursuit of Aristotle's sallies into the realm of conjecture, his fallible opinions about invisible factors, such as the longing by the elements to be in their natural place, that he finds deplorable. In his own chosen field he encountered the same sorts of discussion, the same bad Aristotelianism, and proclaimed their irrelevance to the task of understanding physical reality. In his faithfulness to the notion of logically deducing conclusions implicit in general propositions, he refuses to guess at, or otherwise to invent, underlying causes.[12] Thus he was cool to the theories about nuclei and electrons; they are invisible and unfamiliar,

---

11. Duhem, *Medieval Cosmology*, 4.
12. Duhem, *Aim*, pt. 2, chap. 1.

and they are built from guesses that border on the bizarre. Such theories were about factors outside the realm of repeatable experience for all but the very few. Also they were not related to observable facts until Niels Bohr presented his theory, which coincided with facts of spectrometry. Be it noted that Planck was hesitant to accept the hypothesis of molecules and atoms at first. Also Einstein, who put forth the theory of the photon, a particle, to complement the wave theory of light, might well be said to have resisted progress in rejecting the indeterminacy principle because he would not relinquish his belief in a rationally ordered universe.

Louis de Broglie chided Duhem for his reluctance to accept new factors being proposed in the field of thermodynamics, such as the electron. Yet de Broglie himself had to overcome his reluctance in introducing the theory of the wavicle. This involved the belief that an electron has the properties of both a wave and a particle, an apparent self-contradiction.[13]

Duhem merely showed the wise reticence, also practiced by other great minds, in wanting to be sure of the reality of his theorizing. De Broglie felt that he had to overcome the failure of experiment to determine that light is a wave and not a particle. This was a giant step forward for science, in which many brilliant scientists cooperated. However, it increased the gap between the visualizable and the intelligible. The existence of such a gap is of major importance in Duhem's philosophy of science. In retrospect, it appears that both Duhem and de Broglie were right even though different in their approaches. Duhem's faithfulness to deduction from general propositions would surely have brought him to see the validity of some of the conclusions about microparticles and fields had he lived longer in the era when these explanatory factors were slowly gaining currency. Securing progress in physics is often very, very difficult. That Duhem should be unwilling to dabble in what he felt were unfounded conjectures is not surprising in view of his experiences in researching the ancient and medieval cosmologists.

I have maintained that Duhem was influenced by two sorts of Aristotelianism. The text of the *De Anima*, *Physics*, and *Posterior Analytics* set the bare bones of Aristotle's beliefs on the genesis of science in the

---

13. Einstein's analysis of light as photons had thrown the discussion of the wave particle theory wide open. De Broglie, we imagine, reasoned that the electron might have similar dual properties. Because electrons are so small, a very tiny aperture would be needed to be able to interfere with its waves. De Broglie explained how the space between atoms in a crystal ought to be of the right size. Experiments proved that electrons are diffracted by crystal lattices, just as if they are waves.

human mind. I believe that Duhem adhered rigorously to what he found in these works. On the other hand, the texts of scores of medieval philosophers evidenced bad Aristotelianism. Duhem was reinforced by these in his determination to resist all attempts to introduce alien factors into physical theory. Now I present Duhem's version of how to incorporate a good philosophy of nature, with its attendant epistemological considerations, into a correct analysis of what physics was, in his day. Most fundamental in his analysis is the role of the quantification of sensory data. This makes the regularities and the systematic aspects of natural processes most manageable in stating physical laws. It also makes physics a probabilistic endeavor that does not aim at explaining the material universe. By quantification Duhem means representing things by conventional quantitative symbols.

Representing kinds of things by conventional quantitative symbols eliminates the ambiguity of other conventional signs and makes possible the use of strict rules of calculation. Thus every sense quality can be represented by arbitrary symbols, which, being able to signify more and less of the same thing, can represent variations in the intensity of the quality in a very precise way. Causes producing the quality or effects produced by the quality may be suitably quantified, should the quality itself prove difficult to measure. Duhem gives the example of the expansion of mercury in a thermometer as a measuring of the heat surrounding it.[14] The expansion of the mercury is due to the activity upon it of heat, which is equated with the motion of the surrounding molecules adjacent to the glass of the thermometer. Analyzing the motion of molecules is difficult in itself, but it gives rise to an effect that is measurable to some extent. The measuring involves a translation of the physical circumstances into numbers, by the use of measurement. The temperature may be read as 10 degrees or as 9.9 degrees or as 10.01 degrees, and so on, depending on the accuracy built into the thermometer. These are the translations that quantify the effect of the molecular activity. They replace the language of the sensory awareness of warmth by the language of numbers. There is no replication of warmth as such in the 10 degree reading. What is replicated is the amount of heat, only the quantity. It suffices, for ascertaining someone's body temperature, to know how close it is to the accepted norm. A certain amount of deviation is tolerable. A larger deviation is cause for alarm. Approximation tells us what we need to know. We fit the meaning of the deviation into the rest of our estimation of the situation and act accordingly. However, if we were cal-

14. Duhem, *Aim,* pt. 2, chap. 1, 115–16.

culating how a variation in temperature affected the pressure exerted by a gas upon the walls of its closed container, we would be trying to get the most accurate information possible, so as to state the numerical relation between the measure of the temperature and the measure of the pressure. These measures tell us something that is quantitatively true about the gas and the heat applied by approximately replicating their real quantitative aspects. The more accurate the measure the more it replicates the real quantities involved. This scientific knowledge does inform us reasonably accurately about matter. The version of the gas laws involved here does state a real relationship between temperature and pressure and volume, real but still approximate.

Physical reality was lost in the translation inasmuch as that reality is now represented by an abstract symbol that replicates only the quantitative aspect of the physical. Remember Aristotle's telling us that we can separate the quantitative in our consciousness, but nothing real exists as just quantity. Our instruments do indeed report on just the quantitative in many instances, but no one has ever experienced blank quantity in nature or in any other medium but thought. Duhem sees in this lack of correspondence between the symbolized and the symbol a loss of ability of a physical theory to interpret the meaning of what it has collated. It can deal with the physical laws that state the order and the causal dependencies that are found in nature. But any meaning beyond what they reveal in being ranked and correlated must be found outside the physical theory. Its method, which it must follow in order to achieve a precision greater than is found in our everyday knowledge of things, cuts it off from that realm of common sense from which it began. The transforming of sensed sensibles into quantified data eventually yields a highly abstract intelligibility, which is the glory of science. That intelligibility is a most powerful tool for looking at reality once again and seeing order and system and causal connections where before there was only a hodgepodge. The mind can read right into our sensory observations its judgments about the way things are, including causal connections. But the power of physical theory is less than the power of mind. Although it has phenomenal ability to explain in the domain where evidence is certain, it cannot, Duhem tells us, go beyond the appearances that our senses register repeatedly without betraying its goal, the correct classification and collating of physical laws. Mind can transcend the limitation of physical theory by going altogether outside the range of what it is sure of. But then mind is not doing physics.

Although Duhem's series of articles on the nature of physical theory were roughly concomitant with the three famous articles by Einstein written between the middle of March and the end of June in 1905, neither author acknowledged the other. Nevertheless it was by sweeping away unfounded presuppositions about subvisible factors, supposedly involved in heat and light phenomena, that Einstein explained both blackbody radiation and the photoelectric effect in a quantum mechanical way. In similar vein, Heisenberg and Schrodinger and Dirac developed quantitative ways of analyzing the data about the subvisible by leaving aside every aspect of sensed or imagined reality. Thus Duhem's analysis of how to do physical theory, by abandoning the qualitative aspects of matter and sticking to the measurable, is a truism in serious physics today. What is an electron? It is a particle that is characterized by its mass, and its electric charge, and its wave-like properties. It, like other components of chemical atoms, is known as a momentum having an intrinsic angular spin. It is described by four quantum numbers and is the workhorse of the workaday world.[15] It is electric current; it, along with the positive holes resulting from a scarcity of electrons, is solid-state electronics; it is the carrier of the energy involved in chemical reactions; it is the massive currents miraculously carried by superconductors. That the electron is what it does is the only description that we have of it beyond estimating its mass and charge. The other "little things" of today's physics are similarly apprised by deducing and measuring their quantitative aspects. Duhem is right: all we can be sure of are the measurable aspects of what we are working with.

Duhem was stating what he understood to be a fact about how one does physics successfully. The disappearance of the unmanageable qualitative aspects of things is a boon to the required precision of the quantifying process. It also should prevent the wrongheaded attempts to visualize the underlying stuff of things. The quantified results of experiment, and of observation, were safe and sufficient indications of physical reality. Of course, hypotheses went beyond observation. But in a well-constructed physical theory they are not just wild imaginings of possible substrates. Rather they are the sine qua non of physical theory. They not only express in a highly condensed form all of the phenomena expressed in concise fashion by an array of physical laws but also allow the deduction of lawlike behavior not otherwise suspected.[16] Dirac's reasoning to the existence of antimatter, as an implication of $E^2 = M^2C^4$ having a negative root, $-MC^2$, would have

15. Emilio Segre, *From X-Rays to Quarks* (New York: W. H. Freeman and Company, 1980). The discoveries of Rutherford, Bohr, Einstein, Heisenberg, and others, form the chapters of this very readable book.
16. Duhem, *Aim*, pt. 1, chap. 1.

pleased Duhem mightily. It is a vindication of his belief that successful physical theory approaches ever closer to a complete classification of all the laws of physics. This in turn is a replication, although still with a lack of fit, of the real physical world.

Duhem was more apologetic about his natural classification than he needed to be. As an Aristotelian he saw the growth of physical knowledge as making man ever wiser about his world. The uniformities of nature, the causal dependencies, the successful extrapolations constantly expanded man's comprehension of his surrounds. However, as a mathematical physicist, he saw a failure of physical theory to replicate natural things truly as they actually existed. And so, it was as an act of faith that he concluded that physical theory would arrive at a complete classification of the laws of nature.

But a short sketch of how a physical theory does its proper work leads to a different conclusion, and there is substantial evidence to show that Duhem was right. The first step in setting up a physical theory, Duhem says, is to find what is basic, find what is reliably repeatable in our field of observation. To achieve complete economy of thought, analysis of complexes into their constituent parts should arrive at the smallest number of primitive notions. As Aristotle had said, we are on the way to scientific knowledge when we determine the principles and simplest elements of the objects of inquiry. However, as Duhem points out, what is taken for simplest and basic will depend on the state of the art at any given time.[17]

The correlation of the primary factors into physical laws brings a large group of phenomena into explanation. That is the value of science. More thorough analysis or a new discovery may enlarge the scope of the scientific explanation. Duhem uses Maxwell's reduction of white light to electromagnetic activity, as an instance of enlarging the scope of Maxwell's equations, to include a phenomenon waiting to be classified, into a category already established.[18] Duhem sees the process as a constant dialogue between the factual certainty, in the realm of observation and experiment, and the precision and clarity, afforded by quantification and mathematical deduction.[19] In optics the mind of the physicist funnels the facts into laws, which then give a concise representation of a whole area of optical phenomena. These laws are then integrated into an optical theory, from which, by calculation, one can draw out whatever law one wishes to use. As experiment and observation reveal more of a factual nature, the theory incorporates them and probably adjusts somewhat in order to do so.

17. Duhem, *Aim*, pt. 2, chap. 2, 3.
18. Ibid.
19. Duhem, *Aim*, pt. 2, chap. 7, 5.

The correspondence between the theory and the facts grows to the point where there are no known exceptions. But Duhem had been too impressed by the approximate aspect of physical law. It can be a problem, but human ingenuity has constantly surmounted it. Smaller and smaller quantities are constantly being matched by ever-finer measurements. Nanoseconds and picoseconds are measured easily in today's superb optics, and the waves of electrons are being utilized in chip technology.[20] Approximation to reality is not an insurmountable barrier to our cataloguing of nature. In some areas, such as the periodic table of chemical elements, the classification of the elements that occur in nature is fairly complete. The interrelations between their structures are adequately expressed in terms of protons, neutrons, and electrons. Principles that had at one time been proposed as tenable hypotheses are now firmly stated as physical laws. Duhem foresaw the outlines of the physical theory that is being developed and used today.

20. *High Technology,* vol. 9, no. 3, p. 32, on ten-picosecond computing; p. 9 on use of electron waves in resonant-tunneling transistors.

6   Baffling Phenomena
NICHOLAS RESCHER

1. BAFFLING PHENOMENA

This essay will examine a mercifully rare and distinctly uncomfortable but nevertheless highly instructive sort of occurrence, namely *baffling phenomena*. This term is here applied specifically to those eventuations that we encounter in the course of experience that perplex us because they are at odds with our (putative) knowledge of the world. A baffling phenomenon in this sense is an eventuation that cannot be accommodated within the framework of one's understanding of what goes on because it conflicts with our accepted view of the natural order of things. The phenomenon at issue strikes one as a quirk, an anomaly, a puzzle, calling into question not just the completeness but even the correctness of the currently accepted mechanisms of explanatory understanding.

Consider, for example, the classic story[1] of the king of Siam, who refused to believe a traveler from afar who claimed that in countries he had visited, lakes and rivers turned solid at certain times of year. Since freezing weather lay wholly outside the king's experiential range, his reaction is perfectly understandable; even if he had been personally present at such an occurrence and witnessed this phenomenon "with his own eyes," the king would have been baffled, unable, on the basis of his knowledge, to make the least sense of it. The quantum phenomena that indicated both wavelike and particlelike modes of transmission for light quanta totally baffled a physics community that thought they had to behave one way or the other. In this sort of way, baffling phenomena are the stuff of cognitive dissonance. They represent situations that, given one's understanding of how things go in the world, simply should not be there at all.

---

1. Cf. Locke, *Essays Concerning Human Understanding*, book 4, chap. 16, sect. 5.

2. SOME CONTRASTS

Baffling phenomena are not simply a matter of novelty. Something can be entirely new without being baffling. The unfolding discovery of more and more transuranic elements in the twentieth century is an example. On the other hand, something can be long-known and thoroughly familiar without thereby necessarily ceasing to be baffling. (The magnetic behavior of the lodestone is a historical example, and the great rock figures on Easter Island a more recent one.) What matters for the bafflement of a phenomenon is not its novelty but its apparent conflict with our explanatory understanding.

Moreover, it is not just that such phenomena are puzzling. In explanatory situations, puzzlement arises in two predominant ways: first, through the lack and ignorance that reflect an explanatory gap; the phenomenon is inexplicable by available means; we lack the resources for providing an explanatory account; second, through an embarrassment of riches. There is an explanatory surfeit. We have a variety of conjectural alternative possible explanations for the phenomenon but cannot settle on one of them, cannot decide what particular one is correct. (In the present stage of knowledge, the phenomenon of the extinction of dinosaurs is a plausible example of this latter situation.) But what we have here characterized as a baffling phenomenon is not this sort of thing at all. It is not a mere situation of no explanation or even one of a proliferation of alternate possible explanations but a situation of a phenomenon's running clean contrary to our explanatory canon, of its being at odds with our best available understanding of how things work in the world. A baffling phenomenon is exactly one whose every currently conjectured adequate explanation involves abandoning some currently accepted explanatory principle.

Of course we feel uncomfortable with baffling phenomena. We would like to be rid of them. But once we ascertain their authenticity—establishing that they are something reliably identifiable, repeatable, and genuine rather than faked—we have to come to terms with them.

3. RANGES OF OCCURRENCE

In the course of maturing in life, we all repeatedly encounter baffling phenomena, for example, when we first experience optical illusions or, for that matter, the performances of magicians and the tricks of prestidigitators. Indeed there is always something mysterious and "magical" about baffling phenomena.

The collision of different cultures and civilizations affords a fertile source of examples. The encounter between the peninsular Arabs with the remnants of Greek culture that they overran in Persia is a case in point. What impressed the Arabs particularly were the successes of Greek medicine, in particular in the treatment of eye ailments. The Arabs, for whom ailments reflected the decrees of an inscrutable power, could of course make nothing of the Galenic balancing of humors and similar accoutrements of Greek medical theory: to them (as for us) it was all mumbo jumbo. But the comparative efficacy of treatments purportedly based on this theoretical foundation was something they could see clearly for themselves—and that was, for them, a genuinely baffling phenomenon.

Again, it is reliably reported in the contemporary sources[2] that when the great galleons arrived to bring supplies and reinforcements for the initial group of conquistadors, the Amerindians of Panama simply did not see them as identifiable objects, as *boats* of some sort. Apparently they regarded them not as physical objects but as transitory formations like clouds or sea waves, phenomena that would soon vanish as mysteriously as they had appeared. How such things could bring people and horses unto the scene puzzled them endlessly.

But the most familiar source of baffling phenomena undoubtedly lies in the precincts of natural science. The course of scientific progress is paved with new, anomalous, seemingly inexplicable phenomena: think, for example, of Becquerel and the unexposed photographic plates or of Fleming with his seemingly inexplicable mold in a sterile environment. Again, the dematerialization of matter in modern atomic and subatomic physics and its patently nonmechanistic modus operandi at the level of the very small have made quantum theory a gold mine of baffling phenomena.

4. THE PROMINENCE OF BAFFLING PHENOMENA IN NATURAL SCIENCE

There is, in fact, good reason to regard baffling phenomena as playing a crucial role at the very core of progress in natural science, for the enhancement of scientific technology can and invariably does lead to an encounter with new phenomena that do not conform to our extrapolations from preexisting theory.

In developing natural science, we humans began by exploring the physical world in our own locality, not just our spatial neighborhood but our parametric neighborhood in the "space" of physical variables

---

2. William H. Prescott, *History of the Conquest of Mexico* (New York: Harper, 1843).

such as temperature, pressure, and radiation. Near our natural "home base," we are—thanks to the evolutionary heritage of our sensory and cognitive apparatus—able to operate with relative ease and freedom, scanning nature for data with the unassisted senses. But we soon exhaust the range of what can be managed in this way. To do more, we proceeded to extend our interactive probes into nature more deeply, deploying increasing technical sophistication to achieve increasingly high levels of capability. And, as the range of telescopes, the energy of particle accelerators, the effectiveness of low-temperature instrumentation, the potency of pressurization equipment, the strength of magnets, the power of vacuum-creating contrivances, and the accuracy of measurement apparatus increase—that is, as our capacity to move about in the parametric space of the physical world is enhanced—new phenomena come into our perception, with the result of enlarging the empirical basis of our knowledge of natural processes.

We ongoingly seek, and achieve, greater velocities, higher frequencies, lower or higher temperatures, greater pressures, larger energy excitations, stabler conditions, greater resolving power, and the like, because this is what the interests of science require. For the key to the great progress of contemporary physics lies exactly in the enormous strides made in this technological regard. We have pushed ever further out from our evolutionary home base in nature toward increasingly remote frontiers. From the egocentric standpoint of our local region of parameter space, we have journeyed ever further to "explore" in the manner of a "prospector" searching for cognitively significant phenomena along the various parametric dimensions. This picture is clearly not one of *geographical* exploration but of the *physical* exploration, and subsequent theoretical rationalization, of "phenomena" that are distributed over the "space" of the physical quantities spreading out all about us. This exploration metaphor forms the basis of the conception of scientific research as a prospecting search for the new phenomena that, given the empirical nature of natural science, are needed for the realization of significant new scientific discoveries. Only by operating under new and previously inaccessible conditions—attaining extreme temperature, pressure, particle velocity, field strength, and so on—can we realize those circumstances that enable us to put our hypotheses and theories to the test.

But at this point, another aspect of the matter comes to the fore. Scientific theorizing is a matter of triangulation from observations: of inductive generalization from the data. And (sensibly enough) induction constructs the most economical structures for housing the available data comfortably. It discerns the simplest overall pattern of regularity that can adequately accommodate these data regarding cases in hand and then projects them across the entire spectrum of possibilities in order to answer our general questions. As a fundamentally inductive process, scientific theorizing involves the search for, or the construction of, the least complex theory structure capable of accommodating the available body of data. Induction is a matter of projecting beyond the data as is necessary to get answers while staying as close to the data as possible, all the while proceeding under the aegis of established principles of inductive systematization, uniformity, simplicity, harmony, and the rest, that implement the general idea of cognitive economy.

But with the enhancement of technology, the volume of our body of data inevitably grows. Technological progress constantly enlarges the "window" through which we look out upon parametric space. But this is not a lunar landscape where once we have seen one sector, we have seen it all, and where theory projections from lesser data generally remain in place when further data come our way. Historical experience teaches that we must and do expect that the phenomena we encounter in new and heretofore unexplored regions of parametric space would not fit the patterns of regularity that we inductively project on the basis of uniformities encountered in the previously explored regions of parametric space. The technologically mediated entry into new regions of parametric space constantly destabilizes the attained equilibrium between data and theory. Since it is these regularities that canalize our scientific explorations, it is inevitable that such "nonconformist" phenomena will strike people as strange and surprising. The occurrence of baffling phenomena is part of the very lifeblood of natural science.[3]

5. THE WORKS OF MIND

Let us now turn to another direction. It is instructive to shift attention from baffling phenomena in natural science to those we find in the psychological domain. The natural scientist has learned to wel-

---

3. The scientific and general press abound in examples. See, for instance, the article by Walter Sullivan, "Mysterious Particles May Upset Theories on Radiation from Space" in the *New York Times* on 4 Oct. 1988, p. 23. The article observes, "Scientists studying gamma rays in cosmic radiation were astounded when impacts of what they thought were gamma rays were accompanied by unexpectedly abundant showers of subatomic particles called muons. Such debris is typical of impacts of matter, not gamma rays." The article goes on to remark that this observation may force scientists to rethink basic assumptions about matter and energy.

come baffling phenomena as an impetus to progress; the psychologist, however, views them in a very different light. Consider just a few of the fertile ranges of baffling phenomena in this sphere:

Acupuncture. How is it that one should, by suitably jiggling needles around in someone's body, be able to deaden pain and relieve symptoms? Ideally we shall attain some sort of understanding of how intrusive punctures can have these very nonstandard effects, but we certainly do not have one yet. And the explanations that are actually given by the Chinese adepts who are most successful practitioners of this art are enough to awaken in the listener a most lively sense of just how far this range of phenomena goes against the grain of current orthodoxy regarding the workings of the mind.

Yoga. Yogis are patently capable of amazing feats of mind-body manipulation. Lying unfeeling and unharmed on beds of nails, walking unscathed on burning coals, raising people by mysterious levitation, surviving prolonged entombment by slowing bodily functions to a snail's pace, and the like, are featured in the phenomenology of this domain. And orthodox biomedicine for a very long time reacted to such phenomena primarily by not taking them seriously, studiously looking the other way. And the closer one looks at the sorts of "explanation" that the adepts of yoga themselves give for these performances, the more sympathy one feels with this reaction.

Parapsychology. Parapsychologists often claim and seemingly sometimes substantiate decidedly unnatural feats of mind-to-mind and mind-to-body coordination. For example, some people can apparently function effectively as "psychics" in criminal investigations, and others systematically perform statistically implausible feats of card guessing, in either case acquiring information in the absence of any transmission process. The hostility of the orthodox psychological community to the investigation of such phenomena is itself a development that invites psychological scrutiny.

Psychoanalysis. An extensive and varied phenomenology of psychopathology forms the stock in trade of psychoanalytic inquiry: psychosomatic ailments, autosuggestion, the symptomatology of hysteria, placebo effects, and so on. All of these run against the grain of our standard theories of biomedical process. The most systematically developed explanation of this range of phenomena that we have to date is Freudian theory, which, to put it a little unkindly, strikes many a non-Freudian psychologist as being pretty much at the same scientific level as acupuncture theory.

Hypnotism. The case of hypnotism is particularly instructive. In the latter part of the eighteenth century, the German physician Franz

Anton Mesmer mastered and systematized the practices of various earlier investigators for inducing the trance condition that was to become known as "mesmeric" sleep. In this state, human subjects could shed the symptoms of their maladies, through a mere stroking of the affected parts; become anesthetized and able to undergo operations painlessly; feel instructionally induced itches or pains; perform astonishing feats of body-control such as rendering their bodies stiff as boards, regulating their pulse rate, cutting off bleeding, produce automatic posthypnotic responses, and the like. On the received theories of physiological process (then or now) none of these phenomena should occur at all. To explain such occurrences, Mesmer postulated a peculiar variety of quasi-electrical current or fluid, which he called *animal magnetism*. A complex theory was projected as to how this "magnetic fluid" emanated from the brain of the operator to his subject to enable the power to gain control over the latter's body, particularly in the context of medical therapy.

Mesmer and his disciples made a great splash in the fashionable world of prerevolutionary Paris, where a kind of Mesmermania flourished in certain fashionable circles. Official attention was aroused. A two-pronged royal commission of inquiry was eventually appointed by Louis XVI, and its first division was perhaps the most august—and certainly the most ill-fated—body of scientists ever convened for such an inquiry. Its president was seventy-eight-year-old Benjamin Franklin, the American ambassador to Paris. And its members included Antoine Laurent Lavoisier (founding father of modern chemistry), Jean Sylvain Bailly (distinguished astronomer), and the humane physician Joseph Ignace Guillotin (whose colleagues Lavoisier and Bailly were eventually to perish by the instrument he promoted to eliminate the butchery from execution and who himself came within a hair's breadth of doing the same).

The commission construed its mandate narrowly. To his great chagrin, it ignored Mesmer himself, in favor of some of his wilder disciples. And it focused not on the *phenomena* of mesmerism, but on its *theory*, specifically the claim of an etheral fluid or current that passed from the nervous system of the operator into that of the patient. The report of the first commission, issued on 11 August 1784, stated the unanimous judgment of its members:

> The commissioners, having recognized that this animal magnetic fluid cannot be perceived by any sense, and that it has had no effect on them or on the ill shown to them; having assured themselves that the pressing and touching rarely cause changes helpful to the animal organism, and often cause agitation harmful to the imagination; having, finally, demonstrated by decisive

experiments, that the imagination without magnetism produces convulsion, and that the magnetism without imagination produces nothing; they have concluded unanimously, on the question of the existence and utility of animal magnetism, that nothing proves the existence of the animal magnetic fluid.[4]

The commission thus demolished the "magnetic fluid" and attributed the phenomena of mesmerism not to a vaunted "animal magnetism" but to the operation of an overheated imagination. Not that the commission (or anybody else) had any developed theories about the nature and working of this faculty of imagination. Rather, it was as if in shifting "animal magnetism" from the range of physical to that of psychological effects one had removed it from the area of issues in which serious scientists could be expected to take an interest. The commission committed the non sequitur of considering the imagined products of an imagination as imaginary in the sense of nonveridical. On this basis the orthodox scientific establishment, then as now unable to make sense of hypnotic phenomena on accepted physical principles, was vocal with charges of fraud, deceit, and chicanery. Generation on generation, the fact that mesmerism could not be validated through the operation of physical agents or forces led people to dismiss hypnosis and its phenomena as somehow faked.[5] For many years those interested in investigating hypnotic phenomena proceeded at great risk to their careers and reputations in the face of an implacably hostile medical and scientific establishment.

Psychoanalysis forms an interesting exception to the situation that is otherwise a rule among the preceding examples. For in all those other cases (acupuncture, yoga, hypnotism, and so on), we find a situation of a family of perfectly well-attested albeit unnatural-seeming phenomena that, from the angle of scientific orthodoxy, are altogether baffling and that the scientific community inclines to reject as at best peripheral insofar as not actually fraudulent. But in each case there is a body of investigators, seen by the orthodox as constituting a "lunatic fringe," who not only insist on giving these purportedly peripheral phenomena a prominent, indeed central, place in the scientific scheme of things but go on to propound an explanatory theory for them that seems crazy by any ordinary standard, be it common sense or scientific orthodoxy.

Now to all intents and purposes much the same situation seems to obtain with respect to Freudian psychoanalysis. Here too we have the

---

4. Quoted from Vincent Buranelli, *The Wizard from Vienna: F. A. Mesmer* (New York: Coward, McCann, & Geoghegan, 1975), 163.

5. See George Rosen, "Mesmerism and Surgery: A Strange Chapter in the History of Anaesthesia," *Journal of the History of Medicine* 1 (1946): 527–50.

otherwise familiar situation of a perfectly well-established body of otherwise baffling phenomena: informative dreams, psychosomatic ailments, placebo effects, self-disclosing slips of the tongue, psychosomatic ailments and other manifestations of "repressed sexuality," and a vast taxonomically proliferated symptomatology of hysteria and neurotic behavior. On the foundation of this well-established phenomenology, which orthodox psychomedicine is inclined to marginalize, Freudian doctrine erects an elaborate theoretical structure of drives, complexes, and agencies: of *ego, id,* and *quis-scit-quid*. And it represents this strange-looking apparatus as absolutely central, establishing those seemingly perplexing phenomena as windows into the inmost core of the human psyche. From the standpoint of anything like scientific orthodoxy, the whole business has just the same aura of lunacy we associate with the explanatory demarches of the acupuncturists, yogis, mesmerists, and old-line parapsychologists. Why its fate within the medical community has been so very different is something that, on present indications, may well in the end have to be accounted for on the basis of externally cultural and sociological rather than internally rational considerations.

But all this is perhaps no more than a somewhat tendentious digression. Let us return to the mainstream of our discussion.

6. REACTIONS

When confronted with a baffling phenomenon, an individual or a community can react in a significant variety of ways. These reactions cover the following spectrum:

1. *Dismissal.* To reject the phenomenon at issue as illusory and unreal, simply to refuse it recognition as a genuine phenomenon. To treat it as David Hume maintained the sensible man would treat the report of a miracle, a self-annihilating violation of our laws of nature as we understand them. That is, we would simply weigh the phenomenon on the scale against the established body of our experience and find it wanting. (Exactly this was the reaction to hypnotism/mesmerism by the rationalizing scientists of the late eighteenth century, a circumstance mirrored in the contemporary reaction of scientific orthodoxy to parapsychology.)

2. *Degradation.* To accept the phenomenon as real but dismiss it as unimportant and insignificant. To treat the phenomenon as representing a mere fringe development, a quick, irrelevant curiosity that has no bearing on fundamentals. Its violation of our present view of

things is seen as something minor that will eventually be patched up in the natural course of things by some small revision, some trivial alteration in the established body of explanatory machinery. (The reaction of mainstream psychology to acupuncture and autosuggestion seems to run along this road.)

3. *Accommodation.* To concede the authenticity and significance of the phenomena but to deny their being genuinely baffling by insisting that further development will enable the present state of things to come to terms with them (appearances to the contrary notwithstanding).

4. *Resignation.* To accept that the phenomenon is real, significant, and genuinely baffling and to concede that it demonstrates the need for a significant revamping of the established explanatory scheme, while yet continuing to endorse that scheme as the best that is available in the moment, forging ahead with its use in the hopeful expectation that the day will come when it can be expanded or revised to accommodate the baffling phenomenon that presently defeats our pretensions to scientific competency. Accordingly, one would concede, with Hamlet, that there may be more to nature than our present body of science is prepared to contemplate, regarding our science in a developmental and evolutionary light and accepting its present deficiencies in the hopeful expectation that something better will come along, an eventual superior replacement of the established scheme.

5. *Mystification.* To insist that the phenomenon in question represents a mystery, something beyond all human understanding, something that not only is at odds with our present explanatory conceptions but defies any prospects of human rationalization. The baffling phenomena at issue are taken to reveal not just the inadequacy of our existing explanatory scheme but that of any scheme whatsoever.

Mystification is clearly an exercise in know-nothing defeatism. Negativism makes more sense than that. Indeed, one recent theorist, Michael Polanyi, believes that the route of dismissal or degradation is unavoidable for science:

There must be at all times a predominantly accepted scientific view of the nature of things, in the light of which research is jointly conducted by members of the community of scientists. A strong presumption that any evidence which contradicts the view is invalid must prevail. Such evidence *has to* be disregarded, even if it cannot be accounted for, in the hope that it will eventually turn out to be false or irrelevant.[6]

---

6. Michael Polanyi, "The Potential Theory of Absorption: Authority in Science Has Its Uses and Its Dangers," *Science* 141 (1963): 1010–13; see 1012.

But this view is very problematic. There is surely no reason of principle why a scientist's commitment to his theories has to be dogmatic. Quite to the contrary: an open-minded willingness to contemplate new possibilities is surely no barrier to productive work. Dismissal, degradation, and accommodation are strategies that might possibly constitute good tactics in particular cases but seem rather desperate expedients at the strategic level.

In general, the fourth alternative on the list (that of resignation) thus seems to represent the sensible middle way. To be sure, recourse to this resignationist approach calls for a certain particular view of science. It requires us to see science as we have it as a historical phenomenon, as something changeable in its claims and provisional with respect to its assertions. What is stable about science is not its products (findings) nor even its methods (techniques) but its fundamental aims in terms of explanation, prediction, and control. In sum, we are impelled to see science in teleological terms and not as a doctrinally fixed body of laws and principles. And such a perspective suggests the position that there need be nothing permanent about the bafflement of baffling phenomena. As the frontiers of science shift in the wake of scientific progress, there is generally also a marked shift in the boundary separating that which is baffling from that which is not.

7. SOME LESSONS

From this general perspective, the sensible course is to refuse to engage in the mystification to characterize certain problems as inherently intractable but to have confidence in the ability of the science of the future to accommodate the puzzles of the present. Charles Sanders Peirce expressed the salient point with characteristic cogency and force:

> For my part, I cannot admit the proposition of Kant—that there are certain impassable bounds to human knowledge. . . . The history of science affords illustrations enough of the folly of saying this, that, or the other can never be found out. Auguste Comte said that it was clearly impossible for man ever to learn anything of the chemical constitution of the fixed stars, but before his book had reached its readers the discovery which he had announced as impossible had been made. Legendre said of a certain proposition in the theory of numbers that, while it appeared to be true, it was most likely beyond the powers of the human mind to prove it; yet the next writer on the subject gave six independent demonstrations of the theorem.[7]

---

7. Charles Sanders Peirce, *Collected Papers*, ed. C. Hartshorne and Paul Weiss, vol. 6 (Cambridge, Mass.: Harvard University Press, 1929), sect. 6.556.

Peirce is surely quite right here: it is risky to the point of folly ever to categorize particular issues as inherently intractable to science.

Accordingly, there is simply no need for someone devoted to the spirit of the scientific enterprise to shut his eyes to baffling phenomena and to view their claims to reality with the jaundiced eye of implacable hostility. For anyone who has confidence in the power of scientific inquiry, the presence of limits and imperfections in the presently established body of scientific belief is a circumstance that can be faced with equanimity. There is no call for being defensive and dismissive in this regard. One can accept baffling phenomena as reminders of shortcomings in presently established science without any disloyalty or disaffection from the scientific enterprise as such.

On this perspective, those who react to presentations of baffling phenomenon with reflex defensiveness and dismissive hostility are not serving the cause of science well. Short of endorsing unrealistically megalomaniacal claims about the perfection of present-day science as we have it in hand here and now, there is simply no call for a negatively dismissive reaction to baffling phenomena. But, of course, to say this is certainly not to say that the voice of reason calls on us to endorse whatever weird theories may be on offer to account for them—and not even when these happen to be the only ones whose hat is in the ring. And this consideration introduces our concluding theme.

8. PHENOMENA VERSUS THEORIES

In philosophical circles, it is fashionable nowadays to insist upon the basically sensible idea that observation is inevitably theory-laden, that our descriptions of what we observe are always formulated in terms of some background of theoretical commitments. But even if this point is acknowledged, one has to be prepared to recognize that any authentic phenomenon can remain invariant under a variety of different descriptions. And some of these descriptions will always detach the phenomenon for any given theory. (For example, the old-line mesmerists' description of an event as consisting in someone's "redirecting the stream of magnetic influences flowing from the manipulator to the subject" can be described more neutrally as "stroking a part of the subject's body with the manipulator's hand.") On this basis, we can always maintain a line of separation between phenomena and the theories intended to account for them. For those theories do not have a monopoly on the phenomena. That is, those phenomena, however theory-laden, need not be thought of as being inextricable from those *particular* theories in which various enthusiasts enfold them.

Precisely because, by definition, as it were, baffling phenomena go against the grain of the prevailing explanatory canon, the sorts of explanations proposed for them by those who see them as being significant and central are likely to look strange from an orthodox point of view. They look crazy because they are crazy, in the sense of being totally "out of line" with the tenor of prevalent theorizing. But, by contrast, the phenomena themselves are bound to be relatively unproblematic as such: that is, as phenomena. For, in general, it is not so much their evidentiation that is the problem but their explanation. We can and should maintain a line of separation between the phenomena and the environing theories. And we can achieve this not by an injudicious refusal to see the phenomena as theory-laden but by a sensible avoidance of circularity, that is, by disengaging our characterization of the phenomena as such from whatever specific explanatory theories may be woven around them.

This course has much to be said for it. It means that we can be perfectly open-minded and in principle accepting with respect to those baffling phenomena themselves, without thereby undertaking any obligation, however slender, to take a favorable view of whatever bizarre theories may be proposed by the aficionados who see them as somehow pivotal to a proper view of the nature of things. And this yields substantial advantages. For example, if the history of people's attempts to grapple with baffling phenomena in the psychological tradition from Mesmer to Freud teaches any one lesson, it is the great utility of maintaining a distinction between the interesting and impressive symptomatic and therapeutic phenomena on the one hand, and on the other the often extravagant and problematic theories by which people endeavor to account for them.

7 Basic Science Is Innocent; Applied Science and Technology Can Be Guilty
MARIO BUNGE

Once upon a time science was praised for delivering power. Nowadays science bashing has become fashionable for the same unreason. In particular, it is being blamed for the threat of nuclear annihilation, the degradation of the environment, unemployment, and sundry other horrors.

For better or worse basic science has never deserved either the earlier praise or the current curse: basic scientists seek knowledge, not power. Only applied scientists seek useful knowledge, and only technologists design machines, processes, and plans in order to control nature or society, for better or worse.

Therefore, if we wish to pass fair moral judgments on science and technology we must start by distinguishing basic from applied science, and the latter from technology. Even so, we must be careful not to mistake applied scientists and technologists for their bosses, namely business and government. Indeed, the targets of applied scientific research and technological research and development are chosen by managers or politicians, not by scientists or technologists. The latter are only tools of economic or political power: they yield no power except over themselves. As the saying goes, the technologist is always on tap, never on top.

We start by characterizing basic science, applied science, and technology and end by looking into the good and the evil uses of knowledge.

I. BASIC SCIENCE

Basic scientific research seeks truth for its own sake. It is the kind of research performed by mathematicians, physicists, chemists, biologists, psychologists, and social scientists, when primarily motivated by the quest for knowledge rather than practical usefulness. True, when seeking support for their research they often promise the unwary administrator a rich crop of practical results, but as a matter of fact most of them could not care less for such hypothetical results. The natural scientist wants to find new laws of nature, and the social scientist wishes to describe and explain society. Basic scientists, in sum, wish to understand reality, not to dominate it: they are after knowledge, not power.

The sciences form a system every component of which overlaps and partially interacts with some other components. Therefore, when seeking to clarify the idea of science we must keep in mind the entire family of sciences. Moreover, we must remember that science is at the same time a group of people, an activity, and a body of knowledge. We shall stipulate that a family of scientific research fields is a collection every member R of which is representable by the 10-tuple

$$R = (C, S, D, G, F, B, P, K, A, M),$$

where, at any given moment,

C = the research community of R, composed of individuals who have received a special training, hold information links among themselves, and continue or initiate a research tradition.

S = the host society of C, which supports or at least tolerates the research activities of the members of C.

D = the domain of R, composed exclusively of certified or putatively real entities (rather than, say, ghosts) past, present, or future.

G = the general outlook, or philosophical background, of R consists of (1) an ontology of lawfully changing things (rather than, say, one including free-floating ideas or miracle makers); (2) a realistic epistemology (instead of, say, an idealistic or a conventionalist one); and (3) the ethos of the free search for truth, depth, and system (rather than, say, the ethos of faith or that of the bound quest for utility, profit, power, or consensus).

F = the formal background of R, a collection of up-to-date logical and mathematical theories (rather than being empty or composed of obsolete formal theories).

B = the specific background of R, a collection of up-to-date and reasonably well confirmed (yet corrigible) data, hypotheses, and theories and of reasonably effective research methods, obtained in other research fields relevant to R.

P = the problematics of R, consisting exclusively of cognitive problems concerning the nature (in particular the laws) of the members of D, as well as problems concerning other components of R.

K = the fund of knowledge of R, a collection of up-to-date and testable (though not final) theories, hypotheses, and data compatible with those in B and obtained by members of C at previous times.

A = the aims of the members of C, including discovering or using the laws of the Ds, systematizing (into theories) hypotheses about Ds, and refining methods in M.

M = the methodics of R, consisting exclusively of scrutable (checkable, analyzable, criticizable) and justifiable (explainable) procedures, in the first place the scientific method.

Every scientific research field R is subject to two conditions that distinguish it from a belief system (such as an ideology) as well as from a pseudoscience: (1) There is at least one other contiguous and partially overlapping scientific research field, with the same general characteristics as R, and (2) the membership of every one of the last eight components of R changes, however slowly at times, as a result of scientific research in the same field as well as in related fields of scientific inquiry, rather than in response to ideological, political, or economic pressures.

As can be seen from this description, basic scientists have no opportunities for doing harm except through simulation, theft, or sloth—and even so the damage they can do is limited.

2. APPLIED SCIENCE

Applied scientific research seeks truth with a practical potential. The following is a haphazard list of fields of applied science: materials science, analysis of natural products, experimental synthesis of promising polymers, investigation of plants with a possible industrial interest, pharmacology and food science, medical research, pedagogy, and the applications of basic science to investigating social problems such as unemployment, marginality, criminality, drug addiction, bureaucratism, militarism, and political apathy, with a view to designing social programs, law reforms, institutions, or political movements aiming at the eradication of some such social ills.

Like basic science, applied science aims at increasing knowledge, not at designing machines, social programs, or other artifacts. But, unlike basic science, applied science tackles problems whose solution may have practical value. Furthermore, it makes ample use of basic science without, however, following automatically from the latter. Thus, the space scientists who developed new materials and studied human physiology and psychology in conditions of zero gravity and social isolation struggled with problems that could not have been solved with the sole help of existing knowledge, and, sure enough, they did produce new knowledge.

One of the peculiarities of any applied science is that its domain or scope is narrower than that of the corresponding basic science. For example, instead of studying learning in general, the applied psychologist may study the handicaps that a certain human group finds on learning a foreign language. And instead of studying industrial work in general, the applied sociologist or psychologist may study work satisfaction in a Swiss chemical factory, with an eye on possible ways to improving it in the interest of the workers, the management, or both.

Applied science is thus sandwiched between basic science and technology. Moreover, there are no clear borderlines between the three domains: each shades into the other. The outcome of a piece of basic research may suggest a line of applied research, which in turn may point to a technological project. For example, superconductivity was initially studied for its own sake but is nowadays being approached from an applied angle as well, as it holds some industrial promise, for example, in the domain of high-voltage transmission lines. And the converse flux, from technology to basic science, is equally conspicuous though less intense. For example, the neurophysiological study of speech deficits may throw light on the neuronal mechanism of the production and understanding of phrases.

Once in a blue moon we meet an investigator who can span all three domains, particularly if he is a chemist. But more often than not each task demands people with peculiar backgrounds, interests, and goals. Whereas the original scientist, whether basic or applied, is essentially a discoverer, the original technologist is essentially an inventor of artificial systems or processes.

From the preceding description it is obvious that, unlike his basic counterpart, the applied scientist has plenty of opportunities for mischief. Although he does not design anything except his own experiments, he can supply the basic idea for the design of an artifact or process aiming at evil-doing or the use of which has gross evil side effects. Hence by its very nature applied science cannot be morally neutral.

3. TECHNOLOGY

Modern technology may be defined as the design of artificial things or processes of possible utility to some group, with the help of results obtained by applied scientific research. Contemporary technology may be thought of as composed of the following fields: physiotechnology, that is, civil, mechanical, electrical, nuclear, and space technology; chemotechnology: industrial chemistry and chemical engineering; biotechnology: pharmacology, bromatology, medicine, dentistry, agronomy, veterinary medicine, bioengineering, and genetic engineering; psychotechnology: psychiatry, clinical, educational, business, and war psychology; sociotechnology: law, management science, human engineering, city planning, and military science; and knowledge engineering: information science, computer science, and artificial intelligence. How many possible ways of doing good or evil!

The hub of technology is design, not discovery. Hence, though based on applied science, technology does not flow automatically from it. Indeed, the technologist faces problems, and uses means, that do not normally fall within the province of science. His task is not to find out how things are but to invent something new in order to control or alter natural or social processes for the benefit of his employers. Having invented something, he or someone else is supposed to start the development phase, where most inventions sink. The blueprint must be translated into a prototype, or a handful of seeds, or a few milligrams of a new drug, or a detailed plan for a new social organization. And, once this has been accomplished, the test stage begins. This is not a test for truth but for efficiency and reliability. We are now quite far from basic science.

A possible definition of the concept of modern technology is as follows. A family of technologies is a system, every component T of which is representable by the 11-tuple

$$T = (C, S, D, G, F, B, P, K, A, M, V),$$

where, at any given moment,

C = the professional community of T, a social system composed of persons who have received specialized training, hold information links among themselves, share certain values, and continue or initiate a tradition of research into design, planning, or evaluation of artifacts of some kind.

S = the society that hosts T, which encourages the professional activities of the members of C.

D = the domain of T, composed exclusively of certified or putatively real entities, past, present, or future, some natural and others artificial.

G = the general outlook or philosophical background of T, consisting of (1) an ontology of lawfully changing concrete things, in particular of things under possible human control; (2) a realistic epistemology with a touch of pragmatism; and (3) the ethos of the utilization of natural and human (particularly cognitive) resources.

F = the formal background of T, a collection of up-to-date logical and mathematical theories.

B = the specific background of T, a collection of up-to-date and reasonably well-confirmed (yet corrigible) data, hypotheses, and theories; of reasonably effective research methods; and of useful designs and plans, found in other fields of knowledge, particularly in sciences or technologies related to T.

P = the problematics of T, consisting exclusively of cognitive and practical problems concerning the members of the domain D, as well as problems concerning other components of the 11-tuple defining T.

K = the fund of knowledge of T, a collection of up-to-date and testable (though not final) theories, hypotheses and data, as well as of methods, designs, and plans compatible with the specific background B and obtained by members of C at previous times.

A = the aims of the members of the professional community, including inventing new artifacts, new ways of using old ones, and plans for realizing, as well as evaluating, them.

M = the methodics of T, consisting exclusively of scrutable (verifiable, analyzable, criticizable) and justifiable (explainable) procedures, in particular (1) the scientific method (cognitive problem, hypothesis, checking, eventual correction of hypothesis or reformulation of problem) and (2) the technological method (practical problem, design, prototype, test, eventual correction of design or reformulation of problem).

V = the values of T, a collection of value judgments about natural or artificial things or processes, in particular raw materials and finished products, work processes, and sociotechnical organizations.

Every technology T is subject to the following conditions: (1) there is at least one other contiguous and partially overlapping technology with the same general characteristics as T, and (2) the membership of every one of the last nine components of the 11-tuple defining T changes over time, however slowly, as a result of research and development in T itself as well as in related technologies and sciences, and in response to the needs and wants of the users of T.

Note that, unlike our definition of a basic science in the section Basic Science, that of technology includes an eleventh component, namely the value system V. This system includes value judgments resulting from evaluating natural or artificial things or processes in the

TABLE 1. *Some Similarities and Differences between Science and Technology*

Feature	Science	Technology
Main type of problem	Cognitive	Practical
Ultimate goal	Understanding	Doing
Hubs	Hypothesis and experiment	Design and program
Basis	Mathematics	Mathematics and science
Role of theory	Guide to understanding	Guide to action
Role of experiment	Data source and testing ideas	Data source and testing designs or programs
Cost/benefit analysis	Seldom applicable	Always necessary
Conceptual analysis	Necessary	Secondary
Use of prediction	In truth valuation	In planning
Truth	Maximal desirable	Sufficient for practical purposes
Depth	Maximal desirable	Sufficient for practical purposes
Setting of tasks	By researchers	By managers
Social impact	On the rest of culture	On entire society
Owner	Mankind	Employers
Censorship and secrecy	Lethal	Crippling
Ecological constraints	None or mild	Desirable
Economic constraints	On means	On means and ends
Role of discovery	Central	Central
Role of invention	Central	Central
Criticism	Necessary	Necessary

light of the aims of T, which aims are, more often than not, set by the employers of the technologists. Examples: "That bacterium is good for synthesizing protein P," "Protein P is good for treating disease D," and "The treatment of disease D is good for society or for business."

V must be distinguished from the internal value judgments about the worth of any component of the research and development process, such as materials, designs, or even problems. The latter may be called the *endoaxiology* of T, whereas V makes up the *exoaxiology* of T. The endoaxiology of T is made up by the practitioners of T, whereas its exoaxiology is made up by the employers of the technologists as well as by members of the public. Thus a microbiologist or a molecular biologist may describe or conjecture a certain species of bacterium, but he is not competent to offer an expert judgment on the economic value of a process involving those bacteria to synthesize some protein. Table 1 exhibits further differences between technology and science.

To sum up, because technology is a tool for the transformation of the world, it can be put to good or evil use. However, some particular technologies, such as those involved in offensive strategy and in torture, are inherently evil.

4. VALUES AND MORALS

Basic science studies valuation as a psychological process, and it makes value judgments as well. But the latter are all internal: they are about scientific items such as data, hypotheses, and methods, not about their referents. On the other hand, the technologist forms not only internal value judgments but also external ones: he evaluates everything he can lay his hands on. To him everything, process or idea, is good, bad, or indifferent for some practical purpose. Examples: "The top soil of x is poor for cultivating y," "The air in x is dirty," "This piece of glass has too many impurities," "Product x is shoddy," "Black bread is better for your health than white bread," "Alcohol is bad for you," "Poverty is degrading," and "Participative management works better than authoritarian management."

The difference between the value judgments in science or technology, on the one hand, and those in ordinary life on the other, is that the former are supposed to be better grounded or justified than the latter. If an engineer pronounces product x to be shoddy, or a management scientist holds that management style x works better than style y, he does so on the basis of analyses or tests conducted in the light of scientific knowledge. The quality control division of most manufacturing plants makes use of scientific instruments and statistical methods to monitor the properties that make up the quality of the finished products. Evaluation is also essential, though not as rigorous, in the biotechnologies and sociotechnologies. (As a matter of fact, some medical treatments and some social programs have never been carefully evaluated: they are carried out on faith.)

We must distinguish two kinds of technological evaluation: of technical effectiveness and cost efficiency and of social worth. An artifact may be both effective and efficient but socially worthless or even evil. Thus, an offensive weapon may be good for mass murder, but, since the latter is evil, it is socially disvaluable. Technologists tend to overlook social evaluation, thus surrendering their social responsibility: in fact they tend to be better employees than citizens.

Most industrial products are morally neutral or, rather, ambivalent, in the sense that they can be used for good or for evil. A knife may be used for cutting loaves of bread or throats, and a powerful drug to cure or to kill. The great exceptions are weapons: they can be used only for destruction. Given the ambivalence of most artifacts, we should not put the blame on the whole technology for the evil uses to which it is sometimes put: we should blame instead those who control technology, that is, managers and politicians. The technologist is blameworthy only when he knowingly takes part in the design or planning of things or processes that are unambiguously evil. Incidentally, scientists are often praised or blamed for the development of new weapons systems, such as the hypothetical SDI, but this is a typical engineering problem. True, some scientists have lent their brains to help solve problems of this kind, but by so doing they have acted as technologists: it is well known that the direct input of basic science into weapons design is small—in fact, less than 1 percent.

Basic research, the search for new knowledge for its own sake, is value-free and morally neutral. Even concepts such as those of subsistence level (or poverty line) and marginality are value-free. Morals are involved when something can be done for or against the welfare or life of others, which is precisely where the technologist comes in. He should observe what may be called the *technological imperative*: Thou shalt design or help implement only projects that will not endanger public welfare and shalt alert the public against any projects that fail to satisfy this condition.

The technological imperative may conflict with the short-term interest of the private firm or the government employing a technologist. The isolated individual is helpless, and the professional societies are usually unwilling to defend the member who puts the technological imperative before loyalty to his employer. There is but one solution to this moral problem, namely citizen participation in all large-scale technologies projects. In other words, we should strive for the democratic control of technology.

5. CONCLUDING REMARKS

Mankind faces two monstrous and unprecedented problems that are often blamed on scientists. One is the irreversible degradation of the environment, which, unless checked, will render our planet uninhabitable except by a few primitive organisms. The second problem is the nuclear arms race, which, unless terminated, may result in a global nuclear war that would exterminate all terrestrial organisms. Both problems have arisen from a large-scale uncontrolled application of modern technology. However, neither of them can be blamed exclusively on technologists, because these are under orders from the powers that be.

The ecological disaster is a consequence of unbridled industry, not of technology. It is perfectly possible to use technology to clean up the environment, reclaim deserts, and prevent any further pollution of land and the atmosphere. Do not blame the technologist if such corrective measures are not taken soon or energetically enough, let alone if they are given up. Blame instead the shortsighted and greedy managers or politicians. In particular, nowadays blame the self-styled "liberal" (that is, neoconservative) politicians who defend the view that private interests override the public interest, even if the future of mankind is thereby put in jeopardy.

The impeding global nuclear disaster, or omnicide, is a consequence of political expansionism, not technology. Nuclear engineering is not all bad: it is also being used in peaceful (though still dangerous) nuclear plants, and justifiably so in countries poor in alternative energy resources. And applied political science, another powerful technology, need not be machiavellic or work for special interest groups. It is in a position to advise on the negotiations necessary to avert a (the) nuclear war. Do not blame the technologists for the threat of omnicide: blame instead the fanatics intent on imposing their ideology by force, be they politicians or military experts.

To be sure, most technologies are ambivalent: only some are intrinsically evil. But all of them are ultimately controlled by managers or politicians, not by the technologists themselves. Ask a team of competent technologists to produce an artifact or process designed to improve something useful and they are likely to deliver good goods. Ask the same team to design an efficient means of mass extermination, or brain washing, or exploitation, and it is likely to deliver evil goods. Technology is what technologists do, and these do what they are told to do. Technology has no momentum of its own: it can be pushed or stopped at will.

The technologist without a moral conscience is socially irresponsible: he obeys orders. There is not much we can do to change this docile attitude by direct means. But there is much we can do in an indirect fashion: we can minimize the opportunities of doing evil. This we can do by participating in politics and demanding that, unlike basic science, technology be placed under democratic control. Ask the public whether it wants new offensive weapons to impose the true faith or whether it likes to suffer from new ecological disasters, or from taste-making campaigns, or from new reductions in welfare programs. And do not wait for general elections to do so: adopt instead the Swiss method of asking direct questions to the public by means of referenda on every issue likely to affect any ample sector of the population.

In the old times technology, politics, and morality went each its own way. Nowadays technology and politics go hand in hand and they are fraught with unprecedented moral dilemmas, and yet neither of them is under the control of morals. This autonomy of technology and politics with respect to morality is leading us at best to the ultimate ecological disaster, at worst to omnicide. If we wish to avert these very real dangers we must place technology and politics under the control of a rational morality commanding us to preserve the environment and to destroy all nuclear arms. These two commandments follow from a single moral maxim that should be placed at the very top of the moral code of survival, namely *Enjoy life and help live*.

In sum, basic science is innocent, for it seeks only knowledge of what there is, was, or may be. On the other hand, applied science and technology can be either good or evil, according to whether they promote life or, on the contrary, endanger it. Therefore, whereas scientific research should be totally free to pursue its cognitive aims, technology should be given strict guidelines so that it may abide by the maxim *Enjoy life and help live*. To proceed otherwise, that is, to censor basic research or to continue to allow technology to serve evil purposes, is to court the ultimate disaster, namely the destruction of the biosphere.

PART II
HISTORICAL STUDIES

8 Thomas Aquinas on *Phys.* VII.1 and the Aristotelian Science of the Physical Continuum

RICHARD F. HASSING

This essay seeks to investigate a fundamental principle of premodern physics, the motor causality principle, often expressed as "All that is moved is moved by another" (*omne quod movetur ab alio movetur*). The ancient text in which it was first presented, Aristotle's *Physics,* Book VII, Chapter 1 (*Phys.* VII.1), is analyzed, along with the opinions of two medieval commentators, Averroes (1126–98 A.D.) and Thomas Aquinas (1225–74 .A.D.). The interpretation of the latter occupies center stage. According to Aquinas, Aristotle's argument in *Phys.* VII.1 is "about motion in general, and the mobile insofar as it is a certain continuum, not yet applying to determinate natures" (*In phys.*, n. 1067). And the crux of that argument is that

> there is no first in motion—neither on the part of time, nor of magnitude, nor of the mobile—because of their divisibility. Therefore, there cannot be discovered a first whose motion does not depend on something prior: for the motion of a whole depends on the motions of [its] parts and is divided into them, as proven in Book VI. (*In phys.*, n. 889)

The goal of Part I is to understand to the extent possible what Aquinas means by the mobile as continuum and by the divisibility of the motion of a whole into the motions of its parts. The following points are developed. The physical continuum is infinitely divisible and the subject of per se successive change; it is that which is common to all body as such. As subject of per se successive change, it is not amenable to mathematical representation. The meaning of the motor causality principle of *Phys.* VII.1 is that the physical continuum cannot be a source of self-motion; only that which is indivisible and per se unchangeable can be a principle of self-motion in bodies. The associated understanding of body and motion in *Phys.* VI and VII is not fully accessible if approached from within the conceptual structure of post-

Newtonian physics. Indeed, the premodern physical theory here examined can provide an alternative perspective on the modern tradition of physics. Part II and the notes contain reflections on certain elements of post-Newtonian physics as seen in light of our study of Thomas Aquinas on *Phys.* VII.1 and the Aristotelian science of the physical continuum.

I. THE MOTOR CAUSALITY PRINCIPLE OF *PHYS.* VII.1 AND ITS INTERPRETATION

The motor causality principle appears not only in *Phys.* VII.1 but also in *Phys.* VIII.4 and again in *Phys.* VIII.5. It is a crucial component in the Aristotelian cosmological argument for a first unmoved mover. As such it was discussed extensively from late antiquity through the medieval period in regard to both physical and theological issues. It remains a subject of controversy among contemporary scholars in the history of philosophy and natural science. It thus behooves us to delimit the scope and textual basis of the present inquiry and to indicate relevant background.

Aristotle's account of the relation between mover and moved in *Phys.* VII.1 has two parts. The first is the proof of the motor causality principle (241b24–242a16, textus alter 241b34–242a46); the second is the proof of the impossibility of infinite regress in moved movers and thus of the necessary existence of a first moved mover (242a17–243a3, textus alter 242a50–243a33). These proofs are, as we shall see, species-neutral in that they do not refer to the species or kinds of bodies but only to body as subject of per se successive change,[1] thus

---

1. In *Phys.* V.1, 224a21–33, Aristotle makes a threefold division of changes and changers (causes of change) into (1) accidental (κατὰ συμβεβηκός; *per accidens*), (2) through a part (κατὰ μέρος; *per partem*), and (3) through itself primarily (καθ' αὑτό πρώτως; *per se primo*). At 224b26–27, accidental change is omitted from further discussion, which accordingly covers change *per se primo* and *per partem*. In *Phys.* V.2, Aristotle explains that successive change or motion strictly understood (κίνησις) occurs only in the categories of place, quality, and quantity: "Since, then, there can be no motion of a substance or of a relation or of acting or of being affected, it remains that there can be a motion only with respect to quality or quantity or place, for there is a contrariety in each of these" (226a23–26). The translation is by H. G. Apostle, *Aristotle's Physics* (Grinnell, Iowa: Peripatetic Press, 1980), 94. In *Phys.* VI.4, 234b10–20, Aristotle gives a demonstration that the subject of motion (κίνησις) is divisible into quantitative (thus spatially extended) parts. Now indivisible (unextended) mathematical points can undergo local motion by (somehow) being in something that carries them around. (See Aquinas, *In phys.*, n. 1051. The modern science of kinematics is about the local motion of points.) This, however, is motion *per accidens*—excluded from further treatment in the *Physics*—not motion *per se primo* or *per partem*. The divisibility of the movable is, as we have indicated, a crucial part in the proof of the motor causality principle in *Phys.* VII.1. Thus the contents of Aristotle's argument in *Phys.* VII.1 and his delimitations

to something that all bodies have in common.² The motor causality principle is stated and proved again in *Phys.* VIII.4. This account is not species-neutral, for the distinction between living things and the elements explicitly enters the argument (254b8–256a3). Indeed, for the application of the motor causality principle, the elements present "the greatest difficulty": What is that by which they are moved in their natural motions? (254b34–255a6) It is here that Aristotle presents his

---

of subject matter in *Phys.* V.1 and V.2 make it clear that *per accidens* change and substantial change are excluded from the account of *Phys.* VII.1. Therefore, in the formulation with which *Phys.* VII.1 opens, "All that is moved is necessarily moved by something" (Ἅπαν τὸ κινούμενον ὑπό τινος ἀνάγκη κινεῖσθαι; *Omne quod movetur, necesse est ab aliquo moveri*), the word *moved* refers to per se successive change.

2. This argument thus affords an opportunity to compare the species neutrality of early modern science or philosophy with that of premodern philosophy of nature: How does body as conceived in *Phys.* VII.1 by Aristotle and his commentators compare with the conceptions of body found in Descartes and Newton? Each of the latter thinkers has a theory of body cast in terms of what all bodies, regardless of their kind, have in common. This type of universality we refer to as species neutral in contrast to the traditional universal, for example, "cat," which is specific, or belongs to one natural kind of body but not another. The distinction between the two types of universal is brought out by Spinoza as well as anyone: "That which is common to all [such as extension], and which is equally in a part and in the whole, does not constitute the essence of any particular thing" (*Ethics* II.37, in Spinoza, *On the Improvement of the Understanding: The Ethics, Correspondence*, trans. R. H. M. Elwes [New York: Dover, 1955], 109). Descartes's well-known universals are "figure, extension, [local] motion." See, for example, *Regulae* XII, in Haldane and Ross, eds., *The Philosophical Works of Descartes* (Cambridge: Cambridge University Press, 1973), vol. 1, 41. For Newton, the universals are "extension, hardness, impenetrability, mobility and inertia." See *Principia* III, "Rules of Reasoning in Philosophy," Rule III, in Andrew Motte and Florian Cajori, trans., *Sir Isaac Newton's Mathematical Principles of Natural Philosophy and His System of the World* (New York: Greenwood Press, 1969), vol. 2, 398–400. In post-Newtonian physics we have force, mass, velocity, acceleration, momentum, and energy.

William A. Wallace has discussed the role of species-neutral terms in the constitution of equations in physics; see "Newtonian Antinomies Against the '*Prima Via*'" in Wallace, *From a Realist Point of View* (Washington, D.C.: University Press of America, 1979), 341–43.

The comparison between Aristotle's reasoning from the physical continuum and the early modern theories of Descartes and Newton is worthy of study. Although both accounts (premodern and modern) involve species neutrality, they go in quite different directions. We shall see in Part I of this essay that the premodern account reasons from what all bodies have in common to a negative conclusion about motion: the physical continuum cannot be a principle of self-motion; just as sensible properties are specific, so also the motions of the various kinds of bodies able to move themselves are specific and can only be explained from specific principles. In fundamental contrast, the modern theories reason from the new species-neutral universals—mass, charge, momentum, energy—to an open-ended program for the explanation of all natural phenomena. How was it thought possible for the modern species-neutral theories to do that which, in the Aristotelian species-neutral theory, is proved, in virtue of its species neutrality, to be impossible, namely, explain the specific? We conjecture that the answer is intimately involved with the modern notions of particle and law. (See also n. 30.) A fuller account of this issue lies beyond the scope of this essay.

controversial[3] twofold solution, namely, (1) the elements have within them no agent but only a patient principle of their natural motions (255b29–31), and (2) the requirement that there be a mover for all that is moved is met, in the case of the elements, by the generator (255b34–256a3), that is, the agent through which the element received its substantial form.[4] This solution is not derived from the reasoning of *Phys.* VII.1 but from an examination of the structure and motion of animals and elements (255a6–21)[5] and from the distinction between first and second potency (255a32–255b29). Indeed, the question bears remarking whether the motor causality principle as extended (here in *Phys.* VIII.4) to include substantial generation could be brought within the argument of *Phys.* VII.1, which is restricted to motion proper, that is, successive change.

Following the second presentation of the motor causality principle, Aristotle again argues against the possibility of infinite regress in moved movers (256a18–19, 256a21–257a32). There must accordingly be a first moved mover. The analysis of the first moved mover into an unmoved moving part and a moved part that need not move another is given in *Phys.* VIII.5 (257a32–258b9). This analysis involves yet a

---

3. William A. Wallace has shown that the causality of the natural motion of the elements was a subject of study and debate in the commentaries down to the time of Galileo. See Wallace, *Prelude to Galileo* (Boston: D. Reidel, 1981), 110–14 and 286–93, and *Galileo and His Sources* (Princeton: Princeton University Press, 1984), 175–78.

4. According to a common interpretation, the motor causality principle requires universally an agent cause of motion continuously present and in contact with the moved, that is, a *motor conjunctus*. See J. A. Weisheipl's review (and criticism) of this position in "The Principle *Omne quod movetur ab alio movetur* in Medieval Physics," *Isis* 56, no. 1 (1965): 29–34. (For an interesting current example, see M. Wolff, "Philoponus and the Rise of Preclassical Dynamics" in Richard Sorabji, ed., *Philoponus and the Rejection of Aristotelian Science* [Ithaca, N.Y.: Cornell University Press, 1987], 84–120. Wolff says, "According to the Aristotelian principle that everything which is moved is moved by something else, naturally moved bodies are moved by external [efficient or final] causes" (96). Wolff's inclusion of final causality distinguishes his idea from the *motor conjunctus* tradition. Both Wolff and the proponents of *motor conjunctus*, however, offer an interpretation that, we believe, is difficult to reconcile with Aristotle's understanding of nature, given in *Phys.* II.1, as *internal* principle of motion and rest. It is also difficult to reconcile with the motor causality principle of *Phys.* VII.1, in which internal causes of motion are, as we shall see, precisely the focus of the argument.) It is then argued that the motor causality principle is refuted by the law of inertia, whereby (it is believed) a body moving with constant velocity requires no external cause of motion. It should be clear, however, that (as Weisheipl emphasizes) Aristotle's explication of the motor causality principle as applied to the natural motion of the elements contradicts the *motor conjunctus* doctrine. For the elements, the requirement for a per se mover is met by the generator, and this is not a conjoined efficient cause of motion. This suffices to rule out a certain interpretation of the motor causality principle; it does not, however, resolve the question of the relation between that principle and the law of inertia. We address this issue in Part II, after developing our interpretation of *Phys.* VII.1.

5. Note that Aristotle's account seems to presuppose the perfect homogeneity of the elements.

third statement of the motor causality principle, this time as applied to the first moved mover: it is impossible for that which moves itself to move itself in its entirety (257b2). The proof (257b3–12) is in terms of act and potency, thus in terms of the definition of motion itself (*Phys.* III.1, 201a10–11).[6] This definition is general in that it covers both substantial change and motion, that is, change in the categories of accident: quantity, quality, and place. Now it is obvious that the motion of a thing that moves itself—here the first moved mover—can occur only in the categories of accident: it cannot be substantial change, since no thing generates itself. This raises the question as to why the (more general) argument from act and potency is employed here, in *Phys.* VIII.5, instead of the argument of *Phys.* VII.1, which clearly suffices to cover change of quantity, quality, and place.[7] In general, the three accounts of the motor causality principle differ in type of argumentation and degree of universality. We cannot here pursue the important question as to why the three arguments are composed and placed as they are in Aristotle's text.[8] The more modest intention of this introduction is rather to situate our inquiry on the complex terrain of *Phys.* VII and VIII and to indicate its relation to relevant recent research. The scope of the following investigation will accordingly be limited to the first part of *Phys.* VII.1, to certain texts in *Phys.* V, VI, and VIII that bear directly upon it, and to the commentary of Aquinas, as follows:[9]

6. The definition is also given at *Phys.* III.1, 201a27–29, 201b4–5, and *Phys.* III.2, 202a7–8.

7. Is it perhaps because the argument of *Phys.* VII.1 does not cover the natural motion of the elements as Aristotle has explained it in *Phys.* VIII.4?

8. Aquinas reviews the three arguments for the motor causality principle in *Summa Contra Gentiles* I.13. He does not explain why they are composed and placed as they are in Aristotle's text. He does, however, draw an important distinction between the first unmoved mover that is a part of the first moved mover—to which the *Physics* evidently concludes—and the absolutely first and *separate* unmoved mover, which moves by final causality and is an object of metaphysics. See Thomas Aquinas, *Summa Contra Gentiles* (Turin: Marietti, 1886), Lib. I, cap. XIII, 14; English translation by Anton Pegis, *On the Truth of the Catholic Faith* (Garden City, N.Y.: Hanover House, 1955), Book I, chap. 13, 94.

9. For English translation of Aristotle's *Physics* we shall use Apostle (cit. n. 1), slightly modified for greater literalness, and intercalate important Greek phrases. For Averroes's commentary we shall use the Latin translation of the Juncta edition, *De Physico Auditu libri octo* in *Aristotelis Opera cum Averrois Commentariis* (Venice, 1562–1574; reprint Frankfurt: Minerva, 1962), vol. 4. English translation is by E. M. Macierowski, with whom I have discussed much of this material. For the study of Aquinas's commentary we shall use the Latin of Marietti's Leonine critical edition, *In octo libros Physicorum Aristotelis expositio* (Rome, 1965). Lacking a new critical edition, the Latin lemmata given in Marietti are as close as we can come to the text of the *Physics* used by Aquinas. For English translation we shall use Thomas Aquinas, *Commentary on Aristotle's Physics*, trans. Blackwell, Spath, and Thirlkel (New Haven: Yale University Press, 1963).

Aristotle, *Phys.*	Aquinas, *In phys.*
V.1 224a21–34	nn. 638–40
VI.4 234b10–235a37	nn. 806–16
VII.1 241b24–242a16	nn. 884–90
VIII.4 254b7–256a3	nn. 1021–36
VIII.5 257a31–258b9	nn. 1062–68

Our principal Averroistic text is the opening portion of the commentary on *Phys.* VII.1: Averroes, *In phys.*, 305M–308C.

Among recent writings on the motor causality principle, the works of S. Pines,[10] J. A. Weisheipl,[11] and W. A. Wallace[12] are especially germane. Pines and Weisheipl focus on the motor causality principle in relation to the problem of the elements. *Phys.* VIII.4 is, therefore, their main Aristotelian text, not *Phys.* VII.1, and the argument from the physical continuum. Wallace, apparently unique among modern commentators, emphasizes the importance of *Phys.* VII.1. In this essay we shall follow his lead. Let us briefly review these works.

S. Pines shows that, through the theory of natural inclination, (1) the motor causality principle can be applied to elemental motions such that (2) no extension of the principle to substantial generation is required, and (3) the motion of the inanimate is likened to that of the animate (natural inclination being analogous to soul). He does this as follows.

It is well known that Galen attacked Aristotle's argument in *Phys.* VII.1 and thereby rejected the motor causality principle.[13] Pines analyzes Alexander of Aphrodisias' rebuttal to this attack.[14] This rebuttal consists not in a defense of *Phys.* VII.1,[15] but in a restatement of *Phys.* VIII.4, in which the central issue is the applicability of the motor causality principle to the natural motions of the elements. Alexander thus evidently believed that Aristotle's argument of *Phys.* VIII.4,

---

10. S. Pines, "*Omne quod movetur necesse est ab aliquo moveri:* A Refutation of Galen by Alexander of Aphrodisias and the Theory of Motion" *Isis* 52 (1961): 21–54.

11. Weisheipl, "*Omne quod movetur.*"

12. W. A. Wallace, "Cosmological Arguments and Scientific Concepts" in *From a Realist Point of View*, 313–27.

13. See, for example, Averroes, *In phys.*, 306B, C, G, 307G–I, and Aquinas, *In phys.*, n. 887.

14. Drawing on two Arabic manuscripts, Rescher and Marmura have pieced together and translated the complete text of Alexander's reply to Galen in *The Refutation by Alexander of Aphrodisias of Galen's Treatise on the Theory of Motion* (Islamabad: Islamic Research Institute, 1969). Reference to Galen's attack on Aristotle is first made by Alexander on p. 18 (Carullah MS, 67a27).

15. Alexander attempts to restate *Phys.* VII.1 in what he considers to be a more logical form; Pines, "*Omne quod movetur,*" 29–30.

emended to cover more adequately the case of the elements, is the best argument for the motor causality principle. His emendation consists in this, that, in contrast to the interpretation of Aristotle, the elements possess an intrinsic active principle of their upward and downward motion, namely, natural inclination (*mayl ṭabi'i*). According to Pines,

> Alexander disposes ... of Aristotle's *aporia* concerning the natural motions of the light and heavy bodies. According to the commentator the thesis that everything that is in motion must be moved by something is applicable to these bodies because they are endowed with an intrinsic principle of motion, namely their upward or downward inclination, a principle analogous to the soul of animate bodies.[16]

Alexander's theory of natural inclination is consistent with, but not derived from, the reasoning of *Phys.* VII.1. As noted, it is a departure from *Phys.* VIII.4. Pines then shows that Alexander's interpretation of natural elemental motion passed through Philoponus to Avicenna and the Arabic philosophers, thus constituting a major tradition within the horizon of premodern science.[17]

J. A. Weisheipl presents an alternative interpretation that, following Thomas Aquinas, strictly adheres to Aristotle's rejection of internal agency in the natural motion of the elements, as stated in *Phys.* VIII.4. According to Weisheipl, introduction of an intrinsic agent principle, such as natural inclination, is a deviation from Aristotle incompatible with this text. Specifically, it contradicts the distinction, evident within ordinary experience, between living and nonliving.[18] Aristotle indeed says, "To say that [the elements] are moved by themselves is impossible, for this is proper to living things" (*Phys.* VIII.4, 255a5–7). And this is difficult to reconcile with Alexander of Aphrodisias' assertion

> And if someone says regarding these things that the principle of their motion exists in them with a status similar to that of a soul [belonging] to an animate being this [would mean] that he said in a similar [way] that they are moved by something. For they are moved either by heaviness or by lightness, either of which is other than the body.[19]

For Weisheipl, then, the mover required in the case of the elements

---

16. Pines, "*Omne quod movetur*," 42, also 48 and 53. Rescher and Marmura, *Refutation*, 17 (Carullah MS, 67a18–23).
17. Pines, "*Omne quod movetur*," 51 and 53; Rescher and Marmura, *Refutation*, 2–3. We shall see that, in certain of his texts, Averroes stands in this tradition.
18. Weisheipl, "*Omne quod movetur*," 32.
19. Pines, "*Omne quod movetur*," 42; Rescher and Marmura, *Refutation*, 17 (Carullah MS, 67a22). It is important to note, however, that *De caelo* III.2 contains passages that support Alexander's interpretation; see Pines, "*Omne quod movetur*," 41.

is the generator,[20] and the motor causality principle must, accordingly, be understood to cover substantial change: "*movetur* [in the rule *omne quod movetur ab alio movetur*] must include every coming into being, even of the whole substance whether it be physical or spiritual."[21]

The problem of the application of the motor causality principle to the motions of the elements issues in a dichotomy: Aristotle's solution of *Phys.* VIII.4 (the *generans* is the mover) stands in problematic relation to the argument of *Phys.* VII.1; the solution of Alexander of Aphrodisias (natural inclination is the mover) is compatible with *Phys.* VII.1 but not with VIII.4.[22] This may be one reason why three distinct arguments are given for the motor causality principle. As Weisheipl rightly notes, "A diversity of medieval interpretations [of the principle] is now beginning to be appreciated."[23] For our purposes here, the interpretation presented by W. A. Wallace is most important.

Wallace points out, in the context of a review of major commentators,[24] that (1) the argument of *Phys.* VII.1 "has proved troublesome to practically all commentators and through the centuries has provoked a whole series of arguments and counter-arguments in its refutation and defense" and that (2) in spite of this, Aquinas understood the proof as a demonstration *propter quid*, that is, a strictly valid demonstration through causes.[25] What type of causality then grounds the proof in *Phys.* VII.1? According to Wallace, the argument "is made not through efficient causality but rather through material causality," that is, through the "divisibility of the movable object" and the impli-

20. Natural motion (upward or downward) then follows immediately from the substantial form and in accordance with the final causality of natural place.

21. Weisheipl, "*Omne quod movetur*," 29. The motion of the elements is not the only issue here. If the motor causality principle is taken to include only change in the categories of accident (quantity, quality, place) then one will conclude to a first moved mover and (via *Phys.* VIII.5) to an immaterial source of motion in the first moved mover (a soul of the outer sphere, say) 'which will not necessarily be God as St. Thomas understands Him" (Weisheipl, "*Omne quod movetur*," 29). See n. 8 on Aquinas's account in *Summa Contra Gentiles* I.13.

22. This might make it sound as if *Phys.* VII.1 and *Phys.* VIII.4 are mutually contradictory. They are not: *Phys.* VII.1 states that in whatever moves itself, there must be a distinction between mover and moved. It does not say that the elements do not move themselves. If they did, then there would have to be a distinction within them between mover and moved. *Phys.* VIII.4 then states that living things move themselves and elements do not. Alexander's natural inclination is an internal agent principle of motion that is not identical to the moved element. It, therefore, meets the requirements of *Phys.* VII.1. But in asserting that the elements move themselves in their natural motions (likening them to living things moved by soul), Alexander contradicts *Phys.* VIII.4.

23. Weisheipl, "*Omne quod movetur*," 26, n. 1.

24. Wallace discusses Galen, Alexander, Simplicius, Avicenna, Averroes, Aquinas, and Nifo.

25. Wallace, "Cosmological Arguments," 314 and 315.

cations thereof for motion.[26] This line of reasoning is in turn rooted in *Phys.* VI. Following Wallace, we are thus brought to the quotations from Aquinas on *Phys.* VII.1 with which this essay opens. Let us begin our analysis of Aristotle's account.

The text of *Phys.* VII.1 from 241b24 to 242a16 (textus alter 241b34–242a46) contains the argument for the motor causality principle; that is, it concerns the sources of motion[27] for subjects of successive change. This argument, and with it the text, can be divided into four parts, as follows (textus alter in parentheses):

Principle of Motion and Causality of Parts, 241b24–29 (241b34–39)
Soul, 241b29–35 (241b40–242a34)
Stopping Thesis, 241b35–242a5 (242a35–39)
Divisibility of the Movable and Conclusion of the Argument, 242a5–15 (242a39–46)

A section of Part I is devoted to each of these.

A. *Principle of Motion and Causality of Parts, 241b24–29 (241b34–39)*

Aristotle's argument begins as follows:

All that is moved is necessarily moved by something (Ἅπαν τὸ κινούμενον ὑπό τινος ἀνάγκη κινεῖσθαι). If it does not have the source of motion in itself, it is evident that it is moved by some other [for the mover is the other]; but if it has it in itself, let AB be that which is moved [through itself (καθ' αὑτό) and] not by something of it being moved (μὴ τῷ τῶν τούτου τι κινεῖσθαι).[28]

---

26. Ibid.
27. Final causality is excluded from the reasoning of *Phys.* VII.1; see *Phys.* VII.2, 243a32. Although Aristotle will begin his account in *Phys.* VII.1 with agent or efficient causality in things moved from without (the obvious cases), he will turn immediately thereafter to things moved from within. That the active source of motion in self-movers (think of an animal) is properly and solely an *efficient* cause is less easy to discern; is not form also involved? Our analysis will indeed lead to the concept of natural form as source of motion in things which move themselves. Finally, as Aquinas makes clear in the quotation that appears on the first page of this paper, and as Wallace points out, the divisibility of the mobile and thus a type of material causality is, in the interpretation here presented, at the heart of the motor causality principle. It is thus fair to say that the reasoning of *Phys.* VII.1 and attendant texts is about the relations among material, efficient, and formal causality in things that move themselves.
28. [Textus alter] is given in brackets. The Latin translation of Aristotle's text given in the Marietti edition of Thomas's commentary is: *Omne quod movetur, necesse est ab aliquo moveri. Si igitur in seipso non habet principium motus, manifestum est quod ab altero movetur: aliud enim erit movens. Si autem in seipso, accipiatur AB, quod moveatur secundum se, et non eo quod eorum quae huius sunt, aliquid movetur* (*In phys.* [676, 676bis]).

The Latin translation, given in Juncta of the (lost) Arabic text believed to have been

In any body seen to be in motion (with respect to place, quantity, or quality), what can be said about the mover and its relation to the moved? In certain cases, this relation is obvious, for the mover can be seen outside the mobile doing the moving, as when an animal pushes a rock. In other cases, however, the source of motion is not evident because it is internal to the thing in motion.[29] How, for example, is the animal caused to push the rock?[30] It is to these cases that Aristotle

---

available to Averroes is *Omne motum necessario movetur ab aliquo. Si autem principium motus non fuerit ex ipso, manifestum est, ipsum moveri ab alio: natura motor eius erit aliud. Si autem principium motus huius fuerit ex ipso, accipiatur per se, et sit AB, ita, quod moveatur, non quia aliquid ex eo movetur* (*In phys.*, 305M–306A).

29. Does this passage say that the cause of a thing's motion is either (1) obviously external or (2) internal (and not obvious)? Aristotle himself rules out this interpretation by his treatment of the elements in *Phys.* VIII.4. In the case of the elements, the agent principle of natural motion is neither obvious nor internal (254b33–255a6). Aristotle's intention here, in *Phys.* VII.1, seems not to be to specify an exhaustive division of movers (in terms of their relation to mobiles) but rather to focus on self-movers, that is, on things that have within them a source of agency in their own motion. Animals are the most familiar example, although the account of *Phys.* VII.1 is not restricted to any one kind of body. Indeed, the ultimate application of Aristotle's general theory of self-movers is to the whole cosmos (*Phys.* VIII.6–10).

30. An animal is an individual of a certain species. As such it looks and moves in a way characteristic of that species. The sources of its specific properties and activity are, at least partly, internal. (The cooperating causality of the external environment is of course necessary for it to be alive and healthy; see *Phys.* VIII.2, 253a7–21, and Aquinas, *In phys.*, n. 1002.) At the same time, an animal is a whole composed of parts, and its activity and motion are brought about through the structure, agency, and patiency of its parts. How are the internal principles of its specific changes related to the working of its parts? In the language of medieval science, this is the question of the relations among formal, efficient, and material causality in living things. It is important to note that post-Newtonian physics is widely believed to support a ready-made and simple answer to this question: Whatever a whole is or does is merely a sum of what its simple parts are or do, parts that are simple in that they obey fixed laws of interaction through fundamental forces. Thus matter is adequately described in terms of mass and charge, say, and efficient causes consist in the forces of gravitation and electromagnetism. And since wholes are thus *reducible* to their parts, formal causality is banished from nature. The premodern problem of wholes, parts, and principles of motion is, thus, removed from view by the belief in universal reductionism. We suggest, however, that universal reductionism is not philosophically or scientifically plausible.

First, the inadequacy of the reductionist paradigm in the realm of quantum physics should be familiar. Atomic structure, thus the stability of the chemical species, cannot be explained merely by reduction to electrons and nuclei. "[T]he stability of matter [is] a pure miracle when considered from the standpoint of classical physics.... even after a host of changes due to external influences, an iron atom will always remain an iron atom, with exactly the same properties as before. This cannot be explained by the principles of classical mechanics, certainly not if the atom resembles a planetary system." Werner Heisenberg paraphrasing Niels Bohr in Heisenberg, *Physics and Beyond* (New York: Harper Torchbooks, 1971), 39. In quantum theory, the wave function, uncertainty principle, and Pauli exclusion principle imply a basic revision of the whole-part relation on the atomic scale.

Quantum physics quite aside, the reductionist argument from classical physics (some-

immediately turns and for which he develops his argument in *Phys.* VII.1.

Thus AB is moved from an internal source of motion—it moves itself—but not because a part of it is moved.[31]

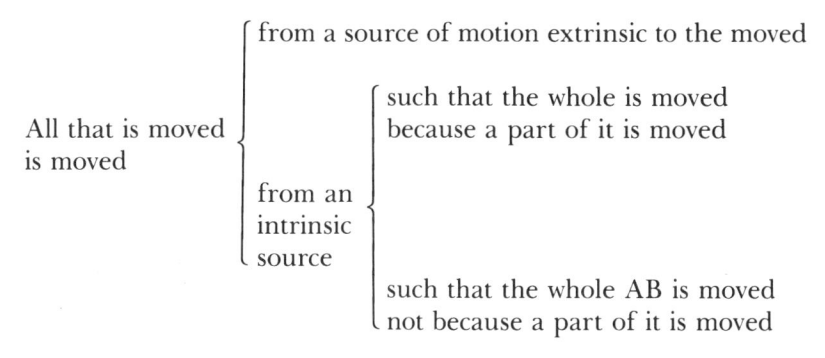

All that is moved is moved
- from a source of motion extrinsic to the moved
- from an intrinsic source
  - such that the whole is moved because a part of it is moved
  - such that the whole AB is moved not because a part of it is moved

The first division, based on what is internal and external to a body, is obvious. The second division, based upon wholes and parts, is not. What does it mean for the whole AB to move itself not because a part of it is moved? To answer this we must look at Aristotle's concept of *first* or *primary* (πρῶτος) as it relates to motion and the causes of motion.

According to Aristotle in *Phys.* V.1,

we say that the body is being healed when in fact it is just the eye or the chest that is being healed, and these are parts of the whole body; . . . [but a body can be] moved neither accidentally nor because something of itself is moved (κινεῖται οὔτε τῷ ἄλλο τι τῶν αὑτοῦ), but because it is itself first moved (ἀλλὰ τῷ αὐτὸ κινεῖσθαι πρῶτον). (*Phys.* V.1, 224a25–28)

---

times called Newtonian-Laplacian determinism) is weak. It is based on a questionable universalization of (1) the parallelogram rule for composition of forces and (2) a way of conceiving matter, simple part, and law first exemplified in Newton's theory of gravitation. See the author's "Wholes, Parts, and Laws of Motion" *Nature and System* 6 (1984): 195–215.

The point here is not that Aristotelian physics is vindicated by the strength of quantum theory and the weakness of classical reductionism. The point is simply that the premodern tradition of physics involves an approach to nature (and a problematic of motion and causality) worthy of study.

31. The word *part* does not appear in the Greek phrase, which is μὴ τῷ τῶν τούτου τι κινεῖσθαι. The article τῷ is a dative of cause. More literally, this phrase reads, "not because of the being moved of something of the things of it." We are justified in using the word *part* by *Phys.* V.1, 224a24–27 and 31–34, in which similar constructions occur and are explicated in terms of parts and wholes. In the dative definite article τῷ, however, there is room for prepositions other than "*because of* the being moved. . . ." It might also mean "by the," "through the," or Apostle's "in the sense that," *Aristotle's Physics*, 127.

As moved, all the parts of AB must be in motion. But clearly for local motion (which suffices for the point we are about to make), this is possible in distinct ways. In one way, the parts of the body remain at fixed distances from each other; thus the body is rigid, as in the case of a stone falling and rotating. In another way, the parts move relative to each other, as in the case of a bird in flight. That which is in local motion by means of its parts appears always to undergo a change of shape, so that its parts move relative to each other.[32] The point is that to say that AB is in motion as a whole, such that all its parts are in motion, says nothing about causes of motion. Yet we are told that AB is moved from an internal principle, that AB moves itself. Indeed, Aristotle explicates in *Phys.* V.1 a further sense of first or primary (πρῶτος), namely, with respect to moving, that is, causing motion:

> It is likewise with the mover, for it may move another accidentally, or it may do so through a part (by something of it) (κατὰ μέρος (τῷ τῶν τούτου τι)), or through itself primarily (καθ' αὑτὸ πρῶτον), for example, the doctor heals.... (224a30–33)[33]

The doctor as healer heals not as a hand that injects medicine but as a whole human substance in possession of the medical art. AB as mover, of itself through the principle within it, moves (that is, induces movement) as a whole. This means that anything less than AB, any part of AB, is not able to move AB. Therefore, AB cannot be divided into a part that moves itself and a remainder moved by that part. Division of AB into parts destroys its self-motive power. This is what it means for AB to move itself primarily, to move itself as a whole not because a part of it is moved.

Two questions need to be addressed: (1) We are speaking here of parts as quantitative parts, not qualitative parts (such as a soul, or a faculty, such as appetition); is it completely clear that this is what Aristotle means? (2) What is an example of AB, an example of what moves itself primarily? Answering these questions requires a further look at the texts.

---

32. According to Einstein, motion must be understood as relative to an observer's frame of reference, and no frame of reference is preferred or singled out by nature (as the ether was thought to be, prior to the Michelson-Morley experiment). Certain types of motion (such as center-of-mass motion at constant velocity) thus have no absolute character. Note, however, that the motions of parts of a whole relative to each other, for instance, the parts of an animal moving itself, cannot be transformed to rest for any observer. Therefore, the type of motion under study here retains absolute character (as does thermal motion) within the physics of Einstein.

33. The Greek πρῶτον is an adjective. Nevertheless, in Marietti's Latin Lemma [465], Aristotle's phrase ἀλλὰ τῷ αὐτὸ κινεῖσθαι πρῶτον is rendered *sed in eo quod ipsum movetur primo*; that is, the adverb is used instead of the adjective *primum*. What moves itself primarily is the first moved.

In *Phys.* VIII.5, Aristotle investigates the structure of a thing able to move itself. He says:

> No thing which moves itself primarily (πρώτως αὐτὸ αὐτὸ κινοῦντος) has one or more parts each of which moves itself. For if the whole is moved by itself (ὑφ' αὐτοῦ), either it will be moved by some part of it (ὑπὸ τῶν αὐτοῦ τινὸς κινήσεται) or the whole will be moved by the whole (ὅλον ὑφ' ὅλου). Now if [it is moved] because a part of it is moved by itself (τῷ κινεῖσθαί τι μόριον αὐτὸ ὑφ' αὑτοῦ), that part would be the primary mover which moves itself (τὸ πρῶτον αὐτὸ αὐτὸ κινοῦν), for if separated (χωρισθέν), it would move itself but would no longer move the whole. But if the whole is moved by the whole, it would be by accident that each of the parts is moved by itself. (257b27–35)

On the basis of this passage, we conclude that the explanation of what moves itself primarily is indeed in terms of quantitative parts.[34] A whole animal, therefore, when it moves itself locally, does not do so primarily, because if certain parts are separated (a tail or an ear, say), it would still be able to move itself locally. What then is an example of AB, a thing that moves itself primarily? Can there be such a thing? The answer to the latter question, we shall argue, is yes and no: yes, in the order of nature; no, in the argument of *Phys.* VII.1. For the argument of *Phys.* VII.1 is about body taken simply as physical continuum without regard to determinate natures. We shall establish this point by recourse not only to the text of Aristotle but also to the commentaries of Aquinas and Averroes. Despite important disagreements between them, these thinkers both agree that *omne quod movetur ab alio movetur*.[35] We shall indeed use their disagreements to elucidate their agreement.

What is an example of AB? Averroes comments as follows on the opening passage of *Phys.* VII.1:

> The moved things which are seen to be moved from themselves (*ex se*), not from without (*ex extrinseco*), are those about which we intend to assert that they are moved by another mover. Therefore, let it be supposed that such a moved [namely AB] be moved through itself (*per se*), not through a part of it (*per partem eius*); that is, let it be moved as a whole (*secundum totum*) not because a part of it moves the whole. For that which is moved as a whole because a part of it moves the whole is moved *per accidens*, as the motion of the whole animal body through the motion of the natural heat or of the muscles. For the first moved through itself (*motum enim primum per se*) in an-

---

34. Aquinas repeats Aristotle's account; see *In phys.*, n. 1060.
35. Both agree that the principle is true. They do not, however, agree on the demonstrative force of Aristotle's proof. For Averroes, the demonstration is true and "of the genus of assured signs (*signorum certorum*), although it is not of the genus of simple [that is, *propter quid*] demonstrations" (*In phys.*, 307K–L). The reason for Averroes's reservation is not entirely clear; see Wallace, "Cosmological Arguments," 318–19. For Aquinas, the demonstration is *propter quid*, thus apodictic (*In phys.*, n. 889).

imals is the heart, which is moved as a whole not because a part of it moves itself (*movet se*) and moves the whole. This is to be understood from the fact that he said "and let AB be moved not because something of it is moved." He said this because that moved which he wants to examine, namely, what is moved *per se*, must be moved as a whole, not as a part (*secundum partem*), [thus not] as was said at the beginning of the fifth book, [in the sense] that something is attributed to the motion of the moved thing because only a part of it is moved whereas the remainder is moved by that part. (*In phys.*, 306E–G)

Averroes here identifies what is moved per se with what is moved *per se primo*; the characterization "moved per se" is here restricted to things that move themselves primarily, to first moved things, such as a living heart. He holds, as a tacit corollary to this, that what is moved *per partem*, that is, because a part of it is moved, is moved *per accidens*. Averroes, therefore, maintains, like Aristotle, that a whole animal does not move itself primarily. He also maintains, unlike Aristotle, that an animal is moved *per accidens*.[36] Since Aristotle does not restrict the meaning of *per se* to *per se primo*, for him, a thing, for example, an animal, can be moved per se without being moved primarily.[37] Indeed, from the Aristotelian perspective, it is remarkable that Averroes should consider a bird in flight, say, as moved *per accidens*. In *Phys.* VIII.4, Aristotle says:

Of things [which move or are moved] *per se* (καθ' αὐτά), some [move or are moved] by themselves (ὑφ' ἑαυτοῦ), and some by others (ὑπ' ἄλλου) . . . That which is moved by itself (ὑφ' αὑτοῦ) is moved according to nature (φύσει), like each of the animals. (254b12–15)[38]

Thus, for Aristotle, a bird in flight is moved (1) per se, (2) by itself, and (3) according to nature. Averroes's comment suggests that, for him (Averroes), the relation between body and soul is *per accidens*; that he understands the unity of natural substances in a different way than Aristotle.[39]

36. Rescher and Marmura attribute this Averroistic view to Aristotle (*Refutation*, 8). In view of 254b12–15 (quoted next in the chapter, and in n. 38), it is difficult to maintain that Averroes's view is Aristotle's.
37. The fact that a whole animal is not itself a first moved part does not mean for Aristotle that, in its natural motion, the animal is not moved per se.
38. The complete quotation is, "Of things [which move or are moved] *per se*, some [move or are moved] by themselves, and some by others; and some according to nature, but others violently and contrary to nature. That which is moved by itself is moved according to nature, like each of the animals (for the animal is moved by itself, and we say that things whose principle of motion is in them are moved according to nature; and so it is according to nature that the whole animal moves itself. . .)" (*Phys.* VIII.4, 254b12–18).
39. It may be germane to note Averroes's well-known and heterodox position on the unity and substantiality of the possible intellect. See, for example, Averroes's commen-

Averroes has thus provided an example of a first moved, of what moves itself primarily, namely, the heart. In *Phys.* VII.1, Aristotle provides no example, nor does Aquinas in his commentary on VII.1. Later in his commentary on this text, Averroes gives two more examples:

> It is necessary for there to be first moveds (*prima mota*) since natural bodies are not divided to infinity inasmuch as they are natural bodies. For example, the first moved in fire (*primum motum in igne*) is the least part that can be fire in act, and likewise the first moved of the natural heat of animals (*primum motum caloris naturalis animalium*) is also the least part which can move that animal. (*In phys.*, 307I)[40]

This passage reveals (1) a disagreement between Aristotle and Aquinas, on the one hand, and Averroes, on the other, concerning the natural motion of fire,[41] and (2) an apparent major disagreement between Averroes and Aquinas concerning the existence of first moved things (*prima mota*). The first of these leads to the complicated subject of Averroes's theory of the motion of the elements[42]; we shall not attempt to provide an adequate treatment of it here. As noted, however, despite their disagreement, Aquinas and Averroes both agree with the motor causality principle. The problem of the elements is thus related to, yet not determined by, the argument of *Phys.* VII.1.[43] For the understanding of that argument, the second of the preceding two disagreements, and its resolution, are most important.

Averroes says, "It is necessary for there to be first moveds...." In contrast, Aquinas, in the conclusion to his commentary on the argument in *Phys.* VII.1, says, "Aristotle has shown in Book VI that there is no first in motion ... there cannot be discovered a first whose motion does not depend on something prior" (*In phys.*, n. 889). There cannot be a first moved, that is, a body or part of a body that moves itself primarily. The existence of the first moved AB is, according to Aquinas, an assumption to be refuted in a *reductio ad absurdum*. This is why he cites no examples of AB in his commentary on *Phys.* VII.1. The crux of the argument (we shall address it in the section "Divisibility of the Movable and Conclusion of the Argument,") concerns the

---

tary on *De Anima* III in A. Hyman and J. J. Walsh, eds., *Philosophy in the Middle Ages* (Indianapolis: Hackett Publishing Co., 1973), 314–25.

40. This passage is also quoted by Pines, "*Omne quod movetur,*" 33, n. 59. See also Averroes, *In phys.*, 384K, on the minimal quantity of fire.

41. On the natural motion of the elements as presented in the *Physics*, Aquinas follows Aristotle. See *In phys.*, n. 1035, also n. 144.

42. See Edward Grant, *A Source Book in Medieval Science* (Cambridge, Mass.: Harvard University Press, 1974), 253–64, esp. 262, n. 35, and 264, n. 8.

43. For the relation between *Phys.* VII.1, VIII.4, and the problem of the elements, see n. 22.

divisibility of bodies and the theory of the continuum given in *Phys.* VI, to which theory Averroes does not refer.[44]

Where does Aristotle stand? In the argument of *Phys.* VII.1, we shall see that he refers to the divisibility of the changeable—this indeed is the link to Book VI—but does not explicitly refer to a dependency of the motion of a whole on the motions of its parts. He speaks of the stopping thesis, Part 3 of the argument. Nor does he deny the existence of a first moved. As we shall see, he uses the stopping thesis to show that the first moved, AB, is moved by something distinct from AB. In fact, in *Phys.* VIII.5, Aristotle asserts,

Nothing prevents [a body that moves itself] from being potentially divisible though actually undivided, and from not having the same power (δύναμιν) if it is divided; and so nothing prevents [self-motion] from being primarily in things which are potentially divisible. (258b1–4)

This is a confusing state of affairs. Aristotle says (in *Phys.* VIII.5) that a first moved can exist; Averroes says (on *Phys.* VII.1) that it must exist; Aquinas says (on *Phys.* VII.1) that it cannot exist. A resolution is possible. In his comment on the preceding passage in *Phys.* VIII.5, Aquinas makes explicit what has thus far been unstated in the argument of *Phys.* VII.1:

It must be noted that Aristotle has proven in Book VI that in motion there is no first, either on the part of the mobile, or of the time, or on the part of that in which motion occurs, especially increase and local motion. This is so because he was then speaking about motion in general and the mobile insofar as it is a certain continuum, not yet applying [his reasoning] to determinate natures (*determinatas naturas*). And according to this it would follow that there is not something which is moved primarily, and consequently there is not something which moves primarily, if the mover is a continuum. Thus there would also not be something which moves itself primarily (*primo movens seipsum*). But now Aristotle is speaking about motion by applying it to determinate natures. Therefore, he holds that there is something which moves itself primarily. (*In phys.*, n. 1067)

The crucial point is that the application of results from *Phys.* VI in the argument of VII.1 presupposes a certain abstraction from determinate natures. The object of study in *Phys.* VII.1 is thus body taken as physical continuum, without regard to kind or specific nature. The physical continuum has magnitude and is infinitely divisible. In this respect, it is like the mathematical continuum. But, unlike the math-

---

44. In his commentary on the motor causality principle in *Phys.* VII.1, Averroes refers to *Phys.* VI once, at 308A, concerning logical matters, not the theory of the continuum.

ematical continuum, it is the subject of per se motion.[45] For this reason it is not mathematizable; it cannot be represented by the real number line or by symbols that give it a certain reality outside the bodies in which it is (as is the case with mass and extension). We shall examine Aquinas's analysis of motion and the physical continuum in the section "Divisibility of the Movable and Conclusion of the Argument."

The argument of *Phys.* VII.1 abstracts from determinate natures. This is not said by Aristotle. The basis of our interpretation must be the coherence it provides to otherwise problematically related texts, namely, *Phys.* VII.1 and VIII.5, and the supporting testimony of our commentators. Thus, at the conclusion of his commentary on Aristotle's argument for the motor causality principle in *Phys.* VII.1, Averroes addresses a certain objection. The objection is based on the fact that the celestial body cannot rest.[46] Averroes says,

For a part of bodies to rest, and concerning which it has been demonstrated that it is impossible that they may be corrupted or come to rest, is in one way possible and in another way impossible. For it is possible according as it is body, to wit neither light nor heavy, but it is impossible according as it is some [determinate] body. And this consideration [in *Phys.* VII.1] is concerned with body according as it is body, since the moved as moved is body. (*In phys.*, 307M).

Averroes's position is now consistent. Body as such, without regard to specific natures and to their changes under quantitative division, is infinitely divisible. In body so considered, unlike natural body, we find no first moved parts. As Averroes says, "It is necessary for there to be first moveds *since natural bodies are not divided to infinity inasmuch as they are natural bodies*" (307I; emphasis added).

Concerning the celestial body, Aquinas makes the same point as Averroes:

Although it is impossible for a part to be at rest with respect to a determinate nature, insofar as it is a body of a certain species, for example, the heavens or fire, nevertheless, this is not impossible if the common character (*ratio*) of

---

45. See n. 1; the physical continuum must be spread out in space; that is, it must be three-dimensional stuff.

We thus have three kinds of magnitude: (1) mathematical continuum, (2) physical continuum, and (3) magnitude of a body of determinate nature. The latter cannot be divided to infinity without corrupting the nature in question. This threefold Aristotelian distinction was discussed among medieval commentators. See Pierre Duhem, *Medieval Cosmology*, trans. Roger Ariew (Chicago: University of Chicago Press, 1985), 35–45, esp. the account of Giles of Rome, 38. Duhem focuses on the problem of natural minima and does not attempt to explain the difference between the mathematical and the physical continuum.

46. Averroes, *In phys.*, 307L.

body is considered. For a body, insofar as it is a body, is not prevented from being at rest or in motion. (*In phys.*, n. 888).[47]

Our inquiry has covered text and commentary in *Phys.* V.1, VII.1, and VIII.5 in order to establish the following points:

1. A first moved or, equivalently, that which moves itself primarily loses self-motive power under (quantitative and actual) division.

2. The argument for the motor causality principle in *Phys.* VII.1 is in terms of body as such, or the physical continuum. Thus the mobile AB will not be considered insofar as it possesses a determinate nature.

3. The crux of Aristotle's argument, as Aquinas will explicate it, consists in the application of results of *Phys.* VI to the physical continuum understood in *Phys.* VII.1. It will be shown that in the physical continuum as such there cannot exist a first moved part.

Thus far in our account, the term *form*, fundamental for the Aristotelian understanding of nature, has not appeared. Let us attempt to elucidate the abstraction from determinate natures, and thus the concept of the physical continuum, in terms of form. To this end, we must take more careful account of the two disagreements, previously noted, between Aristotle and Aquinas, on the one hand, and Averroes, on the other. These are disagreements over (1) the natural motion of the elements and (2) the unity of natural substances.

We have noted in the introduction that the causality of the natural motion of the elements was a major issue in the commentaries down to the time of Galileo. Let us bring out more clearly Averroes's position on this issue as he presents it in his discussion of *Phys.* VII.1. So far, we have seen his assertion that in fire there is a first moved part. This is less than a general statement that all four elements move themselves, that is, possess an internal agent principle. Such a statement is given in the opening sentence of Averroes's commentary on *Phys.* VII.1:

In this treatise he [Aristotle] begins to examine whether every moved has a mover, since it is apparent to sense that some things are moved from themselves (*ex se*) without the mover being distinguished from the moved by sense, as in the four elements. (*In phys.*, 306B)

To be moved *ex se* is contradistinguished by Averroes to being moved *ex extrinseco*:

We do not doubt that they are moved *ex se* and not from an extrinsic mover,

---

47. See also Aquinas, *In phys.*, n. 896: "Aristotle is speaking here [in *Phys.* VII.1] about mobiles and movers in general and is not yet applying [his reasoning] to determinate natures. . . ."

namely, the four elements, and all bodies moved *ex se*. . . . It is also manifest that what is not moved *ex extrinseco* is moved *ex se*. (*In phys.*, 49C–D)

For Averroes, a thing can be moved either *ex se* or *ex extrinseco*. Furthermore, "it is necessary that everything moved *ex se*, if it is not itself a first moved, [then] a first moved is in it" (*In phys.*, 307K).

On this account, the elements are not moved *ex extrinseco*, but rather each contains a first moved part. And this contradicts the canonical Aristotelian position in *Phys.* VIII.4 (255b29–31, 255b34–256a3). Finally, in his famous Comment 28 on *De Caelo* III, Averroes identifies the form of an element as its mover:

[Since] motion is primarily and essentially (*primo et essentialiter*) only by a mover, and in no other way, this [natural] motion [of fire] is not first or essential from an external mover but from the form of the moved. (*In De caelo* III, 198I)[48]

Evidently, the form of an element resides in its first moved part.

This is not the only side of Averroes. In his commentary on *Phys.* VIII.4, he agrees with Aristotle, holding that the elements cannot be moved *ex se*.[49] As previously noted, Averroes's position on this issue is, to say the least, complicated, and it is not our intention here to resolve it. The point is simply this: in his commentary on *Phys.* VII.1, Averroes disagrees with Aristotle and Aquinas concerning the agency or patiency, thus the efficacy, of form in the natural motions of the elements. For Averroes, on *Phys.* VII.1, the form of an element is an active principle, whereas for Aristotle, it is a passive principle. Let us bear this in mind while we briefly review the second of the two disagreements listed on the unity of natural substances.

We have seen that, for Averroes, an animal is moved *per accidens*, whereas, for Aristotle, it is moved per se. The issue seems to turn on the relation between soul and body in living beings. Specifically, we shall find (in the next section of this essay) evidence that, for Averroes, and in contrast to Aristotle, soul is not in the whole but in the first moved part of an animal.

These two disagreements can be seen to concern the locus and efficacy of form. Is form in the whole, or in a part, of the thing informed? Is form an active or a passive principle in the natural motion of the elements? Therefore, there can be agreement among Aristotle, Aquinas, and Averroes on the motor causality principle because the

---

48. See also 198L. Edward Grant has translated and commented on this text (as well as Averroes's Comment 71 on *Phys.* IV.8) in *Source Book*, 253–64.

49. Averroes, *In phys.*, 367I–M. See also H. A. Wolfson, *Crescas' Critique of Aristotle* (Cambridge, Mass.: Harvard University Press, 1957), 673.

reasoning of *Phys.* VII.1 is independent of form. The question now is, What form do we mean: substantial, accidental, or some other type?

The reasoning of *Phys.* VII.1 cannot be independent of substantial form. To abstract from substantial form would leave us to consider only primary matter, which lacks all determinacy (*Phys.* I.7, 191a8-14) and cannot, therefore, be divisible in quantity. To begin to see the type of form from which *Phys.* VII.1 abstracts, it is useful to read more of Aquinas's comment on *Phys.* VIII.5. It is there that Aristotle asserts that a first moved can exist (258b1–4; quoted previously). We have read the part of Aquinas's comment in which he explains that the argument of *Phys.* VII.1 is about "motion in general, and the mobile insofar as it is a certain continuum, not yet applying to determinate natures" (n. 1067); from body so considered, Aquinas reasons, as we shall see, to the impossibility of there being a first moved part. Aquinas now goes on to explain that, as natural, that is, as possessing a determinate nature, a body can contain a first moved part:

It is possible that a continuum, whether it be the mover or the moved, have such a nature that it cannot be actually divided (*non possit actu dividi*).... And if it happens that a continuum is divided, it will not retain the same potency to move or be moved which it had before. For such a potency follows from some form. Natural form (*forma naturalis*), however, requires determinate quantity. Hence, if a body is incorruptible, it cannot be divided in act. If, however, it is corruptible, and if it is divided in act, it will not retain the same potency, as is clear in regard to the heart. Hence, there is nothing to prevent a first among things which are divisible in potency. (*In phys.*, n. 1067)

The important term is natural form (*forma naturalis*). The argument of *Phys.* VII.1 abstracts from natural form.[50] We conjecture that this is the abstraction that yields the physical continuum as object of consideration. Any natural body can be understood as a composite of natural form and physical continuum. The elaboration of the concept of natural form in relation to substantial form and primary matter lies beyond the scope of this essay. Let us conclude this section by noting that Aquinas is quite consistent in denying the existence of a first moved in his commentary on *Phys.* VII.1, while affirming it in his commentary on VIII.5. Without natural form there can be no first moved; with it there can be. The physical continuum is infinitely divisible and subject of per se successive change. Since the physical continuum is common to all bodies, it follows from Aquinas's account that what all bodies have in common cannot be a source of self-motion.

50. The term *natural form* (φυσικὸν εἶδος) is used by Aristotle at *Phys.* I.9, 192b1.

This, we believe, is the essential meaning of the motor causality principle in *Phys.* VII.1.[51] Only something other than what is divisible and a subject of per se change can be a source of motion in things that move themselves. And this source must be specific, not common. Now natural form as form is indivisible and either immovable or, like the soul of an animal, moved *per accidens*. "All that is moved is moved by something (ὑπὸ τινος; *ab aliquo*)," and, in anything able to move itself, that "something" can best be understood as natural form.

If a source of self-motion were common to all bodies, then we would find this self-motion in every body and its parts, even under division to infinity. Would there then be a basis on which to claim a distinction between mover and moved? This self-motion would be an activity invariant under division of the bodies in which it is.[52] To claim a

---

51. This interpretation is not new. Maimonides (1135–1204 A.D.) states in his twenty-fifth proposition, "The opinion of Aristotle may be formulated in the words that matter is not the cause of its own motion" (*The Guide of the Perplexed* II, introduction, Prop. 25, given in Wolfson, *Crescas' Critique*, 315; also S. Pines and L. Strauss, eds., *The Guide of the Perplexed* [Chicago: University of Chicago Press, 1963], 239). Wolfson and Pines cite *Meta.* I.3, 984a21–25, and *Meta.* XII.6, 1071b29–30, as the basis of Maimonides's understanding.

Likewise Crescas (1340–1410 A.D.), in his commentary on Maimonides's seventeenth proposition, the motor causality principle, holds the same interpretation. This is brought out clearly in his explication of the principle as applied, following Alexander of Aphrodisias and the Arabs, to the natural motions of the elements: "Things which are moved by nature are found to vary with respect to the direction of their motion; thus, e.g., the tendency of a stone is downward, whereas that of fire is upward. This seems to indicate that the motion of each element is not simply due to the fact that it is a body in the absolute, for, were it so, the elements would not each move in an opposite direction. It must rather be the fact that each element is a particular kind of body that accounts for its particular motion. Now, with reference to corporeality all elements are alike and they all share it in common. Consequently, it is their respective proper forms that must be assumed to bring about their diverse natural motions...." (Wolfson, *Crescas' Critique*, 297–99).

52. Our formulation raises two important questions, one concerning the possibility of specific activity independent of divisibility, the other concerning the Newtonian theory of gravitation. The latter is discussed in Part II of this essay, and by Wallace in "Newtonian Antinomies," 332–51.

As we interpret it, the motor causality principle of *Phys.* VII.1 rules out a strictly common source of self-motion; no single self-motive principle can be present in all bodies. Our formulation, however, leaves open the possibility of a principle of self-motion that is specific but is invariant under division to infinity within that species. Consider, for example, a worm: Cutting it in two produces parts that (usually) act like the whole, but further division kills the worm(s); the parts of the dead worm do not act like the whole they previously composed. Imagine now an "idealized" worm such that, no matter how many times we cut it, the parts continue to wriggle just like the whole. This would exemplify a body with a principle of self-motion that is specific but does not require minimally determinate quantity. Such a body must be perfectly homogeneous. Now Aristotle argues in *Phys.* VIII.4 (in his well-known discussion of the natural motion of the elements) that a perfectly homogeneous body cannot move itself. This argument (which we shall not review here) would seem to complement *Phys.* VII.1 as we have interpreted it. See also n. 22.

distinction between mover and moved, must there not be a relation between activity and divisibility in bodies (that is, division of a body must at some point yield parts that do not act like the whole)? Perhaps this is a way of understanding the co-relative character of form and matter implied by Aquinas's terse yet fundamental formulation: "Natural form . . . requires determinate quantity" (*In phys.*, n. 1067).[53]

B. *Soul, 241b29–35 (241b40–242a34)*

Aristotle:

For one thing, the belief that AB is moved by itself (ὑφ' αὑτοῦ κινεῖσθαι) because the whole is moved and by nothing external is similar to the belief that DEZ is moved by itself (ὑφ' αὑτοῦ κινεῖσθαι) when DE moves EZ and is itself moved, because we do not see which is moved by which, whether DE by EZ or EZ by DE [similar to denying that KM is moved by something (ὑπό τινος) when KL moves LM and is itself moved, because it is not clear which is the mover and which the moved].[54]

    53. It is helpful to compare this with Robert Boyle's apt statement of the uniformity of nature, a notion widely postulated in early modern philosophy: "Both the mechanical affectations of matter are to be found, and the laws of motion take place, not only in the great masses, and the middle sized lumps, but in the smallest fragments of matter. . . . And therefore to say, that though in natural bodies, whose bulk is manifest and their structure visible, the mechanical principles may be usefully admitted, [but] that [they] are not to be extended to such portions of matter, whose parts and texture are invisible, may perhaps look to some, as if a man should allow, that the laws of mechanism may take place in a town clock, but not in a pocket watch" (Boyle, *Works* [1772], vol. 4, 72). This passage is quoted by L. Laudan in "The Clock Metaphor and Probabilism: The Impact of Descartes on English Methodological Thought, 1650–65," *Annals of Science* 22 (1966): 92, and by J. E. McGuire in "Atoms and the 'Analogy of Nature': Newton's Third Rule of Philosophizing" *Studies in History and Philosophy of Science* 1 (1970): 29. Laudan and McGuire discuss the postulate in Descartes and Newton. The uniformity of nature (Newton's "analogy of nature"), in contrast to form-matter correlativity, means that there is no scale of size intrinsic to nature. The twentieth-century revolutions in physics, relativity and quantum theory, overturned the classical postulate of the uniformity of nature through the discovery of Planck's constant and the constancy of the speed of light. See, for example, Werner Heisenberg, *Across the Frontiers* (New York: Harper and Row, 1974), 12.
    54. [Textus alter] is given in brackets. The Latin translation of Aristotle's text given in the Marietti edition of Thomas's commentary is: *Primum igitur, opinari AB a seipso moveri, propter id quod totum movetur, et a nullo exteriorum, simile est sicut si quis, ipso DE movente EZ, et ipso moto, opinetur DEZ a seipso moveri, propter id quod non videtur utrum ab utro moveatur, et utrum DE ab EZ, aut EZ a DE* (*In phys.*, [676bis]).
    The Latin translation, given in Juncta, of the Arabic read by Averroes is *Dicamus igitur primo, si fuerimus imaginati quod AB non movetur ab aliquo, quia secundum totum movetur, et motus eius non est ab aliquo extrinseco, ex quo aliquis est opinatus, cum DE movet EZ, et movetur, quod DZ non movetur ab aliquo: quod non scit quod movet, et quod movetur, utrum ZE movetur a DE, aut DE a ZE*(*In phys.*, 306A and 306D). This translation appears to be based on the textus alter. We have changed the letter *H* (in Juncta) to the letter Z for consistency with the other translations.

This passage is not part of the argument for the motor causality principle. It is rather a remark designed to clarify what that principle means by describing an opinion that contradicts it. AB is moved from within, and not by anything external. To this extent, it moves itself. It would be a mistake, however, to believe that it moves itself identically, that is, such that there is no distinction between mover and moved. Those who hold this mistaken belief deny what the motor causality principle requires, namely, that AB be moved *by something* (ὑπό τινος).[55] A major source of this belief is evidently the inability to decide by sense which is the mover and which is the moved in the most common self-movers, namely, animals. In an animal, one part, the torso, for example, moves another, the leg, but is in turn carried along by it. We cannot tell by sense which is really moving which, that is, how the principle of motion works through the parts. Aristotle's argument is designed to prove that, nevertheless, there must be a principle of motion that can be distinguished by reason from the mobile. Let us look at the comments of Averroes and Aquinas.

Our study in the previous section of this essay has put us on the lookout for indications that Averroes understands the unity of natural substances in a non-Aristotelian manner. Accordingly we ask, what, for Averroes, is the relation between soul and besouled whole, and between soul and first moved part? Does Averroes see DE as either (nonbodily) form or first moved (bodily) part? He comments as follows:

> Therefore, let us say that to think that there are things here which move themselves (*movet se*) because it so appears to sense is insufficient. For those that are seen to be moved as a whole (*secundum totum*) and are continuous can be divided into two parts, namely, mover and moved. And let it be thought that there is in them no mover distinct from the moved. For example, let there be a mover in the thing DE, and the moved EZ, and DZ the moved whole is moved from itself (*ex se*), by which it is thought that the whole moves itself (*movet se*) and is DZ, since it is not sensed which one moves the other. Having presented the cause by which it happens that men doubt about certain moved things and think that they are moved from themselves without a mover (*ex se sine motore*), he begins to explain that every moved has a first mover (*primum motorem*). (*In phys.*, 306H–I).[56]

On the basis of our examination of Averroes in the previous section of this essay, we can see that the Averroistic possibilities for the mobile DEZ are two: either it is a first moved, that is, it is *motum primum per se*, or it is moved *per accidens* and contains a first moved part.

---

55. This is clearest in the textus alter version.
56. Note that the last line of this passage confirms that, in Averroes's account, a first moved part has within it a first mover.

Now Averroes refers to DEZ and its self-motion as apparent to sense. Since all three of Averroes's first moved parts (heart, minimal part of fire, and of the natural heat of animals) are either subsensible or hidden within the bodies they move, it is most probable that DEZ is not itself a first moved. Indeed, if the division referred to by Averroes is quantitative (rather than a division in speech into soul and body), then DEZ could not be a first moved, since quantitative division would destroy its self-motive power. Let us then grant that DEZ is a body moved *ex se* and *per accidens*, which contains the first moved part DE. The first mover (whose existence is to be demonstrated) is here located *in* DE: "let there be a mover in the thing DE (*ut sit motor in illa re DE*)." Although he does not say so, it is hard to see what this mover could be, other than form. If it is form, then, for Averroes, the formal principle would not be a holistic principle, as it is for Aristotle and Aquinas. Rather, the form of a thing moved *ex se* would be located in a bodily part (the first moved part) of that thing. In the case of an animal, for example, the soul would be located in the first moved part of that animal. This accords with Averroes's earlier statement (at 306E) that animals are moved *per accidens* and would be further evidence that he understands the unity and activity of natural composites in a manner fundamentally different from that of Aristotle and Aquinas. Indeed, the remarkable feature of Aristotle's physics is that the visible look of a thing is, or is immediately related to, the specific way it acts. For Aristotle, an *eidos* is an *energeia*. Thus what we are here considering is a radical Averroistic alternative, according to which the visible looks of things are merely *per accidens* and do not give access to the true sources of motion in nature.

Averroes, however, cannot be quite so easily radicalized, for he specifies not one but two first moved parts of animals, namely, the heart (306F) and the first moved of the natural heat (307I). Thus we cannot put the soul into an unambiguous first moved part. It is a large question, unanswered in the texts under study, how these two animate first moveds are related. In any case, there is an alternative interpretation of the soul-body relation. Perhaps, for Averroes, the soul is, after all, a holistic principle, and the mover in the first moved part DE is a qualitative part, or power, of the soul. This would be a more Aristotelian position. The difficulty with it seems to be this: is not a first moved part self-sufficient in causing its own motion and whatever other motion depends on it? According to Aristotle's description at *Phys.* VIII.5, 257b27–35 (quoted previously), if the first moved DE is divided from the whole DEZ, it should retain the power of self-motion. But under this condition (physical separation) a qualitative part or power of the soul could not continue to move DE. Therefore, the mover in DE could only be the soul, or form, itself.

At this point, however, having used Aristotle's own description of first moved part, have we not infected Aristotle himself with the problem of the relation between form and first moved? How can form be a holistic principle if the first moved part is self-sufficient? Aristotle might reply that, in an animal, the first moved is not simply the heart (and natural heat?) but a complex system of heart, brain, blood, and vital organs; thus the animate first moved part is much closer to the whole than Averroes thinks. Indeed, the dependency of animals on the environment, not to mention their corruptibility, implies that although there may be more or less primary moved movers in them, they contain no completely self-sufficient, absolutely first moved part. Perhaps this is another reason why Aristotle and Aquinas do not explicate the motor causality principle in terms of first moved parts.

We cannot here resolve what is clearly a large issue in the Aristotelian philosophy of nature, namely, the relation between form and first moved. Suffice to say that certain of Averroes's assertions suggest the presence in his own thinking of a fundamental and seminal alternative to the Aristotelian understanding. The core of this alternative is that in the natural self-moving wholes that appear to the senses, form is not a holistic principle but rather resides in a first moved part, which is not directly accessible to the senses. Let us turn to Aquinas.

According to Aquinas, the internal principle of motion here, discernible by reason but not by sense, is soul:

[Aristotle] wishes, moreover, that the first mobile, AB, the whole of which is moved (*quod totum movetur*) by an interior moving principle, be understood as a living body,[57] the whole of which is moved by a soul (*quod totum movetur ab anima*). However, he wishes that the mobile DEZ be understood as some body not the whole of which is moved (*quod non totum movetur*), but rather one bodily part moves and the other is moved. In this mobile it is clear that that which is moved is moved by another. And from this he wishes to show something similar of a living body which seems to move itself (*quod videtur movere seipsum*). For this is proper to it insofar as one part moves another, namely, the soul moves the body, as will be more fully shown in Book VIII. (*In phys.*, n. 885)

Aquinas would assimilate the living whole, AB, to the body DEZ in which "one *bodily* part moves, and the other is moved" (emphasis added). In the animate body "one part moves another, that is, the soul moves the body...." But the soul is not a bodily part. Nevertheless,

---

57. In view of our findings in the previous section of this essay, this statement of Aquinas must be understood to apply only to the sentence (of Aristotle) under study, and not to the entire argument for the motor causality principle in *Phys.* VII.1.

the soul moves the body and is in turn moved with the body, just as DE moves EZ. Perhaps this is the similarity to which Thomas alludes.

The comment, however, is puzzling. Both the animal, AB, and the mobile, DEZ, move themselves by means of their parts. How else could the animal as such move itself? Yet the whole of AB is moved (*totum movetur*) but not the whole of DEZ (*non totum movetur*). What does this mean, and what, for Aquinas, is DEZ supposed to be? Perhaps it is a machine, which accordingly lacks a natural unity and so is not one whole self-mover in the sense that an animal is. Indeed, unlike an animal, a machine cannot initiate its own local motion. The point may then be that, in a whole that can move itself and bring itself to rest by means of its parts, there must be a certain principle of motion, distinct from the moved whole and not a bodily part. As Aquinas indicates, this seems to be what is shown in *Phys.* VIII.5.

Here, however, in *Phys.* VII.1, the account will be neutral to the distinction between living and nonliving. Soul will not be presupposed. Rather, the argument will conclude to the impossibility of self-motion without an active specific (as opposed to common) principle, of which soul is one type. The sentence we have been studying in this section is an explanatory remark external to that argument. The first proper part thereof is the stopping thesis.

C. Stopping Thesis, 241b25–242a5 (242a35–39)

Aristotle:

Furthermore, that which is moved by itself (τὸ ὑφ' αὑτοῦ κινούμενον) would never cease being moved because something other stops being in motion (τῷ ἕτερόν τι στῆναι κινούμενον). Necessarily then, if something stops being in motion because something other stops, it is moved by another (ὑφ' ἑτέρου κινεῖσθαι). This having been made clear, everything moved is necessarily moved by something (πᾶν τὸ κινούμενον κινεῖσθαι ὑπό τινος).

[Furthermore, that which is not moved by something (τὸ μὴ ὑπό τινος κινούμενον) need not cease being moved because something else rests (τῷ ἄλλο ἠρεμεῖν), but if something rests because something else ceases from motion, then the former is necessarily moved by something (ὑπό τινος αὐτὸ κινεῖσθαι). If this is accepted, then everything moved will be moved by something (πᾶν τὸ κινούμενον κινήσεται ὑπό τινος).][58]

---

58. [Textus alter] is given in brackets. The Latin translation of Aristotle's text given in the Marietti edition of Thomas's commentary is *Amplius, quod a seipso movetur, nullo modo pausabit cum movetur, in stando aliquid alterum quod movetur. Necesse est ergo, si aliquid pausat quod movetur, in stando aliquid alterum, hoc ab altero moveri. Hoc autem manifesto facto, necesse est omne quod movetur, moveri ab aliquo* (*In phys.*, [677]).

The Latin translation, given in Juncta, of the Arabic read by Averroes is *Et dico etiam,*

Whatever comes to rest because something else comes to rest is moved by something. Or, equivalently, that which is not moved by something would not come to rest because something other comes to rest. Aristotle does not prove this. Evidently he considers it self-evident. Aquinas reports that, for Aristotle, this thesis is *"quasi per se notum"* (*In phys.,* n. 886). We have called it the stopping thesis. It is, for us, not self-evident. The goal of the present section is to discover its meaning. We shall proceed by applying it to various kinds of bodies, to animals and elements, and to various kinds of elements. In each case, we can check how, and whether, it works. We can then ask, given that the argument before us is about body as such, regardless of kind, which interpretation of the stopping thesis is most plausible?

If the mover is external to the moved, then the validity of the stopping thesis is clearest. If I stop pushing the grocery cart, the cart comes to rest. In this case, the other that comes to rest is the other that was moving the mobile. The cart is obviously moved by another. The mobile AB, however, is not moved from without but from an internal source of motion and primarily. For the moment, we shall neglect the fact that it moves itself primarily and consider the more general case of all bodies for which no external mover can be found by sense. Both animals and elements, in their natural motions, fall into this category, and we can use them to probe the meaning of the stopping thesis. We shall attempt to answer three questions in each case: (1) What is the other that comes to rest? (2) Does this coming to rest involve actual separation of a quantitative part from the moved whole? (3) What is the other by which the mobile is, or was, moved? Note that the other that rests need not be the other that caused motion. This is the case when the mover is external to the moved; when it is internal, we must see how things stand.[59]

Begin then with a living body necessarily moving itself by means of its parts. Consider a bird in flight. Stop the wings and the bird stops flying. It cannot move itself without the motion of those parts that are efficient causes of motion in the whole. Now Aristotle and Aquinas hold that the bird is moved proximately by wings and ultimately by a

---

quod omne, quod non movetur ab aliquo, non cessat a motu si aliquid aliud cesset. Ergo necesse est quod omne, quod cessat a motu per cessationem alterius, moveatur ab alio. Quoniam, hoc si fuerit manifestum, necesse erit quod omne motum, cum sit divisibile, moveatur ab aliquo (*In phys.,* 306L–M).

59. W. A. Wallace, "Cosmological Arguments," 317, makes clear the central role of the stopping thesis in the argument of *Phys.* VII.1 for the motor causality principle. Our analysis closely parallels his. In addition to the commentaries of Averroes and Aquinas, however, Wallace also reviews those of Galen, Alexander of Aphrodisias, Simplicius, Avicenna, and Nifo.

soul. Either way it is moved by something other than itself identically. Averroes even goes so far as to say that the bird is moved *per accidens* by its first moved part (or parts). Therefore, all agree that this mobile is moved by something other, and so the stopping thesis works. Here, the other that comes to rest is the wing; bodily separation of the wing from the bird is not involved; the other by which the bird is moved could be either wing or soul. But since we believe the argument of *Phys.* VII.1 does not presuppose the existence of soul, the wing is the more certain other *by which*. In this case, the stopping thesis is about the dependence of the motion of a whole (moved internally) on the efficient causality of its parts.

The stopping thesis, however, can be applied to the flying bird in another sense. Stop the beak, and the bird cannot fly away from what holds the beak. In this case, the other that comes to rest is not the other by which the bird is moved. The beak is not an efficient cause of the bird's flying. Rather, it is carried along with and is attached to the whole bird. Indeed, if the beak were cut off, the bird could continue to fly. Here then it seems that the coming to rest of the other cannot involve bodily separation from the mobile, for if it did, the mobile would not come to rest.

Let us next consider an element, say, a stone (made of earth) as it falls. If we stop one part of it, holding it at a fixed height, clearly the stone stops. This example is similar to that of the bird's beak. The parts of the stone are not efficient causes of motion in the whole. They are, however, stuck together such that stopping one part arrests the whole. Is the stone moved by something other? We have seen that, according to the canonical Aristotelian and Thomistic position of *Phys.* VIII.4, the elements do not possess an internal active principle of motion (255b29–31) and the other by which they are naturally moved is the generator (255b34–256a3). We have, furthermore, seen that, in his commentary on *Phys.* VII.1, Averroes holds that the four elements are moved *ex se* (*In phys.*, 306B). Therefore, they contain a first moved part (307K). Therefore, they have a first mover, for, according to Averroes, *Phys.* VII.1 will show that "every moved has a first mover" (306I), and so, for Averroes, the stone is not moved by itself identically. Thus, within the accounts of all three thinkers, the stone successfully exemplifies the stopping thesis. (This is hardly to say that we could *derive* from the stopping thesis the diverse theories of the natural motion of the elements.) The other that rests is any bodily part, and its resting stops the whole not because it is an efficient cause of motion but because it is attached to the whole. Thus far, we have two senses of the stopping thesis.

The stopping thesis works in the examples we have so far considered, namely, the bird and the stone, either because the part brought to rest is an efficient cause of motion (wings) or because of the cohesion of the parts of a solid body. The adjective *solid* points to an immediate difficulty: How does the stopping thesis work in the case of fluids? A fluid is such precisely because its parts do not stick together. Three of the four elements—air, water, and fire—are fluids. If a part is stopped, does not the remainder flow on its way? How is any of these three elements unified into *one* moved to which the stopping thesis could be applied? Can the motor causality principle itself apply to what is not already one mobile?[60] In the case of fluids, we can unify a part and stop it by enclosing it in a solid container at rest. But, as remarked, the remainder would go on moving. Our conclusion is that the parts of a fluid are neither efficient causes of motion nor stuck together such that stopping a part arrests the whole. According to Aristotle, Averroes, and Aquinas, however, the three fluid elements must be moved by something. (For Aristotle and Aquinas, the mover is extrinsic; for Averroes, intrinsic, but distinct from the moved.)

Do fluids then violate the stopping thesis; that is, is the thesis not universally valid? The answer is yes, unless we can find a further, third sense of the stopping thesis, one that applies to fluids as well as to animals and to solid nonliving bodies. This further sense is that of a *general dependence* of the motion of a whole on the motions of its parts. If all the parts of a fluid do not move, then the whole does not move. Quite generally, if the parts of a body do not move, the whole does not move. The motions of the bird, the stone, and the fluid elements clearly depend on the motions of their parts in a way that is not efficient causality. It seems in fact to be a kind of material causality: the motions of parts are, in a way, the matter of which the motion of the whole is composed.[61] What this means is obscure and needs to be better established. We shall indeed find that it is at the core of Aquinas's understanding of the motor causality principle in *Phys.* VII.1. This issue, the dependence of the motion of a whole on the motions of its parts, will be addressed in the next section, for Aquinas explicates the stopping thesis only as incorporated within the remainder of the argument. Before taking this up, let us look at what Averroes has to say about the stopping thesis and then conclude with a summary of our findings in this section.

60. This would then presuppose the priority of unity and unifying principles to motion. This priority, denied by Descartes and Leibniz, is perhaps the reason why the definition of nature, a principle of change and stability (*Phys.* II.1), precedes the definition of change (*Phys.* III.1).

61. See also Wallace, "Cosmological Arguments," 314.

We shall see that Aristotle applies the stopping thesis to the quantitative parts of the mobile AB.[62] The cessation from motion of a part of AB is, for Aristotle, as well as Aquinas, a cessation from local motion, alteration, or growth and diminution. It is not a substantial change, that is, a cessation from being. Averroes modifies Aristotle's understanding of the stopping thesis with the following comment:

And whether the cessation of the other should be by rest or by corruption, it follows . . . that everything that ceases from motion through the cessation of another is moved by another. (*In phys.*, 307C)

Recall that, for Averroes, *Phys.* VII.1 is about the moved *ex se* (306E), and "it is necessary that everything moved *ex se*, if it is not itself a first moved, [then] a first moved is in it" (*In phys.*, 307K). Averroes's inclusion of corruption, that is, destruction of form, within the stopping thesis seems then to be concomitant with his focus (in *Phys.* VII.1) on the first moved parts of bodies. Specifically, the other that ceases—not from motion but from being—is form. And for Averroes, form is the other by which the first moved part is moved.

The immediate turn to the first moved parts of bodies is characteristic of Averroes's understanding of *Phys.* VII.1 and is not to be found in Aristotle and Aquinas. Correspondingly, Aquinas's emphasis on the role of *Phys.* VI, and the dependency of the motion of a whole on the motions of its parts, is not to be found in Averroes. Let us review.

We have found four senses of the stopping thesis, that is, four ways in which the motion of a whole depends on something other, such that the cessation of the other stops the whole. These can be listed by means of a table. In each row and column is entered the answer to the question whether the stopping thesis holds in the indicated case.

If *Phys.* VII.1 is about body as such, regardless of kind, then it must apply to the four kinds of bodies listed in the columns. Now it is clear that for Aristotle and Aquinas, the stopping thesis, a crucial component in the argument of Aristotle, can apply to animals, and to solid and fluid elements, only if it is taken in Sense 3, that of a general dependency of the motion of a whole on the motions of its parts. The precise meaning of this dependency is as yet unclear. Since substantial change is excluded from the account of *Phys.* VII.1, we are left with Sense 3 as the only viable candidate for the meaning of the stopping thesis. Let us complete our analysis of Aristotle's argument.

---

62. *Phys.* VII.1, 242a5–6.

Does the stopping thesis hold in the following senses?

	Animal	Solid Element	Fluid Element	First Moved Part
Sense 1: Dependency through efficient causality?	Yes	No	No	(Unassessed)
Sense 2: Dependency through cohesion of parts?	Yes	Yes	No	(Unassessed)
Sense 3: Dependency of motion of whole on motions of parts?	Yes	Yes	Yes	To be discussed
Sense 4: Dependency on the form? (Averroes only)	Yes in all cases because cessation of form means destruction of the being itself of the mobile			

D. Divisibility of the Movable and Conclusion of the Argument, 242a5–15 (242a39–49)

Aristotle:

To return, since AB is taken as being in motion, it must be divisible; for all that is moved is divisible (πᾶν γὰρ τὸ κινούμενον διαιρετὸν ἦν). So let it be divided at C. Then while CB is resting, also AB must rest; for if not, let it be in motion. Then, while CB rests, AC might be in motion, and then AB would not be moved through itself (καθ' αὑτό). But it was assumed to be first moved through itself (καθ' αὑτὸ κινεῖσθαι πρῶτον). It is clear then that when CB rests, AB will also rest, and will then cease to be in motion. But if a thing stops and ceases from motion because something other rests, then it is moved by another (ὑφ' ἑτέρου κινεῖται). It is then clear that all that is moved is moved by something (πᾶν τὸ κινοῦμενον ὑπό τινος κινεῖται); for all that is moved is divisible, and if a part rests then also the whole will rest.

[To return, since AB is taken as being in motion, it must be divisible; for all that is moved is divisible (πᾶν γὰρ τὸ κινοῦμενον διαιρετόν). So let it be divided at C. Then, when CB is not in motion, AB is not in motion. For if it is, it is clear that AC would be in motion when CB is resting, and so it would not be moved through itself and a first [moved] (καθ' αὑτὸ κινηθήσεται καὶ πρῶτον). But it was assumed to be moved through itself and a first [moved]. Hence, if CB is not moved, AB must rest. But it was agreed that that which rests when something is not moved, is moved by something (ὑπό τινος κινεῖσθαι). Thus necessarily all that is moved is moved by something (πᾶν ἀνάγκη τὸ κινοῦμενον ὑπό τινος κινεῖσθαι); for the moved will always be divisible, and when a part is not moved, also the whole must rest.][63]

---

63. [Textus alter] is given in brackets. The Latin translation of Aristotle's text given in the Marietti edition of Thomas's commentary is *Quoniam enim acceptum est AB moveri, divisibile erit: omne enim quod movetur, divisibile est. Dividatur igitur in C. Necesse igitur, BC*

This is the cryptic and controversial conclusion of Aristotle's argument for the motor causality principle. We shall here focus on Aquinas's interpretation, which turns on the theory of the divisibility of mobile and motion first elaborated in *Phys.* VI.[64] Briefly stated, Aristotle's argument seems to be this: We have assumed that AB is a first moved. As moved, it is divisible. As first, its self-motive power is lost under division. Therefore, dividing AB at C and bringing CB to rest, it follows that AC must rest. Thus AB ceases from motion at the cessation of another. Therefore, according to the stopping thesis, AB is moved by another. What meat does Aquinas put on this skeleton?

After noting, "There has been much objection to this proof of Aristotle" (*In phys.*, n. 887), Aquinas reports the diverse opinions of Galen, Avicenna, and Averroes. We shall pass over this in order to get directly to Thomas's interpretation of the proof, which begins:

> It seems that it must be said that [this demonstration] is not *quia* [as Averroes thought] but *propter quid*. For it contains the reason why it is impossible for a mobile to move itself (*movere seipsum*). (*In phys.*, n. 889)

There follows, in one paragraph, Thomas's physical explanation of the motor causality principle. We have quoted a part of this paragraph on the opening page of this essay. We must now go through it in its entirety. It begins with an account of the terms *first* and *primarily*:

> To see this [proof of Aristotle] it must be known that a thing's moving of itself is nothing other than its being the cause of its [own] motion. That, however, which is the cause of its [own] something must possess that something primarily.[65] For that which is first in any genus is the cause of the things

---

quiescente, quiescere et AB. Si enim non, accipiatur moveri. BC igitur quiescente, movebitur utique AC. Non ergo movetur per se AB. Sed concessum est per seipsum moveri primum. Manifestum igitur quod BC quiescente, quiescet et AB: et tunc pausabit quod movetur. Sed si aliquid in quiescendo aluid, stat et pausat moveri, hoc ab altero movetur. Manifestum est igitur quod omne quod movetur, ab aliquo movetur. Divisibile enim est omne quod movetur, et parte quiescente, quiescit totum (*In phys.* [677]).

The Latin translation, given in Juncta, of the Arabic read by Averroes is *Quoniam cum videmus AB moveri, necesse est ut sit divisibile, quoniam iam declaravimus quod omne motum est divisibile. Dividatur igitur in C. Ergo necesse est si CB quievit ut AC quiescat. Si igitur non quieverit, moveatur. Ergo CB quiescit, et CA movetur. Ergo AB non movetur per se. Sed positum est ipsum moveri per se. Ergo declaratum est quod, cum CB quieverit, quiescet BA etiam a motu. Sed, cum fuerit aliquid, quod quiescet a motu per quietem alterius, illud movetur ab illo necessario. Ergo manifestum est quod omne motum movetur ab aliquo. Natura omne motum est divisibile, et cum pars quieverit, totum quiescet* (*In phys.*, 306M–307A).

64. As previously noted, Averroes assumes, in his account of *Phys.* VII.1, the existence of first moved parts universally in bodies. He makes use of the stopping thesis to assert that a first moved part is moved by another, but, in contrast to Aquinas, he does not explicate the stopping thesis in terms of *Phys.* VI.

65. The subject of the verb *conveniat* (it belongs to, it fits, it suits; see n. 66 for the

which come afterward. Thus fire, which is the cause of its [own] and others' heat, is the first hot thing. (*In phys.*, n. 889)⁶⁶

Is this explanation the same as the one we presented in the section "Principle of Motion and Causality of Parts"? Recall that there we sought to understand what it means for AB to be moved as a whole not because a part of it is moved. We concluded, with supporting text from *Phys.* VIII.5, that the first moved, AB, could not be divided into a part that moves itself and a remainder moved by that part; division of AB into parts destroys self-motive power. Therefore, the cause or principle of motion in AB resides somehow in AB as a whole; the motion of AB depends on AB as a whole. This characterization is in terms of wholes, parts, and causes of motion.

Aquinas's characterization, in the preceding paragraph, is in terms of causes of properties—motion being one such property, heat another—but there is no mention of wholes and parts. Instead, the description is in terms of genera and of causal priority and posteriority, that is, of causal dependency. Let us try to bring these two characterizations together.

A property is a property *of* something. That of which it is a property is a whole with parts. Furthermore, the property belongs to a genus, motion and heat being the two genera mentioned by Aquinas. Let us consider another property, that of being able to laugh, or risibility. The whole of New York City is risible because of a part of it, namely, man. In the genus of risibility, man is prior to New York City. Is there anything in this genus prior to man? Is man risible because a part of man—a hand or head, say—is risible? It seems not; rather, risibility is in the human whole as such. Man is, therefore, the first risible or, equivalently, risibility belongs to man primarily. This means that (1) the principle or cause of this property of man cannot be located in any part of man,⁶⁷ (2) any whole of which man is a part is not risible primarily but in virtue of its first risible part, namely, man.

If we look in the genus of heat, then, according to Aquinas, fire is

---

Latin of this passage) is not entirely clear. Is it the something (*aliquid*) caused, or is it the property of being a self-causer? Following Wallace, "Cosmological Arguments," 319, we have taken it to be the something caused, for example, heat. This seems to make more sense than the reading of Blackwell, *Commentary on Aristotle's Physics*, 424: "That which is itself the cause of something must primarily agree with it."

66. The Latin is *Ad cuius evidentiam sciendum est, quod aliquid movere seipsum nihil aliud est, quam esse sibi causa motus. Quod autem est sibi causa alicuius, oportet quod primo ei conveniat; quia quod est primum in quolibet genere, est causa eorum quae sunt post. Unde ignis, qui sibi et aliis est causa, est primum calidum.*

67. Our search for first parts is a search among bodies, so that *part* here means quantitative part. Without this restriction to the physical order, one could say that risibility is located in a qualitative part of man, namely, the soul.

the first. Every other whole is hot because it contains fire as a part, and fire itself is not hot because a part of it is hot. Rather, the cause of being hot is in fire as such. What then is required of a first in the genus of motion?

A first moved must be such that the cause of motion in it cannot be located in any part but rather must be situated in the whole as such. Motion and the cause of motion must be specific to the first moved as a whole, just as risibility is specific to man as such and is not a property of the parts of man. Risibility is not divisible into, and dependent upon, the risibilities of man's parts. Now Aquinas completes his explanation as follows:

> However, Aristotle has shown in Book VI that in motion there cannot be found a first—neither on the part of time, nor of magnitude, nor of the mobile—because of their divisibility. Therefore, there cannot be discovered a first whose motion does not depend on something prior: for the motion of a whole depends on the motions of [its] parts and is divided into them, as proven in Book VI. Aristotle thus shows the cause why no mobile moves itself. [It is] because there cannot be a first mobile whose motion does not depend on parts; just as if I were to show that no divisible thing can be the first being, because the being of whatever is divisible depends on parts. And thus this conditional is true: "If the part is not moved, the whole is not moved," just as this conditional is true: "If the part is not, the whole is not." (*In phys.*, n. 889).[68]

Motion as such, that is, successive change in general (local motion, alteration, increase and decrease), is not specific to any body. This is because the divisibility of body, of the physical continuum, implies a divisibility of motion such that the motion of any whole depends upon the motions of its parts. As previously noted, it is only when we stop considering "motion in general and the mobile insofar as it is continuous" and begin to consider "determinate natures" that we can discover certain first moved things (*In phys.*, n. 1067). We must now go back into Book VI and try to understand Aquinas's interpretation of the theory of the physical continuum and the motion thereof. The crucial proposition concerns the relation between the motion of a whole and the motions of its parts.

---

68. The Latin is *Ostendit autem Aristoteles in sexto, quod in motu non invenitur primum, neque ex parte temporis, neque ex parte magnitudinis, neque etiam ex parte mobilis, propter horum divisibilitatem. Non ergo potest inveniri primum, cuius motus non dependeat ab aliquo priori: motus enim totius dependet a motibus partium, et dividitur in eos, ut in sexto probatum est. Sic ergo ostendit Aristoteles causam quare nullum mobile movet seipsum; quia non potest esse primum mobile, cuius motus non dependeat a partibus: sicut si ostenderem quod nullum divisibile potest esse primum ens, quia esse cuiuslibet divisibilis dependet a partibus: ut sic haec conditionalis sit vera: si pars non movetur, totum non movetur, sicut haec conditionalis est vera: si pars non est, totum non est.*

It is necessary to understand what is meant by the division of the motion of a whole into the motions of its parts and the dependence of the former on the latter. The Aristotelian account, which forms the basis of Aquinas's understanding, is given in *Phys.* VI.4. There, Aristotle states, "A motion is divisible in two ways, one with respect to time, the other with respect to the motions of the parts of the moved" (234b22). It is clear that for motion (in the sense of successive change) to occur, a time interval is required, and every time interval is divisible. In this way we can divide the motion into its temporal phases. It is the second way that must be understood: Granted that a whole is divisible into its quantitative parts, how is the motion of the whole divided into the motions of its parts? What is a whole motion in terms of its partial motions? Let us try to answer this question by using the concepts of body and motion most familiar to us.

Begin then with the simplest example, a body of mass m in uniform rectilinear motion with velocity $\bar{v}$. Let it have two parts, 1 and 2, of masses m_1 and m_2. Is the velocity of the whole divided into the velocities of the parts? Can we write $\bar{v} = \bar{v}_1 + \bar{v}_2$, that is, the velocity of the whole is the (vector) sum of the velocities of parts 1 and 2? Clearly we cannot, since the whole and both its parts move with the same velocity: $\bar{v} = \bar{v}_1 = \bar{v}_2$, so that we cannot have $\bar{v} = \bar{v}_1 + \bar{v}_2 = 2\bar{v}$. Velocity is entirely determined by speed and direction. Here, the whole and both of its parts move in the same direction with the same speed. There is no sense in which the velocity of the whole is divisible into the velocities of the parts. Let us try again in terms of momentum.

Is the momentum of the whole divided into the momenta of the parts? Yes, indeed it is: $m\bar{v} = m_1\bar{v} + m_2\bar{v}$. This holds because the mass of the whole is the sum of the masses of the parts. More generally, the momentum of any whole is a simple (vector) sum of the momenta of its parts. This is expressed algebraically as $m\bar{v} = \Sigma_i m_i \bar{v}_i$, where the ith part of the whole possesses mass m_i, velocity $\bar{v}_i$. Have we grasped Aristotle's meaning? The answer is no.

Aristotle offers a proof that the motion DZ of the whole AC is divisible into the motions DE and EZ of the parts AB and BC.[69] Therein he states, "No thing is moved with the motion of another" (234b28) and "no motion which is one is of more than one thing" (234b33). Let our test body, moving with velocity $\bar{v}$, be divided into two parts *of equal mass*, $m/2$. Then the momentum of the whole is, as before, the sum of the momenta of the parts: $m\bar{v} = m\bar{v}/2 + m\bar{v}/2$. But here, each part has the same momentum; therefore, *each part has the*

---

69. *Phys.* VI.4, 234b22–235a11.

momentum of the other. The momentum of part 1 is also the momentum of part 2. For Aristotle, however—and Aquinas follows him[70]—one part cannot have the motion of the other. Our concept of momentum, $m\bar{v}$, is not adequate to what Aristotle means by the motion of a whole. In fact, this is indicated by the definition of motion: Motion is the act of a being in potency, by which act it is such (201a10–11). Although this is difficult to understand, this much is clear: the two different parts of our test body are, and must be, in potency to two different places and thus should have different motions.

We have established only that our concept of momentum and its divisibility is not what Aristotle and Aquinas understand by motion and its divisibility. Note, however, that, according to Aristotle, the motion of a part may be subtracted from the motion of the whole:

If the motion of the whole [AC] is other [than DZ], let us say TI, the motion of each of the parts [of AC] may be separated off from it. (234b34–235a1).[71]

This seems at first glance entirely familiar to us, for we indeed subtract one momentum from another, and write equations like $m\bar{v} - m_2\bar{v}_2 = m_1\bar{v}_1$. But the meaning of Aristotle's "subtraction" is grounded not in the rules of vector algebra but in the subtractability of a part from the whole. After removing the motions DE and EZ of parts AB and BC from the whole motion DZ, Aristotle states

if there be a remainder, say [the motion] KI, this will be a motion of no thing, for [it is] neither [the motion] of the whole nor of the parts, because [the motion] of one thing is one, nor of anything else. (235a4–6)[72]

There can be no remainder of motion because there is no remaining body of which it could be the motion: Having "subtracted" the motions DE and EZ from the whole motion DZ, the parts AB and BC cannot contribute any other motions to DZ, and there are no remaining parts of AC.

Aristotle's concept of motion is, therefore, connected with his concept of the mobile, of the subject of per se change: for Aristotle and Aquinas, one motion can only be of one mobile.[73] How is our concept

70. *In phys.*, nn. 808–10.
71. The Greek is ἔτι δ' εἰ ἔστιν ἄλλη τοῦ ὅλου κίνησις, οἷον ἐφ' ἧς ΘΙ, ἀφαιρεθήσεται ἀπ' αὐτῆς ἡ ἑκατέρων τῶν μερῶν κίνησις.
72. The Greek is εἰ δ' ἀπολείπει τι, οἷον τὸ ΚΙ, αὕτη οὐδενὸς ἔσται κίνησις (οὔτε γὰρ τοῦ ὅλου οὔτε τῶν μερῶν διὰ τὸ μίαν εἶναι ἑνός, οὔτε ἄλλου οὐθενός...).
73. At *Phys.* V.4, 227b23–30, a motion is said to be one when it is of one subject, in one time, and of one species. In the case at hand, we have specified local motion in a given time interval. Hence, what unifies the motion is precisely the unity of the thing in motion.

of momentum related to our concept of the mobile? What makes a momentum one and grounds a relation between one momentum and another? From the momentum $m\bar{v}$, an algebraic product of mass and velocity, what can be inferred about the thing in motion? Can we infer that it is one, that it has magnitude, that it is divisible? We can infer none of these.

We cannot infer that the thing with momentum $m\bar{v}$ is divisible with respect to its magnitude because the symbolic concept of momentum is tailored to fit either an extended body or an unextended mass point. But can a point, an indivisible, be a subject of change? According to Aristotle in *Phys.* VI.4, 234b10–20, the subject of per se change must be divisible. Therefore, a point could be moved only *per accidens*, by being carried around in what is changing per se. This follows since the changing thing cannot be wholly in that to which it is changing, nor wholly in that from which it is changing; it must be partly in one, or the other, or both. The movable must therefore have parts. A point has no parts and cannot be partly in anything.

We cannot, furthermore, infer that $m\bar{v}$ is necessarily *of one mobile*. For whatever possesses momentum $m\bar{v}$ might be actually divided into many parts of masses m_i, so that $m\bar{v}$ is a sum of many momenta. Then $m\bar{v} = \Sigma_i m_i \bar{v}$. Given this equation, there are in fact four possible things that could have momentum $m\bar{v}$:

1. A body of mass m, velocity $\bar{v}$
2. A mass point of mass m, velocity $\bar{v}$
3. A system of N extended mass elements, m_i, $i = 1, 2, \ldots N$, velocity $\bar{v}$
4. A system of N unextended mass points, m_i, $i = 1, 2, \ldots N$, velocity $\bar{v}$

Our symbolic concept of momentum stands in no necessary relation to the mobile and its unity and continuity. It is neutral to whether the thing in motion is many or one and whether the one or many are divisible or indivisible. What makes a momentum one and what relates one momentum to another has no relation to the mobile and its divisibility into parts; it is rather related to the system of concepts called vector algebra. In contrast, the way Aristotle and Aquinas conceive motion is rooted in the natural articulation of things and their changes; motion, mobile, divisibility of the mobile are, for them, intimately related.[74] Our conclusion is that as long as we think of motion

---

74. We, unlike Aristotle and Aquinas, speak of the motion of a system, not of a whole. Perhaps we can now see one reason for this. A system is unified by our choosing to regard it as one, by our assigning to it a total momentum, total energy, and so on.

in terms of velocity or momentum, the concepts most familiar to us, we cannot fully grasp how the motion of a whole is divisible into the motions of its parts. And for this reason we cannot fully grasp Aquinas's account of the motor causality principle. This should come as no surprise. Motion, for Aristotle and Aquinas, is defined in terms of act and potency, not velocity and momentum.[75] Act and potency are probably the deepest concepts in the Aristotelian and Thomistic understanding of nature. Our study shows the fundamental unity of that understanding.

II. THE MOTOR CAUSALITY PRINCIPLE AND THE LAWS OF INERTIA AND GRAVITATION

Comparisons between ancient and modern physical theories are deceptive. It is easy to see that Aristotle's theory of projectile motion in *Phys.* VIII.10, according to which air pushes the projectile, is naive and false. It is another matter to give an account of the relation between the motor causality principle[76] and a fundamental law of post-Newtonian physics that is adequate to the depth and complexity of each. The reflections contained in this concluding section are, accordingly, far from definitive. Our intention is to call into question the widely held belief that the motor causality principle stands in simple opposition to, and is thus refuted by, classical mechanics.[77] To this end we shall argue that the relation between the two is more complex than is often thought to be the case.

A. *Newton's Law of Inertia*

By the law of inertia we mean Newton's first law of motion: *Every body continues in its state of rest, or of uniform motion in a right line, unless*

The unity of a system is an *actio mentis*. Whether it is also an *unum per se*, a natural whole, cannot be determined from within the mathematical description.

75. Consider W. A. Wallace, "Cosmological Arguments," 325: "a full analysis of motion in terms of act and potency, and a careful metaphysical assessment of all facets of the infinite regress problem, are essential for the completion of the cosmological argument. But the starting point of the argument, more than anything else, requires reappraisal in the present day, and to this task the proof from the divisibility of the movable object can still make a distinctive and noteworthy contribution."

76. The motor causality principle is universal. In spite of certain statements in *Phys.* VII.2 and VIII.10 (cited in the following text), it cannot be understood merely in terms of the particular case of projectile motion.

77. For an early example see E. T. Whittaker, *Space and Spirit* (London: Thomas Nelson and Son Ltd., 1946), 45–46. See also Weisheipl, "*Omne quod movetur*," 29–34. Our interest in the examination of alleged antinomies between the motor causality principle and elements of classical mechanics is inspired by, and closely follows, W. A. Wallace, "Newtonian Antinomies."

it is compelled to change that state by forces impressed upon it.[78] Newton's first law states that a body moves with constant speed in a straight line (that is, with constant velocity) if and only if it is subject to no impressed force. Through the second law of motion, we learn that force is whatever effects, or tends to effect, a change in a body's momentum. In nonrelativistic cases, this reduces to the familiar form, force equals mass times rate of change of velocity. Force, momentum, and velocity are vector quantities (they have both magnitude and direction), which can accordingly be resolved into, or composed from, components according to the parallelogram rule. This is made clear by Corollaries I and II, given by Newton immediately after the three laws of motion.[79]

Impressed force is force acting on a body from sources external to the body. It is important to note that a body can be subject to multiple impressed forces which, however, add up (vectorially) to zero net impressed force.[80] Indeed, the mathematical, as opposed to causal, character of force in Newton's physics must be understood if we are to draw a comparison between the first law and the motor causality principle. It must be emphasized that Newtonian force is (1) whatever effects, or tends to effect, change of velocity *regardless of the cause*,[81] and it is (2) mathematically representable as a vector. Because of this, a force in physics after Newton is not the same as an external cause of motion, for a body can move with constant velocity and, therefore, necessarily be subject to no net external force, yet external causes are required to produce the motion. In fact, every attempt to instantiate constant velocity motion in the world as it is, thus in the presence of other gravitating bodies, must involve external causes of motion.[82] To

---

78. Newton, *Mathematical Principles* I, "Axioms, or Laws of Motion," Motte and Cajori, *Sir Isaac Newton's*, 13. Galileo, Descartes, and Kant each formulated a "law of inertia" similar to Newton's first law but distinct from it in important respects. We comment on Galileo's and Kant's formulations in nn. 83 and 90. For a comparison of Descartes's and Newton's laws of inertia, see the author's "Wholes, Parts, and Laws of Motion," 195–98.

79. Newton, *Mathematical Principles* I, "Axioms, or Laws of Motion," Motte and Cajori, *Sir Isaac Newton's*, 14–17.

80. A book lying on a table is a simple example. Since it is at rest, Newton's first law requires that it be subject to no impressed force. In the Newtonian description, two forces act on it: (1) gravity compels it downward, while (2) the table pushes it upward. These two forces are of equal magnitude and oppositely directed, so that they add (vectorially) to zero. In this way the requirement of the first law is met.

81. "I here design only to give a mathematical notion of those forces, without considering their physical causes and seats." Newton, *Mathematical Principles* I, Definition VIII, Motte and Cajori, *Sir Isaac Newton's*, 5. This is quoted by Wallace, "Newtonian Antinomies," 353.

82. "In point of fact, in all observable cases in the real world, an extrinsic mover is needed in order to have a motion that is exactly uniform." Wallace, "Newtonian Antinomies," 358.

see this, consider the most familiar laboratory device used to illustrate Newton's first law, the air track. In the air track, a small metal block rides on a cushion of air along a groove cut in a straight metal track. The air track enables one to reduce the effects of two forces omnipresent in nature, friction and gravitation, as follows. Horizontal alignment of the track eliminates gravitational force parallel to the direction of motion. The upward push of air (blown through small holes cut vertically in the track) eliminates friction between the metal block and the track and counteracts the downward force of gravity, effecting zero net force perpendicular to the direction of motion. After being given an initial impulse, the metal block moves along the track with constant velocity, thus free of net force. Although the vertical flow of air is clearly an external cause required to produce the motion, it does not act, nor does gravity, in the direction of motion: no horizontal forces are required to produce motion along the horizontal air track, nor do any external causes act in the direction of motion. This is the evidence for Newton's first law; this is what the air track is supposed to show. Our experiment is not over, however, because the earth is not flat but round.

Imagine lengthening the air track. Since it is straight and the earth is round, the moving metal block must recede from the earth. As it recedes, the gravitational force exerted by the earth on the block ceases to be perpendicular to the direction of motion. A component of gravitational force parallel and opposite to the direction of motion is introduced. By Newton's second law, the block must decelerate. Constant velocity motion can be maintained only by slanting the air jets in the track such that a component of the force produced by the air cancels out the component of gravitational force parallel to the track. This is the real lesson of the air track: the gravitational effects of bodies in the universe necessitate the introduction of force components and external causes of motion acting along the direction of motion precisely to produce the condition of zero net force corresponding to constant velocity.[83]

---

83. Note that the component of gravitational force parallel to the direction of motion can be permanently removed only by keeping the air track everywhere perpendicular to geocentric vertical; that is, the air track cannot be straight but must go in a circle around the earth. Circular motion at constant speed is not force-free in the Newtonian account but, on the contrary, can be produced only by a net (centripetal) force.

Galileo's argument for his law of inertia is made by way of a well-known thought experiment. In Galileo's idealization, the component of gravitational force along the direction of motion of a body on an inclined plane is progressively eliminated by reducing the inclination of the plane until it is horizontal, that is, perpendicular to geocentric vertical. See *Dialogues Concerning Two New Sciences*, trans. H. Crew and A. de

We must look further at the law of inertia, at the counterfactual description thereof, which begins not from the world as it is (with friction and gravitation) but from a fictitious universe containing only one body. First, however, let us ask, What does the motor causality principle have to say about the law of inertia as thus far explicated?

The motor causality principle states that everything that is moved must be moved by something (ὑπό τινος, *ab aliquo*) distinct from the moved. This "something" may be internal to the moved—and this is the case on which *Phys.* VII.1 focuses—or it may be external. Things moved from within are moved naturally; things moved from without may be moved either naturally or violently. (The elements in their natural motions constitute the problematic category of things moved naturally but from without, by their generator.) This is the classification given by Aristotle in *Phys.* VIII.4, 254b7–255a6. The point is that the motor causality principle must be understood in connection with the distinction between natural motion and violent or compulsory motion: What the principle says depends on the type of motion in question. Is constant velocity motion natural or violent according to Aristotle? Since such motion is never found in nature as we experience it, but only as (approximately) produced through instruments such as the air track, we conclude that it cannot be natural motion and must, therefore, in the Aristotelian account, be violent motion. Now violent or compulsory motion is produced by causes that (1) are external, (2) act continuously, and (3) are in contact with the mobile. In support of this, we have the following statements by Aristotle:

All that is moved locally is moved either by itself or by another (ἢ ὑφ' ἑαυτοῦ ... ἢ ὑπ' ἄλλου). . . . As for those moved [locally] by another, it must occur in four ways; for local motions by another are four in kind: pushing, pulling, carrying, turning. (*Phys.* VII.2, 243a11–17)

Indeed, "in motion according to place there is nothing between mover and moved" (244b1–2). Finally, in *Phys.* VIII.10, Aristotle states

If all that is moved is moved by something, except for what moves itself, how is it that some of them, like things thrown, are continuously in motion when the mover is not touching them? (*Phys.* VIII.10, 266b28–30)[84]

Salvio (New York: Dover, 1954), 153–244; the "law of inertia" is stated on 244. For this reason it is most plausible that Galileo's inertial motion is circular, and thus that his law of inertia is different from Newton's.

84. The Greek begins εἰ γὰρ πᾶν τὸ κινούμενον κινεῖται ὑπό τινός, ὅσα μὴ αὐτὰ ἑαυτὰ κινεῖ (266b28–29). This distinguishes what is moved by something from what moves itself. The difficulty is that we would expect a discussion of projectile (thus compulsory local) motion to follow on the distinction (243a11–12, just given in the preceding text; also 254b12–14) between what is moved by itself (ὑφ' αὑτοῦ), for ex-

These passages cannot be smoothly reconciled with what we have seen of the motor causality principle in *Phys.* VII.1 and VIII.4. The last statement even seems to say that to be moved "by something" is to be moved by an external mover that is continuously in contact with the moved. This cannot be the whole story, for in *Phys.* VII.1, the mover is not external but internal, and in *Phys.* VIII.4, the mover of the elements in their natural motions (the generator) is external but not in continuous contact with the moved. We are thus left with the problem cited in the introduction to this essay; namely, a unified and comprehensive interpretation of the motor causality principle is lacking. But we are also left with solid evidence for Aristotle's teaching on mover and moved in compulsory motion and thus with the answer to our question on the relation between the motor causality principle and the law of inertia (as thus far explicated): The law of inertia says that constant velocity motion is motion under zero net force. Aristotle says that such motion is violent, not natural. Accordingly, the motor causality principle requires an external continuously moving cause in contact with the mobile. Now our analysis of the air track has shown that the production of constant velocity motion in nature always involves external continuously moving causes, which, however, need not be in contact with the mobile. Therefore, there is an opposition not between the motor causality principle as such and the law of inertia but between the latter and the Aristotelian doctrine of contact action in compulsory motion.[85] Gravitational force does not operate by contact, and the component of gravitational force parallel to the air track could presumably be compensated by electromagnetic forces (noncontact) as well as the air flow (contact).[86]

---

ample, animals, and what is moved by another (ὑπ' ἄλλου), such as elements and projectiles. Instead the phrase πᾶν τὸ κινούμενον κινεῖται ὑπὸ τινός is almost identical to the opening line of *Phys.* VII.1, which is the general formulation of the motor causality principle and implies no restriction to violent motion. A resolution of this problem may be possible, based on the phrase ὅσα μὴ αὐτὰ κινεῖ, "except for what moves itself." (See Smyth, *Greek Grammar* [Cambridge, Mass.: Harvard University Press, 1963], n. 2765. Although there is a verb, κινεῖ, we take the phrase as exceptive; that is, it limits the preceding assertion.) The similar phrase τὸ ἅπαν αὐτὸ αὑτὸ κινεῖν is used by Aristotle in his classification of motions at *Phys.* VIII.4, 254b32, to refer to animals and machines (such as ships) that can be moved, in a sense, from within in virtue of a heterogeneity of parts (in contrast to the elements wherein no distinction between moving and moved parts can be found). See also 255a11. This suggests that, in spite of the general formulation, Aristotle intends in this passage to distinguish between what is moved from within and what is moved from without and to address the problem of how projectiles are moved externally. (I am indebted to E. M. Macierowski for assistance with the Greek.)

85. This result applies as well to projectile motion. The problem is not with the motor causality principle but with the doctrine of contact action in violent motion.

86. Are the force fields of post-Newtonian physics subjects of per se change; are

Now Aristotle's teaching on contact action in violent motion is not derived from the motor causality principle. It seems rather to be based on the distinction between natural and violent motion, which is, in turn, rooted in the definition of nature itself (*Phys.* II.1, 192b21–23). Conversely, the motor causality principle covers cases in which contact action is not involved, namely, natural self-movers (*Phys.* VII.1) and the natural motion of the elements (*Phys.* VIII.4). For this reason, we conclude that, as applied to the motion of bodies in the world as it exists, the motor causality principle and Newton's first law are not in conflict.

Two items remain to be discussed: the counterfactual account of the law of inertia and the fundamental question whether the law of inertia even allows for nature as Aristotle understands it.

We have analyzed the law of inertia as it applies to bodies in the world as it exists. It can be argued that this approach fails to draw out the full implications of the law, thus falling short of revealing the opposition between the law of inertia and the motor causality principle. For in a universe devoid of all but one body, thus devoid of friction and gravitation, constant velocity motion not only would be force-free but would be wholly without need of external causes (none could exist). Because of this, the law of inertia and the motor causality principle are truly irreconcilable.

What does Aristotle's *Physics* have to say about motion in an imaginary one-body universe?[87] Is this motion natural or compulsory? It cannot be compulsory since nothing external to the body exists (except absolute space?). Can it be natural when it exists only in the mind? Can there be motion, in the account of post-Newtonian physics, without a frame of reference, and can there be motion in Aristotle's sense if a (Galilean) transformation from one frame to another brings the

---

they somehow divisible? What is the relation between the electromagnetic field and the theory of the physical continuum in *Phys.* VI and VII?

87. In an extremely interesting article, Amos Funkenstein calls our attention to *Phys.* IV.8, wherein Aristotle argues from motion as we experience it to the impossibility of the void; "The Dialectical Preparation for Scientific Revolutions," in R. S. Westman, ed., *The Copernican Achievement* (Berkeley: University of California Press, 1975), 165–203. As Funkenstein observes, part of Aristotle's argument seems indeed to anticipate inertial motion (*Phys.* IV.8, 215a19–22), the possibility of which is rejected by Aristotle because of the indeterminacy of such motion; inertial motion and real motion are "incommensurable" (Funkenstein, "Dialectical Preparation," 173, 186). Regarding the law of inertia in the history of subsequent science, Funkenstein says that it is "nothing but a *methodological guide as to where one can refrain from the search for causes*" (177; his emphasis). We agree with this for the inertial principle prior to Newton. It will be clear by the conclusion of the present section, however, that, for the law of inertia as taken up within Newton's three laws of motion, we would modify Funkenstein's formulation by replacing the word *causes* with *net forces*.

body to rest? Must not a frame of reference involve material points, and therewith gravitational forces, that, in turn, demand external movers to produce constant velocity motion?[88] It is in fact extremely difficult, as N. R. Hanson has made clear, to give a logically coherent and physically adequate account of the law of inertia in terms of an imaginary one-body universe.[89] There is really no common ground and thus no dialogue between the latter and the motor causality principle. Let us then turn to the last item of business, the question whether Aristotle's concept of nature can coexist at all with the philosophic implications of the law of inertia.

The argument of *Phys.* VII.1 focuses on bodies moved from an internal source of motion. This includes animals, which can initiate and stop their own local motions—they are self-accelerators—as described by Aristotle at *Phys.* VIII.4, 255a6–11. According to the law of inertia, however, a body cannot depart its state of rest, nor stop its motion, unless it is pulled or pushed from without, that is, unless it is subject to an impressed force. On this account, no body can start or stop its own motion; terms of what can proceed from internal sources, it can only be rest or uniform motion in a straight line. Beyond this minimal sense, internal agency in the motions of bodies is ruled out by the law of inertia.

Taken in this way, the law of inertia calls into question the very concept of nature as an internal principle of motion and rest (*Phys.* II.1, 192b21–22). Perhaps a notion of form and matter as strictly passive principles could survive, but form as active principle could not. And this would eviscerate the Aristotelian domain of natural wholes characterized by diverse ways of changing and stabilizing, proceeding from internal and specific principles.

We have argued elsewhere that this interpretation is proper only to the law of inertia as incorporated within Descartes's physics, not Newton's.[90] Let us review the essential idea. We must take seriously the challenge posed to the law of inertia by the animals: they appear to initiate their own local motion all the time. Thus the everyday phenomenon of animate local motion contradicts the law of inertia. How is this contradiction resolved? In the physics deriving from Newton, the resolution is simple.

88. We are free to imagine that these gravitational forces may be minimized such that they produce an arbitrarily small perturbation in constant velocity motion. This, however, is philosophically irrelevant.

89. N. R. Hanson, "Newton's First Law: A Philosopher's Door into Natural Philosophy," in R. Colodny, ed., *Beyond the Edge of Certainty* (Englewood Cliffs, N.J.: Prentice Hall, 1965), 6–28.

90. Hassing, "Wholes, Parts, and Laws of Motion," 195–98.

When an animal initiates its own motion by pushing or pulling on an environing body, thus accelerating from rest, Newton's first law requires a net external force (related to the animal's acceleration by the second law) acting on the animal. This requirement is met by the reaction force of Newton's third law: the environing body pushes or pulls the animal. To accommodate animate local motion, Newton's first law has merely to be understood as incorporated with the other two laws of motion. Now the animal's push on the ground and the ground's push on the animal are a pair of forces that, in terms of Newton's three universal laws of motion, are of perfectly equal status. That is: these three laws make no commitment as to the causal priority of one force over the other in the animal's interaction with the ground. They are silent with respect to the question of how motive forces are initiated, whether in the moved or from without. (Newton's first law does not require that the animal's pushing be externally caused; it requires only that the animal's change of velocity be related, in accordance with the second and third laws, to the simultaneous push of the ground on the animal.) Newton's first law is, therefore, compatible with internal agency in the motion of bodies.

In fundamental contrast, Descartes lacks a law of action and reaction and must, therefore, save his law of inertia from the phenomena by appeal to subsensible parts, or corpuscles, each of which strictly obeys his law of inertia.[91] Descartes's physics is indeed incompatible with the Aristotelian concept of nature. But our own tradition of mathematical physics derives from Newton, not from Descartes.

91. Descartes's law of inertia, or first law of nature, is "[E]ach individual part of matter always continues to remain in the same state unless collision with others compels it to change that state" (*Le Monde*, trans. M. S. Mahoney [New York: Abaris, 1979], chap. 7,61); also "[E]ach thing, insofar as simple and undivided, always remains in the same state, so far as in it lies, and never changes except by external causes" (*Principles of Philosophy*, trans. V. R. Miller and R. P. Miller [Dordrecht: Reidel, 1983], Pt. II, prop. 37, 59). These formulations are more general than Newton's first law in that they require an external cause for every change of matter, not merely a push or pull correlated to a change of velocity. For Descartes's necessary turn to corpuscularism, see *Le Monde*, 67—69. Newton's three laws of motion are compatible with, but do not entail, corpuscularism.

In view of the difference between Descartes's and Newton's laws of inertia, the interpretation of Kant is noteworthy: "The inertia of matter is and signifies nothing but its *lifelessness (leblosigkeit)*" (*Metaphysical Foundations of Natural Science*, trans. J. Ellington [New York: Library of Liberal Arts, 1970], 105). Kant's statement of the law of inertia is most revealing, for he simply conjoins Descartes's formulation with Newton's: "Every change of matter has an external cause. (Every body remains in its state of rest or motion in the same direction and with the same speed unless it is compelled by an external cause to forsake this state.)" (*Metaphysical Foundations*, 104). Kant sees no essential difference between the two laws of inertia. What this reveals, we suggest, is that Kant brings to Newton's laws of motion Cartesian philosophical presuppositions.

Let us summarize. In our analysis of the law of inertia, here taken as Newton's first law, and the motor causality principle, we have looked at air tracks and animals. The crucial result in both cases is the *causal neutrality* of Newton's three laws of motion and the associated concept of force. The absence of net impressed force on a body does not rule out external causes of motion, and the presence of net impressed force does not rule out internal causes of motion. For this reason, the motor causality principle, complex and problematic within the ancient and medieval tradition, is not refuted by Newton's first law. Rather, the opposition between the premodern and modern accounts of motion is situated in the Aristotelian teaching on contact action in compulsory motion.

B. *Newton's Law of Gravitation*

The Newtonian theory of gravitation is clearly of interest within the present perspective. Although it is not a source of self-motion in any one body (gravitation is a two-body interaction, as is clear from the equation $F = -GMm/R^2$), it can be a principle of the relative motions of mutually attracting bodies, such as the solar system or binary stars. When viewed against the background of *Phys.* VII.1 as we interpret it here, the salient feature of Newtonian gravitation is this: it is common to all bodies, as mass is common to all bodies. Mass and gravitational force are thus modern species-neutral universals having some relation to the production of motion. (This is not true of Cartesian extension, which is completely passive.) What then can be said about Newtonian gravitation in relation to the motor causality principle?

The mathematical law $F = -GMm/R^2$ expresses the force of attraction between any two bodies of masses M and m, separated by a distance R. The form of this equation is unchanged as the bodies become arbitrarily small. In this sense, gravitation is a type of activity independent of divisibility. This makes possible the point-mass model of gravitational systems: Because the manner in which any given body attracts other bodies is independent of its size, calculations can be carried out as if the body were an unextended point at which all the body's mass were concentrated. In a point-mass model of the universe, the question of the relation between activity and divisibility cannot arise since the sources of activity in nature are taken to be indivisible. This does not, however, suffice to refute the motor causality principle of *Phys.* VII.1. The reason is that although Newton's gravitational theory is *applicable* to nature, or useful for the solution of certain problems, it is not *adequate* to nature.

For the simplest illustration of what we mean by the applicability but inadequacy of gravitational theory, consider two bodies accelerating toward each other along the line joining them, under gravitational force. Given enough time, they bump into each other. To describe their motion from this point on, the impenetrability of real extended bodies must be brought into the account, and this cannot be explained in terms of gravitational attraction. Some principle of repulsion is needed to explain the phenomenon of impenetrability. The gravitational theory is, thus, applicable to those problems in which the distances between bodies exceed their diameters such that contact does not occur (for example, the solar system; in these cases, the point-mass model can be used), or for which the impenetrability of bodies is presupposed (thus not explained) as a boundary condition (for example, statics problems).

In fundamental contrast, the motor causality principle was never understood by Aristotle or Aquinas to be applicable to nature only within certain problem contexts. It was understood to be simply true of all bodies and bodily motions and, in this sense, adequate to nature.

The Aristotelian theory of *Phys.* VII.1 fits nature in a different manner than Newton's mathematical theory of gravitation. The former is about body as such, as it really exists in nature. As such, body is necessarily divisible, that is, spread out in space. The Newtonian gravitational theory takes body insofar as describable in terms of mass. Within this theory, a body need not be taken as divisible; for many calculations of interest, it can be taken as a mass point. Newtonian gravitational theory is really not *theoria* in the ancient and medieval sense; it seems to be closer to *techne* (even though many of the questions concerning astronomical motion it answers are motivated by sheer curiosity devoid of utility). And this makes it extremely difficult to form a simple comparison between the two.

Much more must be said about the relation between Newtonian gravitation and the motor causality principle. Unfortunately, a comprehensive treatment is here precluded by the breadth and complexity of both subjects. By way of briefest summary, the gravitational theory of Newton covers both terrestrial and celestial motions. It thus impinges on three classic problems of premodern science: fall, projectiles, and the celestial body. It is a mathematical theory based on a measurable property of all bodies (mass) but unable to account for the extension and impenetrability of any body. The motor causality principle of *Phys.* VII.1 is about the common *ratio* of body, or the physical continuum. More generally, the motor causality principle is stated and proved three times in *Phys.* VII and VIII, each time in a different way. Its physical, metaphysical, and theological ramifications motivated a diversity of interpretations among ancient and medieval commentators.

9 Philoponus on Separating the Three-Dimensional in Optics

JEAN DE GROOT

I

The history of optics in antiquity consisted of two unreconciled elements: geometrical optics and philosophical ideas about light. Geometrical optics, exemplified in the treatises of Euclid and Ptolemy, was the mathematical treatment of perspective and reflection, based on the hypothesis of imaginary lines originating in the eye and terminating at the visible object. Questions concerning the nature of light arose in the context of philosophical discussions about sense perception. In these discussions, light was defined in terms appropriate to the explanation of sensation.[1] The history of optics in late antiquity was dominated by a physical theory of light and vision based on the emission of visual rays from the eye, partly because it was difficult to combine the basic rules of geometrical optics with any theory of vision that denied visual rays.[2] John Philoponus made just this denial in proposing his own reconciliation of geometrical optics with an intromission theory of vision based on Aristotle's treatment of light in *De Anima* II.7. Philoponus said it makes no difference whether the lines

---

1. See Plato, *Timaeus* 45b2–d2, and Aristotle, *De Anima* II.5–7. For an analysis of the Stoic fragments on light and vision, see Robert B. Todd, "ΣΥΝΕΝΤΑΣΙΣ and the Stoic Theory of Perception," *Gräzer Beitrage* 2 (1974): 251–61.

2. Lecturing on Euclid in the fourth century, Theon of Alexandria argued against an intromission theory. See his *Recensio*, prologue (*Euclidis Opera Omnia* VII, ed. I. L. Heiberg and H. Menge [Leipzig: B. G. Teubner, 1895], 144–54). For the Platonic theory of vision that was ascribed to Euclid and Theon, see Paul ver Eecke, *L'Optique et Catoptrique* (Paris: de Brouwer, 1938), xiii–xiv, xxvi–xxvii. David Lindberg has pointed out that there are assumptions present implicitly in Euclid's theorems that militate toward a physical interpretation of visual rays. See his *Theories of Vision from Al-Kindi to Kepler* (Chicago: University of Chicago Press, 1976), 13–14. For the influence of the visual ray hypothesis in late antique Stoicism, see H. G. Ingekamp, "Zur Stoischen Lehre von Sehen" *Rheinische Museum für Philologie* N.F. 114, no. 3 (1971): 240–46. He argues that the Stoic theory of vision was mistakenly interpreted in late antiquity as involving an emission from the eye.

of the visual cone proceed from the eye to the object (extromission) or from the object to the eye (intromission). Considering the dominance of extromission theories of vision in late antiquity, this assertion is striking. What view of the nature of mathematical demonstration and its relation to physical explanation makes this denial of visual rays plausible?[3]

Philoponus' own theory for the propagation of light and color was the cornerstone of his rejection of visual rays as a necessary part of geometrical optics. Since this theory in effect reversed the direction of the rays between eye and object, a brief consideration of it is necessary to answer the question before us. Philoponus presented this theory in his long commentary on *De Anima* II.7, 418b9 (*In de an.* 324.23–342.16).[4] In *De Anima* II.7, Aristotle defined light as the actuality of the transparent, qua transparent. In his general exegesis of the passage (*In de an.* 324.23–35), Philoponus paraphrased this definition, introducing a shift in its meaning. For Aristotle, the actuality of transparency and actuality of light were identical. Philoponus considered light to be something that a medium can receive and transmit, if it possesses the trait of transparency. When light supervenes (ἐπιγενόμενον), then it is possible to see through a transparent medium. Ranging light with color and separating it from transparency, he now defined transparency in terms of its ability to act as a carrier for light

---

3. Philoponus' treatment of optics may well reflect Geminus' view that optics does not treat physical questions. It is concerned only with whether the different physical theories of vision are consistent with the mathematical explanation of perspective that geometrical optics provides. See the extract from Geminus in Damianus, *Optical Hypotheses (Damianos Schrift über Optik)*, Griechisch und Deutsch, hrsg. von Richard Schöne (Berlin: Reichsdruckerei, 1897), 24.

Father Wallace has shown how demonstration in a mixed science, optics, is related by subalternation to mathematical demonstration, yielding *propter quid* mathematical demonstration of a natural phenomenon (*The Scientific Methodology of Theodoric of Freiberg* [Fribourg, Switzerland: University Press, 1959], 49–50, 177–79). See also "A Thomistic Philosophy of Nature," in *From a Realist Point of View* (Lanham, Md.: University Press of America, 1983), 40, and his remarks about optics in "Discussion: Galileo and the Continuity Thesis" *Philosophy of Science* 51, no. 2 (June 1984): 508. The history of late antique optics I have traced and Philoponus' contribution to it comprise a stage in the history of optics when all the elements of this Thomistic solution are not yet assembled. In particular, the relation between light and vision is not yet settled. Philoponus' contribution on this question anticipated medieval explanations of the propagation of light by "multiplication of species." Compare Philoponus' theory for the propagation of light, detailed below, to Roger Bacon, *The 'Opus majus' of Roger Bacon*, ed. J. H. Bridges (Oxford: Clarendon Press, 1897–1900), II.71–72, and John Pecham, *John Pecham and the Science of Optics: Perspectiva communis*, ed. David Lindberg (Madison: University of Wisconsin Press, 1970), I.27. Relevant passages from various medieval authors pertaining to the nature and speed of propagation of light are collected in Edward Grant's *Source Book in Medieval Science* (Cambridge, Mass.: Harvard University Press, 1974), 393–97.

4. Commentaries consulted are listed by author at the end of the paper.

and color. The transparent has a power for conveying color, although it is itself colorless.

Philoponus compared the transmission of light and color to the eye to the way in which a fire warms us, even when it lies some distance away. The fire does not come up to us, but rather it warms the air nearest itself, and this air in turn warms the air next to it, which also passes on the effect, until things very distant from the fire receive the effect and are themselves warmed. The same thing happens in the case of light:

> The sun acts directly on the body neighboring it and in contact with it and makes it actually transparent. And that [body], having become [actually transparent], possesses the power so that it also acts on the things nearby and makes them [actually transparent], and in this way, the illuminating power proceeds forward out to the limits, not by the actuality of the sun travelling immediately to the limits, but by those nearby that are acted upon primarily being able themselves to act with a similar action on those capable of receiving it. (*In de an.* 330.8–14)

On this explanation, light is propagated not by a movement from place to place but by a succession of effects. Once it has received the effect, each member of the succession possesses the power to affect its neighbor in a similar way. Philoponus went on to claim that this transmission takes place all at once and without the passage of time (*In de an.* 330.14–15). He said this should not be surprising, seeing that the actuality is incorporeal.[5]

This theory for the propagation of light and color is the vehicle for Philoponus' reconciliation of geometrical optics with an intromission

---

5. Aristotle's distinction between motion and true actuality is central to Philoponus' assertions about the incorporeality of light and its speed of transmission. On the implications of the distinction in Neoplatonic metaphysics, see my article "Philoponus on *De Anima* II.5, *Physics* III.3, and the Propagation of Light" *Phronesis* 28, no. 2 (1983): 177–96.

For the sake of clarity, I have emphasized the changes Philoponus made in Aristotle's theory of light. These changes are less of a departure from Aristotle's treatment than they may appear in this brief analysis. Philoponus still maintained that light is the actuality of transparency. His separation of light from the ability of the medium to receive light is part of the commentary tradition developing the implications of true actuality as something supervening on another entity. See Aristotle's description of pleasure in *Nicomachean Ethics*, X.4, and Alexander of Aphrodisias' comparison of the actualization of perception to pleasure (*In de sen.* 125.12–26.1).

The move away from the identification of light with the actuality of transparency is carried further in later explanations of the relation of light to the medium. The actuality of transparency survives in these later explanations primarily as the power of the medium to receive and transmit light. See, for instance, Alhazen's "Discourse on Light" in the French translation by R. Rashed, "Le «Discours de la lumière» d'Ibn al'Haytham (Alhazen)" *Revue d'histoire des sciences et de leurs applications* 21, no. 3 (July–September 1968): 197–224, in particular, 208–10.

theory of vision. Taking Aristotle's theory without modification, Philoponus said, every part of the transparent should be filled with the colors of visible objects from every direction, and we should be able to see even the things behind us. To solve this problem, Philoponus said he would make use of the same supposition the visual ray theorists use:

> So, just as those [philosophers] suppose that visual rays and [light] rays are sent out along straight lines and are reflected from smooth bodies at equal angles, so also do we suppose that actualities of colors, and furthermore, even light, are sent out along straight lines and reflected from smooth bodies at equal angles. Then for this reason also, images in mirrors appear, not because our visual rays are reflected at the visible objects, but because their actualities come to us (*In de an.*, 331.3–10).

Light and color proceed along straight lines from their sources, but we see only those visible objects that lie on straight lines with the eye. This is why we do not see the things behind us, even though their actualities are in the air (331.14–15). Philoponus extended the explanation to reflection, saying our visual rays are not reflected from mirrors, but rather light and color traveling from visible objects are reflected and proceed along straight lines from the mirror to the eye. He asserted that all the basic principles of the visual ray theory can be assimilated to an Aristotelian viewpoint:

> And to put it simply, whatever they say concerning visual rays, we say the same things in precisely similar terms concerning actualities, saving the appearances. For what difference does it make whether straight lines come to the mirror proceeding from the eye or are reflected from the mirror to the eye? Then, if these are held in common by those [philosophers] and the doctrine of Aristotle, but the one in terms of actualities, the others in terms of visual rays, and myriad impossibilities follow from the supposition of visual rays, one must rather choose the supposition of Aristotle, which both saves the appearances and avoids the impossibilities. (331.25–33)

Philoponus presented, in the commentary on 418b9, a battery of arguments designed to show (1) the compatibility of his theory with the basic principles of rectilinear propagation of rays and their reflection at equal angles and (2) the superiority of Aristotle's theory on physical grounds alone.

By means of this physical theory for the propagation of light, Philoponus combined Aristotle's theory of light with the basic principles of geometrical optics. The question still remains, though, as to what view of the nature of optics and its relation to physics makes this reconciliation plausible. A full answer to this question would involve Philoponus' treatment of optics as a subalternate science, in his commentary on the *Posterior Analytics*.⁶ One part of the answer, however, must address the physical basis for mathematical demonstration in optics. If the visual rays of geometrical optics have no counterpart in an extromission theory of vision, what are we to think of the directionless mathematical lines Philoponus believed are compatible with either an intromission or an extromission theory of vision? Are we to suppose anything in nature corresponds to them? If not, how is optics a science conveying true knowledge about the physical world? Considered in Aristotelian terms, these are questions about the ontological status of quantity in a mixed science.

To answer these questions, we can turn to Philoponus' commentary on *Physics* II.2, one of the texts where Aristotle discussed the subject matters of mathematics, physics, and the mixed sciences such as optics. What we shall find is that Philoponus reworked Aristotle's thinking on the separability of mathematical objects so as to allow for the separability in thought of "the three-dimensional," which was a hypostasized version of Aristotle's bare continuity. Philoponus asserted that the forms of physical things are separable in thought from the three-dimensional, in a way that accords with matter-form distinctions present in the order of nature. This belief about the separability of physical forms from three dimensionality is the methodological precedent to his separation of the directional component of visual rays from the mathematical lines of the visual cone. For separating in thought the subject matter for mathematical demonstration makes possible the consideration of the purely mathematical characteristics of rays of any kind. Then the geometrical properties of the visual cone and the angles it makes at an object or mirror may be considered without regard to the direction of the rays. Once this is accomplished, it follows that rival physical theories may be evaluated in physical terms alone, as Philoponus urged in his commentary on 418b9. At this superficial level, then, the hypostasizing of three dimensionality makes plausible Philoponus' treatment of optics in the *De Anima* commentary.

However, considerable problems attend this solution. With his *snub-concave* distinction, Aristotle ruled out the separability even in thought of physical forms from matter. Philoponus affirmed and reiterated the import of this distinction but outlined a different manner of separability suitable to the forms of physical things. This paper will evaluate Philoponus' claim for the separability of the forms of physical things,

6. See Philoponus' commentary on *Posterior Analytics* I.7–9. I treated this topic in my doctoral thesis, "Aristotle and Philoponus on Light," Harvard University, November 1979.

in relation to Aristotle's thinking on quantity, continuity, and the subject matter of mathematics. Only with such an evaluation will it be possible to judge Philoponus' fidelity to or departure from the Aristotelian tradition in science.[7]

II

The manner of separability of various characteristics of body was a very important issue for Philoponus. His treatment of this issue distinguishes him from other Neoplatonic commentators, such as Simplicius. This issue also plays a role in his argumentation about the void. He approached the issue most straightforwardly, however, in his commentary on *Physics* II.2, when he commented on Aristotle's criticism of Plato. Aristotle criticized those who hypothesize Ideas for assuming that physical things are separable from body in the same way mathematical objects are separable (193b25–194a7). He said that man, flesh, and bone must be treated like "snub nose" and not like "concave." The snub-concave distinction has two elements. The first is that we cannot talk about snub noses and snub bowls as we can talk about red noses and red bowls. Snub is inseparable from nose. The second is that snub is found in no other body besides nose. In the set of things that are snub, there is only one member: nose. "Red," on the other hand, may apply to many different kinds of material things. In this respect, "concave" is like "red." "Flesh," "bone," and "man" are all like "snub." In the set of things that are Man, there is only one member: man, meaning individual men. Aristotle thought that Plato had ignored both elements of the snub-concave distinction. He thought that Plato's mistake was born of treating physical things as if they are just like mathematical objects.[8]

In his initial exposition of *Physics* II.2, Philoponus echoed Aristotle's view that the forms of physical things cannot exist apart from the bodies in which they reside, but he expounded the problem in terms of the kind of separability that characterizes the forms of different kinds of things. This separability is a measure of whether or not the object possesses independent existence. It is impossible even to imag-

---

7. Richard Sorabji argues that Philoponus' innovations in philosophy and science constitute a rejection of Aristotelian science. See his *Philoponus and the Rejection of Aristotelian Science* (Ithaca, N.Y.: Cornell University Press, 1987), chap. 1.
8. Other passages relevant to Aristotle's discussion of the snub-concave distinction in relation to separating the subject matter of mathematics and physics are *De Anima* I.1, 403b7–16, III.4, 429b10–22, III.7, 431b2–17; *Metaphysics* E.1, 1025b30–26a10, K.3, 1061a28–b4.

ine flesh or bone without the mixture of underlying elements that is the matter for each:

> If I tried to define flesh, for instance, I might say it is a warm, moist, bloody, soft body, having such and such actualities. But as soon as I have said this, I have included the underlying matter. (*In phys.* 224.28–31)

It is not even possible to define a simple body, like water, without reference to matter. We conceive it as moist, fluid, and cool, but this is a description of water as a compound (σύνθετον) and necessarily involves the combination of form with its material base. Philoponus agreed with Aristotle that this is an argument against ideal Forms (225.4–5). There is no Man apart from the corporeal man. Philoponus recognized that the mathematician legitimately separates shapes and their attributes from physical objects by disregarding the matter in which they reside (*In phys.* 224.17). But mathematical objects are separable from physical objects only in thought. They do not possess an independent existence. Physical forms are not even separable in thought, however, since it is impossible to disregard their matter in defining them. Platonists made the double mistake of separating in thought forms that are not separable in this way and then granting independent existence to them as well (224.8–11). Mathematical objects are separable in thought (κατ' ἐπίνοιαν) but not in existence (καθ' ὑπόστασιν). Physical objects, however, are separable in neither way (225.2–3).

After this initial interpretation of the text, Philoponus went on to explain the extent to which he agreed and disagreed with Aristotle. He began by specifying that this criticism of Aristotle's was directed against Plato.[9] He agreed with Aristotle under the following conditions:

---

9. Simplicius said instead that Aristotle's criticism was directed against the popular conception of Plato's theory of Ideas. According to this popular conception, there are Ideas for everything that exists in the Demiurge's mind just as they exist here below, along with matter. The relation between things and their ideas is one of sameness, rather than similarity between an image and its paradigm (*In phys.* [Simpl.] 295.12–18). Simplicius was convinced that Aristotle believed the causes of things in the generable world preexist as Ideas in the Demiurge's mind (295.21–32). Like Philoponus, he thought that physical forms could not even be separated in thought (293.31–294.9). Nevertheless, these forms are similar to Ideas in the Demiurge's mind, and their definitions are really the definitions of these Ideas. The definition of snubness, for example, must be given in terms of concavity (294.12–18). There is no definition of "nose" at the level of the Ideas. Later Simplicius admitted that it is possible to separate physical forms in thought, as witnessed by the fact that we discuss the form of a thing apart from its composite substance. What we discuss is not the exemplar, however, but something merely similar to it (296.10–25). Philoponus made no reference in his commentary on this passage to the causes of physical things preexisting in the mind of the Demi-

I say that if Aristotle charged him with separating in existence the forms of physical things, the accusation is reasonable (for it is impossible that things having being in a substratum ever exist in themselves), but if he means that it is impossible to separate form from matter in word or in thought, it seems to me that it is not reasonable. For even if substantial forms (οὐσιώδη εἴδη) are themselves difficult to imagine in themselves, nevertheless reason can separate these too. (*In phys.* 225.5–11)

By substantial form, Philoponus meant the form of the compound that is the physical object. Aristotle was correct in thinking that this compound cannot be conceived apart from body. Its essence must include matter. Nevertheless, Philoponus insisted these same forms are separable from matter in thought. He clearly had in mind a different kind of separability in thought. If it is possible to distinguish form from matter for physical objects, then it must also be possible to designate this matter:

We say form is different from matter, and that matter, while remaining one and the same, receives differences in turn, since the forms are different from it. And what do I say is matter? The secondary substratum, then, by itself—and this is the three-dimensional—[which] is different from flesh and bone and all the remaining forms, being in itself unqualified. (225.11–16)

He separated the forms of physical things in thought, by taking this secondary substratum as matter. But why does this manner of separability not violate the snub-concave distinction? How does the separability in thought of physical forms differ from the separability in thought of mathematical objects?

A clue to the difference between the two kinds of separability is that all physical forms are generated in a matter that is a mixture of elements specific both qualitatively and quantitatively to one particular form. Because of this, there is an indivisible and least quantity of any thing (*In phys.* 97.23). The separability in thought of the forms of physical things is achieved as a separation from the aspect of quantity. In contrast, mathematical objects are simply considered apart from any matter whatsoever. In the few references Philoponus made to the process of abstraction, he interpreted it as the separation of traits that could exist in a variety of bodies (*In de an.* 62.24–27). Aristotle reserved for mathematical objects a particular substratum: continuity or multitude. Furthermore, even the substratum of geometrical ob-

---

urge. Having once established the separability in thought of physical forms, he went on to hypothesize an independently existing three-dimensionality as the matter for these physical forms. Simplicius referred to three-dimensionality only in relation to the subject matter of mathematics and did not grant it independent existence as Philoponus did.

jects he treated as abstractable.[10] In contrast, Philoponus defined mathematical objects without reference to a substratum at all. For Philoponus, mathematical objects have a great deal in common with ordinary accidental attributes. He made this explicit in pointing out the difference between snubness and concavity:

> Just as if we define not snubness but simply concavity, we do not take note of matter at all, in this way also defining accidental attributes, we do not include the substratum in the definition. (*In phys.* 226.21–23)

Accidental attributes, like mathematical traits, are not inextricably bound up with the substratum in which they reside as are physical traits. As a result, they may be attributes of a variety of different kinds of bodies.

In the passage immediately following this comparison of concavity and accidental attributes, Philoponus considered the mixed sciences, optics, astronomy, and harmonics, in order to show that even they cannot conceive their subject matters as simply mathematical objects apart from matter. Optics treats the properties of the visual cone in a purely geometrical way, but since it takes the lines and their properties as actually existing (ἐνεργείᾳ ὑφεστηκότα), it does not take them apart from motion and matter (226.27–227.14). Philoponus' concern, in this passage, is Aristotle's criticism of Plato, so he is concerned with things that can exist separately. The mathematical traits treated by the mixed sciences are always inseparable, when taken as existing. How much more must it be the case, then, that physical forms are inseparable in existence.

This passage throws additional light on the manner of separability of physical forms. In particular instances, physical forms can never be separated, even in thought, from the specific quantities that contribute to their natures. This is why they cannot be treated separately in

---

10. See, in particular, *Metaphysics* Z.10, 1029a16–19, 11.1036a30–b3. On whether the continuous should be treated as the genus of mathematical objects or kept as substratum in a different sense than genus, contrast Ian Mueller, "Aristotle on Geometrical Objects" *Articles on Aristotle*, vol. 3, *Metaphysics*, ed. J. Barnes, M. Schofield, and R. Sorabji (London: Duckworth, 1979), 104, and Robert Sokolowski, "Matter, Elements, and Substance in Aristotle" *Journal of the History of Philosophy* 8, no. 3 (July 1970): 279. The implications of this difference are considerable for our understanding of how the matter for mathematicals is in the world. Although much of Philoponus' account of the three-dimensional is consistent with Mueller's outline of Aristotle's position, Philoponus would not go on to identify Aristotle's extension with a rationally apprehended space, as Mueller suggests (107), but rather with quantity as secondary substratum. We might describe Philoponus' position as being more physicalistic than rationalistic, concentrating on extension as the stuff for physical forms. To substantiate this meaning of extension, Philoponus needed something like space but only in the ancillary role detailed in Section III.

optics. Philoponus amplified this point in treating an objection to his hypostasization of quantity as three-dimensionality:

> It is impossible, then, that any given form exist in any magnitude whatsoever, as it was shown in the first book of this treatise, but flesh and man and bone and all the other physical forms would not exist except in a determinate quantity, but of the quantity in which flesh can exist, when it is corrupted, the form is corrupted along with it. (*In phys.* 578.19–23)

Philoponus was combatting the objection that quantity, as an attribute of substance, is dependent on substance for its existence. He said we could as easily maintain that substance is dependent on quantity, because of its reliance on a particular quantity for its makeup. The important point is that, even though quantity appears inseparable from substance in particular cases, this does not prevent our separating the aspect of quantity in some way. Particular quantities are separable from physical things only in the manner of accidental attributes or mathematical objects. But quantity taken generally is separable in a more fundamental way.

Separability from the aspect of quantity receives its full meaning as part of a theory of the layers of matter characteristic of the order of nature. In his commentary on the *Categories*, Philoponus said of quantity that it is second only to substance among all the kinds of existing things. This is due to the fact that three dimensionality is preceded only by prime matter as the most basic in the hierarchy of matters:

> For prime matter, as has often been said, being incorporeal and without form and shape, first having been expanded, receives three dimensions and becomes three-dimensional, what Aristotle calls secondary substratum; then in this way, it receives qualities and produces elements, so that quality has the third place among existing things and the fourth, things in relation. (*In cat.* 83.14–19)

Philoponus invoked these layers in the order of nature in his commentary on *Physics* II.2. He said there are many matters of the same thing, some nearer and others more distant. He gave as an example the matters for the human body:

> For example, the nearest matter of the human body is the dissimilar-parted things of the whole body, as he himself says, but the matter before these is the similar-parted things. For these underlie in the order of matter those serving as organs. And before the similar-parted things are the humors, and before the humors the elements, and before the elements the three-dimensional, and before this prime matter.... (*In phys.* 232.1–6)

This doctrine of proximate and more distant matters shows that the manner of separability Philoponus defined for physical forms reflects distinctions present in the order of nature. The reason that physical forms are separable in thought is that they have a matter that exists independently, though not separately.

Physical forms are separable in thought from the three-dimensional, because one is form and the other matter. However, the separability of the forms of physical things really only *follows* from the separability in thought of the matter for physical forms. Quantity is separable in thought because it is both a matter and a categorical mode of existing. It is the peculiar situation of quantity's being a matter that makes possible the manner of separability Philoponus highlighted here. It is important to notice that in this new mode of separability, the discriminator of separability is different from that at work in Aristotle's original distinction. In the snub-concave distinction, the discriminator is the way in which something exists, when it exists separately or as a part of what exists separately. In Philoponus' separation of physical forms from quantity, however, separability in existence is not the issue. Rather, it is our ability to *conceive* something in the manner in which it is capable of existing. We could not conceive a quality, for example, a color, as existing apart from a substratum in which it resides. At the very least, we must conceive a color along with an extension that it colors. Quantity, however, can be conceived separately.

In spite of this difference from the snub-concave distinction, Philoponus' mode of separability still follows from Aristotle's criticism of Plato. The forms of physical things are not separable from quantity simply by virtue of our deciding to think of them in this way. Even separability in thought requires that at least one of the elements being separated be capable of being conceived as it exists when separated in thought. The separable element may be taken as separate in existence, like substance, or as existing independently but not separately, like quantity. When the separable element is substance, we have separability in thought in the manner of the concave. When the separable element is quantity, we have separability in thought in the manner of secondary substratum.

If quantity must be taken as existing to be separable at all, then there is a problem in interpreting Philoponus' remarks about optics. As we have seen, in the commentary on *Physics* II.2, Philoponus said that as soon as the lines of optics are taken as existing, they are inseparable from physical forms. So as soon as a specific quantity is taken as part of an actually occurring instance of vision, it is inseparable from the physical facts of how vision takes place. Hence, at the level of true explanation in optics, the lines of the visual cone do have a direction, because the lines are the rays of light and color proceeding into the eye. However, this manner of inseparability applies even to physical explanation. To take a quantity as existing puts explanation in the realm of the snub-concave distinction. So how can we say quantity is taken as existing, when it is separated as secondary substratum?

The problem cannot be solved by saying that quantity at the level of secondary substratum is taken in some general way, reserving specificity for physics alone. It must be possible to separate a specific quantity from physical forms. For the quantity of which Philoponus spoke in the commentary on the *Categories* is not indefinite. The layer of matter known as the three-dimensional or unqualified body already has a quantitative form. It has this by virtue of being a particular quantity and a matter for some particular thing. It is from this quantified matter that the forms of physical things are separable in thought. So the manner of separability Philoponus spelled out for physical forms must apply even to optics. It is simply working on a different level. Presumably, this level may never contravene the requirements of the snub-concave distinction. Then how are we to account for the separability of forms from quantity? The quantity is in principle specific, because of being the sort of thing that is matter. But at this level, it is undiscriminated, because it is not taken as existing in a physical way. Nevertheless, it is taken as existing in some way, because this is precisely the reason why separability in thought is possible at all. How do we conceive a quantity as specific, without violating the snub-concave distinction?

III

We might think physical forms are separable from three dimensionality taken as limited but without quantitative form. Philoponus argued for the existence of such a three dimensionality in his *Corollarium de Loco*. And his manner of argumentation there reflects his concern with how we legitimately separate three dimensionality from physical things. He argued for place's being incorporeal three-dimensional space, coextensive with but different from the bodies in it. He made very clear, however, that he did not mean by this that space could exist devoid of all body or in any way separate from body. Just as matter is different from form but cannot exist apart from it, so space is different from body but always accompanies some body while remaining itself immovable. Are space and body distinguishable according to the manner of separability of the three-dimensional and physical forms?

To answer this question, we must take into consideration the difference between the three dimensionality of the *Categories* commentary and the three-dimensional extension of the *Corollarium de Loco*. Three dimensionality, in the commentaries on the *Categories* and *Physics*, is body without qualities (σῶμα ἄποιον), while spatial extension (τοπικὸν διάστημα) is incorporeal. Body without qualities possesses a quantitative form and has a matter, prime matter. Three dimensionality, understood as spatial extension, has no quantitative form and no matter. Its limits are defined by the quantity of the body it measures. These limits do not constitute a form but merely a place. The connection to the concept of place is thus crucial to maintaining the incorporeality of this sort of quantity.

That spatial extension is incorporeal means it falls outside the scheme of proximate and distant matters. Consequently, it cannot be distinguished from body in the way three-dimensional unqualified body is distinguished as the base from which physical forms are separable. However, this means that Philoponus' claim for the separability of incorporeal three dimensionality is more tenuous and he recognized this. He compared spatial extension to secondary substratum, which insofar as it is in its power, exists by itself (ὅσον ἐφ' ἑαυτῷ δυνάμενον καθ' αὑτὸ ὑποστῆναι), even though it never exists without qualities. His claim for the separability of spatial extension from body proceeds by analogy to secondary substratum:

Then even if, insofar as it were in its power, spatial extension too could have existed by itself, (for what prevented there being space void of body, as we said, if we conceived the jar as containing no body inside?), nevertheless, it never does remain void of body by itself.... (579.6–10)[11]

He reinforced the analogy to secondary substratum with an analogy to matter:

...just as in the case of matter, when form is corrupted another form straightway supervenes, similarly also in the case of the void, the change of place of bodies never leaves behind empty space, but as soon as one body departs, another takes its place. (579.10–13)

Philoponus made no claim for a special mode of separability of space as he did for the separability of physical forms. But at the same time,

11. The parenthetical remark indicates that Philoponus used past tenses in this passage because he was referring to a previous discussion. Rendered in the present tense, the nature of Philoponus' claim for the separability of space is clearer: "Even if, insofar as is in its power, spatial extension too can exist by itself, ... nevertheless it never does remain void of body by itself." The εἰ καὶ ... ἄν is concessive rather than truly conditional.

the separability of space and body cannot share the mode of separability of physical forms, because space is not in the scheme of matters and form.

Should we conclude that Philoponus' hypostasizing of space falls altogether outside the Aristotelian scheme of the commentaries and that it is unrelated to the issue of separability of traits treated in *Physics* II.2? Such a neat separation of the two kinds of three dimensionality is not possible, because Philoponus consistently described both unqualified body and spatial extension as quantity and called each by the name τὸ τριχῇ διάστημα. It is difficult to escape the conclusion that what Philoponus was most interested in was the separation of the three-dimensional as such. In accomplishing this separation, spatial extension plays a role unqualified body cannot, because of the latter's involvement with the forms of existing things. In Philoponus' treatment of quantity, spatial extension does hold the place of providing for the actual existence of a specific quantity apart from the requirements of the snub-concave distinction. But it does not perform this function simply by being a specific quantity without form. For there is no formless quantity. In being a specific quantity taken apart from any form, spatial extension is always allied with unqualified body. Its specific quantity is exactly that of the unqualified body it measures. Measure is thus crucial in the relation of spatial extension to the distinctions of *Physics* II.2. Because of the reliance of measure on what it measures, spatial extension's claim to existence derives from unqualified body, as Philoponus' arguments in favor of its separability suggest. To understand how spatial extension works in this way, we must explore the relation of both unqualified body and spatial extension to the category of quantity. It is not possible to treat this subject fully here. For our present purposes, let it suffice to show that measure was a central concept in Philoponus' conception of space and that he himself thought of the measuring function of space in terms of the distinctions of *Physics* II.2.

Philoponus believed that the concept of place as the three-dimensional measure of a body is an obvious and natural sense of place and that the void quite naturally corresponds to this (568.22–69.17, 576.12–77.9). To argue against Aristotle's conception of place as the surface of the containing body, he used the exchange of water for air that takes place when a jar is emptied. The water that changes places with the air must be of the same amount as the displaced air:

Then, since the measure is as much as also what is measured (τοσοῦτόν ἐστι τὸ μέτρον ὅσον καὶ τὸ μετρούμενον), if the air is ten cubic units (πήχεις στερεούς), it is absolutely necessary that the space (χώραν) to receive it also be of such an amount. Then, [space] would itself be ten cubic units, [an amount] which evidently it also yielded up to the body being moved which is also as much as itself. But this was the place. For [the bodies] change place with one another. Clearly, place is a kind of solid (στερεόν τι), and by solid, I mean the three-dimensional (τὸ τριχῇ διαστατόν). And also place is the measure of the things in place; thus it is also equal [to them]. (568.8–14)

He went on to argue that neither the surface of the containing body nor its shape could be what receives the air, because neither could be the measure of it. The measure must be equal to what is measured, and hence, must be a solid (στερεόν τι). Philoponus described this measure alternatively as the three-dimensional, the void, and spatial extension.

As Philoponus described it here, we encounter spatial extension first in measuring. Place is itself the measure of the bodies in it. This is why it must be the three-dimensional. Nevertheless, even while identifying spatial extension, measure, and the void, Philoponus still followed Aristotle closely in identifying extension with body. His remarks along these lines show that, even in the *Corollaria*, he held to the distinctions he described in the commentary on *Physics* II.2. For instance, Philoponus said it is impossible to separate body from corporeal extension. When qualities are removed from body, unqualified body remains. But from the resulting extension it is impossible to remove body:

Therefore, when the matter is subtracted, straightway the body's form is gone too, for it is in matter that it has its being. Then, just as by calling white "what is capable of dilating vision" we mean this only belongs to it when it is in body as substratum . . . , so too, also, if you conceive a corporeal extension without matter, it will no longer be in a place (for it is no longer physical), nor could one say of such a thing that it does not pass through a body. But neither will it be in any way extended, except in definition; or rather, no such body in any way exists (οὐδὲ ἔστιν ὅλως τοιοῦτόν τι σῶμα ἐν ὑποστάσει), unless one is speaking of the paradigm or definitional account, which are not the subject of our present discussion, since our investigation is about physics. (688.8–25)

To take matter from extension violates the manners of separability we have seen obtain in physics. From unqualified body only quantitative form could be subtracted in thought, yielding prime matter. To separate void as incorporeal extension, however, violates none of the distinctions proper to physics. Furthermore, it is not without reason or function (οὐδὲ μάτην) that void exists, since it is the place of bodies. And it is not qua extension that one extension is in another, but it is qua corporeal that a corporeal extension is in a spatial extension (688.27–31).

We have just seen that the "reason" for the void is the necessity of a measure in the exchange of place of bodies. Now we see that conceptualizing this exchange does not entail separating extension from body, because it is not insofar as it is extension that void is separable. Rather, it is insofar as it is place, that is, measure, that void is separable. We could gloss this in the language of *Physics* II.2 by saying: It is insofar as a specific quantity is both distinguishable as unqualified body and existing as part of a physical thing that it is corporeal. But it is insofar as a quantity is both distinguishable as unqualified body and measurable without form that it is spatial extension. As a measure, spatial extension is never independent of the corporeal extension belonging to what it measures. This quantity, since it is enmattered, could never be a measure, except in the crude sense of a physical yardstick, itself depending on a prior sense of measure. Spatial extension provides the measure of a specific quantity, a measure that is independent of any material thing.

It is necessary as an adjunct to unqualified body precisely because of the distinctions that are and are not possible in physics. As we saw early on, unqualified body must be both specific and a matter for a physical thing. When taken as existing, it is subject to the exigencies of the snub-concave distinction. Spatial extension is both specific and taken as existing apart from physical things. The separation of spatial extension thus complements and completes the manners of separability elaborated in the commentary on *Physics* II.2. The separation of spatial extension allows us to reflect upon the separability of the unqualified body that is inseparable from physical things in particular instances. However, the principle underlying the separation of spatial extension is not as strong as the principles underlying the snub-concave distinction or the separation of physical forms from the three-dimensional. The conceptual necessity of measure is not a part of physics in the way matter-form distinctions are. Nevertheless, measure is an aspect of quantity that cannot be completely assimilated to unqualified body. It is inevitable that what holds the place of measure should have some sort of existence, albeit incorporeal, inseparable from unqualified body and allied with place. This is why Philoponus made space something that exists independently, though not separately.

Most importantly, something like spatial extension is necessary for our grasping unqualified body in thought. When we conceive the separability of forms from the three-dimensional, our thought readily splits off into treating quantity either like snub or like a quality. In his commentary on *Physics* II.2, Philoponus was meticulous in insisting that quantity considered in optics is always a specific quantity that goes along with a unique physical interpretation. Nevertheless, when we separate unqualified body, we think about the three-dimensional as purely mathematical. When we think about unqualified body in this way, we use measure.

IV

In attempting to determine how Philoponus could reconcile a mathematical explanation of perspective based on visual rays with an intromission theory of vision, we have proceeded from the issue of the directionality of the rays to a consideration of the bare dimensionality underlying physical things. We have seen that this dimensionality presents itself to us in several ways, most commonly like a quality. But when we must think about the subject matters of physics and the mixed sciences, we must consider quantity as it really exists. Continuous quantity, in its categorical mode of existing, is secondary substratum. The separation of continuous quantity in this way makes plausible Philoponus' reversal of the rays of geometrical optics, because it allowed him to consider the mathematical characteristics of the visual cone apart from the direction of the rays.

It is important to notice why the additional manner of separability Philoponus introduced into *Physics* II.2 is possible at all. Though difficult to imagine apart from body, the forms of physical things are separable because their matter, unqualified body, can be conceived separately. Unqualified body, quantity, can be conceived separately because, as a categorical mode of being, it exists independently though never separated. The result is that unqualified body is not only a logical entity but is also genuinely matter. Our ability to make per se mathematical demonstrations in science depends on a separability that is present first in the order of nature. It is interesting that this manner of separability relies on our being able to conceive something separately in the manner in which it is capable of existing. We see displayed here, in a simple and rudimentary fashion, how a metaphysical analysis functions in the grounding of mathematical science. The simple test Aristotle used against Plato has ramifications for our understanding of why a mathematical explanation may be compatible with different physical theories while finally being inextricably bound up with only one.

This last point is the important legacy of Philoponus' addition to the snub-concave distinction. Quantity may be conceived separately because it is a matter and a true existent. But as a specific quantity, it is always part of a unique physical interpretation. It is in thought that quantity is separable, and its separability there depends on spatial extension for its articulation. Philoponus made spatial extension really exist because its separability follows upon that of corporeal extension. That there are two extensions for one body is, in Philoponus' hands, the last implication of Aristotle's criticism of Plato.

Finally, let us consider whether Philoponus accepted or rejected Aristotelian science in the case we have considered. It is important to note that, in his commentary on *De anima* II.7, Philoponus argued at great length in favor of what he called the "Aristotelian hypothesis" on the nature of light. It is more important, though, to grasp the profoundly Aristotelian character of the analysis underlying his remarks about optics. Even his argument for the existence of space is partly a development of his separation of the three-dimensional as such. Philoponus' development of this separation proceeds on the foundation of the distinctions of *Physics* II.2 and never violates the manner of separability Aristotle recorded there. Philoponus analyzed how we think about quantity, given the order established by the snub-concave distinction.

COMMENTARIES CONSULTED

Commentaria in Aristotelem Graeca, edited under the authority of the Prussian Academy of Letters. Berlin: G. Reimer, 1882–1909.
Alexander of Aphrodisias.
   III.1. In librum De Sensu, ed. by P. Wendland, 1891.
John Philoponus.
   XIII.1. In Aristotelis Categorias, ed. A. Busse, 1898.
   XIII.3. In Aristotelis Analytica Posteriora, ed. W. Wallies, 1909.
   XV. In Aristotelis De Anima, ed. M. Hayduck, 1897.
   XVI. In Aristotelis Physicorum libros tres priores, ed. H. Vitelli, 1887.
   XVII. In Aristotelis Physicorum libros quinque posteriores, ed. H. Vitelli, 1888.
Simplicius.
   IX. In Aristotelis Physicorum libros quattuor priores, ed. H. Diels, 1882.

10 Ludovico Carbone's Commentary on Aristotle's *De caelo*

JEAN DIETZ MOSS

Ludovico Carbone is an enigmatic figure who published numerous works on logic, theology, and rhetoric and who, perhaps deliberately, furnished a link through his text on logic between the "father of modern science" and the Jesuits of the Collegio Romano. William A. Wallace has carefully documented the surprising correspondences between an unpublished treatise of Galileo, Manuscript 27 (MS 27), a commentary on Aristotle's *Posterior Analytics*, and two published commentaries on the same text, one by Carbone and the other by Paulus Vallius, a Jesuit professor at the Collegio Romano.[1] Carbone's commentary was published in his *Additamenta ad commentaria doctoris Francisci Toleti in logicam Aristotelis* of 1597 and Vallius's in his *Logica . . . duobus tomis distincta* of 1622. Wallace shows that a statement by Vallius in the preface of his *Logica* to the effect that a version of his lecture notes of 1588 had been plagiarized and published some twenty years earlier was actually a reference to Carbone's *Additamenta*.[2] Vallius writes that "a certain individual," whom he does not name, had thought so much of his notes that the man appropriated them and had them printed under his own name.[3] Wallace argues that around 1589 Galileo, then teaching or preparing to teach at the University of Pisa, probably copied the same lecture notes (those preserved as MS 27) in order to improve his own understanding of Aristotle's logic.

Unfortunately Vallius's lecture notes no longer exist in that early

---

1. In *Galileo and His Sources* (Princeton: Princeton University Press, 1984), Wallace gave a preliminary account of the origin of MS 27, which is written in Galileo's own hand. Since then, in collaboration with William F. Edwards, who transcribed the autograph, he has written an introduction and commentary on it in which he explores in great detail the interconnections between the three treatises. See Galileo Galilei, *Tractatio de praecognitionibus et praecognitis* and *Tractatio de demonstratione* (Padua: Editrice Antenore, 1988).
2. The discovery of the preface is related in *Galileo and His Sources*, 18–19.
3. Ibid., 19.

form and have to be inferred from the edition of Carbone and the later version of Vallius, which the Collegio professor mentions was altered from its original ordering by Carbone. The text is not as difficult to reconstruct as one might expect, however, first, because of the two published versions and, second, because of the correlations in text and structure of Galileo's manuscript, and, more importantly, because the notes were part of an ongoing series of lectures regularly given at the Collegio on logic and natural philosophy. Wallace, after examining the lecture notes of other professors at the Collegio from 1560 to 1598, was able to describe in detail the similarities and innovations of individual professors there. The resultant analysis discloses teachings further advanced and substantially different from those offered at the University of Pisa, where Galileo had studied, making it unlikely that a very young Galileo could have derived his manuscript notes from lectures there or from his earlier instruction at the monastery of Vallombrosa.

Now this peculiar linkage between Vallius and Carbone and between Carbone and Galileo through the appropriated teachings of Vallius is sufficient to arouse one's curiosity about Carbone himself and about his other writings. Vallius had also implied in his mildly outraged comments in the preface to his *Logica* that the plagiarist had issued other works based on Collegio lectures. The possibility that Carbone might have published books on rhetoric occurred to me upon hearing of my colleague Professor Wallace's discoveries regarding the preface to the *Logica*. Subsequently I was able to find six published treatises on rhetoric, in addition to two on logic, one on philosophy, and five on theology.[4]

We know by Carbone's own testimony that he was a student at the Collegio Romano, probably during the second decade after its establishment in 1551, and that he was singularly impressed by the quality of his education there. In the preface to one of his books on rhetoric, he mentions that through this publication he wants to demonstrate how much he has benefitted by the excellent lectures of his professors

---

4. The rhetorical books are *De oratoria et dialectica inventione vel de locis communibus* (Venice, 1589); *Tabulae Rhetoricae Cypriani Soarii*, a two-part work that includes Carbone's commentary on this popular Jesuit rhetoric, *De arte dicendi* (Venice, 1589); *De dispositione oratoria* (Venice, 1590); *De octo partium orationis* (Venice, 1592); *De caussis eloquentiae* (Venice, 1593); *Divinus orator, vel De rhetorica divina* (Venice, 1595). The other works on logic, philosophy, and theology include the *Additamenta* mentioned earlier (Venice, 1597); *Introductio in logicam* (Venice, 1597); *Introductio in universam philosophiam* (Venice, 1599); *Fons vitae et sapientiae, vel ad veram sapientiam acquirendam hortatio* (Venice, 1588); *De pacificatione et dilectione inimicorum iniuriarumque* (Florence, 1583); *Introductio in sacram theologiam* (Venice, 1589); *De praeceptis Ecclesiae opusculum utilissimum* (Venice, 1590); *Introductio ad catechismum sive doctrinam Christianam* (Venice, 1596).

at the Collegio.⁵ He does not elaborate on the extent of the debt, and particularly on whether it includes the content of his publications, although one might infer that his compliment is an attempt to acknowledge their influence on his work. Evidently he felt it his mission to try to preserve and convey their teachings beyond the Collegio's halls. The expression of his gratitude is found in a guide and commentary to the very popular rhetoric by the Spanish Jesuit Cypriano Soarez, which was widely used as a text in Jesuit colleges for two hundred years after its initial publication in 1562. Carbone mentions that he had seen Soarez's text before it was published, presumably when he was a student at the Collegio, where the text was introduced and later revised by another Jesuit, Petrus Perpinian.⁶

Title pages and prefaces to Carbone's books provide almost the only biographical details we have about him. They record that he was a native of Costaciaro and affiliated with the German College, which was a part of the Collegio, and that he subsequently obtained a doctorate in theology. Although he did not become a Jesuit himself he seems to have joined one of their primary confraternities, the Congregatio Beatae Mariae Annuntiatae.⁷ The title page to his *De Oratoria, et Dialectica Inventione* (1589) proclaims him "Academico Parthenio & Sacre Theologie in almo Gymnasio Perusino olim publico Professore." As public professor at Perugia he was not far from Rome and could have visited his alma mater frequently, availing himself of the lecture notes professors regularly deposited in the college library. It is possible that he actually met Galileo at the Collegio, where the young mathematician is known to have visited Clavius in 1587. If so, it is not hard to imagine that Carbone would have praised the instruction he had received from his professors and that he may well have inspired Galileo to avail himself of notes that had been so helpful in his own teaching at Perugia. Carbone may have been reading at the library of the Collegio through the late 1580s and early 1590s to prepare the publications in theology and in rhetoric that subsequently appeared from 1583 to 1596. The texts in logic were published in 1597, the year Carbone died. This was a dozen years before Galileo attained renown through his discoveries with the telescope.

5. Carbone states this in the *Tabulae Rhetoricae Cypriani Soarii* (Venice, 1589); the *De rhetorica* of Soarez had 134 printings from 1562 to 1735 and stimulated many commentaries.
6. I have discussed these matters and the teaching of rhetoric generally at the Jesuit College in "The Rhetoric Course at the Collegio Romano," *Rhetorica* 4 (1986): 137–51.
7. Marc Fumaroli, in his discussion of Carbone's treatment of sacred oratory, notes Carbone's membership in the confraternity, *L'Age de l'Eloquence* (Geneva: Librairie Droz, 1980), 182–83.

Wallace's contention that both men probably used a set of Vallius's lecture notes in composing their logical writings is supported by the marked similarities in content, structure, wording, and citations of authorities between Carbone's published text and Galileo's manuscript. That Galileo copied from the text of Vallius's notes and not from Carbone's *Additamenta* is convincingly demonstrated by evidence of departures from the order and content of the *Additamenta,* as well as by parallels with the later published work of Vallius and the lecture notes of other professors at the Collegio.[8]

A recent discovery, the subject of this essay, adds further evidence of Carbone's considerable debt to the Roman College. In 1986, while searching in the Rare Book Collection of the Biblioteca Nazionale Centrale in Florence for other rhetorical writings of Carbone, I happened instead upon a manuscript commentary on Aristotle's *De caelo* and *De generatione* that was written by the Perugian professor.[9] It was preserved in a collection of works that until 1985 had remained uncatalogued. The treatise bears the date 1594 and also seems to be derived from Jesuit notes, apparently again those of Vallius and others in the Jesuit College. On obtaining a microfilm copy of the manuscript, Professor Wallace noted similarities between the newly discovered Carbone commentary and Jesuit sources he had previously studied in his analysis of another of Galileo's youthful treatises, MS 46, likewise concerned with the matter of *De caelo* and *De generatione.*[10] In his *Galileo's Early Notebooks: The Physical Questions,* published in 1977, Wallace had argued that MS 46 was copied by Galileo from lecture notes emanating from the Collegio Romano, just as he was later to suggest in his discussion of MS 27, which he termed the "Logical Questions" to distinguish them from the "Physical Questions" of MS 46.[11] In his study of the "Physical Questions" he found correspon-

8. Wallace, *Galileo and His Sources,* 50–53.
9. The manuscript bears the signature BNF CL XII,64 Theatini.
10. This contention is supported in a comparison by Wallace of the coverage of the recently discovered Carbone manuscript, lecture notes of Jesuits at the Collegio on *De caelo* and *De generatione,* and Galileo's MS 46, in his "The Dating and Significance of Galileo's Pisan Manuscripts," in *Nature, Experiment, and the Sciences: Essays on Galileo and the History of Science in Honour of Stillman Drake* (Dordrecht-Boston: Kluwer Academic Publishers, 1990), 28–29.
11. *Galileo's Early Notebooks: The Physical Questions* (Notre Dame, Ind.: University of Notre Dame Press, 1977), 1–24. MS 46 was thought by Favaro to have been composed while Galileo was a student at the University of Pisa, and so Favaro labeled the notes *Juvenilia* when he published his transcription of them in the National Edition of Galileo's works, *Le Opere di Galileo Galilei,* ed. Antonio Favaro, 20 vols. in 21 (Florence, 1890–1909; rpt. 1968), vol. 1, 7–177. The "Logical Questions," MS 27, Favaro did not transcribe and he included only a brief summary and a few excerpts, calling the work *Saggio di alcune esercitazioni scholastiche di Galileo,* vol. 9, 273–92. Wallace discusses the omission in *Galileo and His Sources,* 4–5.

dences between Galileo's manuscript and the lecture notes of Vallius, as well as those of other Jesuits, including Antonius Menu, Mutius Vitelleschi, and Ludovicus Rugerius. Each of these Jesuits lectured on much the same topics in successive years. Their lecture notes, still available in manuscript form though scattered among various libraries throughout Europe, build on the materials of their predecessors. Wallace concluded from his earlier study that Galileo, when writing out his MS 46, probably used a set of notes also no longer extant but one that bears notable resemblances in content and even identical correspondences in syntax to certain exemplars in the series.

In this essay I have undertaken to describe the *De caelo* part of the Carbone manuscript in some detail because of its striking resemblances to Galileo's MS 46. (Limitations of space prevent my discussion of the similarities that exist in their treatments of *De generatione*.) I think that a discussion of the content and the manner in which Carbone's work resembles and departs from the treatment by Galileo, and Jesuit lecture notes generally, strengthens Wallace's case for the interrelationships between Carbone and the Collegio. In the process such an analysis also serves to illuminate the character of the author himself. If nothing else, the comparison discloses Carbone's ingenuity in adapting the Jesuit teaching materials to the needs of his own students. Since it is a manuscript for which no printed copy has turned up, we might assume that it represents Carbone's teaching notes of the sort that he must have used in composing his textbooks. He may have intended to publish this work as well, for at times his remarks imply as much. In chapter 1 of the second treatise he explains, for example, "This treatise on the heavens . . . will be recalled from the introductory chapters. . . ." Although remarks such as the following are commonplace, one tends to believe Carbone's statement in one of his printed works that students and friends have so urged him to publish his lectures, that he "sweats day and night" to ready his notes for publication.[12]

That Carbone was a master teacher is evident from an examination of the books he published. They are clearly written and contain extensive illustrative materials. The manner in which he organized the texts shows that, despite their derivation from Jesuit lectures, he did not simply convey their contents verbatim but presented them in his own way.

Carbone's manuscript is 197 folios in length and contains two commentaries, one on *De caelo* and the other on *De generatione*. On the title

12. The preface to the *Tabulae* records his efforts.

page of the manuscript, in keeping with his membership in the confraternity dedicated to the Blessed Virgin, Carbone voices a prefatory plea, "The Virgin Mother of God be with me!" Below the prayer the description of the text reads, "Commentaries and Questions on the four books of Aristotle's *De caelo,* by the author Doctor Ludovico Carbone of Costaciaro."

Both Galileo's MS 46 and Carbone's text treat the same material in *De caelo* and *De generatione* and follow the order of Aristotle's work. The organization of both texts is as follows:

CARBONE	GALILEO
De caelo	
Prologue to the four books De Caelo (Three chapters)	Introductory Treatise (Two chapters)
Treatise on the Universe (Nine chapters)	Treatise on the Universe (Four chapters)
Treatise on the Heavens (Thirteen chapters)	Treatise on the Heavens (Six chapters)
De generatione	
Treatise on Alteration (Four chapters)	Tractate on Alteration (Three chapters)
Treatise on the Elements (Thirteen chapters)	Tractate on the Elements (Ten chapters divided into an introduction and two parts)

Apart from these somewhat obvious similarities, Carbone's manuscript contains much more material than does Galileo's. Part of the difference in their two treatments undoubtedly derives from their different objectives in writing out the materials they appropriated, as will be discussed later. Also noteworthy is the fact that Galileo's MS 46, about half the length of Carbone's (100 folios, as compared to Carbone's 197), is obviously incomplete: it is mutilated at the beginning; an unknown number of folios is missing at the juncture of the commentaries on *De caelo* and *De generatione*; and an unknown number of folios is missing at the end.[13] A detailed comparison of the contents of the two manuscripts will be found in Appendices I and II, which provide detailed outlines, respectively, of Carbone's and Galileo's works.

Some of the additional material in Carbone's manuscript seems to be derived from other Jesuit lectures—those of Rugerius, Vitelleschi, and Menu especially—and some of it may have come from Carbone's own reflections or perhaps from other sources unknown to us. One can imagine Carbone's sitting in the library of the Collegio taking

---

13. These details are discussed by Wallace in "The Dating and Significance."

detailed notes from the lectures of its professors, drawing from one or the other to satisfy what he perceived to be the particular needs of his own students. As he explains in the preface to his *De Oratoria, et Dialectica Inventione*, he is hurrying to get this work into print because no published texts treat the matter very well.

Let us look more closely at some of the content in the first part of Carbone's *De caelo*. After the prolegomena three introductory chapters follow, the first of which sets forth the relationship of the four books of *De caelo* to preliminary writings in Aristotle's *Physics*. Chapter 2 of the prefatory material shows marked similarities to the first question of Galileo's MS 46. (As can be seen from Appendix II, Galileo's manuscript is divided into questions rather than chapters.) Both bear similar titles: Galileo's is "What Is Aristotle's Subject Matter in His Books *De caelo*?"; Carbone's is simply "On the object of these books."[14] The content of Galileo's first question is treated in a different order from that of Carbone. Galileo begins by discussing various opinions regarding the object of the work, which he eventually shows to be erroneous. The view of Alexander (Alexander of Aphrodisias) is mentioned first, followed by those of Simplicius, Zimara, Averroes, and St. Thomas. Then the opinions of Galileo (or of his exemplar) are given, for example: "But I say first: the universe is not the subject of these books. The conclusion is Aristotle's, in the third *De caelo* at the beginning, and in the first *Meteors*...." The text goes on to offer four conclusions and follows this with five objections. After these are expressed, each is refuted in turn. Thus the subject is approached by first considering what it is not; then it is defined. After this, arguments that might be brought against the conclusions just reached are given and refuted. Such was the traditional style of disputation, still the most common pedagogical method of the day.

Carbone, on the other hand, treats the same material in a more compact, more cogent fashion, and in what might be called a freer humanistic style. He appears to be conscious of an audience whom he wants to aid in understanding some very difficult material, whereas the author of the disputational form seems to be concerned mainly with casting the material in the approved form, preserving carefully

---

14. Here and in what follows I have used the English translation by Wallace of MS 46 in *Galileo's Early Notebooks*. When locations of citations may be difficult for the reader to find, I have used Wallace's paragraph numbering system and inserted the appropriate references in the text. Professor Wallace has recently transcribed and translated much of Carbone's *De caelo* manuscript and has made both of these available to me. I have used his English translation in this text for the most part, editing and comparing it at times with the Latin transcription. Readers who are interested in delving further into the respective teachings of Carbone and Galileo should be able to locate further particulars with the aid of the data on foliation provided in my two Appendices.

all of the authoritative opinions. Carbone begins, "There are various opinions pertaining to their [the books'] object, which we will set forth in the following conclusions." He then offers the conclusions, each usually prefaced by an opinion (or opinions) he declares to be erroneous at the outset. Only two of the objections Galileo raises are discussed, and these but briefly in two paragraphs at the end of the chapter.

The interesting parallel between the texts is not only that Carbone's four conclusions and two objections address the same content as twelve of the twenty-one parts of Galileo's manuscript but that Carbone's also names many of the same authorities and often ranks them in the same order. For instance, Carbone mentions Alexander first and then Simplicius and St. Thomas. He reverses the order of Iamblichus and Syrianus Magnus in noting their treatment of whether Aristotle is speaking of the heavens, which he discusses in the next section, but both authorities on the same point are addressed by Galileo. Averroes, Albert, and Nifo are cited by both men in the same context. In fact, only one authority noted by Galileo is not referred to by Carbone, Zimara. Since Zimara was an Averroist and Carbone had already mentioned Averroes, he may have simply omitted him in order to simplify the material.

In sum, regarding this sample of the treatments of the first question in the two commentaries on *De caelo,* we may say that Carbone's offers a more succinct summary of opinions concerning the purpose of Aristotle's work. At the same time his discussion preserves the major opinions in the literature, passing over repetitions and some distinctions. Not only the near-uniform citations of the authorities but the consonance of the conclusions argue convincingly that both men are working through the same material. We are drawn to conjecture that the differences in treatment are the result of different purposes behind both men's writing. Galileo seems to have made the notes he has in order to learn the material himself, probably in the way it was presented by the Jesuit professors. Carbone appears to be well acquainted with the subject matter and is concerned to reorder it so as to present it to his students in the most accessible manner. In that regard, a further comment of Vallius is germane on the appropriation of his lectures on logic in what is now known as Carbone's *Introductio ad logicam* (1597). Vallius says that the miscreant "changed only the ordering (disordering it, in my judgment), along with the introductions and conclusions."[15] In the case of Carbone's manuscript notes on *De caelo,* as we have seen in the excerpt just analyzed, the same

---

15. Wallace, quoting Vallius, *Galileo and His Sources,* 19.

technique is evident. We can surmise also that the courses Carbone gave as public professor were not intended to be as rigorous as those provided at the Collegio. As a doctor of sacred theology he had interests quite different from those of Galileo, who was already a practicing mathematician.

Returning to the content of Carbone's manuscript, in the first two chapters of the Treatise on the Universe, I could find few precise parallels in the text of the corresponding part of Galileo's *Physical Questions*. An exception is the discussion in the first chapter of the names of the universe. In the first paragraph both consider the meaning of the same terms, *world* and *universe*; both cite Pythagoras and Plato; both note that the universe is so called because it contains all things; and both mention that it was said to be ornate. Thereafter the two diverge, Carbone discussing the divisions of the universe, Galileo airing the opinions of the ancients regarding the eternity of the universe. In chapter 2, for instance, although Carbone is concerned with the causes of the world and Galileo with the origin of the universe, the material is quite different in content. Galileo mentions causes in passing while treating the existence of an uncaused cause in five conclusions, an objection and reply, and a final conclusion giving the age of the universe. Carbone organizes and limits his discussion to the four causes of the universe. The subject, again, is presented in a less pedantic way by Carbone. He extracts the purpose of the arguments, gives them a more general treatment, and throughout evinces a theological concern. For instance, Carbone concludes, in developing the material cause:

As some have said, it was made from chaos as from its first matter, as some ancient philosophers and poets have held; but in truth, as the true and Christian philosophy teaches, it was made from no preexisting material whatever; whence Paul, in his second [letter] to the Hebrews: we know by faith that the ages were formed by the word of God.

Galileo offers authorities only in the fifth proof. These are "the authority of Holy Scripture," "the determination of the Lateran Council," and a citation of a passage from Aristotle's *Metaphysics*.

The matter of the third and fourth chapters, which treat of the perfection of the universe, is even more obviously prepared with an eye to its use by students of theology. These chapters are drawn from material that Galileo considers in his third question: "On the unity and perfection of the universe." Carbone delays discussion of unity to a later chapter, taking up perfection first and devoting seven chapters to an examination of it. Galileo treats both topics in twenty-three paragraphs: his text throughout is dialectical, containing questions and distinctions and answering arguments. In his discussion, Carbone explains at the outset that he intends to describe certain fundamentals that explain the perfection of the world, and he treats these through simple definitions. He notes that three things especially aid one in understanding the perfection of the world: "the completion and beauty of individual things," "the differentiation of things and the variety of their degrees," and "the order and disposition of the parts." Each of these is given a short paragraph. For the last, order, he cites works of theological significance: Augustine's *De civitate,* the Book of Wisdom, and Dionysius.

The continuation of the discussion of perfection in chapter 4 presents the summary conclusions of the author. The religious-humanistic orientation of Carbone is displayed best by quoting his first conclusion:

The universe is perfect in its kind. Proof, first: the world was made by the supreme Artist; therefore it is perfect. The deduction is valid, from the attributes of the cause to the attributes of the effect. Here pertains that most elegant hymn of Boethius in Carmine 3 of *De consolatione,* meter 9:
> All things Thou bringest forth from Thy high archetype;
> Thou, height of beauty, in Thy mind the beauteous world
> Dost bear, and in that ideal likeness shaping it,
> Dost order perfect parts a perfect whole to frame.[16]

The rest of the conclusions are grounded in the authority of Augustine, Ambrose, and Aristotle. In the third conclusion Carbone focuses on the Last Judgment and the final stage of perfection of the universe.

In this part of our discussion of Carbone's text, we have been concerned to show some of the deviations from the source Galileo followed as Carbone adapted similar materials for his own purposes. What follows is an example of how closely Carbone followed the Jesuit lecture notes in other instances.

In chapter 6 of his commentary on the first treatise of *De caelo,* Carbone takes up discussion of the unity of the world, treated by Galileo earlier in his third question. This question concerns an issue fraught with difficulties from the time of the Condemnations of 1277. Since it treats a doctrinal point and one grounded in theoretical physics, an area in which Carbone was not an expert, he may have decided to stick closely to the discussion in the Jesuit notes.[17]

---

16. Boethius, Carmine 3, is from Book III, part 9. I have given the translation by V. E. Watts, *The Consolation of Philosophy* (London: Penguin, 1969), 97.

17. Wallace finds that most of the text in Galileo's manuscript is so close to the lecture notes of Antonius Menu that parts appear to have been copied from them: *Galileo and His Sources,* 259.

Although he has reordered the overall treatment, Carbone states the proposition or question and offers arguments whose parts follow in almost the same order as Galileo's, at times using wording identical to that in Galileo's text. He begins, "That the world should not be one, as Aristotle has provided, is urged by the following arguments." Both note the view of Democritus that many worlds exist, and both cite Plato, Aristotle's *Metaphysics* 2, and Albert; to these Carbone adds Trismegistus. It is in the clarification and amplification of the more scholastic treatment of Galileo that the two differ. The young mathematician declares simply, "It cannot be demonstrated that there is only one universe, although it is certain that there are not more." Carbone makes the same point but separates his reasoning into two conclusions rephrased in a more elegant style:

The first conclusion: Philosophically speaking, the unity of the world can be construed only with probability. I say "with probability," because no proof can be offered on the basis of natural principles.

Second conclusion: Theologically speaking, that is, from principles known by faith, one can affirm most certainly that there are not many worlds, and to assert the contrary is either a heresy or erroneous.

He then cites the same authority as Galileo: Holy Scripture's allusions to one universe.

Chapter 7, entitled "Can there be many worlds?" continues to treat related issues, all discussed by Galileo in his third question. The presentation of the problem is quite similar:

Carbone: "Since Aristotle was not able to prove sufficiently that the world is one, but even tried to prove that it is impossible for many [worlds] to exist, I propose to examine this difficulty."

Galileo: "The arguments of Aristotle . . . by which he thinks he has demonstrated the unity of the universe, can easily be answered."

And where Galileo says, "It is not impossible that many universes could have been created by God," Carbone states unequivocally, "God can make many worlds."

In his subsequent discussion of the secondary perfection of the world, in chapter 8, Carbone makes many observations similar to those found in Galileo's third question. For example, Carbone's conclusions read as follows:

Third conclusion: With regard to its secondary perfection the world can be made more perfect in all its species. Explanation: God can give earth a greater force of movement, and water likewise, and this is an accidental perfection.

Fourth conclusion: The universe can be made more perfect by the addition of integral parts. Explanation: God can create new species in every genus of things, in simples, in compounds, in animate objects. . . . The reason: because there is no implication [of contradiction], if this were truly done, since this universe as it now is would be related to that more perfect universe as part to whole.

A comparison of Galileo's text at paragraphs fourteen and fifteen of the third question shows similar lines of argument:

> Note, for an answer: a thing can be said to be perfect in two ways, absolutely or in a qualified way. . . .
> I say, first: the universe taken in the first sense is perfect absolutely, since God contains what is most perfect within himself; and second: the universe in the three other meanings is perfect in a qualified way, but not absolutely. . . . and God could have created another universe that is more perfect, and many more perfect species.

The final chapter of the series on perfection takes up a question just answered in the fifteenth paragraph of Galileo's third question: "Can God make other worlds that are more perfect?" Carbone elaborates on the point by noting that God could do so because of his infinite virtue and power and because there is no reason to deny this divine power. Here again, the theologian finds that these problems require more expansive treatment.

Carbone does not treat the fourth question that Galileo takes up: "Whether the universe could have existed from eternity?" Since an affirmative position might be regarded by some as heretical, Carbone may not have thought it important to record the opinions related to it.

The next treatise, "On the Heavens," contains questions of theoretical astronomy that were already much discussed and were to become increasingly important in the next century. That Carbone considers the treatise to be important is obvious from its lengthy treatment and his caution in treating opinions. In an introductory chapter he outlines the matter that will be covered: the nature and substance of the heavens; their quantity, properties, and position; and the number of the heavens. Galileo's treatment of the topic is also quite extensive, as would be expected of a mathematician whose discipline included questions of theoretical astronomy. Because of the significance of the subject matter for the history of science, I shall provide more examples of its substance.

The composition of the heavens is the first question to be considered by both scholars. Galileo devotes considerably more space to the subject than Carbone, but their conclusions agree. Both say that the heavens are not composed of the four elements and offer some of the same proofs: that they do not exhibit rectilinear motion, that they are superior in their position and in their nature, and that since they are the largest body they cannot be composed of elements. Many more opinions are offered by Galileo.

Carbone postpones a consideration of the fourth question treated by Galileo, the incorruptibility of the heavens, and takes up in the next chapter a discussion of whether the heavens are composed of matter and form. As might be expected, Galileo covers that subject in far greater detail and in the traditional fashion presents opinions, one by one, citing specific writings from which they are drawn. Carbone reorganizes the material, greatly simplifying it. He notes that the question really has two parts—whether the heavens are composed of matter and form and whether the matter is of the same kind as that of inferior bodies—but he states that he will treat it as one question. Through transitional phrases he prepares his reader for the opinions that follow. Carbone first takes up the authorities who believe the heavens are composed of matter and form and so are composed of the same corruptible matter as treated by Aristotle in the *Physics*. Among these he simply mentions Empedocles, Plato, Anaxagoras, and Avicenna, without developing their views; all but Empedocles are also recorded by Galileo. Next Carbone cites a second opinion, that of Giles of Rome, who believed that the heavens are composed of matter and form but that the matter is incorruptible. This is so, Giles thought, because the form is perfect and as such has no appetite for more form; it lacks contrariety or any external agent that could corrupt it; its form and matter have such unity that there is no disposition that would permit it to be corrupted. Galileo develops Giles's opinion at greater length, but along parallel lines.

The third opinion treated by Carbone is that of St. Thomas and those who are in agreement with him: Capreolus, Soncinas, and Cajetan. They think that the heavens are composed of matter and form but that the matter is pure potency in the order of being. This is contrasted to the matter of inferior bodies, which is ever directed by an agent to this or that form, and so its appetite is never exhausted, having a potency of contradiction and a privation associated with it. The matter of the heavens is only in potency to its form, which is of the highest perfection, so it has no impulse to take on other forms. Thus, because of their form and matter, the heavens are incorruptible. In this way it is different from the matter of lower bodies. The final point—though, as Carbone notes, perhaps not an opinion of Aquinas—is that the matter of which the individual orbs are composed is not the same as that of the first orb. In Galileo's account St. Thomas's opinion is not as clearly separated from the others.

A fourth opinion offered by Achillini and the Doctors of Bologna (also noted by Galileo) is briefly summarized. They think also that the heavens are composed of matter and form, that the matter is simple act with no potency, and that the form is an intelligence.

Carbone then summarizes, saying that all of the opinions agree that the heavens are composed of matter and form. He suggests that this position can be argued persuasively and provides proofs from Aristotle to support it, which we will not rehearse here but which are also aired in Galileo.

Finally, Carbone presents the opinions of those who hold that the heavens lack any "essential composition of matter and form"; these were treated first in Galileo's account (K1, 9).

By considering the opinions as a group and providing a summation of them at the end of the question, Carbone vastly simplifies the matter; Galileo's source, on the other hand, continues to provide systematic and exhaustive explications of positions, replying to each of the opinions in turn. Both, however, are in agreement on the essential points. Carbone concludes first by stating that all of the opinions except Achillini's can be defended by probable argument and can be reconciled with Aristotle's view. His second conclusion is "The heavens do not have matter of the same kind as these inferior bodies," and Galileo says similarly, "The heavens are not composed of matter of the same kind as the matter of inferior bodies" (K1 30).

The next chapter of Carbone's work, "Whether the heavens are animated," is treated by Galileo also, in his sixth question. The difference in the approaches of the two men is well illustrated by the first part of each. By his prefatory remark, one of the few in the manuscript, Galileo shows more concern with mastering the interrelationships of the material than in assessing its significance for an audience: "Having explained what pertains to the matter of the heavens, it remains for us to consider what pertains to their form." Carbone places the question in context: "At one time there was a celebrated controversy among all philosophers on this matter, concerning which they held various opinions." He goes on to assess and define the problem: "The difficulty can be understood in regard to the entire universe, in which there is a certain kind of form which is its soul, or in relation to the orbs themselves, and it is especially concerning these that the difficulty is usually raised."

Carbone then exposes the opinions of the first sort, that the heavens have a soul, noting the Chaldeans, Egyptians, and Arabs, and, surprisingly, "even indeed some of our own [*ex nostris*] . . ." among its advocates. The remark might be taken to indicate that by "some of our own" Carbone meant certain Jesuits who argued for a world soul, and, if so, that he here considers himself a Jesuit. (The phrase *ex nostris* was frequently used by the Jesuits to indicate a member of their order.) Unfortunately I could discover no corroborating passage in Galileo's manuscript; however, Galileo does mention that some Church Fathers, namely Origen and St. Jerome, held that opinion (L10), so one might alternatively surmise that Carbone was referring only to the Christian tradition.

Various opinions are rehearsed, which have parallels in Galileo, but it is in some of the conclusions that the manuscripts are most similar. As we can see in the discussion that follows, the content of the conclusions of the manuscripts is almost identical, except where Galileo makes a qualification that Carbone does not.

Carbone summarizes all of the foregoing material in his first conclusion: "The world is not animated." This is followed by a proof. These have no counterpart in Galileo. In the second through the fourth conclusions, however, the two are almost identically expressed:

In the second, Carbone: "The heavens do not have a vegetative soul." Galileo: "I say first, there is no vegetative soul in the heavens" (L6).

The next conclusion, in Carbone: "The heavens do not have a sensitive soul." In Galileo: "I say, second, in the heavens there is no sensitive soul having either an internal or an external sense" (L7).

Carbone's fourth conclusion: "The heavens are not informed with an intelligent soul." The same point is found later in Galileo's discussion: "I say, first, apart from intelligences no other souls are constituent in the heavens" (L25).

Carbone's next two conclusions have a counterpart, but also a more carefully articulated distinction, in Galileo:

Carbone's fifth conclusion: "The heavens do not have a motive soul. . . . In sum, therefore, the heavens are not informed by any informing soul. . . ."

Galileo: "I say, second: although it may not seem completely improbable, according to Aristotle, that intelligences are forms simply informing, nevertheless, according to Aristotle and the truth, it is more probable that they are assisting forms" (L29).

The theological interests Carbone has evinced in previous questions are again paramount in his final conclusion. It reads: "to affirm that the heavens are informed by a rational soul, if not a heresy, is at least erroneous. Scholastics treat this in 2 *Sentences,* dist. 14, Irenaeus, book 1 *Contra Hereses,* Jerome, and others; it is also condemned in a certain article of Paris [the Condemnations of 1277]." This conclusion has no counterpart in Galileo. Perhaps between the time Galileo found his exemplar and Carbone combed the materials, the quasi-heretical nature of the position had once more come to trouble theologians.

The subject of the next question, "Whether the heavens are corruptible," is one in which the two manuscripts also contain similar content, although some differences are apparent in the positions. Carbone's expression of his conclusion is much more conservative. His views are given as unqualified absolutes, implying demonstrative proof, whereas Galileo's opinions are expressed as probabilities. The change in measure may be a result of a shift in Jesuit opinion.

Carbone says that the heavens are corruptible by divine power, but this, he notes, is an improper way of speaking for they really have no intrinsic property that would allow them to corrupt. It is better to say "that they can be corrupted by the power of God." Galileo makes the same distinction between the nature of the heavens as they were created and God's absolute power, but he continues: "I now say, first: if we speak of the heavens according to their nature, and if corruptible be taken to signify anything that has in itself a passive potency whereby it can be corrupted by an active power proportioned to it, it is probable that the heavens are corruptible" (J12–13).

In his second conclusion Carbone states, "The heavens are absolutely incorruptible. The doctrine is Aristotle's in the second book of *De caelo,* and it is confirmed from the common teaching of theologians and philosophers." Galileo casts the conclusion dialectically: "I say second: it is more probable that the heavens are incorruptible by nature" (J18). Galileo's proof is extensive and is drawn from Aristotle, the commentators, and the Church Fathers.

Concerning the eternity of the heavens, Carbone holds in his third conclusion: "The heavens have a perpetual duration, and so they will not corrupt at the end of the world...." Here, Galileo offers a different, more nuanced conclusion: "The heavens, according to the testimony of Holy Scripture, will be changed from the state they now have and will perish in a qualified way..., but not with regard to substance; and neither will the elements" (J35). He adds, "The heavens have finite power but they can, by finite power, endure for an infinite time."

The question that one might expect would prompt the most lively opinions, given the publication of Copernicus's *De revolutionibus* some forty years before, "On the number and order of the heavens," prompts Carbone only to a pallid exposition touching on ancient and contemporary conservative opinions. Perhaps he thought it best to leave the controversy to the consideration of mathematicians and astronomers. Galileo does treat the opinion of Copernicus; his discussion occurs in the separate question he devotes to the order of the heavenly orbs. Carbone compresses the material, which he acknowledges in his prefatory remarks: "Although much could be said by repeating materials from the astronomers, we will reduce the much to a little." In this and the remaining parts of the commentary the tangential interest of Carbone in astronomy is quite apparent. Since the subject matter by its nature demands a specialized vocabulary and a prescribed order of discussion, it is not surprising that Carbone's text is almost identical in language and in structure to that part of Galileo's that deals with the topic (G1–11).

The Carbone text reflects the opinions and order of Galileo's discussion precisely, beginning with the first opinion that there is only one heaven, through those holding the existence of eight, nine, ten, and eleven heavens. Both agree that there are ten movable heavens and an eleventh, immovable one. But Carbone is more interested in describing the importance of the eleventh to Christian doctrine as "the empyrean heaven, so called from light, where the Blessed Spirits dwell" and where "the Angels were created."

The last chapter of Carbone's *De caelo* to bear a marked resemblance to Galileo's MS 46 is the eleventh, concerned with the cause of the motion of the heavens: "Are the heavens moved by some intrinsic or extrinsic principle, or by an Intelligence, or by God?" Several of the opinions and two of the conclusions are in agreement with Galileo's treatment in his sixth question. Carbone examines those who say the heavens are moved by chance, by the will of God, and by a proper form. The last of these possibilities is noted by Galileo, as is the conclusion that they are moved by an assisting intelligence. In commenting on the Intelligences and their method of moving the heavens, Carbone diverges from Galileo, his discussion becoming very theological in nature: "Hence it is that theologians say that all bodies obey Intelligences in order to local motion. . . . But this motive power is not really distinct from the substance of the Angel, but only formally, as the powers of the soul [are related] to its essence." The philosophical term *Intelligence* has been converted by Carbone, unwittingly, into a theological one: *angel*.

Since the provenance of the rest of *De caelo* is not clear and it bears no strong parallels to Galileo's MS 46, I will curtail my discussion of the content at this point, referring the reader to the annotated Appendices for further details. From what I have shown of Carbone's commentary, however, some final observations about it would seem to be in order. First, in particular, it appears obvious that both Galileo and Carbone are working from the same group of notes in the Collegio series. Also, it may be surmised that Carbone, whose manuscript is dated 1594, may have had later exemplars at his disposal. Emphases and concerns may have shifted by that time and so found their way into Carbone's manuscript. And, as we have observed, his interests are different from Galileo's and also from those of the professors whose notes he used. They were primarily philosophers; he was a theologian who was concerned with providing general instruction in other areas as well, especially in rhetoric.

In general, I would add that, in my previous writings on Galileo, I have noted how his failure to achieve demonstrative certitude led him to make more and more use of rhetoric and dialectical reasoning when advancing his claims in support of the Copernican system. In Carbone's achievement we can see something of the converse at work. Not a scientist in any sense, but one well versed in the grammatical, rhetorical, and logical arts, Carbone toward the end of his life tried to clarify Aristotle's thought on the most difficult subject taught in the Renaissance, the nature of the heavens. Perhaps it is not too much to suggest that the merging of these two talents, those of the scientist and the humanist, respectively, was a stronger factor than has hitherto been recognized in the birth of the modern era.

Our examination of Carbone's manuscript also offers further testimony to the remarkable influence the professors of the Collegio Romano had on its students, an influence that carried far beyond their own college and the schools and colleges of the order. Certainly Carbone added much of his own in style and content to his writings, but he would have been the first to acknowledge the breadth and depth of the insights of the Renaissance Jesuits in subjects ranging from rhetoric and logic to natural philosophy and theology. That he was an extraordinary pupil, appreciative of his teachers while himself being gifted with sensitive pedagogical talent, is a judgment reinforced by his Commentary on Aristotle's *De caelo*.

APPENDIX I: SUMMARY OF THE CONTENTS OF
CARBONE'S MANUSCRIPT

1r   The Virgin Mother of God be with me! Commentaries and Questions on the four books of Aristotle's *De caelo*, by the author, Doctor Ludovico Carbone of Costaciaro, in the year 1594

2r   *Prolegomena to the four books* De caelo
       Chap. 1. On the relationship of these books to the foregoing
2v   Chap. 2. On the object of these books
       Four conclusions, three objections with replies.

3v	Chap. 3. On the inscription of these books
	Chap. 4. On the importance of this science *De caelo*
4r	Chap. 5. On the division of these books
4v	Chap. 6. On the division of the first book
5r	ON THE FIRST AND SECOND BOOKS *DE CAELO*
	Summary of the text of the first book
8r	Summary of the text of the second book
10v	*First Treatise: On the Universe*
	Chap. 1. On the name and division of the universe.
11v	Chap. 2. On the causes of the world and of its definition or description
	Definition through the four causes.
12v	Chap. 3. On the perfection of the universe, or of certain fundamentals required for explaining the world's perfection
	Four fundamentals.
13v	Chap. 4. Of certain conclusions with which one responds to the proposed difficulty
	Four conclusions.
15r	Chap. 5. Certain difficulties are proposed and solved.
16v	Chap. 6. On the unity of the world
	Three arguments to the contrary; two opinions; three conclusions; replies to the arguments
18v	Chap. 7. Can there be many worlds?
	Arguments to the contrary; two opinions; single conclusion; replies to the arguments.
20r	Chap. 8. Whether this world is so perfect that it cannot be made more perfect?
	Three arguments to the contrary; ten conclusions; replies to the arguments.
22r	Chap. 9. Can God make other worlds that are more perfect?
	Single conclusion; three doubts and their solutions.
23r	*Second Treatise: On the Heavens*
	Chap. 1. On the order of this treatise
	Chap. 2. Whether the heavens are composed of the elements, or whether they are a kind of fifth substance
	Five arguments in favor of elemental composition; two opinions; single conclusion; replies to the arguments.
25r	Chap. 3. Are the heavens composed of matter and form?
	Five opinions; seven conclusions; replies to difficulties
31r	Chap. 4. Whether the heavens are animated
	Arguments for the affirmative; three opinions; seven conclusions; replies to the arguments.
33v	Chap. 5. Whether the heavens are corruptible
	Arguments to the contrary; a single fundamental; three conclusions; replies to the arguments.
35v	Chap. 6. Whether the heavens are the most perfect of all bodies
	Arguments in favor of both sides; three opinions; two fundamentals; four conclusions; replies to the arguments.

38r	Chap. 7. On the [continuous] quantity [of the heavens] Seven conclusions, interspersed with objections and replies.
41v	Chap. 8. Whether there is a difference of position in the heavens Three opinions; two fundamentals; two conclusions
43v	Chap. 9. On the number and order of the heavens Difficulties; five opinions; five conclusions; replies to the difficulties.
45v	Chap. 10. On the motion of the heavens Difficulties; three opinions; two conclusions.
46r	Chap. 11. Are the heavens moved by some intrinsic or extrinsic principle, or by an Intelligence, or by God? Arguments in favor of both sides; four opinions; four conclusions; replies to the arguments.
51v	Chap. 12. What kind of motion is found in the heavens Four conclusions relating to circular motion; difficulties; three additional conclusions.
53r	Chap. 13. On certain difficulties concerning the nature of the stars Six difficulties, with their solutions.
55v	*Third Treatise: On the Action of the Heavens on Inferior [Bodies]* Chap. 1. Whether the heavens act on inferior [bodies] through motion Four statements explaining Aristotle's opinion; three conclusions, interspersed with objections and their solutions.
58r	Chap. 2. Whether the heavens act through light, by heating Three conclusions; doubts, with their solutions.
59v	Chap. 3. Whether, if the motion and influx of the heavens were to cease, inferior [bodies] here would perish Three opinions; three conclusions.
61r	Chap. 4. Whether the heavens act on inferior [bodies] here through influences Two opinions; four conclusions.
66v	ON THE THIRD AND FOURTH BOOKS *DE CAELO* Chap. 1. On the relation of this second part with the foregoing
67r	Chap. 2. On the division of the third book Summary of the text of the third book
69r	Summary of the text of the fourth book
70r	*Treatise on the Elements* Chap. 1. whether there are elements Single conclusion.
71r	Chap. 2. On the number of the elements Difficulties; five conclusions; replies to the difficulties
74r	Chap. 3. On the essence of the elements Description and definition; single conclusion.
74v	Chap. 4. On the forms of the elements Difficulties; two conclusions; replies to the difficulties.
76r	Chap. 5. On nobility, whether fire is more noble than the other [elements] Arguments in favor of each element; conclusion in favor of fire.

76v	Chap. 6. On the quantity of the elements and of their qualities
	Two statements on their quantity; four on their qualities
77v	Chap. 7. On the [motive] qualities with regard to their sufficiency
	Three statements.
	Chap. 8. On the definition of these qualities
	Definitions of gravity and levity.
78r	Chap. 9. On the intension and remission of these qualities
	Six conclusions.
79r	Chap. 10. On the terminus of these qualities
	A difficulty; a single conclusion replying to it.
79v	Chap. 11. On the connection and ordering of the motive [and active] qualities
	Three conclusions, interspersed with objections and replies.
80r	Chap. 12. Whether the motive qualities of the elements differ in species
	A difficulty; a single conclusion replying to it.
81r	Chap. 13. On the application of these [motive] qualities to the elements themselves.
	Difficulties relating to earth, water, and air; three statements.
85r	ON ARISTOTLE'S BOOKS *DE GENERATIONE*
86r	*Prolegomena to the books* De generatione
	Chap. 1. On the object of these books
88v	Chap. 2. On the division of these books
89r	*Treatise on Generation*
	Chap. 1. Whether there is generation, and whether substantial generation differs from accidental generation
90v	Chap. 2. What is generation
94r	Chap. 3. What is the terminus of generation
98v	Chap. 4. On the subject of generation
107v	Chap. 5. How secondary and particular causes concur in generation
115v	Chap. 6. How God concurs here in the actions of inferior [bodies]
120v	*Treatise on Corruption*
	Chap. 1. Whether corruption is natural
122v	Chap. 2. Whether the generation of one thing is the corruption of another
126r	Chap. 3. Whether generation and corruption are motions
129v	*Treatise on Alteration*
	Chap. 1. On the name and definition of alteration, and whether it is subalternated to generation
	Explanations of the three topics in the title.
131v	Chap. 2. What is alteration, and of the terminus and subject of alteration
	Explanations of the three topics in the title.
134v	Chap. 3. How intension and remission take place in qualities
	Two opinions; three fundamentals; four conclusions.
145v	Chap. 4. Whether alteration is a continuous change
	Three notations; three opinions; three conclusions.

151r	*Treatise on Action*
	Chap. 1. What is action, and what does Aristotle teach on it
157r	Chap. 2. Whether all action is effected through contact
164v	Chap. 3. Whether a thing can act on itself, and similars on similars
171r	Chap. 4. Whether every agent while acting also reacts
179r	*Treatise on Compounds*
	Chap. 1. On the nature of compounds
181v	Chap. 2. Whether the forms of the elements remain in each minimal part of the compound
186r	Chap. 3. Whether the forms of the elements remain formally in the compound
187v	*Treatise on the Four Qualities*
	Single Chapter: On Certain Difficulties
188r	First difficulty: Are two qualities active and two passive
	Six conclusions.
189r	Second difficulty: Which of the qualities is more active
	Three conclusions.
189v	Third through thirteenth difficulties
	Statements of the difficulty and a simple response to each.
196r	Index of treatises and chapters contained in this volume

APPENDIX II: SUMMARY OF THE CONTENTS OF
GALILEO'S MANUSCRIPT 46

[Mutilated at the beginning, folios possibly missing]

4r	[QUESTIONS ON ARISTOTLE'S *DE CAELO*]
	[*Introductory Treatise*]
	Quest. 1. What is Aristotle's subject matter in his books *De caelo*
	Six opinions; four conclusions; six objections, with replies.
6v	Quest. 2. On the order, connection, and title of these books
	Three opinions; a single conclusion, with proofs and replies to arguments contained in opposing opinions.
7v	*Treatise on the Universe*
	Quest. 1. On the opinion of ancient philosophers concerning the universe
	Five opinions; an objection and reply; two conclusions.
8v	Quest. 2. The truth concerning the origin of the universe
	Seven conclusions, including a last dating the origin.
10v	Quest. 3. On the unity and perfection of the universe
	Six queries, with replies to each.
13r	Quest. 4. Could the universe have existed from eternity
	Four opinions; three conclusions, with proofs and confirmations.
16v	*Treatise on the Heavens*
	Quest. 1. Is there only one heaven
	Five opinions; a single conclusion, with proofs; three notations; replies to arguments in the opposing opinions.

22r	Quest. 2. On the order of the heavenly orbs
	Two opinions and their rejection; a single conclusion, with proofs; objections, with their replies.
26r	Quest. 3. Are the heavens one of the simple bodies or composed of them
	Three arguments in favor; two opinions; two conclusions, with objections and replies; replies to the three arguments in favor.
30v	Quest. 4. Are the heavens incorruptible
	Two opinions; a distinction; two conclusions, with proofs, difficulties and replies; refutation of arguments for the first opinion.
34r	Quest. 5. Are the heavens composed of matter and form
	Two general opinions; two conclusions; a subsidiary query and its reply.
51r	Quest. 6. Are the heavens animated
	Four opinions; three preliminary conclusions; three additional positions; two propositions; difficulties, with replies.

[To 56v, after which folios are probably missing . . .]

57r	[QUESTIONS ON ARISTOTLE'S *DE GENERATIONE*]
	[*Tractate on Alteration*]
	[Quest. 1. On alteration]
	A fragment on the terminus of alteration.
	Quest. 2. On intension and remission
	Authorities who have treated this; three notations; four conclusions, with proofs, objections, and replies.
63r	Quest. 3. On the parts and degrees of quality
	Six notations; a query and its reply.
65v	*Tractate on the Elements*
67v	First Part: On the Quiddity and Substance of the Elements
	Quest. 1. On the definitions of an element
	Two notations, explanation of Aristotle's definition.
68v	Quest. 2. On the material, efficient, and final cause of the elements
	A causal analysis of the elements.
69v	Quest. 3. What are the forms of the elements
	Four opinions; three conclusions, with arguments against the opposing opinions.
71v	Quest. 4. Do the forms of the elements undergo intension and remission
	Two opinions, with arguments in favor of the second; to folio 74v, patently an incomplete exposition.

[Folios missing between 74v and 75r]

75v	[Quest. 5. On the number and continuous quantity of the elements]
	Title and introduction missing; concerned with the two queries in the title, plus the maxima and minima of elements, on which there are eight notations, four opinions, ten conclusions, and replies to the arguments favoring the first opinion.
88v	Second Part: On Primary Qualities
	Quest. 1. On the number of primary qualities
	Three notations, each with objections and replies.

90r   Quest. 2. Are all four qualities positive, or are some privative
       Four opinions; three conclusions, with proofs; replies to the arguments in support of the first opinion.
92v   Quest. 3. Are all four qualities active
       Source of the difficulty; six notations, including objections and replies.
96v   Quest. 4. How are primary qualities involved in activity and resistance
       Three conclusions; three corollaries; four notations and the beginning of a fifth; incomplete.

[To 100v, after which folios are again missing]

11   Foscarini's Defense of Copernicanism
RICHARD J. BLACKWELL

In February 1616 the Catholic church decided to condemn Copernican heliocentrism as false and contrary to the Scriptures. More specifically two Copernican propositions were censured by the Consultors of the Holy Office as follows:

1. The sun is the center of the world and is completely immobile by local motion.

Censure: All agreed that this proposition is foolish and absurd in philosophy and is formally heretical, because it explicitly contradicts sentences found in many places in Sacred Scripture according to the proper meaning of the words and according to the common interpretation and understanding of the Holy Fathers and of learned theologians.

2. The earth is not the center of the world and is not immobile but moves as a whole and also with a diurnal motion.

Censure: All agreed that this proposition receives the same censure in philosophy; and in respect to theological truth, it is at least erroneous in faith.[1]

The reason for the weaker condemnation of the second proposition is that it was considered to be contrary to the Scriptures only indirectly by inference from the explicit words of the Bible.

This decision had to be promulgated publicly before it could become official, which was accomplished by a decree issued by the Congregation of the Index on 5 March 1616. The relevant section of this decree reads as follows:

It has come to the attention of this Sacred Congregation that the Pythagorean doctrine of the mobility of the earth and the immobility of the sun, which is false and completely contrary to the divine Scriptures, and which is taught by Nicholas Copernicus in his *De revolutionibus orbium coelestium* and by Diego de

---

1. Sergio M. Pagano, *I documenti del processo di Galileo Galilei* (Vatican City: Pontificia Academia Scientiarum, 1984), Scripta Varia 53, 99–100. All translations in this paper are by the author.

Zuñiga in his *Commentary on Job*, is now being divulged and accepted by many. This can be seen from the letter published by a Carmelite priest, entitled *Letter of Fr. Paolo Antonio Foscarini on the Opinion of the Pythagoreans and of Copernicus on the Mobility of the Earth and the Stability of the Sun and on the New Pythagorean System of the World*, Naples: Lazzaro Scoriggio, 1615. In this letter the said Father tries to show that the above-mentioned doctrine of the immobility of the sun in the center of the world and of the mobility of the earth is both in agreement with the truth and is not contrary to Sacred Scripture. Therefore, lest this opinion spread further and endanger Catholic truth, it is ordered that the said Nicholas Copernicus' *De revolutionibus orbium* and Diego de Zuñiga's *Commentary on Job* are suspended until corrected; also that the book of the Carmelite Father Paolo Antonio Foscarini is completely prohibited and condemned; and also all other books teaching the same thing are prohibited, as the present Decree prohibits, condemns, and suspends them all respectively.[2]

It is evident from the wording of this decree that Foscarini's *Letter*[3] was considered to be the main offender because it explicitly attempted to reconcile Scripture with the new astronomy. Unlike the writings of Copernicus and of Diego de Zuñiga, which were judged to be correctable[4] (actually no "corrected" version of either book was ever published), Foscarini's *Letter* was seen as beyond the pale of correction, condemned with no hope of redemption.

Yet despite the undeniably prominent role of Foscarini's *Letter* in this condemnation, Galileo scholars have almost completely ignored it.[5] This is doubtlessly due in some degree to the inexplicable fact that Favaro did not include the *Letter* in his definitive edition, *Le Opere di Galileo Galilei*.[6] The purpose of this paper is to begin to fill this void

---

2. Ibid., 102–3.

3. The full title of the *Letter* is *Lettera sopra l'opinione de' Pittagorici e del Copernico della mobilità della terra, e stabilità del sole, e del nuovo Pittagorico sistema del mondo, al Reverendiss. P. M. Sebastiano Fantone, generale dell'ordine carmelitano, nella quale si accordano ed appaciano i luoghi della Sacra Scrittura, e le proposizioni teologiche, che giammai possano addursi contro di tale opinione.* It was dated 6 January 1615.

4. The correction for Diego de Zuñiga's book would have been simply to drop the few pages on Job 9:6 from his *Commentary on Job* (1584). The corrections for Copernicus's book, announced in "Monitum Sacrae Congregationis ad Nicholai Copernici lectorem" (1620), consisted of (1) omitting a disrespectful remark about Lactantius in the Dedicatory Preface, (2) dropping isolated assertions that the earth moves, and (3) eliminating the whole of Book I, Chapter 8, which is devoted to refuting the traditional Aristotelian-Ptolemaic arguments for an earth at rest in the center of the universe.

5. We have been able to find no studies of the *Letter* in English and only two article-length papers in Italian: Bruno Basile, "Galileo e il teologo 'Copernicano' Paolo Antonio Foscarini" *Rivista di Letteratura Italiana* 1 (1983): 63–96; and Stefano Caroti, "Un sostenitore napoletano della mobilità della terra: il padre Paolo Antonio Foscarini," in *Galileo e Napoli*, ed. F. Lomonaco and M. Torrini (Naples: Guida, 1987), 81–121.

6. Twenty volumes in 21 (Florence: G. Barbèra Editore, 1890–1909). Hereafter referred to simply as *Opere*.

by examining the argument of the *Letter* and its role in the Galileo affair.

THE AUTHOR AND HIS LETTER

Paolo Antonio Foscarini was born in Montaltro Uffugo in Calabria. His birth date is given variously as 1565 or 1580, and his death as 1615 or 10 June 1616. There is disputed evidence indicating that his original surname was *Scarini* but that he changed it to *Foscarini* to associate himself gainfully with the prominent and noble Venetian family of that name.[7] We do know that he was a Carmelite priest, that he was trained as a theologian and served as a professor of theology for his order, that he was twice appointed Provincial of the Carmelite Order in Calabria, and that he was reputed to be learned in many areas, including mathematics and astronomy. From his writings it is clear that he was not professionally trained in astronomy. But he was well informed about developments in that field, including the recent telescopic discoveries made by Galileo, for whom he had a great admiration. We have not been able to find any information as to what occasioned him to write his *Letter,* which appeared as a total surprise to Galileo and his friends.

The first edition of the *Letter* was rigorously suppressed after the Decree of 5 March 1616, and as a result copies of it are rather rare.[8] There were three later publications of the Italian text: Fiorenza in 1710, Milano in 1811, and Firenze in 1850.[9] A Latin translation by David Lotaeus[10] appeared in Northern Europe after Galileo's trial in *Systema cosmicum di Galileo Galilei,* which went through numer-

---

7. For this evidence and both sides of this dispute, see Antonio Favaro, "Serie nona di scampoli galileiana #63: Paolo Antonio Foscarini," in *Accademia Patavina di Science, Lettere ed Arti, Atti e Memorie* (Padua: 1894), vol. 10, 33–36; and P. Anastase de Saint-Paul, "Paul-Antoine Foscarini," in *Dictionnaire de théologique catholique* (Paris: Letouzey et Ané, 1933), vol. 12, 53–55.

8. We have not located any copies of the first edition (Naples: Lazzaro Scoriggio, 1615; 64 pp.) in the United States, but do know of two copies in Rome, one in the Biblioteca Apostolica Vaticana, the other in the Biblioteca Nazionale Centrale. The latter copy was originally in the Jesuit library of the Collegio Romano, which was taken over by the Italian state government in the nineteenth century.

9. The 1850 edition is the best Italian text. It is located in *Opere di Galileo Galilei, prima edizione condotta . . . ,* ed. d'Alberi (Florence, 1842–56), vol. 5, 455–94. Quotations from the *Letter* given later in this paper are taken from this 1850 edition.

10. It might be noted that Lotaeus abridged two brief remarks (both appearing on p. 475 of the 1850 edition mentioned in note 9) acknowledging the infallibility of the pope. Salusbury's English version was made from Lotaeus' Latin text and so reflects the same deletions.

ous editions from 1635 to 1699. Thomas Salusbury prepared an English version,[11] now quite archaic and florid in style, from the Latin text.

THE CONTENT OF THE LETTER

In the first few pages of the *Letter* Foscarini is crystal clear about his intentions. He wishes to show that the newly revived heliocentric astronomy is not inconsistent with various biblical passages and theological doctrines that at first sight may seem to assert a geocentric model of the universe. Put positively, he wishes to argue that these scriptural texts and theological doctrines can be easily reinterpreted along Copernican lines. He is quite aware that his undertaking was bold and daring. As he explicitly says, "As far as I know, and may it be pleasing to God, I am without doubt the first one to undertake this project."[12] The fact that the *Letter* was a direct attempt at biblical reinterpretation is undoubtedly the reason why the *Letter* was condemned so totally by the church a year later.

Foscarini's main point is that if this reinterpretation is published, and if at some later time Copernicanism is proved to be true, then the church can use his work to prevent the scandalous implication that the Bible contains error. Nowhere in the *Letter* does Foscarini say that heliocentrism is already established as true. Rather he claims only that it is at least as probable as geocentrism. It is obvious that his sympathies lie with Copernicanism, and toward the end of the *Letter* he concludes, "It is very clear that the opinion of Pythagoras and Copernicus is so probable that it is perhaps more likely than the common opinion of Ptolemy."[13] But that is as far as he goes.

Unfortunately Foscarini is less clear in his conception of the relations between science and Scripture. In some places he seems to argue that human reason alone can never attain certitude and hence should be viewed as inferior to, and correctable by, the certain content of revelation.[14] But in several other places he indicates that it is possible for natural knowledge, and specifically astronomy, to attain full certitude.[15] In such cases he adopts the old Augustinian principle that

11. In Thomas Salusbury, *Mathematical Collections and Translations* (London: Wm. Leybourn, 1661), vol. 1, 473–503. The present writer has prepared a modern English translation, which he plans to publish in the near future.
12. *Lettera...*, in *Opere di Galileo Galilei, prima edizione condotta...*, ed. d'Alberi (Florence, 1842–56), vol. 5, 461.
13. Ibid., 489.
14. For the clearest example of this, see ibid., 458.
15. The most explicit of such passages is at ibid., 461.

the Bible should then be reinterpreted accordingly. Foscarini as theologian leans toward the former view, Foscarini as the amateur scientist leans toward the latter view, and the tension remains unresolved. It would seem, however, that the latter view must have predominated, at least when he wrote the *Letter*, for otherwise there would really be no need to reinterpret Scripture.[16]

This brings us to the substantive content of the *Letter*. Foscarini argues that there are six classes of biblical passages and theological doctrines that seem to conflict with Copernicanism. These potential objections in some way say the following (the fourth and sixth are not biblical but theological):

(1) The earth is stationary and does not move (for example, "You have made firm the orb of the earth, which will not move." Psalms 93:1).

(2) The sun is moved and rotates around the earth ("The sun rises, and sets, and returns to its place; reborn there, it rotates through the south and is curved toward the north." Ecclesiastes 1:5–6).

(3) The heavens are at the top and the earth is at the bottom ("I will display portents in heaven above and signs on earth below." Joel 3:3).

(4) Hell is in the center of the earth (a common opinion of theologians).

(5) The earth is contrasted with the heavens as a center to a circumference. ("The first man, being from earth, is earthly; the second man, being from heaven, is celestial." 1 Corinthians 15:47–48).

(6) After judgment day the sun will stop in the east and the moon in the west (a common opinion of the Fathers and theologians).[17]

Foscarini's strategy is simply to show that the basic principles of biblical exegesis allow a reading of the preceding groups of scriptural texts and theological doctrines that agrees with heliocentrism. To accomplish this he introduces next six principles of interpretation[18] (not

---

16. Caroti, "Un sostenitore napoletano," argues that Foscarini may well have become personally convinced of Copernicanism in about 1614 (while he was writing his seven volume encyclopedic survey of the arts and sciences), but he treats Copernicanism in his writings only as a probable hypothesis for strategic reasons.

Bruno Basile, "Galileo e il teologo," takes the opposite point of view. Basile, however, is quite correct in his main thesis, namely, that there was a close and profound relationship between Foscarini and Galileo, although Galileo was forced by prudence to remain silent on this because of the strong negative reaction to Foscarini's *Letter* and its subsequent condemnation.

17. These six groups of objections are located in the *Letter*, pp. 462–65, of the 1850 d'Alberi edition, which we have been quoting.

18. Ibid., 465–89.

in a one-to-one correspondence with the six groups of objections), which he uses to discuss the objections in considerable detail. But oddly enough only the first of these is a theological principle of exegesis; the remaining five are philosophical principles of a scholastic and quasi-Aristotelian character.[19] He seems unaware of the objection that this raises: namely, if his own philosophy is less than certain, then like astronomy, it should not be used on Augustinian grounds to reinterpret Scripture to find its true sense.

At any rate his "first and most important" principle, which breaks no new ground, is the following:

> When Sacred Scripture attributes something to God or to any creature which would otherwise be improper and incommensurate, then it should be interpreted and explained in one or more of the following ways. First it is said to pertain metaphorically and proportionally, or by similitude. Secondly . . . it is said according to our mode of consideration . . . Thirdly it is said according to the vulgar opinion and the common way of speaking. . . . Fourthly it is said under the guise of some human aspect.[20]

After applying this principle in great detail to the six sets of objections to heliocentrism, he draws the main conclusion in the *Letter* as follows:

> Coming thus to our main point, and using the same argument, if the Pythagorean opinion were true, it would be easy to reconcile it with those passages of Sacred Scripture which are contrary to it, and especially those passages of our first and second groups, by using our principle; that is, by saying that in those places Scripture speaks according to our mode of understanding, and according to appearances, and in respect to us. For thus it is that those bodies appear to be related to us and are described by the common and vulgar mode of human thinking; namely, the earth seems to stand still and to be immobile, and the sun seems to rotate around it. And hence Scripture serves us by speaking in the vulgar and common manner; from our point of view it seems that the earth stands firmly in the center and that the sun revolves around it, rather than the contrary. The same thing happens when people are carried in a small boat on the sea near the shore; to them it seems that the shore moves and is carried backward, rather than that they move forward, which is the truth.[21]

Foscarini's last five philosophical principles are worthy of a quick summary if only to illustrate how completely the mode of argumentation changes. His second principle is that God has implanted in all

---

19. Caroti, "Un sostenitore napoletano," 104ff., has shown that Foscarini based these five principles on his reading of Copernicus' *De revolutionibus*, Book I, esp. chap. 8.
20. *Letter*, 465–66.
21. Ibid., 472.

things an immutable law governing their being, nature, and motions. Thus the motions of the earth are stable and fixed; that is what the Scriptures mean when they say that the earth is immobile. The third principle is that if only a part of a thing is moved, it cannot be said to be moved simply and absolutely. For example, if a glass of sea water is moved, the sea itself cannot be said to have moved. So when part of the earth changes in substance, quality, or quantity, as in the cycle of life and death, it is not changed as a whole. Thus the earth is immobile. The fourth principle is that nothing as a whole can be moved from its natural place, although its parts can be so moved violently. Now the natural place of the earth is to be in the fixed path of the third orbit; so again the earth is immobile, as the Bible says. The fifth is that the earth is a perpetual, not a contingent, creature. Thus its parts cannot be separated from itself as a whole, and hence it is stable and immutable. The sixth and last principle is that a comparative predicate is properly attributed to a thing when it is related to the whole (or nearly all) of its class. For instance, a person is said to be tall in relation to the average height of all humans, not just pygmies or giants. Hence the earth is said to be low in comparison to the whole universe, and not just in relation to a few of the planets. Thus the Scripture properly says that the earth is low because it is rather close to the center and even though it is above the sun, Venus, and Mercury. This is also used to explain how Christ could "descend" to earth and "ascend" into heaven, and the sense in which hell is in the center of the earth.

The last pages of the *Letter* contain a Neoplatonic description of the sun as a majestic god ruling in the center of the three heavens, and an arcane discussion of a series of biblical passages that supposedly indicate heliocentrism, including a long symbolic analysis of the candelabra constructed for the Temple, which is described in Exodus 25:31–35. Despite the disjointed character of the discussion in these last pages, Foscarini has not lost sight of his main objective, as he makes a final judgment about Copernicanism.

> From it one can derive the most precise system, and the hidden constitution, of the world in a way which is more solidly based on reason and experience than is the common opinion. It is also quite clear that the new opinion can be explained in such a way that there is no longer any need to be concerned whether it is contrary to passages of Sacred Scripture or to the justification of theological propositions.[22]

---

22. Ibid., 489.

THE CONTROVERSY OVER THE LETTER

The reactions to Foscarini's letter were immediate and mostly hostile, the main exception being those of Galileo and his friends, some of whom were ecstatic.[23] A reconstruction of the sequence of events in this hostile response is revealing. Initially someone must have registered a formal complaint at the Holy Office against the *Letter*. This can be inferred from the fact that there exists an undated and unsigned document[24] giving a theological opinion on the orthodoxy of the *Letter*, a normal early step in processing such complaints. This theologian's negative opinion is disappointingly superficial. In addition to calling Copernicanism a rash opinion and to disputing a few textual interpretations, the author of the document simply says, "His [Foscarini's] reconciliation contorts the Sacred Scriptures, and explains them contrary to the common explication of the Holy Fathers, which agrees with the more common, indeed the most common, and most true opinion of almost all astronomers." In short Copernicanism was not the received view at that time: neither a new nor a helpful point to make.

This document must have been seen by Foscarini, because he wrote, probably in late March or early April 1615, a strongly worded *Defense*[25] of his *Letter* that replied directly to the unnamed theologian's report. In many ways the *Defense* was Foscarini's finest hour. The style is more vigorous and the content more substantive than in the *Letter*. After first registering a bitter complaint about the theologian's characterization of Copernicanism as a "rash" opinion, he immediately raises a new and central question: what is the status of the authority of the Fathers of the Church in this issue of heliocentrism? His answer is unequivocal. One must distinguish carefully between matters that pertain to faith and morals and other matters that pertain to natural

---

23. On 7 March 1615 Prince Cesi sent a copy of Foscarini's *Letter* to Galileo, along with his own letter (*Opere*, XII, 150), in which he says, "This book could not have appeared at a better time." So Galileo must have read the *Letter* by mid- or late March, when, as we know from other sources, he was in the midst of composing his own *Letter to the Grand Duchess Christina*, which treats of the same topics. For a study of the relations between Foscarini's *Letter* and Galileo's *Letter*, see Basile, "Galileo e il teologo." Galileo carefully avoided mention of Foscarini by name since he had reason to believe (from a letter from Campoli, 21 March 1615 [*Opere*, XII, 160]) that Foscarini's *Letter* would in time be condemned by the Holy Office, which proved to be true.

24. The Latin text of this document, probably written sometime in March 1615, can be found in Domenico Berti, "Antecedenti al processo galileiano e alla condonna della doctrina copernicana," in *Atti della R. Accademia dei Lincei* 1881–82, Serie terza, Memorie della classe di scienze morali, storiche e filologiche (Rome: Coi Tipi del Salvicuci, 1882), vol. 10, 72–73.

25. Ibid., 73–78.

human knowledge. The authority of the Church Fathers extends only to the former, and not to the latter; indeed some of them deliberately avoided the latter to devote themselves more completely to the word of God. Second, the heliocentrism-geocentrism debate is definitely not a matter of faith or morals. As a result the authority of the Church Fathers is irrelevant in regard to heliocentrism, and one not only can but should disagree with them if and when reason and experience establish a different view of the natural world. This is the core of the *Defense*. As a justification Foscarini quotes the Church's own documents.

But this latter restriction [that is, to matters pertaining to faith and morals] is most correctly stated by the Council of Trent, Session IV, and before that by the Second Lateran Council under Leo X, and by many other Councils, with the urging and assistance of the Holy Spirit. For all the Councils declare that the very words which I introduced above [that is, the authority of the Holy Fathers prevails] should be understood as referring to matters which pertain to faith and morals. However in matters which pertain to the natural sciences and which are discovered and are open to investigation by human reason, the Sacred Scripture ought not to be interpreted otherwise than according to what human reason itself establishes from natural experience and according to what is clear from innumerable data.[26]

Granting this distinction between matters of faith and morals versus matters of natural knowledge as a distinction between the domains of religion and of science, Foscarini proceeds to make effective use of Augustine's warning that in the latter area one should not be rigidly committed to one point of view, since natural knowledge grows and changes, especially if one wishes to use that knowledge in the interpretation of Scripture. For in the latter case outmoded natural knowledge can cause a scandal to the faithful. The application of this maxim to the astronomy debate is obvious.

[I]n matters pertaining to the sciences acquired by human effort, no one ought to be so addicted to a philosophical sect, or to defend some philosophical opinion with such tenacity, that he thinks that the whole of Sacred Scripture should henceforth be understood accordingly. For otherwise, since something new is always being added to the human sciences, and since many things are seen with the passage of time to be false which previously were thought to be true, it could happen that, when the falsity of a philosophical opinion has been detected, the authority of the Scriptures would be destroyed since that authority has been based on an interpretation which we had thought was true and correct (but nevertheless it was not). Therefore we should not be so tenaciously committed to the philosophy of Aristotle or to Ptolemy's world system that we seem to wish to defend them as we would home and hearth.[27]

26. Ibid., 75.
27. Ibid., 77.

Foscarini's main theological principle of exegesis in the *Letter* is the notion that the meaning of the Bible is often stated in terms accommodated to human language and understanding. This is expanded in the last pages of the *Defense* with an elaborate but traditional discussion of the levels of meaning in the Scriptures: literal or historical versus spiritual, with the former subdivided into proper and figurative. The question then becomes whether the geocentric language of the Bible is to be taken as proper or figurative, with Foscarini obviously opting for the latter. This not only supports the main argument of the *Letter* but also grounds his view more firmly in the established tradition, including Cardinal Bellarmine's parallel discussion in his *De controversiis*, I, 3, "On the Interpretation of the Word of God."

When Foscarini wrote his *Defense*, his strategy was to send it, along with the *Letter*, to Bellarmine for the cardinal's judgment on the matter. This he did, probably in early April, and Bellarmine's letter of reply to Foscarini, dated 12 April 1615,[28] was precisely to the point, although it was not what Foscarini wanted to hear. Bellarmine's letter makes three points, the second of which was particularly devastating. First he congratulates Foscarini (and also Galileo by name[29]) for assigning a hypothetical, rather than a realistic, status to the Copernican theory, a point of view that is said to "contain nothing dangerous." This was probably intended more as a piece of prudential advice than as a factual report on the convictions of the two men.

The second point in Bellarmine's letter deals with the critical issue of the extent of the authority of the Fathers of the Church. After pointing out that all the Fathers agree on a literal, geocentric reading of the Scriptures, Bellarmine proceeds to reject Foscarini's use of the notion of matters of faith and morals.

> Nor can one reply that this is not a matter of faith, because even if it is not a matter of faith because of the subject matter [*ex parte objecti*], it is still a matter of faith because of the speaker [*ex parte dicentis*]. Thus anyone who would say that Abraham did not have two sons and Jacob twelve would be just as much of a heretic as someone who would say that Christ was not born of a virgin, for the Holy Spirit has said both of these things through the mouths of the Prophets and the Apostles.[30]

---

28. *Opere*, XII, 171–72. This famous letter has been studied in detail by Galileo scholars but surprisingly not in its proper context, that is, the specific discussions in the two documents by Foscarini, the *Letter* and the *Defense*, which in the first sentence Bellarmine acknowledges having received for his evaluations.

29. This explicit mention of Galileo, who was not a party to the correspondence, may well mean that Bellarmine was using this exchange with Foscarini to communicate his advice or warning indirectly to Galileo.

30. *Opere*, XII, 172.

The origin and significance of this principle of exegesis introduced by Bellarmine are matters that are too complex for analysis here. Suffice it to say that according to this principle everything said in the Scriptures is a matter of faith, from the mere fact of having been stated in the texts of the Bible. If so, the main point of Foscarini's *Defense* has been abolished.

The third item in Bellarmine's letter is much less controversial and could have been agreed to by all concerned. Copernicanism had not yet been proved to be true, and as a result it would be premature at present to reinterpret Scripture accordingly. But the latter would be needed if and when heliocentrism was established by reason and experience.

Foscarini must have been surprised and disappointed by Bellarmine's assessment. But he was not disheartened. For he subsequently turned his efforts toward composing another, more definitive treatise on the whole issue. Galileo's unpublished point by point notes[31] on Bellarmine's letter were most likely prepared to assist Foscarini in readdressing the dispute. As late as 20 June Cesi wrote to Galileo from Rome expressing optimism on Foscarini's progress.

> The treatise by the Father [Foscarini] will arrive soon, and will be a great help because of the care which he has taken to reply fully to all the objections raised here to the contrary. . . .[32]

But we do not know whether Foscarini ever finished, for his new book never appeared, and there is no known manuscript of it or record of what happened to it. At this point the story simply ends. One year later Foscarini had died, of unknown causes, his *Letter* having been placed on the *Index* a few months earlier.

In retrospect the historical importance of Foscarini's *Letter* consists in the central role that it played of voicing the arguments in favor of a reconciliation between Copernicanism and Scripture when this issue was first considered in a formal way by the Catholic church. The church officials who decided instead on a condemnation of Copernicanism in February 1616 certainly knew the *Letter,* and most probably Foscarini's *Defense* as well. They would also have known of Galileo's *Letter to Castelli* (21 December 1613), which had earlier argued for reconciliation. Did they take into account Galileo's much more substantial *Letter to the Grand Duchess Christina,* which was completed in the summer of 1615 but not published until 1636 and so would have been available to them only through private circulation? Furthermore

31. *Opere,* V, 367–70.
32. *Opere,* XII, 189–90.

it is quite unlikely that Campanella's *Apologia pro Galilaeo* influenced their deliberations.[33] As a result Foscarini's *Letter* and *Defense* were, for all practical purposes, the main briefs in favor of reconciliation before the Congregation of the Index as it decided on its fateful Decree of 5 March 1616. On the other hand the quite unexpected publication of Foscarini's *Letter* may also have inadvertently provided an excellent opportunity for the Holy Office to send a forceful, albeit indirect, message to Galileo by placing the *Letter* on the *Index*.

33. Campanella's *Apologia pro Galilaeo, mathematico florentino,* was first published in 1622 in Frankfurt. The date of its composition is unknown, and there is considerable dispute among scholars as to whether it was written before or after the condemnation of Copernicanism in the Decree of 5 March 1616. Campanella wrote his *Apologia* in response to a specific request from Cardinal Boniface Caetani for an evaluation of the new astronomy in relation to the Scriptures. Cardinal Caetani was the curial official charged with formulating the needed corrections to Copernicus' *De revolutionibus* mentioned in the Decree of 5 March 1616. On this see Bernardino M. Bonansea, "Campanella's Defense of Galileo," in *Reinterpreting Galileo,* ed. William A. Wallace (Washington, D.C.: Catholic University of America Press, 1986), 205–39.

12   Galileo and Probable Arguments
EDITH SYLLA

In the final hearing of his trial, Galileo said (Giorgio de Santillana's translation):

> A long time ago, i.e. before the decision of the Holy Congregation of the Index, and before the injunction was intimated to me, I was indifferent and regarded both opinions, namely, that of Ptolemy and that of Copernicus, as open to discussion [*disputabili*], inasmuch as either one or the other might be true in Nature; but after the said decision, assured of the wisdom of the authorities [*prudenza de superiori*], I ceased to have any doubt [*ambiguita*]; and I held, as I still hold, as most true and indisputable [*verissima et indubitata*], the opinion of Ptolemy, that is to say, the stability of the Earth and the motion of the Sun.[1]

A little later in the same hearing, Galileo said with regard to his *Dialogue on the Two Chief World Systems*:

> As regards the writing of the published dialogue, my motive in so doing was not because I held the Copernican doctrine to be true [*non mi son mosso perche io tenga vera l'opinione Copernicana*], but simply, thinking to confer a common benefit, I have set forth the arguments [*raggioni*] from nature and astronomy which may be brought on either side; my object being to make it clear that neither the one set of arguments nor the other has the force of conclusive demonstration [*di concludere dimonstrativamente*] in favor of this opinion or of that; and that therefore, in order to proceed with certainty [*per procedere con sicurezza*], we must have recourse to the decisions [*determinatione*] of higher teaching, as may be clearly seen from a large number of passages in the dialogue in question. I affirm, therefore, on my conscience [*dento di me medesimo*], that I do not now hold the condemned opinion and have not held it since the decision of the authorities.[2]

Despite these statements, Galileo was found guilty of vehement suspicion of heresy. In addition to the suspicion that he believed and held

---

1. Giorgio De Santillana, *The Crime of Galileo* (Chicago: University of Chicago Press, Phoenix Books, 1955), 302. Antonio Favaro, ed., *Le Opere di Galileo Galilei* (Florence: S.A.G. Barbera Editore, 1890–1909, reprinted 1929–39), vol. XIX, 261.
2. De Santillana, *Crime of Galileo*, 303; Favaro, *Opere*, XIX, 361–62.

the doctrine "that the sun is the center of the world and does not move from east to west and that the earth moves and is not the center of the world," he was convicted of believing that

> an opinion may be held and defended as probable after it has been declared and defined to be contrary to the Holy Scripture [*si possa tener e difendere per probabile un'opinione dopo esser stata dichiarata e diffinita per contraria alla sacra scrittura*].[3]

In this paper I attempt to explain how it may have come about that Galileo was found guilty of holding and defending as probable an opinion declared contrary to Holy Scripture. My argument is that in part by writing in letter and dialogue form, Galileo entered into forms of expression in which rhetorical methods and criteria were assumed to hold sway. Galileo, having been trained in philosophy and mathematics, thought in terms of the epistemology of demonstrative sciences, combining with the ideas of Aristotle's *Posterior Analytics* and commentaries thereon considerations more proper to mathematical or Archimedean sciences. In Aristotelian or Archimedean demonstrative sciences, probable or persuasive arguments had little or no weight. When, on the other hand, Galileo addressed physical and religious questions within a rhetorical context, he could not avoid seeming to have a greater commitment to probable arguments than he may have recognized as scientifically justifiable. Although he may not agree with my conclusions, I would like to dedicate this paper to William A. Wallace, in whose honor this volume has been compiled, and for whose scholarship and good judgment I have always had the highest respect.

THE ARISTOTELIAN MODEL

In his *Nichomachean Ethics* Aristotle made a clear distinction between subjects in which certainty is possible and those in which it is not:

> Our discussion will be adequate if it has as much clearness as the subject matter admits of, for precision is not to be sought for alike in all discussions, any more than in all the products of the crafts. . . . We must be content, then, in speaking of such subjects and with such premises to indicate the truth roughly and in outline, and in speaking about things which are only for the most part true and with premises of the same kind to reach conclusions that are no better. In the same spirit, therefore, should each type of statement be *received*; for it is the mark of an educated person to look for precision in each class of things just so far as the nature of the subject admits; it is evidently equally foolish to accept probable reasoning from a mathematician and to demand from a rhetorician scientific proofs.[4]

3. De Santillana, *Crime of Galileo*, 310; *Opere*, XIX, 405.
4. Aristotle, *Ethica Nicomachea*, trans. W. D. Ross, in R. McKeon, ed., *The Basic Works*

For Aristotle, then, certain sciences, such as mathematics and physics, aimed for certainty and scientific demonstrations or proofs, whereas in other areas, such as ethics, the most one could hope for was probable reasoning, where probable reasoning was such as would convince most people or the wisest and most experienced or prudent individuals, although lacking absolute proof.

MEDIEVAL VARIANTS ON THE ARISTOTELIAN MODEL

Thomas Aquinas mirrored this view in the *Summa Theologiae*:

In human affairs it is not possible to have demonstration and infallible proof; but it suffices to have some conjectural probability (*coniecturalis probabilitas*) such as the rhetor uses to persuade.[5]

Since on an Aristotelian view each science is distinct and based on its own principles, Aristotle and Aquinas could advocate one style of argumentation in physics and another in ethics without obvious difficulty. In the thirteenth and fourteenth centuries, when Aristotelianism flourished in the universities alongside Christian theology, natural philosophy could still claim to be autonomous and not subject to theology. In the opinion of such "Averroist" authors as Boethius of Dacia in the thirteenth century and William of Ockham in the fourteenth, there is no problem in saying that certain things are true in natural philosophy that are not true according to Christian belief. Thus one can say that *naturally* it is impossible for something to come into existence out of nothing, but *supernaturally* God can create the world out of nothing, since God is the author of the laws of nature and, as such, capable of transcending them.[6]

---

of Aristotle (New York: Random House, 1941), 1094b12–14, 19–28. I have altered the translation slightly. Cf. Glenn R. Morrow, trans., *Proclus: A Commentary on the First Book of Euclid's Elements* (Princeton, N.J.: Princeton University Press, 1970), 150–51, "But perhaps some persons might mistakenly think this proposition deserves to be ranked among the postulates on the grounds that the angles being less than two right angles makes us at once believe in the convergence and intersection of the straight lines. To them Geminus has given the proper answer when he said that we have learned from the very founders of this science not to pay attention to plausible imaginings in determining what propositions are to be accepted in geometry. Aristotle likewise says that to accept probable reasoning from a geometer is like demanding proofs from a rhetorician. And Simmias is made by Plato to say, I am aware that those who make proofs out of probabilities are imposters."

5. As quoted in Douglas Patey, *Probability and Literary Form: Philosophic Theory and Literary Practice in the Augustine Age* (Cambridge: Cambridge University Press, 1984), 9–10. This book provides an interesting view of later theories of probability in a literary context. See also Edmund Byrne, *Probability and Opinion: A Study in the Medieval Presuppositions of Post-Medieval Theories of Probability* (The Hague: Martinus Nijhoff, 1968).

6. Cf. Anneliese Maier, "Das Problem der Evidenz in der Philosophie des 14. Jahr-

In the late Middle Ages, in addition to the "Averroist" view that something can be true (naturally) in natural philosophy but false (supernaturally) according to Christian belief, there was a "probabilist" view, according to which conclusions may be shown to be probable (although not demonstrated) in natural philosophy even though they contradict Christian belief.[7] In this probabilist view, as held, for instance, by Nicolaus of Autrecourt, a natural conclusion is probable if it appears to be true and if the available arguments and evidence tend to support it without proving that it is true. In this probabilist view, then, probability and truth are independent: it may be false but probable that the world is eternal and true but improbable that the world has a beginning in time.

There is an ambiguity within late medieval probabilism that may well be behind Galileo's contretemps on the matter of probable arguments. Simply put, one might consider an opinion as probable *tout court* or as probable within natural philosophy. This ambiguity appears in a passage from Jean of Mirecourt quoted by Julius Weinberg:

> I do not take "probable" as does the Philosopher, but I call probable anything which is neither known nor believed from the Catholic faith nor determined by the Church nor stated by such a one whose statement none ought to deny or to assert its opposite. . . . If it is said that something is not probable because the faith is in opposition, I say: this implication is not valid, for although it follows that a proposition is not true when faith is in opposition, yet it does not follow that the proposition is not probable. Indeed, the opposites of articles of faith are more probable to us than are the articles themselves.[8]

This may be compared to a similar statement by Pierre Ceffons:

> Although it is erroneous to say that God is not three and one and that the world had no beginning, it is nevertheless not erroneous to assert that, faith aside, it is more *probable* that God is not three and one or that the world never began than to assert their opposites. For nothing prevents some false propositions from being more probable than some true ones.[9]

Thus, both Mirecourt and Ceffons say that a proposition contrary to the faith may be probable despite being false. And yet both authors qualify this conclusion slightly. Ceffons says that, for example, the

---

hunderts," in *Ausgehendes Mittelalter* (Rome: Edizioni di Storia e Letteratura, 1967), vol. 2, 367–418, esp. 398–412. Also Edith Sylla, "Autonomous and Handmaiden Science: St. Thomas Aquinas and William of Ockham on the Physics of the Eucharist," in J. Murdoch and E. Sylla, eds., *The Cultural Context of Medieval Learning* (Dordrecht: Reidel, 1975), 349–96.

7. Cf. Julius Weinberg, *Nicolaus of Autrecourt: A Study in 14th Century Thought* (Princeton, N.J.: Princeton University Press/University of Cincinnati, 1948), esp. 114–126.

8. Ibid., 120–21.

9. Ibid., 116–17.

eternity of the world is more probable *faith aside*. Mirecourt's position is apparently more complicated since he excludes Christian beliefs from probability, presumably because they are believed fully, yet does not exclude what is opposed to Christian beliefs from probability. Possibly Mirecourt means, like Ceffons, that such views are probable to us faith aside, but he does not explicitly say so.

Thus in the medieval Averroist and probabilist views of the relation of natural philosophy or reason to theology or revelation there are two alternative modes of accommodating human knowledge to Christian faith. The Averroists take both natural philosophy and sacred doctrine as certain even when they appear to contradict each other. But they do not really say that mutually contradictory propositions can both be true at the same time, because they understand that all propositions within natural philosophy carry the tacit proviso "according to natural principles."[10] The probabilist, on the other hand, accommodates reason and revelation by accepting that the propositions of natural philosophy are only probable, not certain, and may be false though they are as well confirmed as natural propositions are capable of being.

Jean Buridan exemplifies a typical fourteenth-century position on the relation of natural philosophy to absolute truth somewhere on the spectrum between the Averroism of a Boethius of Dacia and the probabilism of a Nicholaus of Autrecourt. In his commentary on the *Metaphysics* in reply to the question "whether concerning things the comprehension of truth is possible for us," Jean Buridan replies in the affirmative that comprehension of the truth with certainty is possible for us, arguing in part that this must be so because we have a natural desire to know and nothing so basic in nature is in vain. Comprehension might be defined, he says, to mean simply the mental understanding of a proposition or it might include assent or adherence to the proposition. In the latter case our adherence might be simply willful or it might be based on appearance or evidence and the proposition itself might be absolutely true or true in the normal course of nature. The propositions that the heavens move or that fire is warm and other propositions of natural science are true in the normal course of nature notwithstanding the fact that God could make fire cold, and so on.

The firmness with which we assent to a proposition, without appre-

---

10. See Edith Sylla, "Averroism and the Assertiveness of the Separate Sciences," to appear in the proceedings of the VIIIth International Congress in Medieval Philosophy, Helsinki, Finland, 1987.

hension that the opposite might be true, can occur in three ways, according to Buridan:

> In one way [we assent] voluntarily without [reading *sine* for *sive*] any natural appearance and in this way the Christian assents and adheres firmly to the articles of the Catholic faith and in the same way some heretics adhere to their false opinions to the extent that they would rather die than deny them.... In a second way firmness of assent arises in us from natural appearances and various arguments and in this way we can also assent not only to truth, but also to falsehood....
>
> In a third way assent arises from evidence and the evidence of a proposition is absolute when from the nature of sense or understanding a person is compelled or necessitated to assent to the proposition, so that dissent is impossible, and this sort of evidence, according to Aristotle, belongs to first principles.... But in another way evidence is taken *secundum quid* or *ex suppositione*. As was said previously, a common course of nature is observed in things and in this way it is evident to us that all fire is warm and that the heaven moves, although the contrary is possible by God's power. This sort of evidence suffices for the principles and conclusions of natural science. Indeed there is an even weaker evidence that suffices for acting well morally, namely when one has seen and inquired into all the circumstances which a diligent person can inquire into. If one judges according to the exigency of such circumstances, that judgment will be evident with an evidence sufficient to acting well morally even if the judgment is false because of unavoidable ignorance of some circumstances....
>
> As a corollary it is concluded that those people speak very badly who want to destroy natural and moral sciences on the grounds that there is no absolute evidence for many of their principles and conclusions since they can be falsified by cases that are supernaturally possible. Absolute evidence is not required for such sciences; rather evidence *secundum quid* or *ex suppositione* suffices. Therefore, Aristotle speaks well in the second book when he says that mathematical exactness is not to be looked for in all sciences.[11]

Thus for Buridan absolute certainty is not required in natural philosophy, but certainty *ex suppositione* or *secundum quid* is sufficient. In writing in this way Buridan is assuming the Aristotelian model of distinct sciences, each science having its own principles and conclusions.

But what if one were to inquire absolutely about certainty or evidence, not confining oneself within the bounds of any one science within which certain principles may be assumed? We can get an inkling of what might occur by looking at Nicole Oresme's French vernacular commentary on Aristotle's *De caelo*, where because a lay audience is assumed, everything said does not assume the standpoint

---

11. Johannes Burdinaus, *In Metaphysicen Aristotelis* (Paris: Badius, 1518; reprinted, Frankfurt: Minerva, 1964), BBiir–BBiiir. On demonstrations *ex suppositione* in their various versions, see William A. Wallace, "Aristotle and Galileo: The Uses of ΥΠΟ-ΘΕΣΙΣ (*suppositio*) in Scientific Reasoning," in Dominic O'Meara, ed., *Studies in Aristotle* (Washington, D.C.: Catholic University of America Press, 1981), 47–77.

of an *ex professione* natural philosopher. In the *Livre du ciel et du monde*, Oresme ends his treatment of the possible rotation of the earth with a rather subtle methodological point, which may be summarized as follows: To explain the apparent daily motion of the heavens from east to west one may assume either that the heavens rotate east to west or that the earth rotates west to east. Having considered all the arguments that can be made in favor of one or the other of these hypotheses, one could well believe the earth rotates rather than the heavens, though it cannot be proved either way. And yet at first glance the rotation of the earth seems as much against natural reason as many of the articles of Christian faith. Consequently, to the nonbeliever who wants to argue rationally against the tenets of Christianity, one can respond that propositions that seem at first sight unreasonable may in fact be quite defensible by rational argument.[12] As far as the rotation of the earth is concerned, Oresme declares that he believes the earth does not rotate: "For God hath established the terrestrial ball which shall not be moved."[13] And yet earlier he concluded that to say that in the time of Joshua the earth really stopped and the sun only appeared to stop seemed more reasonable [*semble plus raisonnable*] than to say that the sun stopped as the Bible, literally interpreted, stated.[14]

Although the twist Oresme's argument takes at the end is confusing, one may interpret his position to be that on the basis of natural reason there are no conclusive arguments as to whether or not the earth moves and a reasonable person, on the basis of available arguments (*persuasions*), could believe that the earth rotates. Nevertheless, he and most other people are not convinced and do not believe that it rotates. Why not? Perhaps because the Bible says that God hath established the terrestrial ball, which shall not be moved.[15]

I suppose that Oresme's position on the epistemological status of natural philosophy was similar to Buridan's. Thus for him natural philosophy would not be absolutely certain, but it would be sufficiently certain *ex suppositione*. Pace Edward Grant, I do not believe that Oresme "sought to humble reason and show that physical arguments could not establish a relatively simple physical problem."[16] Yet in writ-

12. A. D. Menut and A. J. Denomy, eds., *Nicole Oresme: Le Livre du ciel et du monde* (Madison: University of Wisconsin Press, 1968), 536–39.
13. Ibid., 536, my translation.
14. Ibid., 530.
15. Cf. Stillman Drake, "Reexamining Galileo's *Dialogue*," in William A. Wallace, ed., *Reinterpreting Galileo* (Washington, D.C.: Catholic University of America Press, 1966), 161.
16. Edward Grant, *A Source Book in Medieval Science* (Cambridge, Mass.: Harvard University Press, 1974), 510, n. 61.

ing for a lay audience, even in the format of a commentary on Aristotle's *De caelo,* Oresme felt compelled to go beyond what he might say *as a natural philosopher* to say what he believed *tout court.*

There is a tendency among certain recent historians to praise Copernicus, Kepler, Galileo, and other early modern scientists for having believed that their physical theories were really true, whereas most late medieval natural philosophers are supposed to have developed multiple imaginative hypotheses, to none of which they fully subscribed.[17] The inference is drawn that such medieval philosophers were *glad* to show that science is uncertain, so that certainty could be reserved for items of faith and doctrine. This, so far as I can see, does not fit the likes of Buridan and Oresme, and yet the Middle Ages bequeathed succeeding generations an ambiguous legacy with regard to the "probable." To call an ethical, rhetorical, or dialectical argument probable was to praise it as worthy of acceptance, but in natural philosophy a probable argument could be espoused or it could be considered second best to a demonstration, as it would have been for Aristotle.

THE LETTER TO THE GRAND DUCHESS CHRISTINA

For all his use of mathematics and experiment, the point of departure for many of Galileo's assumptions about the nature of science was Aristotle's *Posterior Analytics* as its interpretation had been developed in the Middle Ages and Renaissance.[18] This being the case, it is ironical that Galileo often chose the letter or dialogue as the format within which to express his views, since these formats were adapted to the use of rhetorical or probable rather than demonstrative arguments. In recent years Maurice Finocchiaro and Jean Dietz Moss have each studied the influence of rhetoric on Galileo's mode of presentation, Moss in the *Letter to the Grand Duchess Christina* and Finocchiaro in the *Dialogue on the Two Chief World Systems.*[19] In this paper, rather

17. See, e.g., Benjamin Nelson, "The Early Modern Revolution in Science and Philosophy: Fictionalism, Probabilism, Fideism, and Catholic 'Prophetism'" *Boston Studies in the Philosophy of Science* 3 (1967): 1–40.

18. Cf. William A. Wallace, *Galileo and His Sources* (Princeton, N.J.: Princeton University Press, 1984), 99–148.

19. Jean Dietz Moss, "Galileo's *Letter to Christina*: Some Rhetorical Considerations" *Renaissance Quarterly* 36 (1983): 547–76; M. A. Finocchiaro, *Galileo and the Art of Reasoning: Rhetorical Foundations of Logic and Scientific Method,* Boston Studies in the Philosophy of Science, vol. 61 (Dordrecht and Boston: D. Reidel, 1980). I tend to agree with Moss's view of how rhetoric functions in Galileo's works rather than Finocchiaro's: that is, I do not think that for Galileo dialogue is a scientific method of discovering truth. Cf. C. J. R. Armstrong, "The Dialectical Road to Truth: the Dialogue," in Peter Shar-

than recapitulating what Moss and Finocchiaro have said about Galileo and rhetoric in general, I want to concentrate solely on his use of the idea of probable rather than demonstrative arguments.

Galileo was a mathematician and philosopher but not a theologian. Because of this, I believe, the arguments in his *Letter to the Grand Duchess Christina* might have seemed more reasonable to a mathematician or philosopher than to a theologian. We know that Galileo first set out his views of the relation of science and Christianity in an open letter to Benedetto Castelli that was later expanded and readdressed to the Grand Duchess Christina. Castelli could be considered an expert, as were the church officials who Galileo clearly hoped would also read the letter. The Grand Duchess Christina, on the other hand, was obviously considered a layperson and nonexpert, though from the viewpoint of the 1990s it certainly seems doubtful, even so, that she would have responded favorably to Galileo's quotation of Jerome in condemnation of those who "led on by pride, weigh heavy words and philosophize amongst women concerning holy Scripture. Others—oh shame!—learn from women what they teach to men. . . ."[20]

Because Galileo was writing in letter form and to a layperson, the reasoning of his letter could be expected to be rhetorical rather than demonstrative. Moreover, he was not limited to addressing his subject from the viewpoint of any one science or discipline but would be expected to take up points from any discipline or from common sense.

To schematize, Galileo's underlying argument in the letter is as follows:

1. No two true propositions can contradict each other.

2. In sciences such as physics some propositions can be demonstrated to be true by sense experience and necessary demonstrations.

3. The Bible sometimes makes statements that are not literally true because it is accommodated to the understanding of ordinary readers.

4. If a demonstrated proposition in science contradicts the literal sense of Scripture, then the Bible should be reinterpreted so that it no longer contradicts demonstrated scientific truth.

This much of Galileo's position would have been unexceptionable to many if not all of the theologians of his time. A similar position

---

ratt, ed., *French Renaissance Studies, 1540–70* (Edinburgh: Edinburgh University Press, 1976), 36–51. Galileo's written dialogues do not function as medieval disputations.

20. Stillman Drake, trans., *Discoveries and the Opinions of Galileo* (Garden City, N.Y.: Doubleday and Company/Anchor Books, 1957), 191.

was stated by Cardinal Bellarmine in his letter to Foscarini.[21] The difficulty of Galileo's position arises in his precepts concerning what is to be done when science lacks proofs but has only probable arguments, and, at the same time, contradicts the literal sense of Scripture. In such cases, a further distinction might be made among the types of statements included in the Bible: some relate to faith and morals, whereas others do not. One should presumably be more circumspect in proposing reinterpretations of passages relating to faith and morals than of passages not so related. In a decree of 8 April 1546, the Council of Trent had declared:

> Nobody has the right, basing himself on his own prudence, in matters of faith and morals that concern the edification of Christian doctrine, to violently divert the Holy Scripture toward his own opinion and to interpret it contrary to the sense that Holy Mother the Church holds and has held, to whom it belongs to judge the true meaning and interpretation of the Holy Scriptures, or even contrary to the unanimous agreement of the Fathers.[22]

As Galileo pointed out, this decree applies only to matters of faith and morals and not to every statement in the Bible. The Holy Scriptures were not written to teach astronomy. Yet Galileo went so far as to concede a further proposition in his letter to Christina:

> 5. Yet even in those propositions which are not matters of faith, the authority of Holy Scripture ought to be preferred over that of all human writings written not with a demonstrative method, but either with simple narration or also with probable arguments [*scritte non con metodo dimostrativo, ma o con pura narrazione o anco con probabili ragioni*].[23]

From the point of view of theology, this would seem to be a dangerous precept, because by following it one would run the risk of asserting strongly on one day, if the motion of the earth were discussed without proving it, that the Bible states the truth when it says that the earth shall not be moved, and of having to admit the next day that

---

21. Roberto Bellarmino a Paolo Antonio Foscarini, in Galileo, *Opere*, XII, 171–72. For Bellarmine the fourth proposition should perhaps be stated in a more clearly counterfactual way: "Dico che quando ci fusse vera demonstratione . . . allhora bisogneria. . . ." But see also Ugo Baldini and George Coyne, eds., *The Louvain Lectures (Lectiones Lovanienses) of Bellarmine and the Autograph Copy of his 1616 Declaration to Galileo* (Vatican City: Specola Vaticana, 1984), 21: "Si vero aliquando evidenter constiterit, stellas moveri ad motum coeli, non a se, hoc videndum erit, quod recte intelligantur scripturae, ut cum ea perspecta veritate non pugnent. Certum enim est verum sensum scripturae cum nulla alia veritate sive philosophica, sive astrologica pugnare."
22. François Russo, "Galileo and the Theology of his Time," in Paul Cardinal Poupard, ed., *Galileo Galilei: Toward a Resolution of 350 Years of Debate—1633–1983* (Pittsburgh, Pa.: Duquesne University Press, 1987), 120; cf. *Discoveries*, 203; *Opere*, V, 337.
23. Cf. *Discoveries*, 183; *Opere*, V, 317. I have attempted a more literal translation than Drake's.

the literal interpretation of the Bible is incorrect in this case, if someone succeeded in proving that the earth moved. Perhaps it would seem acceptable if theologians had no real expectation of science's succeeding in proving new truths, but I doubt that this was the case universally.

Galileo himself, on the other hand, quoted Augustine on the dangers of asserting too strongly the truth of any given interpretation of Scripture. We may take this as an alternative plank in Galileo's manifesto on the proper relations of science and faith:

5 alt. Now keeping always our respect for moderation in grave piety, we ought not to believe anything inadvisedly on a dubious point, lest in favor of our error we conceive a prejudice against something that truth hereafter may reveal to be not contrary in any way to the sacred books of either the Old or the New Testament.[24]

The cause of tension in Galileo's view is the assumption that propositions at one point in time only probable may later be proved. This was a possibility that Aristotle had not considered when he said that we expect proofs from a mathematician but only probable arguments from a person discussing ethics. Thus Galileo argued:

Among physical propositions there are some with regard to which all human speculation and discourse cannot supply more than a probable opinion and a truth-like conjecture in place of sure and demonstrated science; for example, whether the stars are animate. Then there are other propositions of which we have (or may firmly believe [*credere*] that we can have) undoubted certainty through experience, long observation, and rigorous demonstrations; for example whether or not the earth and sun move, or whether or not the earth is spherical. As to the first sort of proposition, I have no doubt that where human reasoning cannot reach—and where consequently we can have no science but only opinion and faith—it is necessary in piety to comply absolutely with the strict sense of Scripture. But as to the other kind, I would believe, as said before, that first we are to make certain of the fact, which will reveal to us the true senses of the Bible, and these will most certainly be found to agree with the proved fact, even though at first the words sounded otherwise, because two truths can never contradict each other. I take this to be an orthodox and indisputable doctrine insofar as I find it specifically in St. Augustine. . . .[25]

In this passage Galileo went beyond his initial position to the extent that he put into the second class of propositions not only those proved true but also those concerning which we may firmly believe that we can have undoubted certainty, though we have not presently achieved it. This would greatly expand the number of biblical propositions to

24. *Discoveries*, 199; *Opere*, V, 331–32; see also *Discoveries*, 188–89; *Opere*, V, 321.
25. Cf. *Discoveries*, 197–98; *Opere*, V, 330. I have modified Drake's translation.

be taken into account in avoiding overextension of the literal interpretation of the Scriptures. Moreover, it essentially undermines the significance of what I have numbered the fifth proposition in Galileo's *Letter*. In fact, given the alternate fifth proposition, one could understand the range of "human writings written not with a demonstrative method," as referred to in Galileo's initial fifth proposition, to be much narrower than it may appear at first sight. The Bible is to be preferred to nonscientific human writings. But if a proposition is proved scientifically or appears likely to be proved scientifically in the near future, for example, if it can be examined with a scientific method even if not demonstrated absolutely, then one should be cautious not to assert a literal interpretation of the Bible that contradicts it.

In the letter to Christina, this extension of the realm in which theology should beware of asserting senses of Scripture contrary to those proposed by science was moderated by the apparent implication that the heliocentric system had already been proved:

They know that as to the arrangement of the parts of the universe, I hold the sun to be situated motionless in the center of the revolution of the celestial orbs while the earth rotates on its axis and revolves about the sun. They know also that I confirm this position not only by refuting the arguments of Ptolemy and Aristotle, but by producing many counterarguments; in particular some which relate to physical effects whose causes can perhaps be assigned in no other way. In addition there are astronomical arguments derived from many things in my new celestial discoveries that plainly confute the Ptolemaic system while admirably agreeing with and confirming the contrary position.[26]

But however it is interpreted, the position on the relation of Christianity and science that Galileo advocated in the *Letter to the Grand Duchess Christina* has implicit difficulties for theology if a scientific proposition may gain increasing confirmation until it is finally proved. On the one hand, the theologian seems to be advised to continue to assert dogmatically the literal truth of Scripture until the moment of proof of a contrary scientific proposition, when it suddenly becomes his task to show that the literal interpretation is to be rejected. Alternatively, if one also takes into account those unproven scientific assertions that scientists firmly believe can ultimately be proved by experience and demonstrations, the range of biblical propositions open to doubt is vastly expanded, perhaps taking in all assertions about the nature of the world open to empirical investigation. Given the long Aristotelian tradition of dividing sciences by their methods as well as by their subject matters, it seems likely that Galileo leaned toward the

---

26. *Discoveries*, 177; *Opere*, V, 331. Drake's translation slightly modified.

alternative version of his position, according to which biblical interpreters should be diffident in asserting the interpretation of any passage related to the physical world, whether or not scientists have yet demonstrated anything on the subject.

Thus in the *Letter to the Grand Duchess Christina,* Galileo claimed that the Bible need not be reinterpreted because of merely probable arguments, but he implied that the stability of the sun and motion of the earth had been, or at least were very near to being, proved. Soon after the letter, however, Copernicus's book was placed on the Index and his view of the stability of the sun and motion of the earth was declared to be absurd philosophically and, in the case of the stability of the sun, formally heretical. In the *Dialogue on the Two Chief World Systems,* therefore, one would not expect to find Galileo's still claiming or implying that the Copernican system had been proved.[27]

DIALOGUE ON THE TWO CHIEF WORLD SYSTEMS

Possibly because it was revised over a period of time in order to meet the censors' demands before publication, the *Dialogue*'s positions are not wholly consistent. Thus the title page asserts that the work proposes indeterminately the philosophical and natural arguments for either side, but in the preface Galileo explains why he has taken the Copernican side. In the *Dialogue* itself, when one follows the tone of the discussion, the Copernican system is very obviously favored, and yet it is repeatedly asserted that the Copernican side has not been and cannot be proved true. Whereas in the *Letter to Christina,* probable arguments are treated as if they had very little weight, in the *Dialogue* some probable arguments are treated as approaching very near to certainty or geometrical demonstrations. Thus the argument from the apparent motion of sunspots and, even more so, the argument from the tides are treated as coming close to proving the sun's rest in the middle of the orbit of a rotating earth. Yet at crucial points, the char-

---

27. After I had completed this paper, Richard Blackwell kindly allowed me to see a copy of his paper on Foscarini, which appears elsewhere in this volume. In the *Letter of Fr. Paolo Antonio Foscarini on the Opinion of the Pythagoreans and of Copernicus* (Naples, 1615), Foscarini suggested how the Bible could be reinterpreted to agree with the Copernican system while claiming only that the Copernican system was very probable, not proved true. Although Galileo does not mention Foscarini by name in his *Letter to the Grand Duchess Christina,* it is almost certain that Galileo's arguments and the church's reaction to them were influenced by Foscarini's letter and by the fate of his work. When taken together, both Foscarini and Galileo at this time appeared to want to reinterpret problematic biblical passages in advance of any demonstration of the truth of the Copernican system.

acters in the dialogue reiterate the difference between probable arguments and proofs.

Having shown that the annual variations in the pattern of sunspot motions are very naturally explained by assuming that the sun rotates in the center of the earth's orbit and having argued that to produce the same effects on the assumption that it is the sun rotating about the earth will require attributing to the sun four different motions, Galileo has Simplicio foreswear any decision between the two possibilities on the grounds that it is beyond his capacity.[28] Sagredo praises Simplicio for this and supports his view that "only that which is derived from the highest wisdom and supreme authority may be embraced with complete certainty."[29] Nevertheless, Sagredo goes on,

> But so far as human reason is allowed to penetrate, confining myself within the bounds of conjecture and of probable arguments, I shall indeed say (with a little more boldness than Simplicio exhibits) that I have not, among all the many subtleties that I have ever heard, met with anything which is more wonderful to my intellect or has more decisively captured my mind (outside of pure geometrical and arithmetical proofs) than these two conjectures, one of which is taken from the stoppings and retrograde motions of the five planets, and the other from the peculiarities of movement of the sunspots.[30]

And he continues in this positive vein of support. Salviati, however, takes a more cautious view:

> I do not give these arguments the status of either conclusiveness or of inconclusiveness, since (as I have said before) my intention has not been to solve anything about this momentous question, but merely to set forth those physical and astronomical reasons which the two sides can give me to set forth. I leave to others the decision, which ultimately should not be ambiguous, since one of the arrangements must be true and the other false. Hence it is not possible within the bounds of human learning that the reasons adopted by the right side should be anything but as clearly conclusive as those opposed to them vain and ineffective.[31]

After the later discussion of the causes of some properties of the lodestone, Sagredo again responds enthusiastically, "The entire argument looks convincing to me, and I rank these experiments . . . very little lower than mathematical proof,"[32] and this time Salviati maintains enthusiasm,[33] although he had previously expressed his disap-

---

28. Galileo Galilei, *Dialogue Concerning the Two Chief World Systems*, trans. Stillman Drake (Berkeley and Los Angeles: University of California Press, 1962), 355; *Opere*, VII, 382–83.
29. *Dialogue*, 356, translation modified; *Opere*, VII, 383.
30. *Dialogue*, 356, translation modified; *Opere*, VII, 383.
31. *Dialogue*, 356, translation modified; *Opere*, VII, 383.
32. *Dialogue*, 408; *Opere*, VII, 434.
33. *Dialogue*, 408–409; *Opere*, VII, 434–35.

pointment that Gilbert lacked grounding in mathematics that would have permitted more rigorous argument.[34] Sagredo then goes on to remark that since the argument "concerns a physical problem, I suppose Simplicio is also convinced as fully as permitted by natural science, in which he is aware that geometrical evidence cannot be demanded."[35] Simplicio responds, "Truly, I think that Salviati's eloquence has so clearly explained the cause of this effect that the most mediocre mind, however unscientific, would be persuaded."[36]

PROBABLE ARGUMENTS

Previous discussions of the attitudes of Copernicus or Kepler or Galileo toward scientific demonstration have made it seem that there were only two alternatives: either skepticism, hypotheticalism, and saving the phenomena or straightforward demonstrations of scientific truth.[37] Whereas Osiander in his notice to the reader at the start of the *De Revolutionibus* is understood to have argued that the Copernican system should be taken only as a mathematical hypothesis and basis of calculation, Copernicus, Kepler, and Galileo are all claimed to have taken the Copernican system as a scientific truth. Although this contrast is valid, as far as it goes, it omits a third alternative, which is my concern here, namely whether or not the motion of the earth and stability of the sun are *probable*, which should not be lumped together indiscriminately with the issue of whether they are to be taken as a mathematical hypothesis that saves the phenomena à la Ptolemaic astronomy.

In a mathematical argument one may derive consequences of an original assumption, for example, that the earth rotates and travels around the sun or that the weights in a balance move downward on parallel paths, without concerning oneself with the question whether the assumption is true.[38] But whether or not such an assumption is probable is a different issue. A probable assumption, unlike Ptolemy's assumption of epicycles or the equant, should fit all or most of the

34. *Dialogue*, 406; *Opere*, VII, 432.
35. *Dialogue*, 410; *Opere*, VII, 436; cf. *Opere*, VII, 14; *Opere*, VII, 38.
36. *Dialogue*, 410.
37. Cf. Edward Grant, "Late Medieval Thought, Copernicus, and the Scientific Revolution" *Journal of the History of Ideas* 23 (1962): 197–200. See also Benjamin Nelson, "Copernicus and the Quest for Certitude: 'East' and 'West,'" in Arthur Beer and K. A. Strand, eds., *Copernicus Yesterday and Today: Vistas in Astronomy* 17 (1975): 39–46.
38. Cf. Edith Sylla, "Galileo and the Oxford *Calculatores*: Analytical Languages and the Mean-Speed Theorem for Accelerated Motion," in William A. Wallace, ed., *Reinterpreting Galileo* (Washington, D.C.: Catholic University of America Press, 1986), 100.

available evidence, even if it is not proved by this evidence. It should at least be a viable candidate for truth status.

Thus, there were more than two alternatives open to Copernicus, Osiander, Kepler, and Galileo with regard to the status of the Copernican system. For Osiander, not only were the hypotheses of the Copernican system not a true physical description of the world, they were not even probable [*verisimiles*], that is, not candidates for truth status, since they included assumptions or implications known to be false, for instance, that the distances of planets from the earth vary as greatly as the deferent/epicycle models require.

Copernicus, writing for other astronomers, could present the mathematical details of his system, which may well have been sufficient to make him lean toward believing it was a correct representation of the physical world, and yet not commit himself absolutely on this subject. The fact that astronomers before Kepler did not detect a serious inconsistency between Osiander's prefatory note and the body of Copernicus's work is evidence that the work does not stress that the system asserts a physical truth.

Kepler, also writing for other scientists and mathematicians, has a very sophisticated theory of the progress of science and of the process by which scientific hypotheses may reveal or show signs of their own truth. Whereas Copernicus may not emphasize his commitment to the truth of his hypotheses, Kepler carefully describes how and why a scientist may gain confidence in a theory.[39] It is clear in the case of Kepler that there are at least three factors to be considered: the scientific theory under consideration, the arguments and evidence for and against it, and the scientist's commitment to the theory, the latter affected but not totally determined by the arguments and evidence. Likewise with Sagredo, Salviati, and Simplicio, Galileo portrays different responses to the same arguments and evidence, Sagredo perhaps being more easily persuaded, Salviati suspending judgment.

By writing in letter or dialogue form, and with the expectation of lay as well as expert readers, Galileo committed himself more to the task of persuasion than Copernicus, who might let the evidence speak for itself to experts. He very obviously used not only arguments (*logos*), but also the rhetorical tools of credibility of the speaker (*ethos*) and emotional appeals (*pathos*).[40] Although the dialogue form is "fictional,"

39. See Nicholas Jardine, *The Birth of History and Philosophy of Science* (Cambridge: Cambridge University Press, 1984).
40. Cf. Jean Dietz Moss, "Galileo's Letter to Christina" (n. 18) and *eadem*, "The Rhetoric of Proof in Galileo's Writings," in William A. Wallace, ed., *Reinterpreting Galileo* (Washington, D.C.: Catholic University of America Press, 1986), 179–204.

any reader would naturally suppose that an author who made the Aristotelian spokesman, Simplicio, appear to be a fool, while portraying the advocate of Copernicanism, Salviati, as invariably astute, must favor the Copernican side.

Why, then, did Galileo open himself to condemnation by the church when he was careful to state explicitly that none of his arguments proved absolutely that the Copernican system was true? For Galileo, as I have argued, what really mattered was scientific demonstration.[41] He hoped to prove that the Copernican system was true, if not by the evidence of the tides, then in some other way. At the very least he firmly believed that he could have undoubted certainty about the motion of the earth through experiences, long observations, and rigorous demonstrations. On the other hand, there is little doubt that in advance of having such experiences, long observations, and rigorous demonstrations, Galileo himself did in some sense "believe in" the motion of the earth. Thus, when Galileo stated in his trial that he held as most true and indisputable the opinion of Ptolemy and, later, that his motive in writing the *Dialogue* was not that he held the Copernican doctrine to be true, he was likely not giving a true representation of his psychological-belief state as we would understand it in the twentieth century. Like Oresme, Galileo may indeed as a scientist have admitted that there was (as yet) no conclusive proof that the Ptolemaic system was false and the Copernican system true, but, unlike Oresme, he seems to have "believed," if beliefs can be inferred from actions, that the Copernican system was true.

What, then, about the probability or improbability of the Copernican system? If Galileo had treated Copernicanism only as a mathematical hypothesis, as Cardinal Bellarmine had supported his doing,[42] then he would only have affirmed that if the earth moved and the sun stood still, then the apparent astronomical motions could be "saved" or accounted for. But to claim in a rhetorical context that a theory is probable goes further than claiming that if it were true the evidence could be accounted for, because to say in a rhetorical context that a theory is probable implies that it is worthy of belief. Moreover, if probability only comes into consideration when proof or full belief is lacking, a much wider range of evidence may be appealed to beyond "experiences, long observations, and rigorous demonstrations." In particular, the opinion or testimony of prudent and highly respected individuals is a type of evidence to be taken into account. As indicated

---

41. Cf. text in *Dialogue*, 53–54; *Opere*, VII, 78, quoted in Moss, "Rhetoric of Proof," 204.

42. Galileo, *Opere*, XII, 171.

by the decree of the Council of Trent quoted previously, the "unanimous agreement of the [Church] Fathers," or the positions of the "Holy Mother Church" were presumed to have great weight in the correct interpretation of Scripture.

For a person to say after 1616 in a rhetorical context that the Copernican system is probable, therefore, would naturally be taken as tantamount to saying that the arguments and persuasions in its favor outweigh the declaration of the eleven *consultores* in 1616, which said that the proposition that the sun is in the center of the world and completely immobile in local motion

> is foolish and absurd in philosophy and formally heretical inasmuch as it expressly contradicts the doctrine of Holy Scripture in many passages, both in their literal meaning and according to the general interpretation of the Holy Fathers and Doctors of Theology; and that the proposition that the earth rotates and moves around the sun is likewise absurd in philosophy and at least erroneous in the faith.[43]

In the *Dialogue on the Two Chief World Systems*, if one makes the most natural inferences about Galileo's position given the way in which he portrays Simplicio, Sagredo, and Salviati, Galileo certainly seems to consider the Copernican system as probable or worthy of belief.[44] In discussing the arguments of Chiaramonti against the motion of the earth, Galileo, through the mouth of Salviati, makes it clear that probability or improbability may be specific to the individual:

> He puts it down as a very improbable thing [*cosa molto inverisimile*] that an evanescent and corruptible body such as the earth could move perpetually with a regular motion, especially since we see animals finally exhaust themselves and stand in need of rest. And to him this improbability is increased by the motion being immeasurably greater in comparison with that of animals. Now I cannot understand why he should be disturbed at present about the speed of the earth, when that of the stellar sphere, which is so much greater, causes him no more considerable disturbance than does that which he ascribes to a millstone performing only one revolution every twenty-four hours.[45]

In a later passage not untinged with irony, Galileo has Salviati point out that the evidence of the Bible ought to carry heavy weight:

> *Salviati*: All of this is satisfactory to me except his [the unnamed author of a booklet against Copernicus] having mixed passages from the ever venerable and mighty Holy Scriptures among these apish puerilities, and his having

---

43. Jerome Langford, *Galileo, Science, and the Church*, rev. ed. (Ann Arbor: University of Michigan Press, 1971), 89 (some changes in translation).

44. See the inferences about Galileo's position made by Augustinus Oregius, Melchior Incofer, and Zacharias Pasqualigus in *Opere*, XIX, 348–60.

45. *Dialogue*, 273; *Opere*, VII, 297; cf. Weinberg, *Nicholas of Autrecourt*, 117–18.

tried to utilize sacred things for wounding anybody who might, without either affirming or denying anything, philosophize jokingly and in sport, having made certain assumptions and desiring to argue about them among friends.

Simplicio: Truly he scandalized me too, and not a little; especially later, when he adds that if indeed the Copernicans answer these and the like arguments in some distorted way, they still will not be able to answer satisfactorily some things which come later.

Salviati: Oh, that is worst of all, for he is pretending to have things which are more effective and convincing than the authority of Holy Writ. But let us, for our part, revere it, and pass on to physical and human arguments.[46]

Here, I think, is just the source of Galileo's problem with the church over the matter of probable arguments. First of all, for Galileo probable arguments are inferior and not worthy of much attention in comparison to "experiences, long observations, and rigorous demonstrations." But by writing in a rhetorical genre Galileo was raising the expectation that his conclusions were not limited to what could be shown within natural philosophy but also relied on wider considerations. This was exactly the assumption of those who examined the *Dialogue* with the question whether it revealed that Galileo held, defended, or taught the Copernican system in it.[47] Although we may be convinced by Galileo's caricaturing of them that some of the theologians who argued against him were of mediocre intellect, nevertheless the overall impression given is that Galileo had very little respect for contemporary theologians or even, for example, for the decrees of the Council of Trent. He paid lip service to statements of the Church Fathers when they supported his cause—and St. Augustine seems actually to have supplied him with strong arguments in favor of his position on the proper relation of science to scriptural exegesis—yet he essentially counted the literal interpretation of the Bible, even when supported by the unanimous interpretation of church leaders, for nothing at all in comparison to "experiences, long observations, and rigorous demonstrations." Whereas, if one were engaged in physics or natural philosophy, the limitation of evidence to experience, observations, and demonstrations might be justified, Galileo, writing in the vernacular, in dialogue form, expecting an audience including lay people, would be expected to pay attention also to the other sorts of evidence assumed to have weight in that larger context. As Bellarmine had said many years earlier, in the case of the Bible there is the issue of credibility *ex parte dicentis*, corresponding to *ethos* in the rhetorical scheme.[48]

46. *Dialogue*, 357–58; *Opere*, VII, 384–85.
47. See *Opere*, XIX, 348–60.
48. Bellarmine, Letter to Foscarini, in Galileo, *Opere*, XII, 172.

This is why, I think, the judges at Galileo's trial could condemn him, even giving them the benefit of the doubt and assuming that they were not taking an extreme view of church authority. If one were operating solely within a scientific context, then either probable arguments would be misplaced, as in Aristotle's view, or they might have weight *ex suppositione*, assuming the natural course of events, with no divine intervention, as in the viewpoints of Buridan or Autrecourt. On the latter alternative, as we have seen, there was good scholastic precedent for the judgment that a conclusion such as the earth's rotation could be more or less probable from the natural science point of view based on appearances and yet false. This was, in fact, Oresme's position, as I have indicated, and it also appears to have been the position of Niccolo Riccardi, master of the Sacred Palace, who was responsible for approving the publication of Galileo's *Dialogue* in Rome. When it became apparent that for various reasons Galileo was determined to publish the *Dialogue* in Florence rather than Rome, Riccardi wrote to Giacinto Stefani, the consultor of the Inquisition in Florence:

Signor Galileo plans to print there one of his works ... in which probable reasoning is given concerning the Copernican system with regard to the motion of the earth....

Stefani could, Riccardi wrote, go ahead and send the book forth or not, without further approval from Rome,

remembering, however, that it is the intention of the Holy Father that the title and subject of the book not be presented as concerning the tides, but rather absolutely concerning the mathematical consideration of the Copernican position with regard to the motion of the earth and with a goal of showing that except for God's revelation and sacred doctrine, the appearances could be saved by this position, resolving all the contrary persuasions that experience and the peripatetic philosophy could adduce, so that the absolute truth should never be conceded to this opinion but only hypothetical truth, without the Scriptures.[49]

Although this passage could be understood as emphasizing the hypothetical mathematical approach usually associated with the Ptolemaic and Copernican use of epicycles and the like and referred to by Bellarmine in his letter to Foscarini, I think it goes further than that to allow that Galileo might show that the motion of the earth in the Copernican system would be probable given all the observations or arguments that the Peripatetics might adduce were it not for God's revelation and sacred doctrine.

49. *Opere*, XIX, 327; cf. Jerome Langford, *Galileo, Science and the Church*, 131, and Drake, "Reexamining Galileo's *Dialogue*," 161.

To meet Riccardi's condition, the "medicine of the end" of the *Dialogue* was not sufficient, where Simplicio is made to repeat what had been the pope's own argument, that one can never be certain that a given physical explanation corresponds to reality because God in his infinite power and wisdom could always have accomplished the same result in another way.[50] This caveat might for some individuals, as it seems to have for Simplicio, imply that no science is ever certain, and, in fact, Salviati adds to Simplicio's point the further doctrine that human beings can never discover the work of God's hands or penetrate the profound depths of His infinite wisdom.[51] A more common response, however, which was likely Galileo's own, was to claim with Jean Buridan that despite such absolute caveats, what was demonstrated in science by many experiences, long observations, and well-founded arguments was nevertheless sufficiently reliable, probable, and worthy of acceptance.[52]

If Galileo agreed with Buridan on this point, then despite Pope Urban VIII's or Simplicio's argument that we cannot be sure of any natural philosophical conclusion because God could have done things otherwise, Galileo would have held that the conclusion was nevertheless highly probable and very near certainty. In his unpublished notes on Bellarmine's letter to Foscarini, Galileo had claimed to be willing to meet very high standards of probability:

Not to believe that a proof of the earth's motion exists until one has been shown is very prudent, nor do we demand that anyone believe such a thing without proof. Indeed, we seek, for the good of the holy Church, that everything the followers of this doctrine can set forth be examined with greatest rigor, and that nothing be admitted unless it far outweighs the rival arguments. If these men are only ninety percent right, then they are defeated; but when nearly everything the philosophers and astronomers say on the other side is proved to be quite false, and all of it inconsequential, then this side should not be deprecated or called paradoxical simply because it cannot be completely proved. . . .[53]

By the time of the *Dialogue*, then, Galileo seems to have thought that the Copernican system was very very close to being demonstrated, even if not absolutely so. If it were proved, then Scripture would need to be reinterpreted accordingly. In the meanwhile, he apparently thought there was no harm in weighing relative probabilities and in attempting to convince people that the Copernican system was correct.

50. *Dialogue*, 464; *Opere*, VII, 488.
51. *Dialogue*, 464; *Opere*, VII, 489.
52. Cf. Maier, "Das Problem der Evidenz," 398–400; Weinberg, *Nicolaus of Autrecourt*, 176–77.
53. Drake, *Discoveries*, 169; *Opere*, XII, 368–69.

There would be no harm in showing the Copernican system probable, even if it was contrary to the Bible, because a physical theory can be probable and yet false. While he was doing this, Galileo apparently understood himself to be arguing as a scientist.

Since, however, Galileo was operating in a wider rhetorical context and writing for lay readers as well as professional scientists, then one might well have expected from him Riccardi's view that the Copernican system might have been probable were it not for the Church's determination otherwise in 1616. In fact the preface to the *Dialogue* repeats Riccardi's view:

> It is not from failing to take account of what others have thought that we have yielded to asserting that the earth is motionless, and holding the contrary to be a mere mathematical caprice, but (if for nothing else) for those reasons that are supplied by piety, religion, the knowledge of Divine Omnipotence, and a consciousness of the limitations of the human mind.[54]

Giving Galileo the benefit of the doubt, we may suppose that Galileo as a professional natural philosopher consciously suspended judgment concerning the Copernican system seeing that it was not proved true, and as a Christian he could well have believed it false. Considering Buridan's description of the proper human response to articles of faith, we may understand that believing an article of faith, which may well be improbable from a rational or natural point of view, requires an act of will. Insofar as it was in his power to make choices where a matter of willing was involved, Galileo may have chosen to accept as true what the church declared to be true.

Melchior Incofer and the other church officials who examined the *Dialogue* inferred from the acerbity of its characterization of Aristotelians and other like evidence that surely Galileo must have believed the Copernican view.[55] In contrast to Incofer, Buridan in the passage cited had used as evidence for firmness of adherence or belief whether or not a believer was willing to give up his life rather than his belief. If we read between the lines of the *Dialogue* we may well conclude that its author believed the Copernican system true. Galileo himself, reading over his work after a lapse of time, acknowledged that the work read in places as if he believed the Copernican system true.[56] Never-

---

54. *Dialogue*, 6; *Opere*, VII, 30.
55. Cf. *Opere*, XIX, 353, "Nisi sententiae de motu terrae firmiter adhaereret Galilaeus tanquam putatae verae, nunquam tam acriter pro ea decertaret, nec tam viliter haberet contrarium sentientes, ut non putet numerandos esse inter homines. . . . Certe, nisi hoc sit defendere opinionem cui quispiam firmiter adhaeret, nescio an (praescindendo a Fede) ulla futura sit discerniendi nota, huius aut illius esse quempiam opinionis, etsi omni conatu eam defendat."
56. *Opere*, XII, 343.

theless on the evidence of his adjuration, given Buridan's criterion, the possibility is left open that as a matter of free will and choice, Galileo did not adhere as a matter of faith to the Copernican system.

Thus there is little question that in the *Dialogue* Galileo seemed to present the Copernican system as probable both on the basis of natural evidence and arguments *and absolutely*. One might argue on the basis of medieval probabilist positions like that of Nicholaus of Autrecourt that there is nothing wrong in declaring a position probable even if it is known to contradict Christian doctrine, because it is perfectly possible for a proposition to be both probable and false, but that this is a probability *faith aside*.

Might there have been a conflict between the Jesuits and the Dominicans on this issue, presumably with the Jesuits' accepting a wider application of the description "probable," and the Dominicans' wishing to exclude propositions known to be false from probability?[57] According to Edmund Byrne, Thomas Aquinas never explicitly referred to a proposition as both true and at the same time improbable or as both false and at the same time probable. Yet Aquinas did call Aristotle's argument for the eternity of the world probable, whereas we know he believed the world not eternal.[58] Indeed, Aquinas appears to have conceded that Aristotle's arguments for the eternity of the world were probable in the sense of being efficacious against the position of those who had argued that the world had been generated.[59] In like manner, Galileo argued in the preface to the *Dialogue* that he had striven by every artifice to show that the Copernican view was "superior to supposing the earth motionless—not, indeed, absolutely, but as against the arguments of some professed peripatetics."[60]

I leave for further research the discussion of how Dominicans and Jesuits at the time of Galileo's trial may have differed in the connotations they attached to the qualification "probable." However this may sort out, I think the fact remains that by his move to writing in the vernacular, in rhetorical genres, and to a lay readership, Galileo, without quite realizing it himself, moved out of the context of the Aris-

---

57. See Rivka Feldhay, "Catholicism and the Emergence of Galilean Science: A Conflict Between Science and Religion?" *Knowledge and Society: Studies in the Sociology of Culture Past and Present* 7 (1988): 139–63; William Ashworth, "Catholicism and Early Modern Science," in David Lindberg and Ronald Numbers, eds., *God and Nature: Historical Essays in the Encounter Between Christianity and Science* (Berkeley: University of California Press, 1986), 136–66, esp. 157–58; and William A. Wallace, "The Certitude of Science in Late Medieval and Renaissance Thought" *History of Philosophy Quarterly* 3 (1986), 281–91, esp. 287–88.
58. Byrne, *Probability and Opinion*, 156.
59. Ibid., 245.
60. *Dialogue*, 6; *Opere*, VII, 29–30.

totelian and scholastic conception of separate demonstrative sciences and so naturally encouraged the likelihood that his readers would infer—despite the denial of the preface—that he held the Copernican system to be both ultimately true and at the very least currently probable on the basis of all available evidence. If, indeed, Kepler and others could understand that Copernicus believed his system to be true despite the denial of Osiander's prefatory note to the reader, so too Galileo's readers could discount a preface meant to ward off hostility and see that the body of the work really told a different story.

13 Bacon's Critique of Ancient Philosophy in *New Organon* I

RICHARD H. KENNINGTON

Bacon makes a sustained critique of ancient philosophy in *New Organon*, part I, which has largely escaped thematic scrutiny. Initially this critique is said to be directed against three points of the "ordinary logic" (*logica vulgaris*), the tradition descended from Aristotle's *Organon*. Bacon asserts that his art, which is "a kind of logic" that he calls "interpretation of nature," differs from this traditional logic "in three points especially": "in the end aimed at, in the order of demonstration, and in the starting point of inquiry."[1] The combined scope of these rubrics obviously extends beyond the *Organon*. Indeed, Bacon's discussion of each is not limited to Aristotle but applies generally to all his predecessors and even includes pretheoretical or "ordinary human reason."[2] Nevertheless, he never considers the medieval scholastic philosophers and scarcely alludes to Telesius and Renaissance philosophers.[3] Bacon's critique is primarily concerned with "the form of inquiry and discovery that was in use among the ancients"[4]; it is only of the ancients that he expressly asks after their form of inquiry. Only ancient philosophers are mentioned, apart from Gilbert, in what is perhaps the most penetrating part of the critique, the *Idola mentis*.

This critique is unique: it has no rival in length or comprehensive-

---

The author is grateful to the Earhart Foundation and the National Endowment for the Humanities for financial support for his research.

Text references to Bacon are cited from the standard edition of J. Spedding, R. L. Ellis, and D. D. Heath, *The Works of Francis Bacon*, 14 vols. (London, 1857–74; Stuttgart-Bad Canstatt, 1963). References to the *New Organon* (hereafter *N. Org.*) are (1) to Book and Aphorism number of the work, (2) to pages in the Latin original (vol. I), and (3) to the English translation in this edition (vol. IV).

1. "Plan of the Great Instauration," *Works* I, 135; IV, 23–24. The *New Organon* was published in 1620 in one volume together with the "Preface" and "Plan of the Great Instauration" of which it was to be the second of six parts.
2. *N. Org.* I, 26; *Works* I, 161; IV, 51.
3. *N. Org.* I, 115; *Works* I, 211; IV, 103.
4. *N. Org.* I, 125; *Works* I, 219; IV, 111.

ness in the writings of the seventeenth-century philosophers, for example, Descartes, Hobbes, or Spinoza. Although Descartes is notorious for his failure to discuss the views of Aristotle and other predecessors, the ancients fare little better elsewhere in the founding writings of early modern philosophy. On the other hand, the effect of Bacon's critique is widely visible in the philosophic writings of his immediate successors. However, to see this effect, we must recognize that the critique of the ancients in part I is the necessary preparation for the method itself in part II of the *New Organon*. The interest in method in the sixteenth century is of course widespread in such figures as Ramus, Bodin, and Acontius. Yet before Bacon no modern philosopher advocated the necessity for, or himself composed, a treatise on a universal method for seeking truth in the sciences. After the *New Organon* of 1620, treatises on method are produced, although often left incomplete or unpublished, by Descartes, Hobbes, Spinoza, Locke, and Leibniz, all well-known readers of Bacon.

Yet these treaties differ greatly from the *New Organon*. The real consequence of Bacon's advocacy of method lies in the supporting theses that emerge from his critique of the ancients: of their end of knowledge, order of demonstration, and starting point. These theses reappear not only in treatises on method but also in such metaphysical writings as Descartes's *Meditations*; indeed theses often regarded as the innovations of Descartes can be shown to receive their first statement in the *New Organon*. It is Bacon who first replaces the ancient order of knowing that ascends to first causes or principles by the demand for certain foundations at the outset of the order of knowing. Modern "foundationalism" and the related problem of "mirroring nature" have their origin in the Baconian critique of the ancients.[5] Bacon's critique of the ancient starting point of philosophy in the "anticipations of nature" is the repudiation of the notion of "mirroring nature," which he makes explicit.[6] This repudiation is then repeated by Descartes in the first chapter of *Le Monde*.[7] Theoretical reason, or *theoria*, receives its first detailed critique in the *New Organon*. Of the goal of philosophy as mastery of nature in Descartes's *Discourse on Method*,

---

5. See Richard Rorty, *Philosophy and the Mirror of Nature* (Princeton, N.J.: Princeton University Press, 1979), introduction; 42.

6. *N. Org.* I, 26 ff.; *Works* I, 161; IV, 51. "The human understanding is like a false mirror, which receiving rays irregularly, distorts and discolors the nature of things, mingling its own nature with it" (*N. Org.* I, 41; *Works* I, 163–64; IV, 54). It is the modern rejection of mirroring that makes the turn to foundations necessary.

7. R. Descartes, *Le Monde ou Traité de la Lumière* (*Oeuvres de Descartes*, ed. Adam-Tannery), 11 (Paris: Cerf, 1909), 3–4.

Bacon is the acknowledged source[8]; the ancient speculative or theoretical goal is nowhere asserted in the Cartesian writings. These preliminary indications suggest that a scrutiny of Bacon's critique of the ancients illuminates the modern origins.

Bacon's statement that there are "two ways of contemplation" indicates the premise underlying his critique of the ancients. This assertion, first published in the *Advancement of Learning*, appears in three other major Baconian texts, including the "Author's Preface" to the *New Organon*.[9] One of these ways of contemplation is the ancient one; the other is Bacon's new way. To contemplate for the ancients, as for Bacon, means to consider or behold that which is. The term is somewhat more informally used than the classical *theorein* but never bears a nontheoretical meaning, except perhaps in the rare phrase "contemplative prudence."[10] Thus Bacon's intent is to wage a contest with the ancients on their own chosen ground, the true way of considering that which is. Of course, we do not often think of Bacon as a contemplative philosopher, but that is because the term (and its near equivalent *speculative*) has become dominated by the meaning stamped on it by the great tradition of Platonic and Aristotelian philosophy, ancient and medieval.

One extreme of Baconian interpretation takes him as the originator of a modern tradition that repudiates not only the contemplative goal of classical philosophy but contemplation as such, the knowing of that which is. This is the road of interpretation that takes "mastery of nature" in Bacon, but also in Descartes and Hobbes, as the characteristic and definitive goal of the founding modern philosophers. Against these students of Bacon we appeal to the texts cited previously in which Bacon speaks of "two ways of contemplation"; to his proposal in the *Advancement* that "contemplation and action ... be more nearly and straitly conjoined and united together than they have been,"[11] which implies two types of contemplation; and to his constant endeavor to show that his new approach provides a superior access to knowledge of that which is.

The opposite extreme of Baconian interpretation takes its bearings from Bacon's rare but undeniable assertion of the priority of contemplation to every practical goal. "Assuredly the very contemplation of

---

8. E. Gilson, *René Descartes, Discours de la méthode, Texte et Commentaire*, 3d. ed. (Paris: J. Vrin, 1962), 443–45.

9. *Advancement of Learning*, Works III, 293; *Valerius Terminus*, Works III, 250; "Proem" to *Magna Instauratio*, Works I, 122; IV, 8; Pref. *N. Org.*, Works I, 153; IV, 42. (Ellis's translation does not correctly render "duae similiter contemplantium ..."), Works I, 152.

10. *N. Org.* I, 58; Works I, 170; IV, 60.

11. *Advancement of Learning*, Works III, 294.

things as they are, without superstition or imposture, error or confusion, is in itself more worthy than all the fruit of inventions" at *New Organon* I, 129. Confronted by this statement, scholars have assumed that Bacon means to refer here to the ancient contemplative goal of philosophy: they tacitly assume that there is but one primary meaning of contemplation in Bacon's writings.[12] This leads to the acute paradox that Bacon, having asserted in I, 129, that his goal is the conquest of the things of the universe, now suddenly in the same aphorism I, 129, reverts to the ancient primacy of contemplation in the Platonic-Aristotelian sense. They have failed to ask, In which of the two senses of contemplation is Bacon here speaking? It is impossible to think that Bacon has spent almost a hundred pages giving a critique of ancient contemplation only to return to it abruptly in the end.

Both extremes of interpretation accept a disjunction of knowledge and action, or contemplation and action, the one insisting that Bacon sacrificed theory to action, the other that he reverted to the ancient priority of theory to action. To deny this disjunction is a principal purpose of Bacon's critique of the ancients. The conjoining together of contemplation and action proves to be just the clue to Bacon's claim that his contemplative way is superior to that of the ancients.

1. THE LIMITS OF THE CRITIQUE: PRELIMINARY

Bacon gives a preliminary indication of the limits of his critique in the "Author's Preface." The "two ways of contemplation" are indeed alternative ways of philosophy, but they do not simply exclude each other. His own philosophy, Bacon observes,[13] will not be much available for the practical business of life. It will therefore be legitimate to preserve and cultivate the old philosophy for practical life. The ancient and the modern philosophies could thus divide the domain of philosophy, the modern, methodical philosophy being the theoretical phi-

---

12. See Jerry Weinberger, *Science, Faith and Politics: Francis Bacon and the Utopian Roots of the Modern Age* (Ithaca, N.Y.: Cornell University Press, 1985), 176; "The remarkable assertion [in I, 129] of the superiority of theory to practice accords with the ancient utopian critique of the productive arts...." Remarks such as "Contemplative truth, not technological advance is the main goal of Baconian science" by L. Jardine, in *Discovery and the Art of Discourse* (Cambridge: Cambridge University Press, 1974), 116, remain unclear since they do not distinguish which Baconian sense of contemplation is meant.

Howard B. White, in *Peace Among the Willows: The Political Philosophy of Francis Bacon* (The Hague: Martinus Nijhoff, 1968), raises the question "whether contemplation means the same thing to Bacon that it means to Plato" (198ff.) and makes valuable clarifications but does not recognize that Bacon himself distinguishes two kinds of contemplation.

13. *Works* I, 153–54; IV, 42.

losophy of nature, the ancient philosophy being available for practical life. This passage is not without laborious irony, but we should not allow this irony to hide from us a serious point. Two considerations especially support its seriousness. Negatively, Bacon's critique of the ancients is limited to the order of demonstration and the starting point: it does not offer a critique of the end, for example, of the ancient view of the good. It excludes a critique directed at the practical philosophy of the ancients. Positively, the Baconian contemplative way promises a methodical natural philosophy, in which the law of nature is the central concept, but not a methodical philosophy of the human things. Thanks to this limit of the new philosophy, the contest over the interpretation of the human things will be waged on the basis of nonmethodical knowledge of both parties, the ancient and the modern contemplative ways.

2. THE ORDER OF DEMONSTRATION

We begin with the order of demonstration since it is the most comprehensive of the three points at issue in the critique. It proves to be identical with "the form of inquiry and discovery that was in use among the ancients," which Bacon considers in *New Organon*, I, 125: "This form appears on the very face of their writings." The ancient order of demonstration was, in the first place, an ascent. "From a few examples and particulars (with the addition of common notions and perhaps of some portions of the received opinions which have been most popular), they flew at once to the most general conclusions or principles of the sciences." From these principles followed the descent. "Taking the truth of these as fixed and immovable, they proceeded by means of intermediate propositions to educe and prove from them the inferior conclusions."

Bacon's description of the twofold ancient order of inquiry has a recognizable accuracy up to a point. In a well-known passage in the *Nicomachean Ethics,* Aristotle remarks that Plato rightly asked whether the discussion was proceeding from or leading up to first principles.[14] He alludes to the distinction between the order of our knowing that begins with what is first to us and ascends to what is first simply, and the order of nature that begins with what is first simply and descends to particulars. We can suggest further that the necessity of beginning with what is "first to us" is the Socratic correction of his predecessors that is a guiding premise of classical Greek philosophy.

14. *Nicomachean Ethics* 1095a30 ff.

The gravamen of Bacon's charge is that the initial ascent in the order of knowing is a "flight," or as he calls it at *New Organon*, I, 104, "a leap." (The use of these verbs anticipates the further assertion, to which we shall come, that the contemplative philosophers of antiquity were corrupted by religion.) To support this charge, it would seem that Bacon ought to point to important examples of "flight" and name the questionable first principles that resulted therefrom. This problem will receive some clarification when Bacon turns to the issue of final causes. In the present context, we must take Bacon at his word: the ancient form of inquiry and therefore the "flight" is evident in some manner on the face of the ancient writings.

So we must suggest our own possible examples. Does not Socrates ascend arbitrarily, hence by a flight, when, in *Republic* VI, he turns from the good, which is the good for man, to "the good" as the first principle of the superhuman whole?[15] Or consider an example from Aristotle's *Physics*. In Book II Aristotle contends for his assertion that nature is a principle or cause of motion and rest in those things to which it belongs primarily and not incidentally. His proof is a consideration of the difference between artificial and natural things. But the induction given is based on a limited number of examples; possibly difficult cases are unaddressed. Bacon's frequent objection to the ancient induction is that it generally decides "on too small a number of facts"; a "just scale of ascent" (*New Organon*, I, 104) is lacking.

In the *Idola mentis* Bacon deepens his objection to the ancient order of demonstration by relating it to first causes, final causes, superstition, and religion. The character of the ascent is questioned in the first of the *Idola*, the *idola tribus*. The idols of the tribe are of the innate type, in which the human mind in forming its notions "mixes up its own nature with the nature of things."[16] The natural characteristic of the human mind is its restless quest for ultimate or first causes. At *New Organon* I, 48, we learn that of every principle the human understanding discovers it demands a further cause that is "prior in the order of nature." Bacon makes a distinction between the generality of principles and their causal character. What is reasonable is to seek principles of maximum generality; what is shallow is to be dissatisfied with general principles so long as they cannot be referred to a cause. The quest for principles of greater generality seeks the evidence from the widest possible induction; it is the quest for a "just scale of ascent." This is a first indication of what a Baconian methodical ascent means.

15. *Republic* 505bff.
16. "Plan of the Great Instauration," *Works* I, 139; IV, 27.

The quest for a first cause, on the other hand, cannot be brought to a rest without the introduction of the final cause. The final cause is an anthropomorphism that "has relation clearly to the nature of man rather than to the nature of the universe," as is said in the same context. The natural desire of the human understanding is not for knowledge but for assurance or reassurance that all that is is for the sake of a purpose or for the good. In the sequel it is assimilated to religion or the desire for a benevolent and comprehensive divine power.

The step to religion is taken in the *Idola theatri*, which are the great dogmas enacted by the philosophers.[17] These are adventitious *idola* that complete or correspond to the innate *Idola tribus*. In the plays of this theater, the artifacts of the philosophers are like those of the poets, which give us the world as one would wish it to be. Final causes and first causes show that "philosophy" has been corrupted by "superstition and an admixture of theology" (*New Organon* I, 65). In Pythagoras, the superstition is coarse; in Plato, "more dangerous and subtle." In natural philosophy, Plato's school was corrupted by "natural theology."[18] The evidence of the corruption by superstition and theology in Pythagoras, Plato, and by implication Aristotle is the presence of first causes and final causes without the intermediate causes or axioms within the ascent that would render them plausible. Moreover, the mutual influence of philosophy and religion proves to be a mutual corruption in Bacon's account. Initially philosophy is corrupted by religion and erects final causes into dogmas, and this process was widespread among the pagan Greek philosophers. But the succession of such philosophic dogmas has ceased because "now for many ages," that is, in the Middle Ages, "men's minds have become busied with religion and theology." Hence the initial corruption of philosophy by religion culminates in the total absorption of philosophy and its teleological dogmas by the Christian religion in the medieval period. As regards final causality, "Aristotle is more to be blamed than Plato," asserts Bacon, in the *De Augmentis*, "seeing that he left out the fountain of final causes, namely God, and substituted Nature for God. ... Aristotle, when he had made nature pregnant with final causes, laying it down that 'nature does nothing in vain, and always effects her will when free from impediments,' had no further need of a God."[19]

Bacon's judgment of final causality is more traditional, that is, sym-

17. *N. Org.* I, 62–68; *Works* I, 173–76; IV, 63–66.
18. *N. Org.* I, 65; *Works* I, 175; IV, 65.
19. *De Augmentis* IV, *Works* I, 570–71; IV, 364–65.

pathetic, in the *Advancement of Learning* of 1605 than in the *New Organon* of fifteen years later. In the *Advancement*, Bacon assigns to "Metaphysique" the inquiry into "formal and final causes," and to "Physique" that into "material and efficient causes."[20] "The handling of final causes mixed with the rest in physical inquiries hath intercepted the severe and diligent inquiry of all real and physical causes."[21] Bacon's judgments of metaphysics and physics are revised in *New Organon* II, 9, as is often overlooked by those who take the *Advancement* as the canonical version of Bacon's classification of the sciences. Certainly the revision is not to be explained by some narrowing of subject matter under consideration in the *New Organon*, for the domain considered in the latter is quite explicitly general: "a just division of philosophy and the sciences" (*New Organon* II, 9). Metaphysics here becomes "the investigation of forms [that is, laws of nature] which are (in the eye of reason at least, and in their essential law) eternal and immutable." The laws that are the object of metaphysics are known by experimental method and hence outside the "ordinary course of nature." By contrast "Physics," in Bacon's unusual nomenclature, is not the inquiry into the laws of nature. It is "the investigation of the efficient cause, and of matter, and of the latent process, and the latent configuration (all of which have reference to the common and ordinary course of nature)."[22] The result is a sharp departure from the more traditional *Advancement*: final causes have been excluded from both main branches of "philosophy and the sciences," namely, from both metaphysics and physics. Bacon reserves a place for final causes only in human things, and not in the constitution of human beings but only in their actions (*in hominibus actionibus*) (*New Organon* II, 2).

To understand Bacon's opposition to teleology, we must first acknowledge that the rejection of final causes was at home in the naturalism and materialism of Telesius and other Renaissance thinkers familiar to Bacon (*New Organon* I, 116). Bacon is interested in the teleological issue primarily in the comprehensive causality of the heavens. His critique is directed above all against Aristotle and is most forcefully expressed in *De Augmentis*, as we have seen.

As regards the manner in which nature as a whole is to be understood, the choice of the teleological versus the mechanical view is decided by the manner in which the problems of the heavens and their motion is solved, as Aristotle himself stresses in the *Physics*.[23] The

20. *Advancement of Learning*, Works III, 354, 355.
21. *Advancement of Learning*, Works III, 357–58.
22. *N. Org.* II, 9; Works I, 235; IV, 126.
23. *Physics* 196a25ff; 199a3–5.

solution that Aristotle advances depends upon a physical astronomy that was nonhypothetical and teleological. By contrast, the astronomy of Ptolemy was content with mathematical constructions that "saved the appearances," as is well known, and became the accepted tradition. Thus the physical astronomy on which Aristotle relied had been superseded by the dominant tradition for many centuries by the time of Bacon. Moreover, insofar as the theory of Copernicus remains a hypothetical account, it lends no support to a teleological account, and insofar as it is regarded as nonhypothetical, it nonetheless is not a causal account and so is again unavailable for teleological purposes. Accordingly the Aristotelian teleology lacked the required supporting nonhypothetical and causal astronomy during the centuries from Ptolemy to Bacon. From these background remarks, we can understand Bacon's repeated objection to the astronomical tradition that it is merely hypothetical, a matter of fictitious circles, and the like. On the phenomena of the heavens many hypotheses may be constructed.[24] Copernicus and his modern followers were not of decisive importance for Bacon, as a genuinely nonhypothetical account would have to be a causal account ("the highest part of physics"), and such an account was not claimed at Bacon's time.[25]

To conclude this part of our discussion, Bacon's reform of the *ordo demonstrandi* means that genuine knowledge is obtainable at any point of the ascent without being grounded in a first cause. Therefore, the object of Bacon's new contemplation will be any principle known at any point in the ascent.

3. THE STARTING POINT

Bacon's critique of the ancient starting point is made through a comparison with the correct starting point. He calls the ancient one "anticipations of nature" and the Baconian one "the interpretation of nature" (*New Organon* I, 26ff.). This opposition remains obscure until the concept of the "law of nature" is introduced. In fact, the preliminary case for the "interpretation of nature" is the best Baconian introduction to his concept of a law of nature.

The true *ordo demonstrandi* required a "just scale of ascent" or "prog-

---

24. *N. Org.* II, 36; *Works* I, 297–98; IV, 183–84.
25. See G. Rees, "Mathematics and Bacon's Natural Philosophy" *Revue Internationale de Philosophie* (fasc. 4) (1986): 414: "[Bacon] was a convinced antifictionalist. He believed that the principal systems of his day, the Ptolemaic, Tychonic and Copernican, were merely arbitrary and competing methodisations of celestial appearances—methodisations which, whatever their predictive value, were worthless because none represented the actual course of the heavenly bodies."

ress in stages of certainty," as we have seen. It therefore supposed a certitude in the starting point, but this issue has not yet been addressed. "Anticipations of nature" refer to ordinary, "immediate and proper," and spontaneous deliverances of the senses, in contradistinction to experimentally controlled deliverances of the senses. The assertion "It is a great error to assert that the sense is the measure of things" is a criticism directed against the "anticipations of nature." To correct the anticipations Bacon provides "helps," namely, instruments (including the telescope), but what is more important, the experiment. "The subtlety of experiments is far greater than that of the sense itself, even when assisted by exquisite instruments."[26] Between the senses and the observed thing is the mediation of the experiment. For "the office of the sense shall be only to judge of the experiment and the experiment itself shall judge of the thing."[27]

The account thus far leaves the impression that "interpretation," that is, utilization of experiment, gives a "more subtle" account of the same thing that "anticipation" or ordinary sensing renders crudely or in some "blurred" fashion. This is misleading: a different object is being sought after in interpretation from that of ordinary sensing, although both involve the senses, in the different ways mentioned.

To approach this difficult issue, we start with an assertion that Bacon often makes: "No one successfully investigates the nature of a thing in the thing itself " (*New Organon* I, 70; cf. I, 80). Rather than adhere to "the thing itself," the inquiry must be enlarged so as to become more general. In the Aristotelian approach, which Bacon is opposing, the thing in question would be a substance or entity of a determinate form or kind. Such a being would be apprehended by what Bacon calls an "anticipation," as distinct from an experimental interpretation. In an anticipation, we encounter what Bacon calls "nature working freely" in the "ordinary course of nature,"[28] in contrast to nature under the "vexations of art" (*New Organon* I, 98) or experiment. These phrases have an informal ring but are in fact technical terms that articulate the pretheoretical world of common human experience. In this life-world, to use contemporary language, it is the natural species that is the articulating principle. "When man contemplates nature working freely, he meets with different species of things, of plants, of animals, minerals. . . ."[29] The inquiry that Bacon is rejecting is then that according to which the thing has a form of a specific

26. "Plan of the Great Instauration," *Works* I, 138; IV, 26.
27. Ibid.
28. *N. Org.* I, 66; *N. Org.* II, 9; *Works* I, 176; IV, 126.
29. Ibid.

kind. The "first state [of nature]" in which nature "is free and develops herself in her own ordinary course" "refers to the species of things," asserts Bacon in the appendix on natural history that accompanied the *New Organon*.[30]

The "thing itself " is the object of sense as referred by our anticipation to its species membership. It is this species reference that Bacon is rejecting as the proper locus of inquiry. He endeavors to shake our trust that to be is to be a being of a certain kind by referring to certain phenomena that are distorted by this species reference, for certain phenomena of great significance, such as heat, light, and the pull of gravity, "cut across" the natural species. To refer them to their incidence in a natural species is just to abstract from their natural coincidence in many species simultaneously. "If a man be acquainted with the cause of any nature (as whiteness or heat) in certain subjects only, his knowledge is imperfect..." (*New Organon* II, 3). For if we study heat in one species of phenomena such as fire, by itself, and in another species of phenomena such as celestial bodies, by itself, we shall not understand heat. It is because of this subject- or species-related inquiry that the error has arisen that "the heat of the sun and of fire are quite different in kind."[31] "We are told (and it seems to be a division quite received and authorized) that there are three kinds [genera] of heat: the heat of heavenly bodies, the heat of animals, and the heat of fire" (*New Organon* II, 35). It is this received opinion that there are different heats that are "in their specific nature different and wholly heterogeneous" (*New Organon* I, 35) that Bacon is rejecting.

Bacon regards the heterogeneity of kinds as theoretically arbitrary and unproven. But he also regards it as an obstruction to operations useful for mankind. If the heat of the sun and fire were regarded as one and the same, then man can accomplish by means of fire or "artificially" what the sun accomplishes "naturally." Men would attempt to imitate and even surpass the work of the sun by the heat of fire (*New Organon* II, 35; I, 75). But this should not lead us to assert that Bacon's concept of the workings of nature is governed exclusively by the humanitarian desire for useful operations. It is here both together, "contemplation joined together with action," that fortify each other in establishing a conclusion, the unity of the phenomena experienced in various contexts as heat, a unity that has since become an axiom in scientific work.

The phenomenally different manifestations of heat may be shown

30. *Works* I, 395; IV, 253.
31. *N. Org.* I, 75; *Works* I, 184; IV, 175.

to belong to a common nature (what Bacon calls a "simple nature") if they can be referred to a single cause. This is the task that Bacon proposes to solve by the tables of his philosophic method. The cause being sought for he calls a "form" using the traditional term "because it has grown into use and become familiar," that is, for essentially rhetorical reasons (*New Organon* II, 2). It is for the sake of precision that he rejects the traditional term and its species-relatedness and prefers the term *law*. Yet he continues to speak of form, sometimes speaks of "form or law" (*New Organon* II, 17), and sometimes says that if there are forms they must be understood as "laws of action" (*New Organon* I, 51). Bacon's apparently first published instance of the notion of law is his reference to a "summary law of nature" in *Advancement*,[32] which he calls the *magna forma* in *New Organon* II, 26, 52.

Bacon is a materialist. "In nature nothing truly exists besides individual bodies [*corpora individua*] performing pure individual acts according to law [*ex lege*]. Yet in the sciences, this very law, and its inquiry and discovery and explanation, is the foundation of knowledge as well as of operation" (*New Organon* II, 2). Bacon is a materialist but not a metaphysical materialist: he denies that there are atoms (*New Organon* II, 8). He therefore does not start from the ultimate, undivided parts of matter, either to derive compounds or to derive the first cause of motion. His science is neutral to the actual dividedness of the bodies of experience; he is a principal source of modern corpuscularism. A Baconian form is not a form of a being or of a kind of being. It is a regular pattern of the motions of corpuscles. Bacon is unable to establish the necessity of this pattern of motions; he offers us an articulated account of the law of nature without any proof of its assumed necessary causal action. An example of a law of nature is the law of heat, to which he devotes his exemplary account of the use of method to establish a law. The law of heat is a regular pattern of the corpuscles acting upon each other, which motion is progressively differentiated from other kinds of motion.[33]

Bacon makes an extraordinary attempt to establish a new ontology of beings, or at least bodies, on the basis of his concept of law. Heat is a quality, of which there is an underlying law. But what of other qualities? Do they not also each have an underlying law? Bacon answers in the affirmative and therefore proposes a momentous reform of the notion of a thing, especially at *New Organon* II, 5. He endeavors to restrict the multitude of qualities to a finite list of "simple natures."

---

32. *Advancement of Learning*, Works III, 265.
33. Cf. Antonio Pérez-Ramos, *Francis Bacon's Idea of Science and the Maker's Knowledge Tradition* (Oxford: Clarendon Press, 1988), 97.

He seeks to establish a complete inventory or catalogue or alphabet of all the simple natures there are. But the attempt to restrict them is not successful in reducing the horde of qualities into classes or grades or priorities. The one limitation appears to be that every simple nature is a quality of a body. A body is defined as "a troop or collection of simple natures" (*New Organon* II, 5). The glaring difficulty here, as Bacon acknowledges, is that a body must be a point of coincidence of the laws that underlie a body's qualities. Since each law is itself a pattern of motions of corpuscles, they must "severally crush, depress, break and enthrall one another, and thus individual forms are obscured" (*New Organon* II, 24). The difficulties that beset this new ontology go far to explain why Bacon's method in part II fails even to suggest how the method could lead to a science of human beings.

With the concept of the law of nature to aid us, we may now clarify the critique of the ancient *ordo demonstrandi*. As indicated previously, Bacon contended that the ancient ascent was a flight or leap because no intermediate steps were given to justify the assertion of first or final causes. So the ancient contemplation fails, but what new reason is there that Bacon's modern contemplative way must also fail to reach a first or final cause? Bacon's concept of law appears to demand that knowledge of law be part of a hierarchy or ladder of laws whose immediately higher rung, that is, more general law, is also known. However this may be—it raises the question of a regress that cannot be carried out—Bacon surely conceives of a hierarchy of laws that culminates in the notion of a comprehensive law, a *summa lex* or *magna forma*. Yet the question arises, Why should the *summa lex/magna forma* preclude first or final causes?

Bacon supplies a biblical origin for the *summa lex* in the *Advancement*. Solomon in *Ecclesiastes* III: 2 "doth insinuate that the supreme or summary law of nature which he calleth *the work which God worketh from the beginning to the end* is not possible to be found out by man."[34] Considered attentively, the passage that Bacon quotes does not say anything about "law," "nature," or "law of nature." And whereas the Bible or Solomon says that this law of nature cannot be found by man, Bacon suggests the contrary possibility. The impediments to attaining to knowledge of the *summa lex* are not necessarily insuperable, a conclusion Bacon also draws in the *New Organon* (II, 26). If then we suppose the *summa lex* is accessible, still precisely as law in Bacon's sense it does not make possible a first or final cause. To assert, as is sometimes done, that any notion of a law must require a lawgiver

---

34. *Advancement of Learning, Works* III, 265.

overlooks the condition that the law show some evidence of its being made by a lawgiver, that is, that it show signs of his purposes. But the Baconian law, or systematic hierarchy of laws, is purposeless. This enables us to understand in a clearer way a passage about ascent in the first Idol that we have already considered. "The most general principles in nature ought to be held merely positive, as they are discovered, and cannot with truth be referred to a cause" (*New Organon* I, 48). The Baconian ascent, warranted by the procedures of experimental method at each step, permits the inclusion of a principle within more general ones but supplies no basis for a reference to a cause. We are justified, then, in speaking of a *lex positiva,* a phrase Bacon actually uses in the fragment *de Principiis atque Originibus* (ca. 1616). Bacon's new contemplative way claims to be genuine knowledge but not to know first beings or first principles.

As indicated, Bacon offers no specific critique of the end, as distinctive from the *ordo demonstrandi* and the starting point of ancient philosophy. Why then did he reject the ancient end of pure contemplation? To address this question, we must use the result of the foregoing discussion that showed that Bacon understood the ancient end as inseparable from the entire "way of contemplation" of the ancients in its tripartite character. By showing that the defects of the ancient *ordo demonstrandi* and starting point were traceable to their purely contemplative end, Bacon has already given his critique of that end; no additional critique specific to that end is required.

But his critique has in fact a double character: he not only traces the ancient defects to their source but also indicates that the "conjoining of contemplation with action" is the remedy for those defects. The ancient ascent is faulty because it is a "leap" in quest of final causality and not a quest for pure knowledge; its remedy is the experimental procedure that guarantees a just scale of ascent. But experimentalism must be directed upon its proper object, the law of nature, before we see how knowledge and action are combined. The law of nature states the underlying cause of a "simple nature" that is encountered in experience, for example, heat. But the experimental process of verifying such a law proves to be the same as the process of the production of heat.

Bacon had therefore already rejected the ancient end by rejecting the ancient *ordo demonstrandi* and starting point. But his correction of the ancient way, which is the conjoining of contemplation with action, as just sketched, leaves Bacon with a great problem, precisely in the realm of practice. The "action" with which theory is combined is limited to the production that is feasible through knowledge of the laws of nature. It excludes knowledge of the ends or goods of human life that would guide the uses of that production. The notable method of Part II of the *New Organon* is exclusively concerned with discovering laws of nature and not with understanding the nature of particular beings such as men and their ends or goals. Thus Bacon's philosophy claims to illuminate "action" only in the sense of "production" and not at all the ends or goods of human life. Therefore, as stated, the ancient moral teaching, at least insofar as it is not derivative from the first causes and principles of contemplative knowing, is a legitimate way of understanding the ends or goods of human life. Moreover, we can speak of a rivalry in this context, insofar as the ancient knowledge of practical life as well as the Baconian remain "prescientific" and are devoid of dependence on modern natural science. Therefore, Bacon's reflection the "excellency of the end" in *New Organon* I, 129, to which we now turn, is not based on that "great mother of the sciences," that is, "natural philosophy," as was his announced program at *New Organon* I, 80, 127.

4. THE QUESTION OF THE END

Bacon concentrates his argument regarding the end in the closing aphorisms of part I, but primarily in I, 129. This famous passage appears to propose two versions of the end that are contradictory. The first and longer discussion contends that the "most wholesome" and "noble" ambition is "to establish and extend the power and dominion of the human race itself over the things of the universe." The second version of the end asserts, "The very contemplation of things as they are, without superstition or imposture, error or confusion, is itself more worthy than all the fruit of inventions." It thus appears that in the same aphorism of some three pages' length we have the new Baconian goal of power over nature side by side with a reassertion of the traditional ancient primacy of the contemplative end. As we have suggested, we meet in *New Organon* I, 129, a critical text for the relation of Bacon to ancient philosophy.

The dispute in recent years over whether Bacon's end is power or contemplation would have proved less troublesome if it had been recognized that Bacon speaks of "two ways of contemplation," as suggested previously. For it cannot be the ancient contemplation that Bacon is praising in I, 129, and in a similar passage in I, 124, which states, "The contemplation of truth is a thing worthier and loftier than all utility and magnitude of works." The ancient contemplative way is a "flight" or "leap" to first and final causes that is traceable to the corruption of religion, as we have seen. Of course, Bacon does not specify which contemplation he has in mind in I, 129, and I, 124. He perhaps expected that his inattentive reader would assume that he means the ancient contemplation, as that with which he is most familiar.[35]

The first thing to notice about these passages at I, 124, and I, 129, is that nothing is said about contemplation of what is first, in the way of first or ultimate causes or principles, as in the pertinent passages in the ancient Platonic and Aristotelian sources.[36] Both Baconian passages omit mention of precisely those ultimate or first beings or causes that are said to be theoretically unjustified and harmful to inquiry in the *Idola* at *New Organon* I, 48 and 65.

In I, 124, Bacon says, after the eulogy of contemplation cited, "I am building in the human understanding a true model of the world (*exemplar mundi*) such as it is in fact, not such as a man's own reason would have it to be." Here he is repeating the exclusion of final causes that he has stressed previously is the defect of the ancient contemplative way: it is hardly conceivable that in this very sentence he is reasserting the truth of the ancient contemplative way.

The ancient contemplation was choiceworthy because of the dignity of the highest things that it understood, regardless of whether accompanied by beneficial results. Bacon, however, does not refer in I, 124, to the dignity of the highest things. What is "worthier and loftier" than "utility and works" is "the contemplation of truth," which produces "serene tranquility." Whereas the ground of the dignity of ancient contemplation had been located in the objective order, in the present contemplation in I, 124, the ground of worth is subjective, tranquility of the human psyche. The same result is obtained from I, 129. What is "more worthy than all the fruit of inventions" is "the very contemplation of things as they are, without superstition or imposture, error or confusion." Thus the details of the contemplation presented in I, 124 and 129, corroborate our conclusion that it is Bacon's own contemplative way that he is praising. It might appear similar in certain respects to the tranquility and freedom from superstition of ancient Stoic and Epicurean thought. But what sets it apart from them is ultimately the same difference that separates it

---

35. In the "Plan of the Great Instauration" Bacon advances the rhetorical principle "He that is ignorant (says the proverb) receives not the words of knowledge, unless thou first tell him that which is in his own heart," *Works* I, 134; IV, 22.

36. *Republic* 484b1–b5; 484c1–d2; *Metaphysics* 981b26ff.

from Plato and Aristotle: the utter absence of any relation to eternal or deathless beings or an order of nature.

Harmonizing mastery of nature with Bacon's own new contemplation in I, 129, proves quite feasible. The methodical ascent, which replaces the "flight" of the ancient ascent, cannot be motivated by some "natural desire to know." The reality of that desire has proved to be the deluded flight to final causes. It is replaced by the contemplation of things as they are, "without superstition or imposture," but without Bacon's saying that this has its source in some natural desire. Bacon makes a universal assertion about human desire that is grounded on his empirical knowledge of human nature: "that whereunto man's nature doth most aspire . . . is immortality or continuance."[37] That statement from the *Advancement* supplies the premise on which the mastery of nature argument is built in I, 129. Men desire immortality or that surrogate that is achievable through procreation or family but above all through honor and glory. The mastery of nature argument combines the humanitarian utility that accrues to all men with the honor and glory that are deservedly given to the human race, or to the philosophic teacher of the human race, for mastering nature to secure that utility.

In simplifying the line of argument for mastery of nature, we have assuredly deprived it of some of its profundity. The exchange of utility to mankind in return for honor from mankind is a mercenary relationship seen from the side of the nonphilosopher. In particular, Bacon leads us to wonder whether the self-esteem of the philosopher who recognizes his own intellectual mastery of nature is not a godlike satisfaction. It is a question whether that satisfaction can be enhanced or diminished by the recognition or neglect by the rest of the human race. Bacon's justification of the superiority of his contemplative way to the ancient way owes more to ancient philosophy than it does to his own philosophic method. At least as regards the question of the end, the terms of Bacon's justification show the superiority of the ancient to the modern contemplation.

37. *Advancement of Learning, Works* III, 318.

14 The Problem of Method in Newton's Natural Philosophy
ANDREA CROCE BIRCH

INTRODUCTION: THE CONTROVERSY OVER
NEWTON'S METHODOLOGY

Newton's often-quoted statement on method—and the source of so much controversy—occurs in Query 31 of the *Opticks*:

> As in mathematics, so in natural philosophy, the investigation of difficult things by the method of analysis ought ever to precede the method of composition. This analysis consists in making experiments and observations, and in drawing general conclusions from them by induction, and admitting of no objections against the conclusions, but such as are taken from the experiments, or other certain truths. For hypotheses are not to be regarded in experimental philosophy. And although the arguing from experiments and observations by induction be no demonstration of general conclusions; yet it is the best way of arguing which the nature of things admits of, and may be looked upon as so much the stronger, by how much the induction is more general. And if no exception occur from the phenomena, the conclusion may be pronounced generally. But if at any time afterwards any exception shall occur from experiments, it may then begin to be pronounced with such exceptions as occur. By this way of analysis we may proceed from compounds to ingredients, and from motions to the forces producing them; and in general, from effects to their causes, and from particular causes to more general ones, till the argument end in the most general. This is the method of analysis: and the synthesis consists in assuming the causes discovered, and established as principles, and by them explaining the phenomena proceeding from them, and proving the explanations.[1]

The opening words of this passage raise the problem. Newton compares the method of analysis and synthesis used in natural philosophy to the mathematical method of analysis and synthesis. Yet he describes a type of analysis and synthesis that does not seem to match the mathematical analysis and synthesis of the ancient geometers.

---

1. Isaac Newton, *Opticks* (New York: Dover, 1952; based on the 4th ed., London, 1730), 404–5.

When referring to the analysis and synthesis of natural philosophy, Hooke actually reverses Newton's definitions:

> The methods of attaining a knowledge in nature may be two; either the Analytic or the Synthetic. The first is the proceeding from the causes to the effects. The second, from the effects to the causes.[2]

Dugald Stewart cites Hooke's words with approval. Stewart argues that the meaning of analysis and synthesis in natural philosophy has a radically different sense than that utilized by the Greek mathematicians or any mathematicians.[3] He explains that in some cases the Greek geometer and the natural philosopher would in fact use the terms in completely opposite ways. Stewart concludes that Newton was inaccurate in drawing a comparison between the method of analysis and synthesis in natural philosophy and analysis and synthesis in mathematics.

According to I. Bernard Cohen, application of the terms *analysis* and *synthesis* to Newton's natural philosophy results in confusion unless one understands Stewart's assessment.[4] Cohen focuses on Newton's description of the "empirical" aspects of the method of analysis and synthesis and disregards what he considers Newton's misleading words, "As in mathematics." Newton's description emphasizes experimentation, observation, and induction. In Cohen's view, since they play a minimal role in the *Principia*, one must conclude that Newton's method of analysis and synthesis cannot be applied to the natural philosophy of the highly mathematical *Principia*.[5] Cohen disagrees with Guerlac's attempt to do so. Like Cohen, Guerlac emphasizes the experimental, observational, and inductive elements in Newton's description of analysis and synthesis.[6] Unlike Cohen, Guerlac argues that Newton's method of analysis and synthesis has a significant part in the *Principia*. According to Guerlac, although Newton's *Principia* appears to be strictly mathematical, it is as firmly based on experimentation, observation, and induction as the *Opticks*.

The purpose of this paper is to resolve the apparent conflict between Newton's "empirical" description of the method of analysis and

---

2. Robert Hooke, *Posthumous Works*, 330, quoted in Dugald Stewart, *Elements of the Philosophy of the Human Mind*, vol. 3 of *The Collected Works of Dugald Stewart*, ed. Sir William Hamilton (Edinburgh: Thomas Constable, 1854), 276.
3. Stewart, *Elements*, 274–75.
4. I. Bernard Cohen, *The Newtonian Revolution* (Cambridge: Cambridge University Press, 1980), 293.
5. Cohen, *Newtonian Revolution*, 14–16.
6. Henry Guerlac, *Essays and Papers in the History of Modern Science* (Baltimore: Johns Hopkins University Press, 1977), 211.

synthesis and his stated association of that method with mathematical investigation. In particular the paper focuses on two issues: the ways Newton's method of analysis and synthesis, as applied to natural philosophy, compares to geometrical analysis and synthesis; and the way Newton's method of analysis and synthesis applies to all of his natural philosophy, both the empirical science of the *Opticks* and the physicomathematical science of the *Principia*.[7]

To wrestle with those issues, the first task of this paper will be to review the key features of a traditionally dominant conception of *geometrical* analysis and synthesis. This review will be followed by a discussion of the features of analysis and synthesis that Newton associates with *natural philosophy*. That discussion will acknowledge the differentiation within natural philosophy between empirical science and physicomathematical science. Specifically, it will identify two types of analysis and synthesis associated with natural philosophy: empirical analysis and synthesis based on suppositions derived from observation of phenomena and physicomathematical analysis and synthesis based on mathematical "idealizations."[8] We will find that there is more than a merely analogous relationship between geometrical analysis and synthesis and the analysis and synthesis Newton applies to natural philosophy in both its empirical and physicomathematical components. Newton's comparison of the analysis and synthesis used by natural philosophers to the method employed by mathematicians is thus neither muddled nor incorrect.

The final section of the paper situates Newton's work within the context of the growing seventeenth-century trend toward differentia-

---

7. Isaac Newton, *Mathematical Principles of Natural Philosophy and His System of the World*, 2 vols., trans. Andrew Motte, 1729, from the 3d ed., 1726; revised and ed. Florian Cajori (Berkeley: University of California Press, 1934). For a discussion of the application of mathematics to the study of nature see William A. Wallace, *From a Realist Point of View: Essays on the Philosophy of Science*, 2d ed. (Lanham, Md.: University Press of America, 1983), 38–39. Wallace locates the seeds of the distinction between the empirical and the physicomathematical sciences in Aristotle. Whereas the study of plants and animals could be based on observation, Aristotle and Aquinas were aware that constructing a science of heavenly bodies or the elemental parts of the universe was more difficult because of their distance from the powers of the human senses. Wallace points out that Aristotle himself utilized mathematical premises for solving problems involving the motion of heavenly and elemental bodies. Aquinas granted the physicomathematical sciences, or the "mixed sciences" as he called them, the status of true sciences. For debate concerning the status of the physicomathematical sciences in Galileo's time see R. Feldhay, "Catholicism and the Emergence of Galilean Science: A Conflict Between Science and Religion?" *Knowledge and Society*, vol. 7, ed. Henrika Kuklick (Greenwich, Conn.: JAI, 1988).

8. William A. Wallace, "Galileo and Reasoning *Ex Suppositione*," *Prelude to Galileo: Essays on Medieval and Sixteenth-Century Sources of Galileo's Thought* (Boston: Reidel, 1981), 135.

tion.⁹ Although struggling to find a unified method, Newton differentiated natural philosophy from mathematics (just as he increasingly separated natural philosophy from theology and alchemy).¹⁰ Within natural philosophy, he differentiated empirical science and physicomathematical science. Within mathematics, he differentiated the formal mathematics of Plato and the physical geometry of Euclid. The particularly problematic issue of applying Newton's empirical description of analysis and synthesis in the *Opticks* to the physicomathematical science of the *Principia* can be resolved by understanding his *differentiated* view of mathematics.

I. GEOMETRICAL ANALYSIS AND SYNTHESIS

Although Aristotle was familiar with Greek geometrical analysis, Pappus of Alexandria (Greek geometer, third century A.D.) was the first to provide an extensive discussion of the method. In book VII of the *Collection* he gives this description of analysis and synthesis:

Analysis, then, takes that which is sought as if it were admitted and passes it through its successive consequences to something which is admitted as the

---

9. The limitations in length and scope of this paper preclude the possibility of adequately tracing the sources and consequences of differentiation. For an introduction to the theme of differentiation see Eugene Klaaren, *Religious Origins of Modern Science: Belief in Creation in Seventeenth-Century Thought* (Grand Rapids, Mich.: William Eerdmans, 1977). Klaaren explains that the voluntarist theology of creation that was dominant in seventeenth-century English thought set the stage for "the structure of modern differentiation" (97). Sharp distinctions began to be drawn between the Creator and creation, between human knowers and the knowable world, and between various disciplines within the traditional body of knowledge. The consequences for science were twofold: nature was considered contingent and based on the will of God (40, 121), and humans had a duty to investigate nature experimentally because there could be no shortcut through human reason, which was only created and limited (121). Cf. R. Hooykaas, *Religion and the Rise of Modern Science* (Grand Rapids, Mich.: William Eerdmans, 1972). Hooykaas contrasts the Greek view (deification of nature and overestimation of human reason) with the attitude latent in the biblical tradition (de-deification of a created nature and a more modest evaluation of human reason in contrast with God's powers).

10. For Newton's views on theology see David Lindberg and Ronald Numbers, eds., *God and Nature: Historical Essays on the Encounter Between Christianity and Science* (Berkeley: University of California Press, 1986); Frank Manuel, *The Religion of Isaac Newton* (Oxford: Oxford University Press, 1974); H. McLachlan, *The Religious Opinions of Milton, Locke and Newton* (Manchester: Manchester University Press, 1941). Newton supported the differentiation between natural philosophy and theology that was institutionalized in the Royal Society (McLachlan, *Religious Opinions*, 170). Klaaren quotes Hooke: "the business and design of the Royal Society is—To improve the knowledge of natural things... (not meddling with Divinity)" (104). For Newton's work on alchemy see Betty Jo Dobbs, *The Foundations of Newton's Alchemy, or "The Hunting of the Green Lyon"* (Cambridge: Cambridge University Press, 1976); M. L. Righini Bonelli and William Shea, eds., *Reason, Experiment, and Mysticism in the Scientific Revolution* (New York: Neale Watson, 1975).

result of synthesis: for in analysis we assume that which is sought as if it were already done, and we inquire what it is from which this results, and again what is the antecedent cause of the latter, and so on, until by so retracing our steps we come upon something already known or belonging to the class of first principles, and such a method we call analysis as being solution backwards.

But in synthesis, reversing the process, we take as already done that which was last arrived at in the analysis and, by arranging in their natural order as consequences what before were antecedents, and successively connecting them one with another, we arrive finally at the construction of what was sought; and this we call synthesis.[11]

Pappus goes on to differentiate two kinds of analysis: analysis of "a problem to prove" and analysis of "a problem to find."[12] We will briefly explain each kind of analysis before enumerating the key features of the method.

The first kind of analysis is used if we have to prove or disprove a specific geometrical theorem. We begin by assuming the theorem, although we do not yet know whether it is true or false. We proceed to derive consequences from the assumed theorem until we arrive at a consequence, usually a theorem, we already have experienced as true. We can then conclude that the assumed theorem from which we deduced the consequence is also true, provided that all the intermediate steps of the derivation are convertible. If we had arrived at a consequence known to be false, we would have had to conclude that the assumed theorem from which it was derived is false. The analytic branch of the proof of a theorem is based on the metaphysical position that truth forms a consistent whole: a supposition leading deductively to a true consequence must be true.[13] The ancient geometers knew that a synthesis was needed to assure the convertibility of the deductive steps and guarantee the proof of the theorem. In synthesis, we begin with the particular consequence about which we have knowledge based on a proven method. We retrace our steps through the particulars, assuming each one as a principle to the degree to which it rests on reliable experience and methods. We finally arrive back at the assumed theorem in question. Whereas in analysis we can terminate the process in any number of conclusions, provided they are known, in synthesis the process is focused and must conclude with the theorem being proved.[14]

11. Thomas Heath, *A History of Greek Mathematics*, vol. 2 (Oxford: Clarendon Press, 1921), 400.
12. See George Polya, *How to Solve It* (Princeton, N.J.: Princeton University Press, 1945).
13. See Stewart, *Elements*, 265.
14. Ibid., 267.

The second kind of analysis, analysis of the "problem to find," is applied to finding the unknown satisfying the conditions of the specific geometrical problem (figure) in question. We do not know whether anything satisfying such conditions exists, but we assume the thing sought and derive from it another unknown that has to satisfy related conditions. We proceed until we come to a last unknown that we can find by some familiar method or until we arrive at an unknown that is part of a problem that cannot be solved. In the former case, if we solve for that last unknown, we can feel confident that we can solve the original problem, assuming convertibility. In synthesis, we put our confidence to the test. After manipulating the form the problem took at the termination of the analysis, we retrace our steps through synthesis, solving each problem with known methods, until we solve the original problem by meeting all of its conditions.

The ancient method of analysis and synthesis provided the geometer with a technique, although it did not diminish the need for intelligence and care at each step. The hallmarks of that technique revolve around six features that analysis of a "problem to prove" and analysis of a "problem to find" have in common.

First, it should not be forgotten that analysis is analysis of something concrete, that is, a theorem applying to geometrical constructions or an actual geometrical figure. The practitioner of analysis has a belief in reality and the consistency (perhaps even simplicity) of truth. Stewart suggests that the root of the term *analysis* lies in the analogy between solving a geometrical problem and unloosening a difficult knot in order to determine how to duplicate it.[15] One would begin with the given knot and then proceed to undo it through its various turns. After carefully untying the knot, one could reverse the procedure and obtain a rule for the solution of the original problem: how to make a particular knot. Hintikka and Remes capture the empirical nature of ancient geometrical analysis through their "instantial interpretation or the analysis-of-figures" explanation of the method.[16]

Second, analysis assumes "that which is sought as if it were already done."[17] If we wish to demonstrate theorems believed to be true or to determine the truth of questionable theorems, we begin from one supposition: that the theorem is true. From that fixed starting point we deduce all the consequences. The fixed starting point serves as a constraint on one end of the procedure, but it allows for the possibility

15. Ibid., 267–68.
16. Jaakko Hintikka and Otto Remes, *The Method of Analysis* (Boston: Reidel, 1974), 32.
17. Heath, *History of Greek Mathematics*, 400.

of pursuing different paths to a variety of conclusions. All that is required is that each path be followed in a step-by-step manner and that the termination point be consistent with known principles. Stewart compares the situation to that of an inland inhabitant who wishes to leave the country via any one of a number of seaports.[18] The inhabitant assumes that a road to a seaport exists and proceeds from his starting point. His journey terminates when he reaches a (any) seaport. In the same way, if we wish to find an unknown in a geometrical figure, we must begin by assuming a solution to the problem exists. That means we also assume that what is required to solve the problem is accessible and has certain relations to the data that the conditions prescribe.

Third, Pappus's description of analysis and synthesis seems to imply that the last step of analysis is the first step of synthesis. The two steps, however, are not identical.[19] The last step of analysis of a "problem to prove" involves a theorem with which we have some familiarity. We must exert some effort to put it into a form that can serve as the first step of synthesis. The last step of analysis of a "problem to find" concludes with an unknown that can (potentially) be found by some known method. Again we must expend effort to find the unknown by some known method before it can be utilized in the synthesis.

Fourth, Pappus's account of analysis indicates that it is a procedure that is often repeated through several stages. Geometers do not usually arrive immediately at a known theorem or an unknown that can be found by a known method. They start with the givens and the thing sought, draw consequences, and consequences from the consequences, until they arrive at a conclusion that can be used as a starting point in synthesis.[20]

Fifth, the analytic branch of the procedure must be employed before the synthetic. Analysis and synthesis are not simply two alternative ways the mind can proceed through processes of reasoning.[21] Rather, the validity of the whole method emanates from both branches of the dual procedure, with analysis always preceding synthesis.

Sixth, although analysis is usually associated with discovery and synthesis with proof, the joint method depends on the mutual operation of analysis and synthesis to arrive at discoveries and demonstrations. Analysis involves discovery of consequences and leads to a tentative proof. Synthesis guarantees the convertibility of the deductions and must itself include innovation and discovery of solutions. Synthesis is

18. Stewart, *Elements*, 267.
19. See Polya, *How to Solve It*, 142–43.
20. Ibid., 142.
21. Guerlac, *Essays and Papers*, 203–6.

not merely an insignificant duplication in reverse of the stages of the analysis.

The six features that characterize geometrical analysis give some indication of its power as a method for solving mathematical problems. Innovative thinkers turned to the method of analysis and its accompanying synthesis as the means of unlocking solutions to other problems, such as those generated by the world of natural phenomena.

II. ANALYSIS AND SYNTHESIS IN NATURAL PHILOSOPHY

Scholars such as J. H. Randall, Jr., and Noretta Koertge have claimed that analysis and synthesis surfaced during the scientific revolution as the effective methodological approach that made possible the contributions of natural philosophers from Galileo to Newton.[22] Garrison suggests caution in making any generalization that the method of analysis and synthesis was the "methodological 'secret' of the heroic age of science."[23] Yet he agrees that this judgment, when applied to Newton, "seems remarkably plausible."[24] Newton himself believed in the power of the joint method of analysis and synthesis for natural philosophy. The method was intended to result in certain knowledge although the natural philosopher was a fallible human who could never completely penetrate the world of nature constructed by God.[25]

Newton gained credibility for his method by connecting it with the

---

22. J. H. Randall, Jr., *The School of Padua and the Emergence of Modern Science* (Padua: Editrice Antenore, 1961); Noretta Koertge, "Analysis as a Method of Discovery During the Scientific Revolution," *Scientific Discovery, Logic, and Rationality*, ed. Thomas Nickles (Boston: Reidel, 1980). See also Zev Bechler, *Contemporary Newtonian Research* (Boston: Reidel, 1982); Ralph Blake, "Isaac Newton and the Hypothetico-Deductive Method," *Philosophy of Science*, ed. Paul Durbin (New York: McGraw-Hill, 1968); Robert Butts and John Davis, eds., *The Methodological Heritage of Newton* (Toronto: University of Toronto Press, 1970); James Garrison, "Newton and the Relation of Mathematics to Natural Philosophy" *Journal of the History of Ideas* 48 (Oct.–Dec. 1987): 609–27; Peggy Marchi, "The Method of Analysis in Mathematics," *Scientific Discovery, Logic, and Rationality*, ed. Thomas Nickles (Boston: Reidel, 1980); E. W. Strong, "Newton's 'Mathematical Way,'" *Roots of Scientific Thought*, ed. Philip Wiener and Aaron Noland (New York: Basic Books, 1957); William A. Wallace, *Causality and Scientific Explanation*, 2 vols. (Ann Arbor: University of Michigan Press, 1972); William A. Wallace, "Newton's Early Writings: Beginnings of a New Direction," *Newton and the New Direction in Science*, ed. G. V. Coyne, S. M. Heller, and J. Zycinski (Vatican City: Vatican Observatory, 1988).

23. Garrison, "Newton and the Relation," 622.

24. Ibid., 623.

25. See Barbara Shapiro, *Probability and Certainty in Seventeenth-Century England* (Princeton, N.J.: Princeton University Press, 1983), 17. Note that Shapiro, who wants to insist on the probabilism of science, has to acknowledge Newton as an exception who strove to move beyond probabilism to certainty in science. She avoids confronting or explaining that reality by focusing on the pre-Newtonian era.

method used in mathematics. The method of mathematical analysis as developed by seventeenth-century mathematicians had deep roots in ancient geometry. Seventeenth-century mathematicians, including Newton, believed that the ancient geometers had had a powerful method for making discoveries. Pappus left some clues, but the process by which actual discoveries had been made was lost. Works surviving from the ancient world were written in the demonstrative language of synthetic geometry. Seventeenth-century mathematicians set themselves the task of recovering analysis as the method of discovering solutions to mathematical problems.[26] Not surprisingly, Newton tried to uncover the essence of analysis and develop a version for discovering solutions to problems in natural philosophy. Newton's own work in natural philosophy demands that we situate his description of the method of analysis and synthesis in a broad context that includes applications to both the empirical and physicomathematical sciences.

Turning to Newton's description of method in Query 31, six features emerge. First, Newton specifically says, "Analysis consists in making experiments and observations" (*Opticks* 404). It is clearly a method that involves actual phenomena. Garrison aptly explains that

> an experiment is an empirical instantiation of a theorem in natural philosophy, just as a geometrical figure is an empirical instantiation of a geometrical theorem; in both the general approach is to study the interdependencies among the various elements of the configuration, those that are known (independent variables) and those that are unknown (dependent variables).[27]

In other words, any particular experiment is one model of the fit or

---

26. Richard Westfall, *Never at Rest: A Biography of Isaac Newton* (Cambridge: Cambridge University Press, 1980), 24. Westfall points out that whereas seventeenth-century mathematicians paid tribute to ancient Greek geometrical analysis, in reality, seventeenth-century analysis depended upon algebra, a form of mathematics that had not been developed by the ancient world. The further seventeenth-century mathematicians advanced in reconstructing "analysis," the more removed their version became from ancient geometry. The central problems of ancient geometry, the solid loci problems (*locus solidus* or conics), provide an illustration. Books VII and VIII of Pappus's *Collection* served as the source on ancient views. Descartes used algebraic techniques to work on the problems in his *Geometry* (1637). Newton tackled the problems, and although his orientation has been considered classical, the techniques he used pointed toward the advancements he had made in the calculus (Westfall, 378–79). Note that Newton's early treatise on the calculus is called "De analysi" (Westfall, *Never at Rest*, 717–20). See David Gregory, "Memoranda by David Gregory" (nos. 444, 445, 461), *The Correspondence of Isaac Newton*, vol. 3, ed. H. W. Turnbull (Cambridge: Cambridge University Press, 1961), esp. 329–33, 385–89; Cohen, *Newtonian Revolution*, 294; D. T. Whiteside, "Introduction," *The Mathematical Works of Isaac Newton*, 2 vols. (New York: Johnson Reprint Corporation, 1964); J. J. Milne, "Newton's Contribution to the Geometry of Conics," *Isaac Newton, 1642–1727*, ed. W. J. Greenstreet (London: G. Bell and Sons, 1927).

27. Garrison, "Newton and the Relation," 620.

lack of fit between a theorem in natural philosophy and the actual phenomena of nature, just as a geometrical figure is one embodiment of actual geometrical constructs flowing from a geometrical theorem.

In the same way, a purely mathematical idealization in the physicomathematical sciences is an instantiation of natural phenomena. Cohen's account of the "Newtonian style" of the *Principia* captures the thrust of Newton's position: mathematical entities are derived from phenomena and must be tested against the phenomena.[28]

Although the physicomathematical sciences are less directly linked to experimentation than the empirical sciences, the point is that Newton's description of analysis and synthesis applies to both the experimentation of the empirical sciences (for example, the *Opticks*) and the mathematical idealizations of the physicomathematical sciences (such as the *Principia*). Moreover, the analysis and synthesis of Newton's natural philosophy as a whole (that is, whether applied to the empirical or physicomathematical sciences) compare to the nature of geometrical analysis and synthesis. The primary difference is that in geometrical analysis and synthesis one is analyzing concrete magnitudes constructed by humans, whereas in natural philosophy one is analyzing concrete phenomena that can be measured experimentally or mathematically idealized by humans but are produced by nonhuman forces (such as God, from Newton's point of view).[29] This difference indicates why the analysis and synthesis of natural philosophy are more difficult and lead to less certain conclusions than geometrical analysis and synthesis. Natural philosophy deals with objects of study that are further removed from human construction and human knowledge. Yet Newton himself never wavers in his belief in reality or necessary causal knowledge in natural philosophy. His metaphysical commitment to the simplicity of nature guarantees truth and the possibility of certain knowledge.[30]

Second, just as geometers assume "that which is sought as if it were already done,"[31] natural philosophers believe in the reality of explanations required by the phenomena. In the empirical sciences they begin by assuming the existence of a cause or general conclusion that

---

28. Cohen, *Newtonian Revolution*, xii–xiii.
29. Garrison, "Newton and the Relation," 620.
30. Recall Newton's "Rules of Reasoning in Philosophy" in the *Mathematical Principles* (398–400). Rule I reads, "We are to admit no more causes of natural things than such as are both true and sufficient to explain their appearances." Newton adds, "Nature is pleased with simplicity, and affects not the pomp of superfluous causes." He goes on to state Rule II: "Therefore to the same natural effects we must, as far as possible, assign the same causes."
31. Heath, *History of Greek Mathematics*, 400.

would account for the phenomena proceeding from it. The conclusion must be put in a form that is worthy and capable of being tested. In the physicomathematical sciences, natural philosophers begin with "nature simplified and idealized, leading to an imaginative construct in the mathematical domain."[32] They use mathematical calculations to deduce consequences that must be compared to experimental data. In both the empirical and the physicomathematical sciences the thing sought is the explanation of the phenomena. Natural philosophers proceed from the belief that the phenomena will admit of an explanation. The phenomena would be accounted for if the explanation or conclusion were true. Recall that Newton makes a statement in the *Opticks* that can apply to both the empirical and the physicomathematical sciences: "if no exception occur from the phenomena, the conclusion may be pronounced generally" (404).

Third, as in geometrical analysis and synthesis, the final step in Newtonian analysis cannot be equated with the first step of synthesis without the application of a known method. Analysis is not a procedure that merely accumulates the results of observations and experiments. It requires a method to formulate generalizations and make sense of the possible chaos of observed phenomena. Some known methods utilized by Newton in the empirical sciences include experimentation, induction, reasoning *ex suppositione*, and *experimentum crucis*. Through carefully designed experimentation, the natural philosopher can try to minimize the interference of accidental causes. Induction describes the capacity of the human mind to formulate generalizations (or causes) on the basis of effects that come before the senses as particular physical phenomena. Often the natural philosopher must consciously reason *ex suppositione*.[33] That is, the natural philosopher must develop an ideal supposition that an effect will be attained and reason to the antecedent causes of that effect. Reasoning *ex suppositione* is not arbitrary because suppositions are derived from observation of what takes place in nature "regularly or for the most part" and those suppositions can be verified by experiment.[34] Although Hooke's arguments often sound Baconian, he understood the persuasive force of even one *experimentum crucis*:

> But, how certain soever I think myself of my hypothesis (which I did not take up without first trying some hundreds of experiments) yet I should be very glad to meet with one *experimentum crucis* from Mr. Newton, that should divorce me from it.[35]

32. Cohen, *Newtonian Revolution*, xii.
33. Wallace, "Galileo and Reasoning *Ex Suppositione*," *Prelude to Galileo*, 132–33.
34. Wallace, *Prelude*, 145.
35. Robert Hooke, paper presented to the Royal Society of London, 1671/72, *Isaac*

Newton, himself, considered his prismatic experiment determining the composition of white light an *experimentum crucis*. He replies to Hooke: "On *this* [*experimentum crucis*] I chose to lay the whole stress of my discourse."[36] The words of Isaac Barrow, Newton's teacher, help to explain Newton's position:

> The truth of principles does not solely depend on induction, or a perpetual observation of particulars, as Aristotle seems to have thought; since only one experiment will suffice (provided it be sufficiently clear and indubitable) to establish a true hypothesis, to form a true definition; and consequently to constitute true principles. I own the perfection of sense is in some measure required to establish the truth of hypotheses, but the universality or frequency of observation is not so.[37]

Clearly, analysis in the empirical sciences does not involve merely collecting data on the basis of observation. When applied to the physicomathematical sciences, analysis relies even less on observation. For example, in the physicomathematical sciences, a supposition or mathematical idealization is not developed through observing what regularly occurs in nature. Rather, suppositions in the physicomathematical sciences have the character of mathematical definitions or mathematical laws that describe mathematical entities moving in mathematical time in geometrical space.[38] Of course, such mathematical suppositions must ultimately be tested against the experimental data. The physicomathematical sciences then share with the empirical sciences the possibility of utilizing the known methods of well-designed experiments, including the *experimentum crucis,* and induction.

Fourth, like geometrical analysis, Newtonian analysis operates through several stages and is always open to revision: "But if at any time afterwards any exception shall occur from experiments, it may then begin to be pronounced with such exceptions as occur" (*Opticks* 404). Such a statement applies to both the empirical and the physicomathematical sciences. Cohen conveys the sense of revision and repetition in his description of the method of the *Principia*.[39] After consequences are deduced from the original mathematical idealization and compared

---

Newton's Papers and Letters on Natural Philosophy, ed. I. Bernard Cohen (Cambridge, Mass.: Harvard University Press, 1958), 111.

36. Isaac Newton, "Answer to some Considerations [of Hooke] upon his Doctrine of Light and Colors" *Philosophical Transactions,* no. 80 (18 November 1672), 5102, in Cohen, ed., *Papers and Letters,* 134.

37. Isaac Barrow, *Mathematical Lectures Read in the Publick Schools at the University of Cambridge,* trans. John Kirby (London, 1734), 116, quoted in Guerlac, *Essays and Papers,* 209.

38. Cohen, *Newtonian Revolution,* xii.

39. Ibid., xiii.

to the experimental data, the original mathematical idealization often must be altered and the process repeated. For example,

> Newton starts out with a mass point in a central force field and deduces a law of areas. Later he will add conditions of a second body mutually interacting with the original one, then still other bodies. He will eventually consider bodies of finite sizes and specified shapes and constitutions rather than essentially mass points, and will even pursue the possibilities of various types of resisting mediums through which they may move.[40]

Future work in science can always uncover exceptions, anomalies, and more data requiring an explanation. Newton did not want to deny either the possibility of certitude in scientific knowledge or the evolutionary, sometimes revolutionary, character of scientific development.

Fifth, as Cotes reminds readers in the preface to the *Principia*, Newton's scientific method comprises two branches, the analytic and the synthetic. The analytic branch must be worked through prior to the synthetic. Cotes explains that natural philosophers who possess Newton's experimental philosophy

> proceed therefore in a twofold method; synthetical and analytical. From some select phenomena they deduce by analysis the forces of nature and the more simple laws of forces; and from thence by synthesis show the constitution of the rest. This is the incomparably best way of philosophizing, which our renowned author most justly embraced in preference to the rest. . . .[41]

Newton's description of the method in Query 31 of the *Opticks* makes it clear that both analysis and synthesis are parts of experimental philosophy. Analysis relies on experiments and observations, generalizes results by induction, and proceeds from effects to causes. Newton writes,

> In the two first books of these Opticks, I proceeded by this *analysis* to discover and prove the original differences of the rays of light in respect of refrangibility, reflexibility, and colour. . . [my emphasis]. (*Opticks* 405)

Synthesis follows analysis and assumes the causes as principles, accounts for the phenomena deduced from them, and therefore proves the explanatory cause. Newton claims he has given an "instance . . . in the end of the first book" where "these discoveries being proved [by experiment], may be assumed in the method of composition [that is, *synthesis*] for explaining the phenomena arising from them" [my

---

40. Ibid.
41. Roger Cotes, "Preface to the Second Edition" (1713) in Newton, *Mathematical Principles*, xx–xxi.

emphasis] (*Opticks* 405). One example at the end of book I is Proposition 8, which states, "By the discovered properties of light to explain the colours made by prisms" (*Opticks* 161).

Newton's description of analysis and synthesis also applies to the physicomathematical science of the *Principia*. Analysis in that case refers to the abstraction from or simplification and idealization of nature that precede any mathematical demonstration or synthesis. Although Cohen recognizes idealization as the first phase of Newton's method in the *Principia*, he refuses to associate it with analysis. Cohen's view of analysis remains too narrowly confined to induction: "In the *Principia* the role of induction is minimal and there is hardly a trace of the analysis which Newton said should always precede synthesis."[42] Yet analysis as "idealization" or "abstraction" in the physicomathematical sciences compares to the essence of what analysis means in the experimental sciences. Note Newton's words in a draft of a letter to Cotes: "Experimental philosophy *reduces* phaenomena to general rules and looks upon the rules to be general when they hold generally in phaenomena" [my emphasis].[43] Analysis to general rules is itself a form of abstraction. Of course, analysis in both the empirical and the physicomathematical sciences must be infused with a way to compare the "general rules" or the mathematical "idealizations" to experimental data. For Newton, neither the explanatory causes (that is, general rules or conclusions) of the empirical sciences nor the mathematical principles or systems of the physicomathematical sciences are equivalent to hypotheses in the sense of romantic fictions or imaginary arguments. In the same draft Newton contrasts experimental philosophy with the hypothetical philosophy that "consists in imaginary explications of things."[44] He claims that he follows the first sort of philosophy, whereas the latter is followed "too much by Cartes, Leibniz and some others."[45]

Sixth, the power of the method of analysis and synthesis in natural philosophy (both the empirical and the physicomathematical components), as in geometry, derives from the operation of both the analytic and the synthetic branches of the method. Although analysis is usually identified with discovery and synthesis with proof, Newton indicates that analysis and synthesis each involve both discovery and proof. As we have seen in Query 31, Newton specifically says: "In the two first

---

42. Cohen, *Newtonian Revolution*, 16.
43. A. Rupert Hall and Laura Tilling, eds., *The Correspondence of Isaac Newton*, vol. 5 (Cambridge: Cambridge University Press, 1975), 398.
44. *Correspondence*, 398.
45. *Correspondence*, 398–99.

books of these Opticks I proceeded by this analysis to *discover and prove* the original differences of the rays of light" [my emphasis] (*Opticks* 405). Synthesis also points to discovery and proof. For example, Newton writes in an unpublished manuscript that after having discovered the law of gravity "from phenomena" he can use it as a principle to predict and discover new phenomena:

> I derived from it all the motions of the heavenly bodies and the flux and reflux of the sea, showing by mathematical demonstrations that this force alone was sufficient to produce all those phenomena, and *deriving from it (a priori) some new motions which astronomers had not then observed but since appear to be true*, as that Saturn and Jupiter draw one another, that the variation of the moon is bigger in winter than in summer, that there is an equation of the moon's mean motion amounting to almost five minutes which depends upon the position of her apogee to the sun. [my emphasis][46]

Although synthesis has some role in discovery, as indicated by the preceding quote, in Query 31 Newton describes synthesis by saying that it consists in explaining the phenomena proceeding from causes and principles and "proving the explanations" (*Opticks* 405).

If looked at separately, analysis and synthesis have similar roles: each can be described as a method of discovery and proof. This observation might clarify why it is natural for the discovery emphasis of analysis to blend with the probative power of synthesis, and the demonstrative emphasis of synthesis to assume the discovery of analysis. The analytic method, although somewhat probative, does not include strict demonstration: argument dependent on induction is "no demonstration of general conclusions" (*Opticks* 404). Analysis requires synthesis to complete the proof and achieve necessary knowledge. Synthesis is not a mere rewriting of analysis. As Stewart explains

> in natural philosophy, a synthesis which merely reversed the analysis would be absurd. On the contrary, our analysis necessarily sets out from *known facts*; and after it has conducted as to a general principle, the synthetical reasoning which follows consists always of an application of this principle to phenomena, *different* from those comprehended in the original induction.[47]

Just as analysis must be conjoined with synthesis, synthesis demands analysis to make Newton's joint method a tool of discovery and proof. In the *Opticks* Newton writes that synthesis "consists in *assuming the causes discovered,* and established as principles, and by them explaining the phenomena proceeding from them, and proving the explanations"

---

46. Newton, Cambridge University Library, MS. Add. 3970, quoted in Guerlac, *Essays and Papers*, 211.
47. Stewart, *Elements*, 275.

[my emphasis] (405). Despite the fact that synthesis proceeds from causes and principles by deduction, its true demonstrative force for natural philosophy emerges only when synthesis is viewed in conjunction with analysis. The power of the joint method for the empirical sciences guarantees that general principles reduced from contingent phenomena explain actual occurrences in nature. In the physicomathematical sciences the joint method of analysis and synthesis keeps mathematical idealizations, such as those that ground the *Principia*, from being merely fictions.

III. GEOMETRY'S EMPIRICAL NATURE

The six features of Newton's method of analysis and synthesis match the six features of Pappus's description of geometrical analysis and synthesis.[48] Both the geometrical method and the method used in natural philosophy work with concrete instantiations; presuppose the reality of the end to be accomplished; rely on other known methods to convert the last step of analysis to the first step of synthesis; proceed through repeated stages, with analysis preceding synthesis; and are powerful tools of discovery *and* proof. Additional comparisons could have been made, but enough has been said to demonstrate the similarity between geometrical analysis and synthesis and Newtonian analysis and synthesis applied to natural philosophy. The parallel drawn by Newton between the analysis and synthesis of natural philosophy and mathematical analysis and synthesis makes eminent sense.

Not only did Newton want to emphasize the parallel between mathematical analysis and synthesis and the analysis and synthesis of natural philosophy but he intended his description of the method of analysis and synthesis to apply to his entire natural philosophy, that is, to both the empirical science of the *Opticks* and the physicomathe-

---

48. See n. 26. The opening words of Newton's "Preface to the First Edition" (1686) of the *Principia* attest to his familiarity with and deep regard for the ancient geometers: "Since the ancients (as we are told by Pappus) esteemed the science of mechanics of greatest importance in the investigation of natural things, and the moderns, rejecting substantial forms and occult qualities, have endeavored to subject the phenomena of nature to the laws of mathematics, I have in this treatise *cultivated mathematics as far as it relates to philosophy*. The ancients considered mechanics in a twofold respect; as rational, which proceeds accurately by demonstration, and practical. To practical mechanics all the manual arts belong, from which mechanics took its name. But as artificers do not work with perfect accuracy, it comes to pass that mechanics is so distinguished from geometry that *what is perfectly accurate is called geometrical*; what is less so, is mechanical" [my emphasis] (*Mathematical Principles*, xvii). In his preface to the *Geometria*, most likely written in 1693, Newton refers to Pappus often. See D. T. Whiteside, ed. *The Mathematical Papers of Isaac Newton*, vol. 7 (Cambridge: Cambridge University Press, 1976).

matical science of the *Principia*. As we have seen, Newton succeeded in his intention. For example, the first step of empirical analysis and the first step of physicomathematical analysis are more than analogous. Empirical analysis starts with a natural supposition derived from observation of contingent physical phenomena. Physicomathematical analysis commences with a mathematical idealization of contingent nature. The potentially problematic issue of applying Newton's empirical description of analysis and synthesis in Query 31 of the *Opticks* to the physicomathematical science of the *Principia* can be resolved by recalling Newton's view of mathematics.

Mathematics stemmed from two traditions, the philosophical and the geometrical. In the philosophical traditions of Plato and Aristotle, mathematical entities did not require matter for their being understood. They could be thought of as having an ideal existence apart from embodiment in matter and therefore as free from change. The increasing application of mathematics to problems in natural philosophy caused thinkers to address the question of the possibility of certain knowledge in the physicomathematical sciences. Viewing mathematical entities strictly as ideal or formal raised two potential problems: it was not immediately apparent what role mathematical entities could play in arguments from effect to cause (the way to argue when dealing with physical phenomena), because in mathematics causes were considered more known than their effects. Moreover, if mathematical entities were not real, natural philosophers did not know how they could use them to guarantee the necessity or absolute truth of physical causes.[49] Newton's solution was to turn to the geometrical tradition in mathematics. In the geometrical tradition of Euclid and Archimedes, mathematical entities had not only an ideal existence but a physical existence. Geometry, after all, was about physical objects extended in space. As Garrison asserts, "For Newton, there was no such thing as an absolutely pure geometry completely devoid of empirical content."[50] Newton's own words from the preface of the *Principia* make his position clear:

> To describe right lines and circles are problems, but not geometrical problems. The solution of these problems is required from mechanics, and by geometry the use of them, when so solved, is shown; and it is the glory of geometry that from those few principles, brought from without, it is able to produce some many things. Therefore geometry is founded in mechanical practice,

---

49. See William A. Wallace, "The Problem of Causality in Galileo's Science" *Review of Metaphysics* 36 (March 1983): 615; and Feldhay, "Catholicism and the Emergence," 145–46.

50. Garrison, "Newton and the Relation," 612.

and is nothing but that part of universal mechanics which accurately proposes and demonstrates the art of measuring.[51]

The mathematical "idealizations" in Newton's geometrically presented *Principia* exist in an empirical context: they are derived from the physical world and are tested against experiential data.

Understanding Newton's realistic insight into the empirical character of geometry and his liberation of the ancient method of analysis and synthesis from strictly geometrical applications resolves the apparent contradictions associated with his statement on method in Query 31. The empirical nature of Newton's geometry allowed him to compare the method of natural philosophy to the method of mathematics meaningfully. When he described the method of natural philosophy in empirical terms, Newton's commitment to the empirical character of geometry gave him confidence that his description could apply to both the empirical science of the *Opticks* and the physico-mathematical science of the *Principia*.[52]

51. Newton, "Preface to the First Edition" (1686), *Mathematical Principles*, xvii.
52. Research for this paper was supported in part by a National Endowment for the Humanities Summer Seminar stipend. I must thank Professor Everett Mendelsohn, the director of the seminar, for helpful advice during the early stages of this paper. The debt of gratitude that I owe to Father William A. Wallace cannot be measured. Since the time I was a graduate student, Father Wallace has been my guide through the history and philosophy of science.

15   Kant's Metaphysics of Nature
DANIEL O. DAHLSTROM

Kant's critical philosophy is repeatedly reproached for having presupposed the validity of the basic principles of Newtonian mechanics. If that reproach can indeed be sustained, contemporary physics's successful challenge to these principles extends (*modus tollens*) to the critical philosophy itself. On this view, study of the system of transcendental principles in the *Critique of Pure Reason* may still be useful to the philosopher of science if only to illustrate the dubiousness of a certain kind of reflection on basic principles employed in (contemporary) physics.[1]

Yet Kant himself construed his transcendental principles as necessary rather than sufficient conditions for the study of nature in general, an *Inbegriff* of objects given in some sense to a finite knower. Though he ultimately rejected the notion that either rational or empirical psychology could constitute a science in the proper sense of the term,[2] he nonetheless acknowledged that both psychology and physics were conceivable on the basis of transcendental philosophy, that is, as sciences corresponding to two sorts of objects, those given to inner sense alone and those given to external sense as well (B873–74; MAN 467; 470). Thus, in order to establish that Kant's transcendental principles are only as valid as his physics, it is necessary to show that, Kant's own views notwithstanding, physical principles play decisive roles in the formulations and proofs of the transcendental principles.

---

1. Though transcendental philosophers of science are today plainly an endangered species, see C. F. von Weizäcker, "Kant's 'First Analogy of Experience' and Conservation Principles of Physics" *Synthesis*, 23, no. 1 (1971): 75–95 and W. H. Werkmeister, "Kant and Modern Science," in *Immanuel Kant: Reflections on his Philosophy,* ed. Werkmeister (Tallahassee: Florida State University Press, 1975).

2. Immanuel Kant, *Kritik der reinen Vernunft* (Hamburg: Meiner, 1976), B876 (hereafter *KrV* B876). The second edition of the *KrV* is cited when the text is the same in both editions. When the text cited is to be found only in the first or in the second edition, the abbreviation is italicized, for example, *A392* or *B425*. Immanuel Kant, *Metaphysische Anfangsgründe der Naturwissenschaften* in *Kants Werke*, Akademie-Textausgabe, Band IV (Berlin: de Gruyter, 1968), S. 471 (hereafter *MAN* 471).

There can be no doubt, on the one hand, that the erection of a distinctive doctrine of physics, though hardly a mirror of Newton's own physics, was one of the goals of the critical philosophy and thus in some sense played a significant role in the genesis and structure of that philosophy from its inception.[3] Indeed, there is at least no prima facie difference between his formulation of certain transcendental principles and his formulation of specific principles in his physics.[4] On the other hand, Kant maintains that there is a clear distinction between transcendental philosophy and physics, including that part of physics drafted in 1786 as *Metaphysische Anfangsgründe der Naturwissenschaft* (*MAN*), an apparent realization of the metaphysics of nature promised in the first edition of the *Kritik der reinen Vernunft* (*KrV*). *MAN* contains synthetic–a priori judgments that involve some sort of application of the transcendental principles, an application not possible in regard to psychology. However, since the principles of *MAN* start from an empirical assumption, they are to be distinguished from the system of *transcendental* principles elaborated in the Transcendental Analytic of *KrV*.[5] In order to sustain the reproach that Kant's transcendental philosophy is a mere *apologia pro sua physica*, only as secure as that physics, the *question of the autonomy of the transcendental philosophy* must be answered: does Kant's articulation of and argument for those transcendental principles succeed without recourse to the principles of his physics? Or, since the empirical concept of matter is placed by Kant at the basis of his physics, is he able to establish (indeed, prove)

---

3. Kant's 31 December 1765 letter to Lambert (*Kants Werke*, Band X S. 53) indicates how early Kant conceived the idea of a metaphysics of nature; see also the letter of 2 September 1770. Prominent among his differences with Newton, Kant countenanced theories of neither absolute space nor absolute motion nor matter as composed of "solid, massy, hard, impenetrable, movable particles" (Newton, *Opticks* 375–76). See *MAN* 523: "das so genannte Solide ... (wird) ... als ein leerer Begriff, aus der Naturwissenschaft verwiesen"; *MAN* 559: "absolute Bewegung, d.i. eine solche, die ohne alle Beziehung einer Materie auf eine andere gedacht wird, (ist) schlechthin unmöglich"; *MAN* 481: "Der absolute Raum ist also *an sich* nichts. . . , sondern bedeutet nur einen jenen andern relativen Raum. . . ." Gordan Brittan argues that Kant's transcendental philosophy is an attempt to give an antireductionist interpretation of Newtonian science; see his *Kant's Theory of Science* (Princeton, N.J.: Princeton University Press, 1978).

4. Perhaps the most notorious instance is Kant's reformulation of the First Analogy (B224) and the "first law of mechanics," as he formulates it in the Second Principle of his Mechanics (*MAN* 541).

5. The task Kant explicitly sets for himself in the *Opus postumum*, namely, the transition from the *Metaphysische Anfangsgründe der Naturwissenschaft* to physics, is not treated in what follows. See Hansgeorg Hoppe, *Kants Theorie der Physik: Eine Untersuchung über das Opus postumum von Kant* (Frankfurt am Main: Klostermann, 1969), and W. H. Werkmeister, *Kant: The Architectonic and Development of his Philosophy* (LaSalle, Ill.: Open Court, 1980), chapter 6 (hereafter, Werkmeister 1980).

the system of transcendental principles without appealing to that empirical concept?[6]

The autonomy question in regard to the transcendental principles (of *KrV*) cannot be suitably addressed without a clear understanding of the principles of Kant's physics and their empirical assumption. However, there is also an *autonomy question regarding the metaphysical principles of natural science* (*MAN*) insofar as these principles involve an application of transcendental principles. Since the transcendental principles have already been established as the conditions of any possible experience, how can the metaphysical principles of *MAN* and their proofs be other than redundant, if not otiose?[7] In an attempt to clarify the distinctive character of Kant's metaphysics of nature, the following paper first examines Kant's explicit accounts of the relation obtaining between the system of transcendental principles and the metaphysical first principles of nature, especially in the Architectonic to *KrV* and in the Preface to *MAN*. The second part of the paper offers an interpretation of the distinctive role played by the empirical concept of matter in the constitution of the *Metaphysical First Principles of Natural Science*. The aim in both sections of the paper is to demonstrate how the thesis of the autonomy of the metaphysics of nature can be sustained, despite its subordinate status within the transcendental philosophy. Demonstrating in this way why Kant saw the need for a metaphysics of nature suggests, in addition, a possible solution to the question of the autonomy of the transcendental philosophy itself.

1. PHILOSOPHY, PHYSICS, AND "SYSTEMATIC ARTS"

The demonstration of the system of transcendental principles purportedly does not rest on empirical assumptions. At the same time, while claiming not to derive his system of principles from his physics, Kant also insists that "empirical laws" grasped in the study of nature, though subject to the categories of the understanding, can never be derived from them (A127; B165). Indeed, since the principles of pos-

---

6. Closely related to these questions is the issue underlying the debate between neo-Kantian and Heideggerian interpreters of Kant: is the experience, for which the conditions of possibility are purportedly established in *KrV*, scientific, prescientific, or nonscientific?

7. This question represents one side of a dilemma suggested by the idea of a *MAN*, a system of synthetic–a priori judgments founded upon an empirical assumption. The question constituting the other side of the dilemma of *MAN* is, Why can the system of transcendental principles (the positive conclusion to *KrV*) be applied to yield a metaphysics of matter but not of the psyche or of chemical bonding?

sible experience must contain nothing empirical, Kant adds, "We cannot anticipate the general science of nature, which is built upon specific fundamental experiences, without damaging the unity of the system" (B213).

Is Kant referring in these passages to the (sort of) physics included in *MAN*? The question cannot be answered straightforwardly. Probably not in the first passage (*A127*), since it refers explicitly to "empirical laws," and it would be misleading to refer to the principles of *MAN* as empirical. For the other passage also composed well before *MAN* (*A171–172*), Kant may have something like *MAN* in mind since he there refers explicitly to the unity of the system and, in that connection, to a "general science of nature, which is built on specific fundamental experiences."[8] The last passage (*B165*), composed after the publication of *MAN*, refers to "particular laws," which, "since they concern empirically determined appearances, cannot be *completely derived*" (*nicht vollständig abgeleitet*) from the a priori laws based upon the categories alone. This passage suggests the derivability of particular laws from transcendental principles, perhaps with the addition of specific principles (premises). Since a distinction between transcendental and particular parts of the science of nature is invoked in the Preface to *MAN*, there is reason to think that here at least—after its publication—Kant indeed is thinking of *MAN*.

Kant does refer to the system of transcendental principles as "pure natural science" (*reine Naturwissenschaft*) in the *Prolegomena* and as "the doctrine of nature of pure reason" (*die Naturlehre der reinen Vernunft*) in *KrV*. However, he insists that the latter be distinguished from the metaphysics of corporeal nature, namely, physics ("*Die Metaphysik der körperlichen Natur heißt* Physik") (B873–76; *Prolegomena* 295[9]). In both disciplines there are synthetic–a priori judgments, but the difference between the two disciplines consists in the difference between *pure* principles, devoid of any empirical assumptions, and principles employing some such assumptions (*impure* synthetic–a prior judgments; see B3). Kant also characterizes this difference as that between the principles and their application. The transcendental principle "substance remains and endures," Kant notes in the *Prolegomena*, is "fully a priori," in contrast to propositions concerning motion and impe-

---

8. A171–72, B213: "Da wir aber hier nichts vor uns haben, dessen wir uns bedienen können, als die reinen Grundbegriffe aller möglichen Erfahrung, unter welchen durchaus nichts Empirisches sein muß; so können wir, ohne die Einheit des Systems zu verletzen, der allgemeinen Naturwissenschaft, welche auf gewisse Grunderfahrungen gebaut ist, nicht vorgreifen."

9. All references to the *Prolegomena* are taken from *Kants Werke* IV (Berlin: de Gruyter, 1968), S. 253–384.

netrability, which are nonetheless a priori and proper to the pure part of natural science, the "general natural science" logically prior to any physics grounded on empirical principles. Kant's discussion here in the *Prolegomena* is cause for some confusion (discussed later), inasmuch as (within the space of three lines!) he first locates notions of motion and matter within "the philosophical part of the pure knowledge of nature" and then adds that such notions are "not completely pure and independent of sources in experience" (*Prolegomena* 295).

Nevertheless, despite the ambiguities, it seems legitimate to conclude from these passages that Kant considered neither the principles of physics derivative from transcendental principles alone nor transcendental principles derivative from the principles of physics. This last claim, to be sure, requires some clarification. Transcendental principles constitute necessary but not sufficient conditions for the principles of physics. Given the physical principles, it is possible, of course, to derive or unpack their necessary conditions, some of which may appear identical to the transcendental principles. However, that such principles are *transcendental,* that is, conditions of *any* possible experience, regardless of the type of objects experienced, is hardly established by such a derivation.

Brittan has argued that there is an inconsistency between the *KrV* and the *Prolegomena* in the way Kant formulates his conception of principles and natural science.[10] In the Introduction to *KrV* Kant refers to principles of matter as synthetic–a priori judgments contained in the "pure part of natural science" (B17–18), whereas in the *Prolegomena*, as noted, he indicates that these same principles are "not entirely pure and independent of sources in experience," such that they cannot be called a "completely pure natural science" (IV 295). Kant's terminology, especially his reference to "pure natural science" and to the "pure part of natural science," is, to be sure, a potential source of confusion (see his own admission of equivocation in the use of the word *pure*[11]). Kant does refer, as noted in the previous paragraph, to the system of transcendental (*pure* synthetic–a priori) principles itself as a "pure natural science." But there is no inconsistency and no confusion if the difference between this pure natural science and the pure

---

10. Brittan, *Kant's Theory of Science,* 131ff. Brittan thinks that the inconsistency "stems not from carelessness but from a deep tension in the position" taken by Kant.

11. At the conclusion of *Über den Gebrauch teleologischer Principien in der Philosophie* in *Kants Werke* VIII (Berlin: de Gruyter, 1968), S. 183–84, Kant excuses himself for using *rein* equivocally in the introduction to the second edition of *KrV* (viz. to characterize a knowing "unmixed" with or devoid of anything empirical and a knowing that, even if mixed, is a priori, that is, valid "independent" of anything empirical).

Chart 1: Outline of the Sciences from the Architectonic to *KrV*

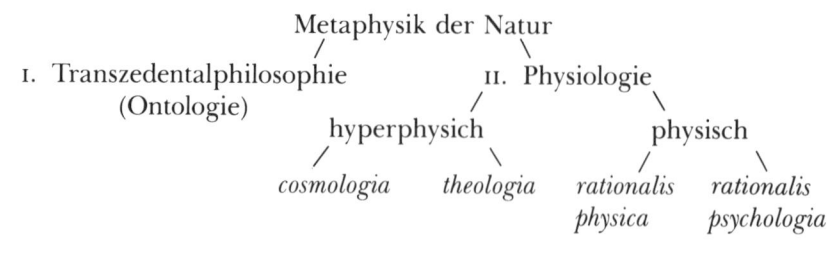

```
                       Metaphysik der Natur
                      /                    \
   I. Transzedentalphilosophie          II. Physiologie
         (Ontologie)                   /              \
                                hyperphysich         physisch
                                /        \          /        \
                          cosmologia   theologia  rationalis  rationalis
                                                  physica    psychologia
```

part of natural science is interpreted as exemplifying the distinction between *pure* and *impure* synthetic–a priori judgments.[12]

This interpretation is confirmed by Kant's schema (Chart 1) of the system of all philosophical knowledge in the Architectonic (B873–76). The *transcendental philosophy* is concerned with "a system of all concepts and principles which refer to objects in general, without assuming objects which *would be given (gegeben wären)*," whereas the *physiology* considers "*nature*, i.e. the conceptual basis (*Inbegriff*) of *given* objects" (B873). Corporeal nature, the object of the outer sense, is the particular conceptual basis (*Inbegriff*) of the "rationalis physica," so named "because it is supposed to contain only the principles of its knowledge a priori" (B874). To the understandable query how one can expect knowledge a priori and thus metaphysics from "given," that is to say, a posteriori objects, Kant replies: "The answer is: we take from experience nothing further than is necessary for an object ... of the outer sense to be *given*. That occurs through the mere concept of matter (impenetrable, lifeless extension). . . ." (B876).[13]

Ostensibly the same distinction between transcendental philosophy and rational physics is invoked in the *Metaphysical Principles of Natural Science*. A *pure rational science of nature* contains only natural laws known a priori.[14]

---

12. Brittan (*Kant's Theory of Science*) himself refers to these distinctions at 132, n. 23, and 137, n. 33.

13. As Gloy points out, Kant's "metaphysics of corporeal nature" is misleading since he has in mind his physics of matter and since "body" signifies "a formed matter." See Karen Gloy, *Die Kantische Theorie der Naturwissenschaft: Eine Strukturanalyse ihrer Möglichkeit, ihres Umfangs und ihrer Grenzen* (Berlin: de Gruyter, 1976), 194Anm30. See also Peter Plaass, *Kants Theorie der Naturwissenschaft: Eine Untersuchung zur Vorrede von Kants "Metaphysische Anfangsgründe der Naturwissenschaften"* (Göttingen: Vandenhoeck & Ruprecht, 1965), S. 92.

14. *Science* is, in general, a systematic whole of knowledge (*Ganze der Erkenntniß*), whereas *science proper* is apodictically certain, treating its object completely according to a priori principles. Science is *rational* when the system is connected according to reasons and inferences (*ein Zusammenhang von Gründen und Folgen*).

Every natural science *proper* thus requires a *pure* part, upon which the apodictic certainty is able to be based, which reason seeks in it. Since this pure part in terms of its principles, in comparison with those which are exclusively empirical, is utterly distinctive, it is at the same time extremely advantageous, indeed—as far as the nature of the matter is concerned—an inescapable duty in regard to the method, to develop that part in its utter completeness, separate and completely isolated from the other as much as possible. In this way one might be able to determine precisely what reason is capable of accomplishing for itself and where its capabilities begin to have need of the aid of empirical principles. Pure rational knowledge on the basis of *concepts* alone is called pure philosophy or metaphysics. (*MAN* 469)

Natural science proper thus presupposes the metaphysics of nature and the latter, Kant adds, may be *transcendental* or *particular*. The *transcendental* part of the metaphysics of nature treats or develops its principles ("laws, i.e. principles of the necessity of what belongs to the *existence* of a thing") "without regard to any sort of specific object of experience" (*ohne Beziehung auf irgend ein bestimmtes Erfahrungsobject*). A "particular metaphysical natural science" is concerned "with a particular nature of this or that sort of things, of which an empirical concept is given." Beyond this concept, namely, the concept of matter, appeal is made in *MAN* to no other empirical principle.

While insisting that natural science proper presupposes a metaphysics of nature (and thus taking aim at Galilean or Newtonian pretensions to a physics founded purely on mathematics), Kant intends neither to deny that mathematics is a necessary condition for natural science nor to oppose mathematics and metaphysics. He insists that there is only as much science proper within a particular study of nature as there is mathematics to be found in it. Knowing a priori, as is required for science proper, means knowing something on the basis of its mere possibility. Such knowing can be achieved only through *logical* considerations of the concept of a thing or through *mathematical* construal of the concept of that thing (*MAN* 470; B741). Mere logical analysis is sufficient for knowing the possibility of thought but not the possibility of some natural object (*Object als Naturding*) which, beyond being thought, must be given. Although a pure philosophy of nature in general (*was den Begriff einer Natur im Allgemeinen ausmacht*) is possible, namely the system of transcendental principles, a pure study of nature concerning specific natural things (*eine reine Naturlehre über bestimmte Naturdinge*) is only possible by means of mathematics.

On the other hand, as the title of *MAN* suggests, mathematics in its application to natural science requires metaphysics and, indeed, both transcendental and particular parts of the metaphysics of nature. The applicability of mathematics to appearances is allegedly assured by the proofs of the transcendental principles of mathematics, namely the axioms of intuition and the anticipations of experience (B221; B206; B199). But these transcendental principles do not indicate how mathematics is applicable to the specific character of objects of external appearances, namely mobile objects in space; hence the need for metaphysical principles of natural science. Accordingly, within natural science proper, mathematics and metaphysics find themselves in a collegiality (*Gemeinschaft*), they "offer each other a hand" (*Man* 470; B754). Yet even in *MAN* (not to speak of *KrV*) there are no mathematical formulas or at least no statements about nature that explicitly presuppose the application of mathematics to specific natural things. Rather *MAN* contains a series of first principles (*Anfangsgründe*), ordered according to the four "titles" (B95) of the table of categories, principles that "mathematics itself inevitably requires in its application to natural science" (*MAN* 479). The four opening explanations (*Erklärungen*) together define matter as the mobile in space (*phoronomy*), filling space (*dynamics*), possessing force (*mechanics*), and capable of being experienced (*phenomenology*). In contrast to empirical studies, these principles of "the possibility of a mathematical account of nature" are complete since corporeal nature is considered "solely according to laws of thinking" (*MAN* 473).

In the Preface to *MAN*, then, Kant outlines three levels of science in the proper sense of the term, in contrast to investigations that fall beneath that rank. There is the transcendental part of the metaphysics of nature, a purely rational knowledge on the basis of concepts alone, what Kant calls "pure philosophy or metaphysics" and "pure philosophy of nature in general." There is also the science that makes the application of mathematics specifically to matter (the movable in space) possible, namely "particular metaphysical natural science" or *MAN* itself. Then there is "a pure doctrine of nature about specific natural things," which is possible only by means of mathematics.[15] Presumably, the latter two sciences are "pure" in the senses cited previously (B17–18; *Prolegomena* 295; see n. 11), without being "completely pure natural sciences." Finally, there are investigations such as chemistry or psychology, which are better construed as "systematic arts" than sciences, since their reasons or principles as well as their laws are empirical. Chart 2 schematizes Kant's account of these levels of science and contrasting enterprises.

15. For this reason (the necessity of mathematization) and other reasons psychology is excluded from the rank of science proper; see *MAN* 471.

Chart 2: Outline of the Sciences from the Preface to *MAN*

Natural Science[16]

Properly so-called (because subject matter treated solely according to principles a priori)

Pure rational knowledge, i.e., metaphysics of nature

Transcendental

Particular
(Application of system of transcendental principles to a single empirical concept capable of construal or depiction (*Darstellung*) a priori, viz. *physica generalis*, i.e., metaphysics of corporeal nature, the systematic presentation of the principles presupposed for the application of mathematics to *Naturlehre*)

Mathematical physics

Improperly so-called (because subject matter treated according to laws of experience)

Applied rational knowledge, i.e., systematic arts (e.g., chemistry, psychology)

(The line above "Mathematical physics" is intended to indicate that mathematical physics is not part of the metaphysics of nature as such, either its transcendental or particular parts, though it does presuppose them and, presumably, does not simply fall under the heading of "Systematic arts." Also, the fact that there is only one particular metaphysics of nature that falls under the transcendental part illustrates the difficulty attending to their distinction, as discussed toward the end of this paper.)

There is some controversy as to how the accounts from the Preface to *MAN* and from the Architectonic to *KrV* cohere. Plaass has identified the transcendental part of the metaphysics of nature with the "transcendental philosophy" (*ontologia*) discussed in the Architectonic. Since that ontology, by Kant's own admission, is yet to be completed, this interpretation would render suspect Kant's claim to absolute completeness in *MAN* (IV 470, 473, 477).[17] If "the particular metaphysical

---

16. A doctrine of nature (*Naturlehre*) may be historical or rational, thus a natural history (psychology) or a natural science (physics).

17. Plaass, *Kants Theorie der Naturwissenschaft*, 67–68; Plaass also argues that derivative pure concepts (predicables, that is, combinations of categories, constituting the ontology) bear the weight in *MAN* such that only the derivation of that ontology explains the crossover of categorial considerations, such as the consideration of intensive magnitude (the transcendental principle under the second group of categories: quality) in

natural science" is the result of the application of transcendental principles, then the incompleteness of the latter seems necessarily transitive. In the face of this deficiency Plaass makes the plausible assumption that the transcendental principles, as developed in the *KrV*, the purported propadeutic to the ontology, are supposed to suffice. Thus for Plaass the transcendental part of the metaphysics of nature, as recounted in the preface to *MAN*, is supposed to refer to the system of transcendental principles, which is to be equated with the "transcendental philosophy" (ontology) described in the Architectonic. Moreover, he construes that ontology in the sense of a system or metaphysics based on concepts alone, utterly independent of intuition (or the assumption of any given objects).[18] On this interpretation, he is able to explain the difference between the transcendental and the particular parts of the metaphysics of nature in terms of the latter's assumption of a specific object.

Hoppe has criticized Plaass's interpretation, insisting that the "pure transcendental part of natural science proper" indicated in *MAN* is equivalent, not to the "ontology" but rather to the "immanent physiology" described in the Architectonic, namely the investigation concerned with nature as the conceptual core (*Inbegriff*) of all objects given to external sense according to conditions a priori. Plaass's critical questions (for example, since the ontology on which it is based has not been completed, how can *MAN* be complete?) accordingly suppose, on Hoppe's interpretation, a misunderstanding of Kant's conception of "ontology" in the Architectonic to *KrV*.[19] In the Architectonic, Hoppe claims, Kant is referring to "ontology" in the sense of "a merely illusory knowledge," namely that of "traditional, pre-Kantian metaphysics" (*eine bloß scheinbare Erkenntnis, ... die Ontologie der überlieferten, vorkantischen Metaphysik*).

Hoppe's dismissal of Kant's references to "ontology" is unconvincing. From Kant's lectures on logic there is considerable evidence for the equation of "ontology" and "transcendental philosophy" made in the Architectonic and, indeed, such that "transcendental philosophy" refers to the system of principles of the possibility of experience.[20]

---

the phoronomy that is the first part of *MAN*, purportedly corresponding to the first group of categories (quantity). So, too, the consideration of force, derived from the category of causality (from the third group of categories), occurs in the dynamics, the second part of *MAN*, purportedly corresponding to the second group of categories (quality).

18. Plaass, *Kants Theorie der Naturwissenschaft*, 69–71.
19. Hoppe, *Kants Theorie der Physik*, 32, 56.
20. See *Kant-Werke*, Band XXVIII, X. 679: "Die transcendentale Philosophie ist die Ontologie ..."; S. 617: "Ontologie ist die Wissenschaft welche Begriffe a priori zur

Moreover, Kant's description of "ontology" in the Architectonic ([*sie*] *betrachtet nur den* Verstand *und* Vernunft *selbst*) is precisely the way Kant characterizes one side of the deduction of the categories in the preface to the first edition of *KrV* (Axvii). To be sure, Kant prefers the label *transcendental philosophy* to *ontology*, especially since the latter traditionally involved the pretension to knowledge of things in themselves (B303). Nevertheless, Kant did not completely eschew *ontology* as a title for the complete system of transcendental philosophy (presumably including the system of transcendental principles as well as all the predicables or derivations from the categories and the (concepts of) pure intuitions of space and time (B108–9; *B109–10*)).

Although Hoppe's dismissal of Kant's references to "ontology" should probably not be countenanced, he is nonetheless correct to criticize Plaass for supposing that the distinction between the transcendental and particular parts of the metaphysics of nature consists in the fact that the latter alone is concerned with objects insofar as they are given to us.[21] Plaass is, of course, aware of this, but he seems to have been misled by the same sentence that (in a different way) misled Hoppe. Kant characterizes ontology as the consideration solely of understanding and reason itself "in a system of all concepts and principles, which refer to objects (*Gegenstände*) in general, without assuming objects (*Objekte*), which *would be given*" (B873). Apparently Plaass takes the last part of this sentence to mean that ontology considers the system of principles referring to objects, regardless of whether objects are given at all or, perhaps more precisely, as though no objects are given at all. However, although the sentence may be so understood, this interpretation conflicts sharply with the system of transcendental principles, that is to say, as much of the transcendental philosophy as is established in *KrV*. Most importantly, the sentence need not be taken in this way. The import of the sentence may be that the transcendental philosophy (ontology) considers the system of principles referring to objects, regardless of *which* objects are given. On this interpretation transcendental philosophy would not assume par-

---

Erkenntnis der Dinge enthält. Sie wird auch genannt Transcendentalphilosophie, ...";
S. 474: "Die Ontologie enthält die ersten Principien aller Erkenntnis, die der Erfahrung korrespondiert. ..." See also S. 7; 174–75; 390; 470; 391; 576; 622; 650–51; 711.

21. The point seems so obvious that it hardly warrants discussion. Both versions of the transcendental deduction turn on the demonstration that the categories make experience possible (A126; *B166–67*). Indeed, the objective validity of the transcendental principles is, Kant alleges, based upon the demonstration that "the conditions of the *possibility* of *experience* in general are at the same time conditions of the *possibility* of *the objects of experience*" (B197). Moreover, in both contexts "human experience" is clearly meant. Plaass, *Kants Theorie der Naturwissenschaft*, 70; Hoppe, *Kants Theorie der Physik*, 36.

ticular objects, though it does assume that some objects (without specifying which) would be given. On this interpretation the meaning of "transcendental philosophy" (ontology) here in the Architectonic is not at odds with the system of transcendental principles in *KrV* and may be equated with the "transcendental part" of the metaphysics of nature alluded to in the Preface to *MAN*.

If my interpretation is faithful to Kant's intentions, then there is no discrepancy between the *KrV* and *MAN* accounts of the relation between his philosophy and his physics. The relation between transcendental philosophy (ontology) and an immanent physiology of nature (specifically, the metaphysics of corporeal nature) announced in the Architectonic of the *KrV* corresponds to the transcendental and particular parts of the metaphysics of nature outlined in the Preface to *MAN* (Chart 3).

Chart 3: Correspondence of Kant's Outlines of the Sciences

KrV		*MAN*
Transcendental philosophy (*ontologia*)	=	Transcendental part of the metaphysics of nature
Metaphysics of corporeal nature (immanent physical physiology, i.e., rational physics)	=	Particular part of the metaphysics of nature

Yet this very consistency highlights a fundamental difficulty. Both the transcendental and the particular parts of that metaphysics of nature (in effect, the transcendental principles of *KrV* and the metaphysical principles of *MAN*) suppose that objects are sensibly given. That and even to some extent how objects are given is already central to the transcendental deduction of the categories and the proof of the system of transcendental principles. Wherein, then, lies the distinction between that system and *MAN*?

In the Architectonic Kant notes that what distinguishes the immanent physiology is its consideration of nature—the conceptual core (*Inbegriff*) of all objects of the senses—"just as it is given *to us*" (*so wie sie uns gegeben ist*). That part of the immanent physiology is called the "metaphysics of corporeal nature" or "physics" insofar as it considers nature as the object of external sense, that is to say, as matter (B874). Similarly in the Preface to *MAN* the particular part of the metaphysics of nature is distinguished from the transcendental part by the former's supposition of the empirical concept of matter, a conception of what corresponds to objects of external sense in general (*MAN* 469–70).

2. THE EMPIRICAL CONCEPT OF MATTER

What precisely is it about the *empirical* concept of matter (the movable in space) that sets off *MAN*, on the one hand, from the transcendental principles in *KrV* and, on the other hand, from "systematic arts" such as chemistry? Indeed, how can a metaphysics of nature, that is to say, synthetic a priori judgments, be erected on the basis of an empirical concept at all?[22]

One response to these questions consists in demonstrating the insignificance of the empirical character of the concept of matter for the necessity of Kant's metaphysics of nature. Several commentators (Plaass, Gloy, and Werkmeister, and not all for the same reasons) contend that the concept of matter or at least its defining characteristic, the concept of motion, can only be understood as a sensibly conditioned but nonetheless derivative concept a priori, specifically a *Praedicabile* (B108).[23] Taking his cue from Kant's remarks concerning the concept of alteration (*Veränderung*), that is, as an empirical concept in one respect, yet derivative of the categories in another (B3, B58, B213, B107), Plaass claims that the entire *content* of the concept of matter is determinable in terms of motion a priori; the concept is empirical only in the sense that experience must be consulted in order to determine, not what matter (an object of external senses in general) essentially is, but that it exists.[24] Relying upon Kant's tendency in *KrV* to refer to the reality of sensation as matter, Schäfer argues, much like Plaass, that its fundamental feature, namely motion, upon which *MAN* is based, is known a priori.[25] Although critical of both Plaass and Schäfer, Gloy continues this tradition of paring down the empirical character of the concept of matter in *MAN*. Like Plaass, Gloy maintains that, unlike empirical concepts, as they are normally understood by Kant,

---

22. M. Glouberman, "The Distinction between 'Transcendental' and 'Metaphysical' in Kant's Philosophy of Science" *Modern Schoolman* 55 (May 1978): 363.

23. Plaass, *Kants Theorie der Naturwissenschaft*, 83–90; Gloy, *Die Kantische Theorie*, 169ff; Werkmeister 1980, 103–4; M. C. Washburn, "The Second Edition of the Critique: Towards an Understanding of Its Nature and Genesis" *Kant-Studien* (1975): 289: "He (Kant) does not mean that the concept of matter, for example, is derived or abstracted from experience but, rather, that its non-emptiness is an empirical question."

24. Plaass, *Kants Theorie der Naturwissenschaft*, 87: "der Inhalt des empirischen Begriffs, durch den die Materie in den M.A. gedacht wird, ist nicht aus der Erfahrung gewonnen, sondern a priori deduziert." See also Plaass, *Kants Theorie der Naturwissenschaft*, 86, 98ff.

25. Lothar Schäfer, *Kants Metaphysik der Natur* (Berlin: de Gruyter, 1966), S. 26–29; 28: "Daß uns ein Etwas zu affizieren vermag, setzt voraus, daß wir uns dem *Bereich*, in dem das Etwas auftaucht, überhaupt zuvor zugewandt haben."

the content of the concept of matter is not dependent upon experience. Gloy argues that *empirical* as an attribute of the concept of matter designates merely an "empirical relatedness" attaching to the concept of motion, matter's basic determination, in contrast to categories and concepts of geometry.[26]

Not all scholars are ready to limit the meaning of *empirical* in this way, as it applies to the concept of matter. Others (such as Hoppe and Walker) insist that, when Kant refers to the empirical concept of matter, he is calling attention to the fact that the concept, both in content and in instantiation, is contingent. Presumably the concept of matter, like any other empirical concept, is conceived through comparison, reflection, and abstraction from empirical intuitions.[27] On this reading the application of transcendental principles in *MAN* may still be considered to yield rational knowledge as demanded in the preface to *MAN*, namely, an apodictic system of reasons and consequences (*MAN* 468). Yet that necessity is in the last analysis not transcendental but conditional, dependent upon the contingent fact that only the movable in space can be the object of human sensibility.

Debate about the *empirical* status of the concept of matter in *MAN*[28] centers on the following sentence: "The fundamental determination of a Something, which is supposed to be an object of external sense, would have to be motion."[29] Leaving aside the troublesome use of the

26. Gloy, *Die Kantische Theorie*, 173: "Der Bezug auf Empirisches unterscheidet den Bewegungsbegriff von gänzlich reinen Erkenntnissen, die nicht nur wie er von nichts Empirischem dependieren, sondern auch auf nichts Empirisches bezogen sind." See also Gloy, *Die Kantische Theorie*, 166–70, for criticism of Hoppe, Plaass, and Schäfer.

27. Hoppe, *Kants Theorie der Physik*, 42–43; 52; 82 ff; Ralph C. S. Walker, "The Status of Kant's Theory of Matter" in *Proceedings of the Third International Kant-Congress* (Dordrecht: Reidel, 1972), 591–96. See *Immanuel Kant's Logik* in *Kants Werke* Band IX (Berlin: de Gruyter, 1968), S. 92: "Der empirische Begriff entspringt aus den Sinnen durch Vergleichung der Gegenstände der Erfahrung und erhält durch den Verstand bloß die Form der Allgemeinheit. Die Realität dieser Begriff beruht auf der wirklichen Erfahrung, woraus sie, ihrem Inhalte nach, geschöpft sind."

28. One major hurdle confronting both lines of interpretation, not addressed here, is the variety of concepts of matter invoked by Kant in *KrV*. In one passage there is reference to "transcendental matter" as an apparent equivalent to "things in themselves" (B182; though this passage from the *Schematismuslehre* is open to other interpretations) and in the *Amphiboly* there is an entire section devoted to the discussion of matter and form as concepts of reflection (B322–24). At several junctures Kant refers to "matter" as what corresponds to the sensation within an appearance (B34), a perception, and even an experience (B209), or as the reality of the sensation (B207). In the proof of the First Analogy, on the other hand, "substance" is placed in apposition to "matter" (B228). Among the commentators Schäfer alone, without considering these many uses, relies rather dubiously on a single use of the word *matter* in the *KrV* for the interpretation of *MAN*, namely "matter" construed as the reality of sensation; see Schäfer, *Kants Metaphysik*, 25.

29. *MAN* 476: "Die Grundbestimmung eines Etwas, das ein Gegenstand äußerer Sinne sein soll, mußte Bewegung sein."

subjunctive here (*mußte Bewegung sein*), one is still left with the problem of interpreting the necessity involved in the attribution of motion to matter (that is to say, to something insofar as it is an object of external sense). Despite their difference, the interpretations of Plaass, Schäfer, and Gloy agree in maintaining that this necessity is more than empirical.[30] Something can be an object of external sense or, in other words, can be experienced in spatial relations (and not merely imagined as in pure geometry) only if that object is movable in space (material). The advantage of this interpretation is patent: *MAN* is assured of the status of science in the proper sense of the term, despite the *empirical* character of the concept at its base.

Nevertheless, as an exegesis of Kant's understanding of the concept of matter, this interpretation is difficult to sustain, and not only because it suggests the collapse of a distinction between *KrV* and *MAN*.[31] Although Kant does mention alteration (*Veränderung*) as an example of a predicable (B108), his reference to motion as an empirical concept shortly after indicating that it is a kind of alteration (*B48*; B58) suggests, contra Gloy, that he does intend to distinguish motion from alteration.[32] Moreover, Kant refers to the concept of matter as something "abstracted" (*abgesondert*, *MAN* 472), a characterization incompatible with the notion of a predicable (a concept derivative solely of the categories alone or the categories together with the pure intuitions of space and time alone) but quite compatible with the account of empirical concepts in Kant's *Logikvorlesungen*. Although Kant does refer to the concept of motion as a predicable in one place,[33] such characterizations are conspicuously absent from lists of predicables in *KrV* (B108) and in the *Prolegomena* (323–26). Moreover, in *MAN* Kant declares "that, since the *mobility* (*Beweglichkeit*) of an object in space cannot be known a priori and without instruction by experience, precisely for that reason it also could not be counted by me in the *KrV* under the pure concepts of the understanding and that this concept as empirical might be able to find a place only in a natural science as applied metaphysics. . ." (*MAN* 481). This declaration is significant since it

---

30. Gloy, *Die Kantische Theorie*, 169: "Die Tatsache, daß sich Bewegung in aller Erfahrung als Fundamentalprädikat der Materie erweist, ist nichts anderes als Ausdruck einer apriorischen Notwendigkeit"; see also 173; Schäfer, *Kants Metaphysik*, 28–29.

31. This criticism is in no way meant to deny that the studies by Plaass, Schäfer, and Gloy have considerable merit as attempts to rethink critically Kant's theory of natural science.

32. As Gloy herself (*Die Kantische Theorie*, 164) must concede, Kant distinguishes motion from the exchange (*Wechsel*), the stream (*Abfluß*), or the succession (*Sukzession*) proper to inner sense (*A381*; *B291*; *MAN* 471). Kant characterizes motion in terms of alteration (*Veränderung des Orts*) at *B48*; *B291–92*.

33. I. Kant, *Gesammelte Schriften* XX (Berlin: de Gruyter), S. 272.

suggests that the content and not merely the instantiation of the concept of a movable object in space are given by experience alone.

Even this last declaration, however, is not free of a certain ambiguity (exploited by Plaass), inasmuch as Kant may have intended only to distinguish the concept of motion from the *original* concepts of the understanding, namely the categories and not the predicables.[34] Perhaps the central problem in this regard is the apparent discrepancy between Kant's characterization of predicables in general and his examples. On the one hand, Kant does not characterize the significance of "predicable" in such a way that it can refer to concepts derived from the categories, yet possessing some empirical content or reference (as Plaass and Gloy in different ways maintain). Yet, although he does not explicitly mention the concept of motion as a predicable in his published writings, the list of predicables certainly contains other concepts, such as resistance (*Widerstand*) or the event of emerging (*Entstehen*), whose derivation without recourse to experience is just as questionable. It is difficult to avoid the conclusion that perhaps Kant himself was unsure or unclear about the status of predicables.

Supposing that the concept of motion can be derived from the complex of space-time in combination with the categories is, in any event, unproblematic if the proof of the system of transcendental principles in *KrV* in fact supposes the concept of motion. Nor is it easy to gainsay that the "alterations" to which Kant alludes in the First and Second Analogies are plainly motions in the sense required for *MAN*, namely bodily alterations in space such as are requisite for human perception. (Consider the examples of fire and smoke [B228], the house [B235], and the ship in the stream [B237].) Nor was Kant unaware of the "remarkable" (*merkwürdig*) fact—as he expresses it in *MAN* and repeats in the second edition of the *KrV*—that recourse to such examples was necessary to understand the transcendental principles (*MAN* 478; B291).

The repetition of this last text in the second edition of the *KrV* may in fact be construed as providing damaging evidence against the autonomy of the transcendental philosophy, relative to *MAN*. Yet in the *Allgemeine Anmerkung zum System der Grundsätze*, where the reference to that remarkableness appears, Kant notes that the appeal to motion was necessary to render alteration intuitive (or observable: *anschaulich machen*). To make something intuitive or observable is not necessarily and, in the present context, is clearly not the same as proving it. Or,

---

34. This possible reading becomes more acceptable if *unter* is taken to mean not "under" but "among" the pure concepts of understanding in *MAN* 483.

as he states it in *MAN*, the examples of motion and other concepts of corporeal nature perform "splendid and indispensable service" to the transcendental philosophy by exemplifying its principles. Exemplification, however, is not to be confused with proof, whether the exemplificatory concept of motion is a predicable or a garden variety empirical concept.

Nevertheless, one might argue that, by characterizing as "indispensable" the appeal to matter (the movable in space) and its principles, Kant is in fact showing his metaphysical hand, that is to say, displaying the physical presuppositions at the base of the transcendental philosophy. After all, is not appeal explicitly made to distinctively human capabilities of perception throughout the proofs for the system of transcendental principles?

One way to rebut these objections is to show that human perception is not the only possible kind of perception (so that Kant's appeals to the concept matter, based upon human perception, remain—necessarily—merely exemplificatory).[35] If another empirical state of affairs regarding the capabilities of perception proper to a finite knower is imaginable, then the necessity of the metaphysical principles of *MAN* is a relative or contingent necessity. In other words, their necessity is contingent upon the fact that humans are only able to perceive, given motions in space. It is certainly difficult to imagine a kind of perception different from human perception in the significant manner, in effect, a spatial-temporal experience devoid of movable matter. Nor does Kant give any hints in this regard, despite the fact that his discussion seems to demand the possibility of another kind of finite knower.[36] Following a suggestion of R. C. Walker, however, it is possible to conceive of a finite knower inhabiting a spatial world in which the knower is conscious of sensible objects externally related though unmoving. The objects might exhibit change (*Veränderung*) of color and, indeed, in such an orderly fashion that they are thought to continue to exist when unperceived.[37]

---

35. Or, to put the matter in another way, it is not enough to show that psychology as well as physics is possible on the basis of the transcendental principles. Since psychology is in the end incapable of being a science, it must be shown that an alternative physical science is possible, even if beyond the purview of human knowers.

36. This stage of the argument has several parallels with Strawson's attempt to explore the "No-Space world," "to imagine ourselves dispensing with outer sense," in *Individuals: An Essay in Descriptive Metaphysics* (Garden City, N.Y.: Doubleday, 1959), 56–80.

37. R. C. S. Walker, *Kant: The Arguments of the Philosophers* (London: Routledge & Kegan Paul, 1978), 169, also pp. 34–37; R. C. S. Walker, "The Status of Kant's Theory of Matter" in *Proceedings of the Third International Kant-Congress* (Dordrecht: Reidel, 1972), 591–96.

The image of a percipient in a world composed solely of color changes is odd, and it is certainly not to be suggested that Kant himself entertained such an image. Nevertheless, it illustrates the sort of alternative that must be countenanced in order to sustain the distinction between the transcendental and metaphysical principles in Kant's theoretical philosophy. The concept of matter distinguishes physics, but the concept is empirical, based upon contingencies of human perception. That the notion of human perception, given the transcendental principles, remains contingent is sustained by the possibility of an alternative spatiotemporal kind of perception. In a (admittedly early) lecture on physics, Kant writes: "Since we know all alterations in the world and of bodies themselves only through the motion of our (sense) organs, everything in physics is to be reduced to motion. Every alteration, which an object-of-the-external sense as an external appearance undergoes, occurs through motion."[38] (Though this text is probably precritical, the reference to "appearance" suggests that there is nothing in it at odds with the critical doctrine, contrary to the interpretations given the passage by Hoppe and Gloy.[39])

In short, there seems to be no sufficient reason to avoid the conclusion that Kant considered the concept of motion in space an empirical concept *in the sense* that the concept's contents as well as its instantiation are dependent upon experience, specifically upon the contingent makeup of human sensibility. On this interpretation, moreover, a clear distinction between transcendental and metaphysical principles of Kant's theoretical philosophy remains intact. The synthetic–a priori principles in *MAN* are "not completely pure"; that is to say, they are necessary principles of corporeal nature insofar as it is experienced by human knowers, but they are not transcendental principles, not conditions of any possible experience, not conditions of experience by any possible knowers.

The autonomy of *MAN* is assured by the same fact that renders its necessity conditional, even while subordinate to transcendental principles. Whereas the latter are the conditions of any possible experience, *MAN* establishes the principles of something in space and perceived by human knowers, namely matter (the movable in space). Since something perceived in space is the object of a possible human

---

38. "Da wir alle Veränderungen in der Welt und der Körper selbst nicht anders erkennen als durch die Bewegung unserer Organe, so ist alles in der Physik auf die Bewegung zu reduzieren. Alle Veränderung, die ein Gegenstand des äußeren Sinnes als eine äußere Erscheinung leidet, geschieht durch Bewegung." "Kants Physikvorlesung," in *Vorlesungen über Enzyklopädie und Logik*, Bd. I, herausgegeben von Gerhard Lehman, S. 95.

39. Hoppe, *Kants Theorie der Physik*, 82ff; Gloy, *Die Kantische Theorie*, 166.

experience, the metaphysical principles remain in some sense (not investigated in this paper) subordinate to the transcendental principles. At the same time by demonstrating that the articulation and proof of transcendental principles are not wedded to the specific sort of object or experience of sensations proper to human knowers, this interpretation provides a means of defending the thesis of the autonomy of *KrV* (relative to Kant's physics).

This observation, moreover, points up the necessity for *MAN*. Transcendental principles (specifically the Axioms of Intuition and the Anticipations of Perception) establish the applicability of mathematics to intuitions and perceptions as ingredient in any possible experience by a finite knower. Indeed, they establish the validity of the application of mathematics even to human experience, since mathematics rests upon the very spatial and temporal intuitions that form human sensibility. However, these transcendental principles do not establish *how* mathematics applies, not to intuitions and perceptions but to the objects of any human experience, that is to say, to sensible objects insofar as they *move in space* and hence can be apprehended in human experience. Herein lies the necessity for metaphysical principles of natural science, namely principles demonstrating the applicability of mathematics to the movable in space as the defining feature of a possible object of human experience.

This interpretation may resolve one side of the dilemma of a metaphysics of nature, namely how, though itself a system of synthetic–a priori principles, it avoids reduction to the transcendental principles and fulfills a necessary function within the framework of Kant's transcendental philosophy. Whereas the proof for the system of transcendental principles in the *KrV* proceeds from a priori conditions of possible experience (apperception, categories, space and time, schematisms), the system of metaphysical principles in *MAN* proceeds from an a posteriori condition of human experience, namely a requirement imposed by the nature of human organs of sensation. Or, to put the matter in Leibnizian terms, whereas transcendental principles constitute the system of real possibilities, that is to say, the conditions of any possible world, the metaphysical principles of natural science define the actual structure of this world, that is to say, the world experienced by humans as it is experienced by humans.[40]

40. The interpretive reconstruction offered here is not intended to gainsay the criticism that Kant in fact quite illegitimately often enlists principles of his physics in the articulation and proofs of the system of transcendental principles. The last clause in the reformulated First Analogy, namely that "the quantum of substance is neither increased nor diminished," seems to suppose spatial motion, as (once again) the examples

Yet if the empirical character of the concept of matter distinguishes metaphysical principles from transcendental principles, it also sharpens the other side of the dilemma announced at the outset of this paper: how a system of synthetic–a priori judgments can be based on an experiential concept. Whence the necessity of a science based upon the contingent fact that human beings only experience objects, given motion in space?[41] These questions not only remain but acquire their specific edge if, in fact, as argued in this paper, the empirical character of the concept of matter provides the key to the respective autonomy of Kant's philosophy and his physics.[42]

---

of wood, ashes, and smoke suggest. Nor am I convinced that Kant would be happy with the reconstruction I (and others) have presented. Perhaps he would have insisted that the fact that there is one and only one a priori science, only one metaphysics of nature, based upon the transcendental principles possible does not militate against the distinction between transcendental philosophy and that science.

41. See Gerd Buchdahl, *Metaphysics and the Philosophy of Science* (Oxford: Blackwell, 1969); for an alternative interpretation and critique of Buchdahl, see M. Glouberman, "The Distinction Between 'Transcendental' and 'Metaphysical' in Kant's Philosophy of Science" *Modern Schoolman* 55 (May 1978): 357–85.

42. Again there is considerable controversy over the method employed in *MAN*, some commentators (Plaass, Schäfer) seizing on Kant's apparent reference to "metaphysical construction" in the Preface to *MAN*, others (Hoppe) challenging whether Kant is describing such a method at all; see Plaass, *Kants Theorie der Naturwissenschaft*, 74–78; Schäfer, *Kants Metaphysik*, 30–38; Hoppe, *Kants Theorie der Physik*, 57–58.

16 The Reidian Tradition: Growth of the Causal Concept
EDWARD H. MADDEN

I

That he started a philosophical tradition attests to the historical importance of Thomas Reid. The members of the tradition in Scotland, France, and the United States included, among numerous others, Dugald Stewart, James Gregory, Sir William Hamilton, Pierre Paul Royer-Collard, Victor Cousin, Théodore Jouffroy, Alexander Campbell, Francis Wayland, Asa Mahan, Henry Tappan, and James McCosh. The Reidian approach to philosophy reigned supreme in France and the United States from 1820 to 1875.[1] After a period of neglect the work of Reid and his successors has received considerable attention. In the past twenty-five years there have been new editions of Reid's work, numerous books and countless articles written on his work, as well as considerable interest shown in the writings of later figures. In addition Reid has significantly influenced numerous contemporary philosophers, particularly those interested in the adverbial view of perceiving and the agent causality resolution of the freedom-determinism issue. Indeed Roderick Chisholm has said that he finds more philosophical truth in the writings of Reid than in that of any other philosophers.[2]

That Reid made significant and lasting contributions to philosophy there can be no doubt. His metaphilosophy of common sense, echoed by G. E. Moore and in a fainter way by the neo-Wittgensteinians, has made a lasting impression, to say nothing of his protoadverbial view of sensing and his agency theory, in which he argues persuasively that

---

1. Todd Adams, "The Commonsense Tradition in America" *Transactions of the C. S. Peirce Society* 24 (1988): 1–31; E. H. Madden, "Victor Cousin and the Commonsense Tradition" *History of Philosophy Quarterly* 1 (1984): 93–109; E. H. Madden and J. W. Manns, "Théodore Jouffroy's Contributions to the Commonsense Tradition" *Journal of the History of Philosophy* 25 (1987): 573–84.
2. In conversation with Professor Chisholm.

motives cannot be construed as causes.[3] The thrust of all Reid's work was against skepticism, frequently against Hume's version of it. However, one cannot help but be disappointed in his specific criticisms of Hume's skeptical analysis of causality, fraught as they are with inconsistencies, and equally disappointed in his own alternative analysis, which seems to fit poorly with his own commonsense metaphilosophy, denying as it does that there are efficient causes in nature. As we shall see, it remained for much later figures in the tradition, most notably Francis Wayland and James McCosh, to criticize Hume's frequency view of causality effectively and to present in its stead a singularist view of causality that one had expected to find in Reid. The singularist view of McCosh particularly has been influential in a recent non-Humean analysis of causality.[4]

McCosh's views and the recent refinements of the singularist view bring the Reidian tradition on the causality issue very close to, though not identical with, the ancient tradition of causes conceived as *rationes essendi* so splendidly described by Father Wallace in his monumental work on *Causality and Scientific Explanation*.[5] Moreover, Stewart to a lesser degree and McCosh to a greater one departed from Reid's rigid inductivism and literal interpretation of Newton's "hypotheses non fingo" dictum to an acknowledgment of causal relations between the entities referred to by theoretical terms in an interpreted hypothetico-deductive system, thereby bringing the Reidian tradition closer to many of the figures considered in Father Wallace's scholarly work.

II

Reid was a persistent critic of Hume's skepticism, perhaps being more thoroughly committed against skepticism than any other philosopher. He saw Hume's skepticism about our knowledge of the external world implicit in Locke's epistemic point of departure. The British empiricists in general, following Locke, claim that the only things we are directly aware of are our own sensations, impressions, ideas, sense data, or whatever, and hence that we can never be directly aware of the external world. Locke's and Berkeley's attempts to say

---

3. Keith Lehrer, "Reid's Influence on Contemporary American and British Philosophy," in *Thomas Reid: Critical Interpretations*, ed. S. F. Barker and T. L. Beauchamp (Philadelphia: Philosophical Monographs, 1976), 1–7. Cf. E. H. Madden, "The Metaphilosophy of Commonsense" *American Philosophical Quarterly* 20 (1983): 23–36, and "Commonsense and Agency Theory" *Review of Metaphysics* 36 (1982): 319–41.
4. R. Harré and E. H. Madden, *Causal Powers* (Oxford: Basil Blackwell, 1975).
5. William A. Wallace, *Causality and Scientific Explanation*, 2 vols. (Ann Arbor: University of Michigan Press, 1972, 1974).

that we are indirectly aware of the physical world, on the one hand, or that the world consists of a cluster of sensations, on the other, are so much chaff in the wind since the ultimate conclusion of Locke's epistemic point of departure is Hume's all-pervasive skepticism. Hume's views in a sense constitute a *reductio* of British empiricism for he denied that we know many things that we all know perfectly well. He rejected conclusively established propositions while in his study but accepted them in the marketplace. To avoid these absurdities, Reid continued, one must reject the Lockean premise that yielded them, namely, the substantive view of sensation, and put in its place a new version of presentative realism. "Sensation" does not refer to any entity at all; rather it refers to a *way* of experiencing. Seeing blue is a way of seeing something, not something seen.[6] Reid then endeavored to show that his new view not only escaped the absurd consequences of Hume's skepticism but also was capable of explaining illusions and hallucinations that often lead philosophers to the substantive view of sensation in the first place.

Reid used the same tactics in dealing with determinism, which he considered a form of skepticism. He pointed out absurd consequences of the determinist's position—can it even be formulated without self-referential difficulties?—and rejected the premise that led to the absurdities, namely, that motives can be construed as causes. His alternative premise that motives provide the point of an action led to a sophisticated form of agent causality.[7]

Reid campaigned against skepticism in numerous other specific contexts. But it must be kept in mind, in order to appreciate his complete commitment against skepticism, that his whole metaphilosophy of common sense can best be construed as a wholesale way of banishing skepticism from the philosophical arena. Not all ordinary judgments, of course, qualify as commonsensical ones; no one asserted this point more strongly than Reid. To be accounted as principles of common sense, judgments must meet certain criteria: they must be universally held; they must be unavoidable, that is, accepted in practice even by those philosophers who, in their closets, affect to dispute their authority; they cannot be either defended or attacked by a disputant except by use of judgments that are neither more manifest nor more certain than the ordinary one in question; and they must be either

---

6. Thomas Reid, *Essays on the Intellectual Powers of Man*, ed. B. Brody (Cambridge, Mass.: M.I.T. Press, 1969), 13–15, 22–23, 37–38, 220–32.

7. Thomas Reid, *Essays on the Active Powers of the Human Mind*, ed. B. Brody (Cambridge, Mass.: M.I.T. Press, 1969), 4–56, 259–303, 309, 313, 319, 323, 329, 333 ff., 341–42.

evident or self-evident. Reid felt that a number of judgments meet these criteria, including, among others, that we are directly aware of physical objects, that Self is identical through time, that every event has a cause, that human agents act freely (because motives are not causes). Any skeptical view or system that undercuts these judgments will have absurd consequences that the commonsense philosopher must uncover and expose. His remaining job is to isolate the premise in the system that gives rise to skeptical conclusions and to replace it by one that avoids such absurdities.[8]

Given his promising campaign against skepticism—both intrinsically interesting and historically important, dominating as it did the philosophical scenes in Scotland, France, and the United States for many years and influencing recent writers as well—it comes as something of a disappointment to discover that Reid did not use his well-defined technique in arguing specifically against Hume's view of causality. To be sure, he did criticize Hume's definition of causality as constant conjunction, but he did not show how this analysis stems inevitably from the faulty epistemic premises with which Hume began or how it contravenes ordinary causal statements. Indeed he is not even consistent in his discussion of Hume's analysis of the causal relation. Constant conjunction cannot be an adequate analysis, Reid averred, since some constant conjunctions are not causal and some causal statements are not constant conjunctions. Day and night are constantly conjoined, yet neither is the cause of the other; and whatever is singular in nature, such as the creation of the world or historical events, is caused without involving constant conjunction. Moreover, on Hume's view anything may be the cause of anything else, so all reasoning from effect to cause and from final causes must be given up as fallacious.[9] In spite of these criticisms, however, Reid allowed that constant conjunctions might be construed as laws of nature, which should be interpreted as rules according to which efficient causes act.[10] This conclusion, however, seems inconsistent with Reid's negative instances of constant conjunctions that are not causal and causes that are not constant conjunctions, instances consistently interpreted by later philosophers as implying that Hume's account could not distinguish between accidental and lawful universals. It was with Reid's neg-

---

8. Thomas Reid, *An Inquiry into the Human Mind*, ed. T. Duggan (Chicago: University of Chicago Press, 1970), 268–69; Reid, *Intellectual Powers*, 30–41, 226, 227, 228. These views of Reid's are reiterated throughout his work.

9. Thomas Reid, *The Works of Thomas Reid*, ed. Sir William Hamilton (Edinburgh: Longmans, 1863), 1, 627.

10. Reid, *Works*, 1, 627–28.

ative instances in mind that J. S. Mill enlarged Hume's definition of cause into "unconditional constant conjunctions."

Reid's alternative analysis of causality unfortunately is no great improvement over Hume's. Although he avoided Hume's problems he seemed to violate his own commitments, for his analysis contravenes ordinary judgments of causality. Moreover, his analysis, for this reason, ill fits the admirable aspects of his philosophy already discussed. As we have indicated, it remained for thinkers much later in the tradition slowly to reach a view of causality that was more in line with Reid's own metaphilosophical principles.

Reid believed that all causality is agent causality. An agent makes something happen and initiates events. An efficient cause is "a being that has power and will to produce an effect."

> The production of an effect requires active power and active power, being a quality, must be in a being endowed with that power. Power without will produces no effect; but, where these are conjoined, the effect must be produced.[11]

On this view, then, paradoxically, only God and, to a lesser extent, men exemplify agent causality. There are no efficient causes (no agency) in the natural world since nature lacks power either to make things happen or to initiate events. However, these consequences of Reid's view are paradoxical given his own metaphilosophy because his analysis of causality contravenes commonsense judgments. We would ordinarily say that an avalanche certainly made something happen; it crushed the buildings in its path. On Reid's view, however, this judgment is false because natural events are totally passive; they are incapable of making anything happen. We are constrained to say that God or his instituted intermediaries crushed the buildings in the path of the bounding boulders. Reid's view has its own *reductio,* for according to it the tractor that furrows the earth and later is crushed by a landslide would be equally passive in both cases. Moreover, he violates the ordinary meanings of words—abuses them, to use Reid's own language—by including the concepts of making something happen and initiating something as jointly necessary for correctly asserting causal judgments.

Further problems for Reid's view of causality arose from James Gregory's effort to distinguish cause-effect and motive-act contexts. Gregory offered what has come to be called the logical criterion of difference between the contexts, a view that has played a prominent role in recent discussions. According to this logical criterion there is

11. Reid, *Works,* 1, 627.

a conceptual relationship between motives and actions; motives guide an action or show the point of an action and hence cannot be referred to without implicit or explicit reference to the action that they explain. On the other hand, there is no conceptual connection between a cause and an effect. Each can be described independently of the other.[12] The symptoms of an illness, for example, and their causes can be independently described. Gregory's criterion, however, is of little value since the claim that the two events can be described independently presupposes the epistemically independent and atomistic epistemology of Hume that the Reidians have no right to use when they find it convenient. Moreover, it is simply false to say there are no conceptual relations in causal contexts, for it makes perfectly good sense to say that the brittleness of the glass caused it to break or the stick of dynamite exploded because it was detonated and dynamite has a certain inner particle structure. The obvious response at this point would be to say that although both cause-effect and motive-act contexts can have conceptual relationships they are quite different in the two contexts: explanatory in the former and both explanatory and intentional in the latter. But this response is not open to Gregory, who shared his friend Reid's view that all efficient causality is agent causality. Hence, paradoxically, there would, on this view, be an explanatory and intentional or teleological dimension in both contexts! So it is necessary to move on to later figures in the Reidian tradition to find a view of causality commensurate with the basic goals of the Scot.

III

Francis Wayland, appointed president of Brown University in 1827, was a graduate of Union College, where he had learned the elements of Scottish philosophy from his teacher Eliphalet Nott; attended medical school after graduation; switched to Andover Theological Seminary and became a successful minister; and had just accepted a teaching position at Union when he received the call to the presidency of Brown.[13]

Wayland's analysis of the concepts of cause and power are intrinsically interesting and instructive as well, falling as they do into an intermediate position between the views of Reid, on the one hand, and those of James McCosh, on the other. Wayland's view acts as a

---

12. For a related argument advanced by Gregory and Henry Tappan see Adams, "Commonsense Tradition," 26–28.

13. Joseph L. Blau, *Men and Movements in American Philosophy* (New York: Prentice-Hall, 1952), 82–83.

connecting link in the development of a singularist theory of causality within the Scottish realistic tradition. Wayland went beyond Reid's view of causality in several significant ways, but, as we shall see, it was McCosh who parlayed these advances into a systematic singularist view of causality.

According to Wayland the concept of cause cannot be understood in isolation; it is inextricably bound up with the notion of power. Power is that element in the cause by virtue of which it produces its effect. Atmospheric conditions of thirty-two degrees Fahrenheit or below have the power to turn water into ice. The notion of power implies invariability and necessity. "It is essential to our conception of power, that under the same conditions it shall invariably produce the same change."[14] A variable antecedent we say at once is destitute of power to produce the effect and hence cannot be the cause. The concept of power determines the difference between constant conjunction and causality proper.

It must not be supposed, however, that because the notion of power implies a stronger bond than mere sequence between cause and effect no reference to experience is required to discover what is the cause of what in the world. It is by experiment only that we are able to discover what is the cause of water's turning into ice or the cause of any other change in nature. Atmospheric conditions have the power to turn water into ice, and when these conditions are present, water (not warmed artificially, and so on) *must* turn into ice, though what these atmospheric conditions are must be discovered experimentally or by some other reliable a posteriori means.[15]

Causal contexts, Wayland continued, vary widely and include both physical and mental events, but in all cases the "tie that binds" together the cause and effect is hidden. We may observe the cause and then the effect, "but a veil in all cases spreads over the nexus between them, which it has not been given to the human mind to penetrate." Nevertheless he sharply contrasts material and spiritual causation. The subject matter in the two cases is entirely different and the results produced are widely dissimilar. What could be more unlike than the freezing of water by a drop in temperature and a change in the moral character of a person by the awareness of a new truth?

Hence, I would ask, may there not be different kinds of causation? May not causation in matter be a totally different nexus from causation in mind?

---

14. Francis Wayland, *The Elements of Intellectual Philosophy* (New York: Sheldon and Co., 1869), 160.
15. Wayland, *Elements*, 161–68.

Were we endowed with faculties capable of knowing perfectly all the phenomena, might we not find them as dissimilar in themselves as they are in their effects?[16]

If a miser is stabbed in the heart in a certain way he inevitably dies; if he is asked to give to charity he inevitably declines. Though the consequence is necessary in both cases, it does not follow that the nature of this necessity is the same in both cases. Indeed, the different contexts require different senses of necessity even though we cannot penetrate the nature of the causal power in either case.

What is the importance of Wayland's discussion for the emerging singularist view of causality in the Scottish tradition? At the outset, unlike Reid, he acknowledged the likelihood of an efficient causality other than agent causality. Indeed the possibility grows into a strong probability when the diversity of contexts and effects is kept in mind. An apple falls off a tree while a man jumps off a diving board, though a man, of course, could fall off a board, in which case his descent would in no way differ from the apple's.

Second, Wayland makes a significant step forward by claiming there is a relation of nonlogical necessity between a cause and an effect whether the events connected be physical or mental. His interpretation of this relation, however, leaves much to be desired. He thought of "power" as an ontological tie that binds together a cause and effect, thereby reifying power into a separate ontological entity in its own right. McCosh vehemently objected to this sort of interpretation and was very careful to say that the concept of power makes sense only as a characteristic of a particular. No one ever made the point more clearly than he: there is no such thing as power but only objects or people acting in a powerful way. Neither through experience nor through intuition do we ever obtain any abstract or general idea of power: "all that we have is a knowledge of a given substance acting."[17] As contemporary writers make this point, there is no metaphysical power that crushes the tin can that has the air pumped out of it; the weight and pressure of the atmospheric blanket constitute the force at work and nothing more. That is all that is meant in saying that the atmospheric blanket is a powerful particular.

None of Wayland's points is more important than his claim that although causal judgments have some sort of necessity, they are nevertheless known to be true only by empirical or experimental means. This point is crucial since, if it can be established, it undercuts a tra-

---

16. Ibid., 158.
17. McCosh, *First and Fundamental Truths* (New York: Charles Scribner's Sons, 1894), 128.

ditional Humean argument. In Hume's argument, "any connection which is necessarily true must be known to be so on a priori grounds" is the major premise; "no a priori knowledge of factual or scientific matters is possible" is the minor premise; and "no necessary relation between factual or scientific matters is possible" is the conclusion. Wayland certainly had no desire to attack the minor premise; indeed, like anyone except rationalists, he insisted that causal connections can only be discovered through careful experimentation. He must be understood as attacking the major premise: he argued that causal propositions both are nonlogically necessary and are known to be true on a posteriori grounds. Wayland, in short, was challenging the Humean assumption that "p is necessary" and "p is a priori," on the one hand, and "p is contingent" and "p is a posteriori," on the other, are materially equivalent.

Unfortunately for his assault on Hume, however, Wayland failed to show why the assumed material equivalencies break down; however, recent commentators sympathetic to Wayland's challenge have tried to show why they do. If there are two competitive explanations of why an event occurred, the choice between them will be made on a posteriori grounds, but, whichever one is accepted as explanatory, the relation between the explanation and the explanans must be necessary or there would be no explanation. The point of any scientific theory is to explain why a body (macro or micro) has the power to make something happen under certain releasing conditions. The relationship between the explanatory inner structure of a stick of dynamite and what it can do under specified conditions of detonation is an intrasystematic necessity. It would be self-inconsistent to say that a stick of dynamite had a structure that *explains* why it exploded when detonated but nevertheless that another stick of dynamite identical in structure with the former one and under the same conditions of detonation might not explode.[18]

Wayland's analysis of the concept of power and, to a lesser extent, that of cause, is clearly in advance of Reid's account even though his discussion is meagre and sketchy. He has whetted our appetite but has presented us with no more intellectual provender than what I have already discussed. We look in vain for a clear relation between his concepts of power and cause, and although he insists that the causal relation is a necessary one, he nowhere gives a clear analysis of what constitutes a cause and an effect—are they events, particulars, events plus particulars, states of affairs, or what? We need to turn to McCosh to find an answer to this crucial question.

18. Cf. Harré and Madden, *Causal Powers*, chap. 1.

IV

James McCosh, appointed president of Princeton University in 1868, was born in Scotland; studied at Glasgow and Edinburgh; taught at Queen's College, Belfast, for sixteen years; and from 1868 on lived out his long life in the United States.[19] The transplanted Scot knew the role he played in the tradition as he carefully formulated a singularist view of causality to supplant the inadequate views of causality that preceded him.

McCosh believed that the concept of powerful particulars is essential to an adequate analysis of the causal relation. When a person sees a boulder rolling down a hill and crushing objects in its path he does not perceive an object in motion and subsequent carnage but perceives a powerful particular at work, an object's making something happen: in short, he apprehends the boulder's crushing the things in its path. To be intelligibly understood such a perception must be construed within the epistemic context of the Reidian tradition. "Making something happen" cannot be learned from experience since it involves a necessity that experience is incapable of yielding. Thus power, like space, is a nativistic input from the intellect itself and is roused into consciousness by the appearance of an appropriate stimulus, say an agent's remembering a forgotten name or a bounding boulder's bearing down on a plow in its path.[20]

We would do McCosh an injustice if we were to think that he reified the notion of power; for him there is no abstract entity "power" but only particulars or substances, objects or people, acting in a powerful way. We never obtain a general idea of power through any epistemic source: "all that we have is knowledge of a given substance acting." Power should never be conceived, along the lines of Wayland, as an unknowable ontological tie that binds. No one ever rejected this view more clearly than McCosh; the exercise of causal power is not a force or power that has some existence of its own but refers only to *forceful objects at work*.[21] In the words of a later writer sympathetic to the point McCosh was making:

Causality is a name for a certain quality of events, it is not a name for the agency behind the events. The agency is there, to be sure: it is the lava flow,

---

19. W. M. Sloane, ed., *The Life of James McCosh* (New York: Charles Scribner's Sons, 1896), chaps. 1–6, 8; J. D. Hoeveler, *James McCosh and the Scottish Intellectual Tradition* (Princeton, N.J.: Princeton University Press, 1981), parts I, II.

20. James McCosh, *Intuitions of the Mind*, new and rev. ed. (New York: Robert Carter and Brothers, 1867), 227, 229.

21. McCosh, *First and Fundamental Truths*, 128; *Intuitions of the Mind*, 233.

the medicine, the light rays, the mechanic's muscles, the tossing waves. There is no other "force," there is no other cause, than just these specific things. But these things are *forceful*: they operate: they produce. And they are forceful and operate and produce in that specific way we call necessary. Causality names that kind of necessary operation.[22]

The concept of a powerful particular, McCosh believed, is an essential dimension of a singularist view of causality, providing, as it does, one of the elements required to produce the necessity of a causal relation. That the concept of causality implies a necessary relationship is clear: given the cause the effect must occur, for if the effect did not occur the causal claim would be automatically withdrawn. This notion of necessity cannot be provided by experience since experience cannot yield any necessary judgment.[23] Hence it must be provided by the concept of powerful particulars: every causal proposition must include reference to a "potent or powerful" substance that is capable of acting on other substances and making something happen to them, where "x made something happen to y" cannot be construed as a contingent proposition. We decide, and must decide, "that every effect proceeds from one or more substances having potency." If a tree falls to the ground or a man's leg is broken we look for powerful particulars as part of our causal explanation, say a hurricane wind's blowing the tree or a tree limb's falling on the man's leg.[24]

However, McCosh cautioned, the notion of a powerful substance (or particular, as we say, since he did not mean by *substance* any metaphysical entity) is not sufficient to explain the necessity between cause and effect. If the dynamite is not detonated it does not explode and blow the boulder to pieces. "That which is necessary to the exercise of power in substance may be called the conditions, and it is only on the conditions being supplied that power is exercised." "A magnet has a power of attracting iron, but it is only when iron is within reach that the property is active."[25] Since the power to do something is part of the nature of a particular and this power is only actualized when the proper external conditions are met, it seems highly legitimate to talk of "latent power." It appears there "may be perfect propriety in speaking of latent power, that is, of a power not in action because the conditions needful to its operations are not supplied."[26]

McCosh's final definition of causality, which results from the pre-

---

22. Sterling Lamprecht, *The Metaphysics of Naturalism* (New York: Appleton-Century-Crofts, 1967), 144.
23. McCosh, *Intuitions of the Mind*, 227.
24. Ibid., 229.
25. Ibid., 230.
26. Ibid.

vious discussion, is this: the powerful particular and the conditions requisite for the manifestation of the power taken together constitute the cause, and the actual manifestation of the power constitutes the effect. Consequently the necessity involved in causal propositions is not simply between a powerful particular and the manifestation of its power, since power remains latent if the conditions are absent. It is only when in combination with a stick of dynamite (not damp, and so forth) an adequate job of detonation is supplied that we say that the effect, the blowing apart of the rock, must occur. "There is a necessary relation between the cause and the effect, arising from the necessity of the cause to produce the effect when the conditions are furnished."[27] It is important to keep in mind, McCosh continues, that, although causal relations are necessary, nevertheless the discovery of which of numerous alternative systems, with different sets of necessary relations, are exemplified in our world is an inductive, scientific matter. McCosh here, it should be clear, was challenging the Humean *assumption* of the material equivalence of "p is a priori" and "p is necessary," on the one hand, and "p is a posteriori" and "p is contingent," on the other. This point was crucial for McCosh since not to recognize it was to become a rationalist, and the Scot was determined to steer a course between rationalism and empiricism.

McCosh thought that the consequences of his view on causality were beneficial. His view explains the occurrence of constant conjunction while that concept totally fails to explicate causality. Even Reid in his clearer moments had shown the latter. Moreover, on his view, causality, containing as it does a noncontingent element, avoids the problem of justifying inductive inference. Reid, McCosh pointed out, included among his principles of common sense the proposition that nature is uniform. McCosh denied that this proposition constituted a basic intuition: indeed, it was not even a principle of common sense in Reid's own terms. It is the sort of fruitless principle that J. S. Mill had to use because his Humean definition of cause provided no other grounds for ensuring the reliability of inductive inference. McCosh prized his own interpretation also because it made sense out of statements about possibility and potentiality (what could, might, would happen if . . .) that Humeans, being epistemically limited to what has happened, are in principle unable to explicate. Another virtue of his own analysis, McCosh felt, was that it avoided the infinite regress of causes attendant upon other views of causality. In his view only *changes* in states of affairs require causal explanation and since such explanations are not

27. Ibid., 232.

themselves changes in states of affairs no further explanation is required.[28]

McCosh's analysis of causality, it seems to me, is a momentous improvement over Reid's and Wayland's. McCosh, it is abundantly clear, rejected Reid's noncommonsensical view that all causality is agent causality and insisted instead, partly under the influence of the new science of thermodynamics, that energy pervades the whole physical world and is capable of making things happen. According to this view all nature is active. McCosh correctly rejected Reid's principle of the uniformity of nature as unworthy of the Scottish realistic tradition.

McCosh's work was also a great advance over Wayland's. Although he agreed with Wayland that the concept of cause cannot be understood without that of power, he carefully avoided Wayland's "unknowable ontological tie that binds" and substituted instead the concept of powerful particulars as nonmetaphysical entities. McCosh, like Wayland, wisely rejected the familiar Humean assumption of material equivalence between modal propositions and how they become known. But the Princeton president gave no more reason why the assumed equivalence is faulty than his Brown counterpart. In McCosh's case, given his degree of sophistication, one can only conclude that he assumed that the lack of material equivalence was obvious. Essentially he shifted the point where contingency enters scientific inference. The causal relations in any system that might be exemplified in our world must be necessary or it would not be a system, but which such systems are exemplified is a contingent matter to be discovered by experiential evidence that is always subject to revision. But even if revised, the new system will still exhibit the relations necessary to make that set of propositions and their referents a system.

McCosh's view on the whole seems a significant rendition of the singularist view of causality. Perhaps only one more step in his analysis is required; in any case, I would add a further one. To say that dynamite has the power to explode when detonated is, after all, only a promissory note. Power statements need to be redeemed (and to redeem them is the task of the physicist) by discovering the nature of the powerful particular that explains why under releasing conditions its power is manifested. In the case of dynamite we need to know the inner structure that explains why this stick of dynamite (which is dry, and so on) when detonated explodes and when not detonated remains in a quiescent or latent state, as McCosh phrases it. Hence the final rendition of a singularist view of causality similar to McCosh's is this:

28. Ibid., 233 ff.

the nature of a particular that explains its power plus the releasing condition constitute the cause, and the manifestation of that power constitutes the effect; and the relation between the cause and effect is a necessary one though it is a contingent matter whether or not this necessary relation is exemplified in our world.[29] Needless to say, numerous other issues would need to be considered to fill out this skeletal view, and the defects of any frequency view of causality must be more thoroughly established, before McCosh's view would be completely acceptable. But that he accomplished a great deal in his own right, I think, cannot be denied.

V

The question persistently arose within the Reidian tradition whether causal relations hold only between observable objects and events or also between theoretical terms and observables in a hypothetico-deductive system. Father Wallace and Professor Laudan have shown convincingly that Reid held a rigid inductivism and emphatically eschewed the use of hypotheses. "Indeed basic to Reid's philosophy, and here the Newtonian influence is quite apparent, was his vehement opposition to the use of hypotheses, conjectures, and even theories that are not induced directly from observation and experiment."[30] Did subsequent members of the tradition follow Reid? What was the overall feeling on this issue during the many years that a singularist view of causality was developing?

It must be kept in mind at the outset that only a handful of the members of the Scottish realistic tradition had sufficient knowledge of biological and physical science to render competent judgments on this issue. Most members of the tradition were trained strictly in philosophy, theology, classical languages, and psychology and were mainly interested in epistemology, metaphysics, agency theory, and moral philosophy. Although they felt in some (never carefully defined) way that psychology, the "science" of consciousness, was inductive and hence "Newtonian," they had no capacity for speculating on the general issue in philosophy of science. The men in the tradition who had firsthand instruction and practice in mathematics and physics were Reid, Stewart, and McCosh; Wayland had a knowledge of biological science gained in medical school.[31] Stewart and McCosh emerge as the two

29. Cf. Harré and Madden, *Causal Powers,* chap. 1.
30. Wallace, *Causality,* 45. See also Larry Laudan, *Science and Hypothesis* (Dordrecht: Reidel, 1981), chap. 7.
31. Reid taught physics and mathematics at both Aberdeen and Glasgow; Stewart

most interesting figures on this issue, departing as they did from Reid's rigid inductivism, Stewart quietly and sometimes implicitly; McCosh, as one might guess, quite completely.

Stewart sometimes claimed that he defended the use of hypotheses only as heuristic devices; yet it is clear that he committed himself to much more than this in his extended and impressive discussions. He thought that rigid inductivists took Newton's dictum *hypotheses non fingo* too literally. After all, Newton advanced numerous hypotheses in his own work but no doubt assumed that his readers would see that his "queries" had experimental consequences and hence could be tested. They are not like Descartes's vortices, which are maintained on a priori grounds. Indeed, *hypotheses non fingo* probably referred only to those hypotheses that, like Descartes's, are immune to falsification. Moreover, Stewart approvingly quoted Boscovich's view that hypotheses are the method best adapted to physics, where legitimate *theories* are generally the slow result of disappointed hypotheses and of errors that have led the way to their own detection.[32]

Stewart's acceptance of Boscovich seems further to confirm the attraction that the hypotheticodeductive method held for him. Boscovich himself argued against an inductive view of science since his own physical theory had concepts that referred to theoretical entities, namely, point-centers-of-mutual-influence. Since Stewart accepted Boscovich's methodology he certainly committed himself, by implication *at least*, to the legitimacy of hypotheses with unobservables as long as they have testable consequences. Stewart was also drawn to, and favored, Boscovich's actual physical theory with its unobservable entities, as well as to his argument that corpuscularian theory is incoherent. Boscovich had argued that interaction cannot be applied to ultimate corpuscles because, being perfectly elastic, they are absolutely incompressible. Hence there can be no transfer of motion between ultimate particles. Stewart was delighted with this outcome because it undercut the atomistic materialism of Hartley and Priestly. However, the joyous reception of Boscovich's argument makes no sense unless Stewart acknowledged the reality reference of the corpuscularian hypothesis. It would be absurd to accept, as Stewart did, Boscovich's theory of point-centers-of-mutual-influence and the corpuscularian theory as legiti-

---

studied physics and mathematics at Edinburgh and taught mathematics there; McCosh read extensively in the natural sciences at Edinburgh; and Wayland studied in medical school for a while before switching to Andover Theological Seminary.

32. E. H. Madden, "Stewart's Enrichment of the Commonsense Tradition" *History of Philosophy Quarterly* 3 (1986): 45–63.

mate competitors and yet on the methodological level to deny that a system with reference to unobservables is ever justified.[33]

Stewart was not unaware of the tensions in his own thinking; he was committed to inductivism as part of the tradition but was sensitive to the existentialist claims as well as heuristic values of hypotheses. He was pulled both ways, and his work constitutes a bridge between the rigid inductivism of Reid and the more modern views of scientific theory and causality held by McCosh, the last great figure in the tradition.

That McCosh departed completely from rigid inductivism and a literal interpretation of Newton's dictum is evident in his ready acceptance of theoretical terms referring to unobservable entities within hypotheticodeductive systems and in his ascription of causal powers to these entities. He thought that the new science of thermodynamics, with its concept of physical energy and its laws of the conservation and dissipation of energy, made evident that unobservable objects have causal powers, can make things happen, and hence once and for all refute Reid's claim that all efficient causality is agent causality. To be sure, agents are active but so are physical particulars whether they are macro or micro in nature.

There is, McCosh wrote, an energy in all physical nature. Moreover, all the physical forces are correlated and can be transformed into one another, so much chemical and electrical power being an equivalent of so much mechanical energy.

> This power is always in objects and can be transferred from one to another depending on the capacities of the bodies. Thus a ball A in motion strikes a ball B at rest, and the power in A is transferred to B, which now moves while A is at rest. It is true that there is a sense in which body is passive. An atom isolated from all other bodies will continue in the state in which it is; it is unable to initiate any action. But if brought into relationship with another body, the one body acts on the other, or rather the bodies mutually affect each other, mechanically or chemically.[34]

Thus viewed, McCosh concluded, matter is active.

It must not be supposed that McCosh explicitly argued in favor of the hypotheticodeductive method as superior to rigid inductivism: far from it. By his time, unless one held a phenomenalistic view, it seemed obvious that the hypotheticodeductive method constitutes the only possible means of dealing with unobservable entities. Even in the case

---

33. Madden, "Stewart's Enrichment," 49–57. Cf. Richard Olson, *Scottish Philosophy and British Physics, 1750–1880* (Princeton, N.J.: Princeton University Press, 1975), 94–98, 106–11.

34. McCosh, *First and Fundamental Truths*, 70, 86.

of macrophysics rigid inductivism yields only "natural history generalizations" that can be overthrown by a single negative instance and scarcely deserve the name of science. "This swan is white because all swans are white" is scarcely the paradigm of inference in theoretical physics.

McCosh had the great merit of consistency on the issue of rigid induction. Occasionally the introspections of consciousness, so dear to the hearts of the members of the tradition, were construed along the lines of instantial induction. We have a basic intuition that this event has a cause, that one has a cause, and so on, and we generalize these intuitions into the maxim that every event has a cause. McCosh rejected this crude inductivism decisively. The intuition that this event has a cause, for reasons we shall not examine, is in the Reidian tradition self-evidently true and hence the generalized maxim that every event has a cause is also a noncontingent proposition and thus is reached by a conceptual and not an inductive procedure. Such a maxim is wholly noninductive in any instantial sense but is rather a "reflexive" generalization, which is quite different from an empirical generalization like "All the apples in this basket are red," which just happens to be true.[35] McCosh's view of how maxims are generalized from basic intuitions reflects the best, and most prevalent, thinking on this issue within the tradition.

The upshot of this discussion is, I trust, clear: Reid began a truly impressive tradition, and the more obvious gaps in his philosophy of nature were gradually filled by, among others, Stewart, Wayland, and McCosh. They all deserve, amply so, the appreciation of the philosophical community, to say nothing of its respect.

35. McCosh, *Intuitions*, 31–80.

Publications of William A. Wallace, O.P.

1941a   "Subsurface Pressure Changes Caused by Waves," Mine Unit Report 365 (November 1941), Naval Ordnance Laboratory, Washington, D.C.

1941b   "Pressure Fields Beneath the U.S.S. *North Carolina*," Mine Unit Report 387 (December 1941), Naval Ordnance Laboratory, Washington, D.C.

1942a   "Pressure Background in Relation to Mine Design," N.O.L.R. 451 (March 1942), Naval Ordnance Laboratory, Washington, D.C.

1942b   "Study of Ships' Hull Vibration and Associated Low Frequency Pressure Fields," N.O.L.R. 509 (May 1942), Washington, D.C.

1942c   "Preliminary Study of Subsonic Background," N.O.L.R. 540 (August 1942), Naval Ordnance Laboratory, Washington, D.C.

1942d   "Maximum Rates of Change of Tides in Various Parts of the World," N.O.L.M. 2159 (August 1942), Washington, D.C.

1942e   "Subsurface Pressure Variations at Kahului Harbor," N.O.L.R. 596 (December 1942), Naval Ordnance Laboratory, Washington, D.C.

1944   "Special Mining Report," coauthored with E. A. Johnson, described in Samuel Morrison [*History of the U.S. Navy in World War II*].

1945   "Tactics of Inner Zone Mining Campaign Against Japan: Operation Starvation," summarized in 1974j.

1946   "Offensive Mining Campaign Against Japan," summarized in 1974i.

1952   "The Origin of the Universe," coauthored with M. J. Davis, *Dominicana* 37 (1952): 25–38, 181–95.

1954a   "Absorption of Finite Amplitude Sound Waves," coauthored with F. E. Fox, *Journal of the Acoustical Society of America* 26 (1954): 994–1006.

1954b   *Physics and God: A Statement and Defense of the* Prima Via *in Light of Modern Science*. Unpublished Dissertation for the Degree of Lector of Sacred Theology, Washington, D.C.: Pontifical Faculty of the Immaculate Conception, 1954.

1956   "Newtonian Antinomies Against the *Prima Via*" *Thomist* 19 (1956): 151–92, reprinted in 1979a, 329–70.

1957   "Some Demonstrations in the Science of Nature," *The Thomist Reader 1957*. Washington, D.C.: The Thomist Press, 1957, 90–118, reprinted in 1979a, 131–59, and in 1983a, 115–43.

1959 *The Scientific Methodology of Theodoric of Freiberg: A Case Study of the Relationship Between Science and Philosophy.* Studia Friburgensia, N.S. 26. Fribourg: University Press, 1959. Pp. xviii + 395.

1961a "Gravitational Motion According to Theodoric of Freiberg" *Thomist* 24 (1961): 327–52; reprinted in *The Dignity of Science*, ed. J. A. Weisheipl. Washington, D.C.: Thomist Press, 1961, 191–216.

1961b "St. Thomas Aquinas, Galileo, and Einstein" *Thomist* 24 (1961): 1–22; reprinted in 1979a, 67–88; enlarged and reprinted as 1963a.

1961c "Theology and the Natural Sciences," *Theology in the Catholic College*, ed. R. Masterson. Dubuque, Iowa: Priory Press, 1961, 167–204.

1962a *The Role of Demonstration in Moral Theology: A Study of Methodology in St. Thomas Aquinas.* Texts and Studies 2. Washington, D.C.: Thomist Press, 1962. Pp. x + 244.

1962b "The Cosmogony of Teilhard de Chardin" *New Scholasticism* 36 (1962): 353–67.

1962c "Science and Religion in the Twentieth Century" *Homiletic and Pastoral Review* 63 (1962): 23–31.

1962d "Place of Science in Liberal Arts Curriculum" *Catholic Educational Review* 60 (1962): 361–76.

1962e "Metaphysics and the Existence of God" *New Scholasticism* 36 (1962): 529–31.

1962f "Natural Philosophy and the Physical Sciences," *Philosophy and the Integration of Contemporary Catholic Education*, ed. G. F. McLean. Washington, D.C.: Catholic University of America Press, 1962, 130–57, 292–97.

1963a *Einstein, Galileo and Aquinas: Three Views of Scientific Method.* Washington, D.C.: Thomist Press, 1963. Pp. 37.

1963b "Existential Ethics: A Thomistic Appraisal" *Thomist* 27 (1963): 493–515.

1963c "Modern Science: A Challenge to Faith?" *Proceedings of the Society of Catholic College Teachers of Sacred Doctrine* 9 (1963): 96–117.

1963d "The Thomistic Order of Development in Natural Philosophy," *Teaching Thomism Today*, ed. G. F. McLean. Washington, D.C.: Catholic University of America Press, 1963, 247–70.

1963e "Nuclear Weapons, Morality, and the Future" *Dominicana* 48 (1963): 7–21; reprinted in 1979a, 247–61.

1963f "Radiation and Social Ethics" *America* 108, no. 25 (22 June 1963): 880–83.

1964a "The Reality of Elementary Particles" *Proceedings of the American Catholic Philosophical Association* 38 (1964): 154–66; reprinted in 1979a, 187–99, and in 1983a, 171–83.

1964b "Theodoric of Freiberg on the Structure of Matter," *Proceedings of the Tenth International Congress of History of Science, Ithaca, N.Y., 1962.* 2 vols., Paris: Hermann, 1964, 1:591–97.

1964c "St. Thomas and the Pull of Gravity," *Science and the Liberal Concept.* West Hartford, Conn : St. Joseph College, 1964, 143–65; reprinted in 1979a, 163–85, and in 1983a, 147–69.

1964d "Cybernetics and a Christian Philosophy of Man," *Philosophy in a Technological Culture*, ed. G. F. McLean. Washington, D.C.: Catholic University of America, 1964, 124–45; enlarged and reprinted in 1979a, 219–45, and in 1983a, 245–71.

1965a "The Measurement and Definition of Sensible Qualities," *New Scholasticism* 39 (1965): 1–25; reprinted in 1979a, 89–113, and in 1983a, 73–97.

1965b "Some Moral and Religious Aspects of Nuclear Technology" *Journal of the Washington Academy of Sciences* 55 (1965): 85–91.

1967a *Cosmogony* [St. Thomas Aquinas, *Summa Theologiae*, Vol. 10 (1a.65–74)]. New York and London: McGraw-Hill Book Co., 1967. Pp. xxiii + 255.

1967b *New Catholic Encyclopedia*, 15 vols. New York: McGraw-Hill Book Co., 1967. [As staff editor for philosophy and related fields, edited some 900 articles comprising about 1,375,000 words; also wrote the following articles:]

"Action at a Distance," 1:96–97
"Atomism," 1:1020–24
"Choice," 3:620–21
"Color," 3:1030–31 (coauthor)
"Cybernetics," 4:557–62 (coauthor)
"Drives and Motives," 4:1063
"Albert Einstein," 5:234–35 (coauthor)
"Emanationism," 5:291–93 (coauthor)
"Form," 5:1013–17 (coauthor)
"Friendship," 6:203–205
"God and Modern Science," 6:568–72
"Hylomorphism," 7:284–85
"Hylosystemism," 7:285
"Symbolic Logic," 8:962–64
"Measurement," 9:528–31 (coauthor)
"Monism," 9:1061–62
"Agostino Nifo," 10:465
"Passion," 10:1052
"Person (in Philosophy)," 11:166–68 (coauthor)
"Philosophy, Articles on," 11:292–94
"Psychology, Articles on," 11:962–63
"Science (Scientia)," 12:1190–93
"Philosophy of Science," 12:1215–19
"Sound," 13:474–76 (coauthor)
"Theodoric Borgognoni of Lucca," 14:22
"Theodoric (Deitrich) of Freiberg," 14:22–24
"Natural Theology," 14:61–64 (coauthor)
"Thing," 14:91–92
"Thomas Aquinas, St.," 14:102–15 (coauthor)
"Uncertainty Principle," 14:385–87 (coauthor)
"Witelo," 14:979

1967c "The Concept of Motion in the Sixteenth Century" *Proceedings of the American Catholic Philosophical Association* 41 (1967): 184–95; reprinted in 1981a, 64–77.

1967d "Il tomismo e la scienza moderna: passato, presente e futuro" *Sapienza* 20 (1967): 429–43.

1968a "The Enigma of Domingo de Soto: *Uniformiter difformis* and Falling Bodies in Late Medieval Physics" *Isis* 59 (1968): 384–401; reprinted in 1981a, 91–109.

1968b "Elementarity and Reality in Particle Physics" *Boston Studies in the Philosophy of Science* 3 (1968): 236–71; reprinted in 1983a, 185–212.

1968c "Toward a Definition of the Philosophy of Science" *Mélanges à la mémoire de Charles de Koninck*. Québec: Les Presses de l'Université Laval, 1968, 465–85; reprinted in 1979a, 1–21, and in 1983a, 1–21.

1968d "Philosophy of the Physical Sciences," *Philosophy and Contemporary Man*, ed. G. F. McLean. Washington, D.C.: Catholic University of America Press, 1968, 50–64; reprinted in 1979a, 23–37.

1968e "Thomism and Modern Science: Relationships Past, Present, and Future" *Thomist* 32 (1968): 67–83; English translation of 1967d.

1969 "The 'Calculatores' in Early Sixteenth-Century Physics" *British Journal for the History of Science* 4, no. 3 (June 1969): 221–32; reprinted in 1981a, 79–90.

1970 "The Case for Developmental Thomism" (Presidential Address) *Proceedings of the American Catholic Philosophical Association* 44 (1970): 1–16.

1971 "Mechanics from Bradwardine to Galileo" *Journal of the History of Ideas* 32 (1971): 15–28; reprinted in 1981a, 51–63, and in 1988e.

1972a *Causality and Scientific Explanation*. Vol. 1. *Medieval and Early Classical Science*. Ann Arbor: University of Michigan Press, 1972. xii + 288 pp. Reprinted in 1981b.

1972b "The Cosmological Argument: A Reappraisal" *Proceedings of the American Catholic Philosophical Association* 46 (1972): 43–57; reprinted in 1979a, 313–27, and in 1983a, 309–23.

1973 "Experimental Science and Mechanics in the Middle Ages," *Dictionary of the History of Ideas*, 4 vols. New York: Charles Scribner's Sons, 1973, 2:196–205; reprinted in 1981a, 196–205.

1974a *Causality and Scientific Explanation*. Vol. 2. *Classical and Contemporary Science*. Ann Arbor: University of Michigan Press, 1974. Pp. xi + 422. Reprinted in 1981b.

1974b "Three Classics of Science: The Reviews of Three Great Books: Galileo, *Two New Sciences*; Gilbert, *The Loadstone and Magnetic Bodies*; and Harvey, *The Motion of the Heart and Blood*." *The Great Ideas Today 1974*, ed. John Van Doren. Chicago: Encyclopaedia Britannica, 1974, 211–72.

1974c "Theodoric of Freiberg: On the Rainbow," *A Source Book in Medieval Science*, ed. Edward Grant. Cambridge, Mass.: Harvard University Press, 1974, 435–41.

1974d "Galileo and the Thomists" *St. Thomas Aquinas Commemorative Studies 1274–1974*, ed. Armand Maurer, 2 vols. Toronto: Pontifical Institute of Mediaeval Studies, 1974, 2:293–330; revised and reprinted in 1981a, 160–91.

1974e "Aquinas on the Temporal Relation Between Cause and Effect" *Review of Metaphysics* 27 (1974): 569–84; reprinted in 1979a, 115–30, and in 1983a, 99–114.

1974f "Aquinas on Creation: Science, Theology, and Matters of Fact" *Thomist* 38 (1974): 485–523.

1974g "Ellis A. Johnson, 1906–1973," coauthored with T. Page and G. S. Pettee, *Operations Research* 22 (1974): 1141–55.

1974h *New Catholic Encyclopedia*, vol. 16, supplement 1967–74. Washington and New York: Publishers Guild, 1974. Articles on
"Cosmological Argument," 105–8
"Contemporary Philosophers," 341–48
"Recent Developments in Philosophy," 348–51

1974i "Offensive Mining Campaign Against Japan," coauthor of previously classified report of the Naval Analysis Division, U.S. Navy, 1946, prepared as part of the U.S. Strategic Bombing Survey, summarized in E. A. Johnson and D. A. Katcher, *Mines Against Japan*. White Oak, Silver Spring, Md.: Naval Ordnance Laboratory, 1974, 21–39.

1974j "Tactics of Inner Zone Mining Campaign Against Japan—Operation STARVATION," coauthor of previously classified report of the Twentieth U.S. Air Force, August 1945, summarized in E. A. Johnson and D. A. Katcher, *Mines Against Japan*. White Oak, Silver Spring, Md.: Naval Ordnance Laboratory, 1974, 137–276.

1975 "The First Way: A Rejoinder" *Thomist* 39 (1975): 375–82; reprinted in 1983a, 325–32.

1976a "Galileo and Reasoning *Ex suppositione*: The Methodology of the *Two New Sciences*" *Proceedings of the 1974 Biennial Meeting of the Philosophy of Science Association,* Dordrecht-Boston: D. Reidel Publishing Company, 1976, 79–104; reprinted and enlarged in 1981a, 129–59.

1976b "Buridan, Ockham, Aquinas: Science in the Middle Ages" *Thomist* 40 (1976): 475–83; reprinted in 1981a, 341–48.

1976c "Six Studies of Causality on the Bicentennial of David Hume" *Thomist* 40 (1976): 684–96.

1976d "El enigma de Domingo de Soto: *Uniformiter difformis* y la caida de los cuerpos en la tardia fisica medieval" *Studium* 16 (1976): 343–67; Spanish translation of 1968a.

1977a *The Elements of Philosophy: A Compendium for Philosophers and Theologians.* New York: Alba House, 1977. Pp. xx + 342.

1977b *Galileo's Early Notebooks: The Physical Questions: A Translation from the Latin, with Historical and Paleographical Commentary.* Notre Dame, Ind.: University of Notre Dame Press, 1977. Pp. xiv + 321.

1978a "Galileo Galilei and the *Doctores Parisienses*" *New Perspectives on Galileo,* eds. R. E. Butts and J. C. Pitt. Dordrecht: D. Reidel Publishing Co., 1978, 87–138; reprinted and enlarged in 1981a, 192–252.

1978b "The Philosophical Setting of Medieval Science" *Science in the Middle Ages*, ed. D. C. Lindberg. Chicago and London: University of Chicago Press, 1978, 91–119; reprinted in 1981a, 3–28.

1978c "Causality, Analogy, and the Growth of Scientific Knowledge" *Tommaso d'Aquino nel suo settimo centenario*, 9 vols. Naples: Edizioni Domenicane Italiane, 1978, 9:26–40; reprinted in 1979a, 201–15, and in 1983a, 213–27.

1978d "Galileo's Knowledge of the Scotistic Tradition" *Regnum Hominis et Regnum Dei*, 2 vols., ed. Camille Bérubé. Rome: Societas Internationalis Scotistica, 1978, 2:313–20; reprinted and enlarged in 1981a, 253–63.

1978e "Causes and Forces in Sixteenth-Century Physics" *Isis* 69 (1978): 400–12; reprinted in 1981a, 110–26.

1978f "El concepto de movimiento en el siglo XVI" *Studium* 18 (1978): 91–106; Spanish translation of 1967c.

1979a *From a Realist Point of View: Essays on the Philosophy of Science*. Washington, D.C.: University Press of America, 1979. Pp. xii + 376.

1979b "Medieval and Renaissance Sources of Modern Science" *Proceedings of the Patristic-Medieval-Renaissance Conference* 2 (1979): 1–17; reprinted in 1981a, 303–19.

1979c "Immateriality and Its Surrogates in Modern Science" *Proceedings of the American Catholic Philosophical Association* 52 (1978): 28–83; enlarged and reprinted in 1979a, 287–312; reprinted in 1983a, 297–307.

1979d *New Catholic Encyclopedia*, Vol. 17. New York and Washington: Publishers Guild Inc., 1979. Articles on "Philosophical Pluralism," 510–12; "Thomism," 665–66.

1980a "The Scientific Methodology of St. Albert the Great" *Albertus Magnus Doctor Universalis 1280–1980*, eds. G. Meyer and A. Zimmerman. Mainz: Matthias Gruenewald Verlag, 1980, 385–407.

1980b "Albertus Magnus on Suppositional Necessity in the Natural Sciences" *Albertus Magnus and the Sciences*, ed. J. A. Weisheipl. Toronto: Pontifical Institute of Mediaeval Studies, 1980, 103–28.

1980c "Galileo's Citations of Albert the Great" *Albert the Great: Commemorative Essays*, eds. F. J. Kovach and R. W. Shahan. Norman, Okla.: University of Oklahoma Press, 1980, 261–83; reprinted in 1981a, 264–85.

1980d *Dictionary of Scientific Biography*, ed. C. C. Gillispie, 16 vols. New York: Charles Scribner's Sons, 1970–80. Articles on

"Albertus Magnus," 1:99–103
"Thomas Aquinas," 1:196–200
"Bernard of Le Treille (Trilia)," 2:20–21
"Theodoric Borgognoni of Lucca," 2:314–15
"Francesco Buonamici," 2:590–91
"Juan de Celaya," 3:171–72
"Pedro Ciruelo," 3:280
"Luis Nuñez Coronel," 3:420–21
"Dietrich von Freiberg," 4:92–95

"Jean Dullaert of Ghent," 4:237–38
"Gerard of Silteo (Sileto)," 5:361
"Giles (Aegidius) of Lessines," 5:401–2
"Gaspar Lax," 8:100
"John Major," 9:32–33
"Domingo de Soto," 12:547–48
"Alvaro Thomaz," 13:349–50
"Ulrich of Strassburg," 13:534
"Vincent of Beauvais," 14:34–36
"William of Auvergne," 14:388–89

1980e "Maritain and the Notion of Scientific Progress" *Notes et Documents* (International Maritain Institute, Rome) 19 (1980): 21–26; 20 (1980): 28–35; reprinted in 1983a, 231–43.

1981a *Prelude to Galileo: Essays on Medieval and Sixteenth-Century Sources of Galileo's Thought.* Boston Studies in the Philosophy of Science, 62. Dordrecht-Boston: D. Reidel Publishing Co., 1981. Pp. xvi + 369.

1981b *Causality and Scientific Explanation.* Vol. 1. *Medieval and Early Classical Science*; Vol. 2. *Classical and Contemporary Science.* Washington, D.C.: University Press of America, 1981. Reprintings of 1972a and 1974a.

1981c "Galileo and Scholastic Theories of Impetus" *Studi sul XIV secolo in memoria di Anneliese Maier,* ed. A. Maierù and A. Paravicini Bagliani. Rome: Edizioni di Storia e Letteratura, 1981, 275–97; reprinted in 1981a, 320–40.

1981d "Aristotle and Galileo: The Uses of *Hupothesis* (*Suppositio*) in Scientific Reasoning" *Studies in Aristotle,* ed. D. J. O'Meara. Studies in Philosophy and the History of Philosophy, 9. Washington, D.C.: Catholic University of America Press, 1981, 47–77.

1982a *Religion and Science: Must There Be Conflict?* Third Annual Moreau Lecture. Wilkes-Barre, Penn.: King's College, 1982.

1982b "St. Thomas's Conception of Natural Philosophy and Its Method" *La Philosophie de la nature de Saint Thomas d'Aquin,* ed. Leo Elder. Studi Tomistici, 18. Rome: Libreria Editrice Vaticana, 1982, 7–27; reprinted in 1983a, 23–43.

1982c "Aristotle in the Middle Ages," *Dictionary of the Middle Ages,* 13 vols., ed. J. R. Strayer. New York: Charles Scribner's Sons, 1982, 1:456–69.

1982d "Comment [on J. A. Weisheipl's 'Avicenna and Aquinas']" *Approaches to Nature in the Middle Ages,* ed. L. D. Roberts. Binghamton, N.Y.: Center for Medieval and Early Renaissance Studies, 1982, 161–69.

1983a *From a Realist Point of View: Essays on the Philosophy of Science,* 2d ed. Lanham-New York-London: University Press of America, 1983. Pp. ix + 340.

1983b "Aristotelian Influences on Galileo's Thought" *Aristotelismo Veneto e Scienza Moderna,* ed. Luigi Olivieri, 2 vols. Padua: Editrice Antenore, 1983, 1:349–78.

1983c "Influssi aristotelici sul pensiero di Galileo" *Aristotelismo Veneto e Scienza Moderna,* ed. Luigi Olivieri, 2 vols., Padua: Editrice Antenore, 1983, 1:379–403; Italian translation of 1983b.

1983d "The Problem of Causality in Galileo's Science" *Review of Metaphysics* 36 (1983): 607–32.
1983e "Galileo's Early Arguments for Geocentrism and His Later Rejection of Them" *Novita Celesti e Crisi del Sapere*, ed. Paolo Galluzzi, Florence: Istituto e Museo di Storia della Scienza, 1983, 31–40.
1983f "Galileo and Aristotle in the *Dialogo*" *Angelicum* 60 (1983): 311–32.
1983g "Galilée et les professeurs jésuites du College romain à la fin du xvi siècle" *Galileo Galilei: 350 ans d'histoire, 1633–1983*, ed. P. Poupard. Tournai: Desclée International, 1983, 75–97.
1983h "Galileo's Science and Trial of 1633" *Wilson Quarterly* 7 (1983): 154–64; abbreviated version of 1983f, reprinted in 1990c.
1983i "Aquinas, Galileo, and Aristotle" (Medalist's Address) *Proceedings of the American Catholic Philosophical Association* 57 (1983): 17–24.
1984a *Galileo and His Sources: The Heritage of the Collegio Romano in Galileo's Science.* Princeton, N.J.: Princeton University Press, 1984. Pp. xiv + 371.
1984b "The Intelligibility of Nature: A Neo-Aristotelian View" *Review of Metaphysics* 38 (1984): 33–56.
1984c "Galileo and the Continuity Thesis" *Philosophy of Science* 51 (1984): 504–10.
1984d "The Philosophical Formation of Dominicans" *Angelicum* 61 (1984): 96–122.
1984e "Galileo e i Professori del Collegio Romano alla fine del secolo XVI" *Galileo Galilei, 350 anni di storia (1633–1983)*, ed. P. Poupard. Rome: Edizioni Pieme, 1984, 76–97; Italian translation of 1983g.
1985a "Galileo's Concept of Science: Recent Manuscript Evidence" *The Galileo Affair: A Meeting of Faith and Science*, eds. G. V. Coyne, M. Heller, and J. Zycinski. Vatican City: Vatican Observatory, 1985, 15–35.
1985b "Nature as Animating: The Soul in the Human Sciences" *Thomist* 49 (1985): 612–48.
1985c Dietrich von Freiberg: *De miscibilibus in mixto*, Latin text with critical apparatus, in his *Opera omnia*, Tomus IV, Schriften zur Naturwissenschaft. Hamburg: Felix Meiner Verlag, 1985, 27–47.
1985d Éloge: James Athanasius Weisheipl, O.P. 3 July 1923–30 December 1984. *Isis* 76 (1985): 566–67.
1986a *Reinterpreting Galileo* (editor), Studies in Philosophy and History of Philosophy 15, Washington: Catholic University of America Press, 1986. Pp. x + 286. "Introduction," vii–x; "Reinterpreting Galileo on the Basis of His Latin Manuscripts," 3–28 (cf. 1985a).
1986b "*Aitia*: Causal Reasoning in Composition and Rhetoric" J. D. Moss, ed., *Rhetoric and Praxis: The Contribution of Classical Rhetoric to Practical Reasoning.* Washington: Catholic University of America Press, 1986, 107–33.
1986c "Galileo's Sources: Manuscripts or Printed Works?" *Print and Culture in the Renaissance: Essays on the Advent of Printing in Europe*, ed. G. B. Tyson and Sylvia Wagonheim. Newark, Del.: University of Delaware Press, 1986, 45–54.

1986d "The Certitude of Science in Late Medieval and Renaissance Thought" *History of Philosophy Quarterly* 3 (1986): 281–91.

1986e "Galileo and His Sources" [Reply to A. C. Crombie] *Times Literary Supplement,* no. 4318, 3 January 1986, 13, 23.

1987a "The Early Jesuits and the Heritage of Domingo de Soto" *History and Technology* 4 (1987): 301–20.

1987b "Thomas Aquinas on Dialectics and Rhetoric" *A Straight Path: Studies in Medieval Philosophy and Culture: Essays in Honor of Arthur Hyman,* ed. S. Link-Salinger. Washington, D.C.: Catholic University of America Press, 1987, 244–54.

1987c "Galileo and the Professors of the Collegio Romano at the End of the Sixteenth Century" in *Galileo Galilei: Toward a Resolution of 350 Years of Debate—1633–1983,* ed. Paul Poupard, trans. Ian Campbell. Pittsburgh, Penn.: Duquesne University Press, 1987, 44–60; English translation of 1983g.

1987d "Science and Philosophy at the Collegio Romano in the Time of Benedetti," in *Cultura, Scienze e Techniche nella Venezia del Cinquecento,* Atti del Convegno Internationale di Studio "G. B. Benedetti e il suo tempo." Venice: Istituto Veneto di Scienze, Lettere ed Arti, 1987, 113–26.

1988a Galileo Galilei, *Tractatio de praecognitionibus et praecognitis* and *Tractatio de demonstratione.* Transcribed from the Latin autograph by W. F. Edwards, with an introduction, notes, and commentary by W. A. Wallace. Padua: Editrice Antenore, 1988. Pp. lxxxix + 330.

1988b "Randall *Redivivus*: Galileo and the Paduan Aristotelians" *Journal of the History of Ideas* 49, no. 1 (1988): 133–49.

1988c "Traditional Natural Philosophy" *Cambridge History of Renaissance Philosophy,* ed. C. B. Schmitt, Quentin Skinner, Eckhard Kessler, and Jill Krage. Cambridge: Cambridge University Press, 201–35.

1988d "Newton's Early Writings: Beginnings of a New Direction," in *Newton and the New Direction in Science,* ed. G. V. Coyne, S. M. Heller, and J. Zycinski. Vatican City: Vatican Observatory, 23–44.

1988e "Mechanics from Bradwardine to Galileo," in *History of Physics: Selected Reprints,* ed. Stephen G. Brush. College Park, Md.: American Association of Physics Teachers, 1988, 10–23; reprint of 1971a.

1989a "Nature, Human Nature, and Norms for Medical Ethics," in *Catholic Perspectives in Medical Morals: Foundational Issues,* ed. E. D. Pellegrino. Dordrecht-Boston: Kluwer Academic Publishers, 1989, 23–53.

1989b "Aristotelian Science and Rhetoric in Transition: The Middle Ages and the Renaissance" *Rhetorica* 7, no. 1 (1989): 7–21.

1989c "The Problem of Apodictic Proof in Early Seventeenth-Century Mechanics: Galileo, Guevara, and the Jesuits." *Science in Context* 3 (1989): 67–87.

1990a "The Dating and Significance of Galileo's Pisan Manuscripts," in *Nature, Experiment, and the Sciences. Essays on Galileo and the History of Science in Honour of Stillman Drake,* ed. Trevor Levere and W. R. Shea. Boston Studies in the Philosophy of Science, 120. Dordrecht-Boston: Kluwer Academic Publishers, 3–50.

1990b "Duhem and Koyré on Domingo de Soto," *Synthese* 83 (1990): 239–60.
1990c "Galileo's Science and the Trial of 1633," in *World History*, Vol. 2: 1500 to 20th Century, 2d ed., ed. David McComb, Guilford, CT: Duskin Publishing Group, 1990, 25–30; reprint of 1983h.
1990d "Aquinas and Newton on the Causality of Nature and of God: The Medieval and the Modern Problematic," in *Philosophy and the God of Abraham,* ed. R. J. Long and W. E. Carroll. Toronto: Pontifical Institute of Mediaeval Studies, in press.

Contributors

Andrea Croce Birch completed her doctoral studies under Rev. William A. Wallace, O.P., at The Catholic University of America. She is currently teaching philosophy at St. Mary's College, Winona, Minnesota.

Richard J. Blackwell received his Ph.D. at St. Louis University, where he has been teaching since 1961. In 1963 he translated Christian Wolff's *Preliminary Discourse on Philosophy in General*, and he co-translated Aquinas's *Commentary on Aristotle's Physics*. His *Discovery in the Physical Sciences* was published in 1969. He is also the author of numerous articles, such as "Descartes' Laws of Motion" in *Isis* and "The Inductivist Model of Science" in *Modern Schoolman*. His compilation, *A Bibliography of the Philosophy of Science, 1945–81,* was published in 1981 and his translation of Christian Huyghens's *The Pendulum Clock or Geometrical Demonstrations Concerning the Motion of Pendula as Applied to Clocks* in 1986.

Mario A. Bunge received his Ph.D. at National University LaPlata in 1952. He has been teaching at McGill University since 1966. His several books include *Causality: The Place of the Causal Principle in Modern Science* (1963), *Foundations of Physics* (1967), *Philosophy of Physics* (1973), *The Furniture of the World* (1977), *A World of Systems* (1979), *The Mind-Body Problem* (1980), and *Scientific Materialism* (1981). Among his numerous essays is "Technology as Applied Science" in *Technology and Culture*.

Francis J. Collingwood received his Ph.D. at the University of Toronto and has been teaching at Marquette University since 1950. Among his publications are *Philosophy of Nature* (1960) and *Man's Physical and Spiritual Nature* (1963) and the essays "Is 'Physical Knowledge' Limited by Its Quantitative Approach to Reality?" in *The Nature of Physical Knowledge,* edited by L. W. Friedrich, and "St. Thomas' Notion of a Physical Science" in *Ithaca*.

CONTRIBUTORS

Jean de Groot received her Ph.D. from Harvard University and has been on the faculty of The Catholic University of America since 1984. Among her publications are "On the Surprising in Science and Logic" in *Review of Metaphysics* and "Philoponus on *De Anima* II.5, *Physics* III.3, and the Propagation of Light" in *Phronesis*.

Jude P. Dougherty received his Ph.D. from The Catholic University of America in 1960. After teaching at Marquette University and Bellarmine College, he returned to The Catholic University of America, where he has served as dean of the School of Philosophy since 1967. In addition to his work as editor of *Review of Metaphysics*, he has authored or edited five books, including *Recent American Naturalism* (1960) and *The Good Life and Its Pursuit* (1984), and has published forty-five articles, which reflect a long-standing interest in the philosophy of science and in social and political philosophy.

Rom Harré, Fellow of Linacre College, Oxford, has published several books, including *An Introduction to the Logic of the Sciences* (1960, 1983), *The Anticipation of Nature* (1965), *The Principles of Scientific Thinking* (1970), *The Philosophies of Science* (1972, 1985), *Causal Powers: A Theory of Natural Necessity* (1975), *The Explanation of Social Behavior* (1976), *Social Being: A Theory of Social Psychology* (1979), and *Personal Being: A Theory of Individual Psychology* (1983). He is also editor of *A History of the Physical Sciences Since Antiquity* (1986) and co-editor of *The Encyclopedic Dictionary of Psychology* (1983).

R. F. Hassing received his Ph.D. in theoretical physics at Cornell University as well as advanced degrees in political theory at University of Toronto and in philosophy at The Catholic University of America. His essays include "Wholes, Parts, and Laws of Motion" in *Nature and System* and "The Use and Non-Use of Physics in Spinoza's Ethics" in *The Southwestern Journal of Philosophy*. He has also co-authored articles published in *Physical Review*.

Patrick A. Heelan received his Ph.D. in geophysics at St. Louis University in 1952 and his Ph.D. in philosophy at Université catholique de Louvain, Belgium, in 1964. He has been teaching at State University of New York, Stony Brook, since 1970. His published works include *Quantum Mechanics and Objectivity* (1965) and *Space Perception and the Philosophy of Science* (1983), as well as several articles, including "Quantum Logic and Classical Logic: Their Respective Roles" in

Synthese and "Hermeneutics of Experimental Science in the Context of the Life-World" in *Interdisciplinary Phenomenology*.

Richard H. Kennington studied at the Sorbonne and the University of Chicago before receiving his Ph.D. from the New School for Social Research. He has been on the faculty at The Catholic University of America since 1975. His essays include "Descartes" in *History of Political Philosophy*, "The Finitude of Descartes' Evil Genius" in *Journal of the History of Ideas*, and "The Teaching of Nature in Descartes' Soul Doctrine" in *Review of Metaphysics*. He has also edited *The Philosophy of Baruch Spinoza* (1980) and *The Philosophy of Immanuel Kant* (1985) for Studies in Philosophy and the History of Philosophy, The Catholic University of America Press.

Edward H. Madden received his Ph.D. at the University of Iowa in 1950 and has been part of the faculty of State University of New York, Buffalo, since 1964. His publications include *Structure of Scientific Thought* (1960), *Causal Powers* (1975), and *Causing, Perceiving and Believing* (1975). He has also been the author of several articles on American philosophy, including William James in *American Philosophical Quarterly*. He has also been the author of several books on American philosophy and, since 1960, has been general editor of the Harvard University Press Series of Source Books in the History of the Sciences.

Jean Dietz Moss is an associate professor and director of the Rhetoric Program at The Catholic University of America. She is the author of a number of essays on the history and interaction of rhetoric and dialectic in the period of the scientific revolution, such as "Galileo's Letter to Christina: Some Rhetorical Considerations," *Renaissance Quarterly* (1983), "The Rhetoric of Proof in Galileo's Writings on the Copernican System," *Reinterpreting Galileo*, ed. William A. Wallace (1986), and "The Rhetoric Course at the Collegio Romano in the Latter Half of the Sixteenth Century," *Rhetorica* (1986). Her publications also include a study of a Reformation sect, *Godded with God: Hendrik Niclaes and His Family of Love* (1981), and a collection of essays on classical rhetoric and the teaching of writing that she edited, *Rhetoric and Praxis* (1986).

Nicholas Rescher received degrees from Queens College (New York) and Princeton University and an honorary degree from Loyola University (Chicago). He has been a university professor of philosophy at the University of Pittsburgh since 1970 and director of its Center for Philosophy of Science since 1981. His numerous books include *Essays in Philosophical Analysis* (1969), *The Coherence Theory of Truth* (1973), *Methodological Pragmatism* (1977), and *Scientific Progress* (1978).

Robert Sokolowski received his Ph.D. at Université catholique de Louvain, Belgium, in 1963. He has been on the faculty of The Catholic University of America since 1963. His numerous publications include the following books: *The Formation of Husserl's Concept of Constitution* (1964, 1970), *Husserlian Meditations: How Words Present Things* (1974), *Presence and Absence: A Philosophical Investigation of Language and Being* (1978), *The God of Faith and Reason* (1982), and *Moral Action* (1985). He has also edited *Husserl and the Phenomenological Tradition* (1988) for The Catholic University of America Press.

Edith Sylla received her Ph.D. in the history of science from Harvard University in 1971. Apart from a stay at Cornell University in 1978–1979 as a fellow of the Society for the Humanities, she has been a member of the Department of History at North Carolina State University since 1970 and has served as assistant dean for Research and Graduate Programs in Humanities and Social Sciences at the same institution since 1985. Her numerous publications include "The A Posteriori Foundations of Natural Science: Some Medieval Commentaries on Aristotle's *Physics,* Book I, Chapters 1 and 2," *Synthese,* 40 (1979): 147–87, "The Oxford Calculators," in Norman Kretzmann, Anthony Kenny, and Jan Pinborg (eds.), *The Cambridge History of Later Medieval Philosophy* (Cambridge: Cambridge University Press, 1982), pp. 540–63, and "Galileo and the Oxford *Calculatores*: Analytical Languages and the Mean-Speed Theorem for Accelerated Motion," in William A. Wallace (ed.), *Reinterpreting Galileo,* Studies in Philosophy and the History of Philosophy, vol. 15 (Washington, D.C.: The Catholic University of America Press, 1986), 53–108.

Index

Achillini on composition of heavens, 188
Acontius, 236
acupuncture, 86
affordances, 15–17
Albert, cited by Carbone, 182, 185
Alexander of Aphrodisias: theory of natural inclination, 114–15; on subject matter of *De caelo*, 181–82
analysis and synthesis: analogy between geometry and physics, 255; in geometry (Pappus), 256–60; in natural philosophy (Newton), 260–68
Anaxagoras on composition of heavens, 187
angel and Intelligences, 191
antirealism, 12
Aquinas: commentary on *Physics* VII.1, 123–46; on subject matter of *De caelo*, 181–82; on composition of heavens, 187; on Aristotelian view of scientific certainty, 213; on probable arguments, 233
Archimedes, 269
Aristotle: intensional hierarchy, 10; continuity with the "new science," 25–26; theory of mind and imagination, 51–52, 56–58, 72; philosophy of nature, 64–70; theory of the senses and their reliability, 65–66; uniformity of nature, 67–68; realism, 69; errors of medieval followers, 70–73; on the genesis of science, 74–75; *Physics*, VII.1, 109–56; theory of light in *De anima* II.7, 158; criticism of Plato in *Physics* II.2, 162–67, 173–74; *Categories*, 166–69; *Posterior Analytics* and the Collegio Romano, 175–76; *De caelo*, 178–92; *De generatione*, 178–80; *Metaphysics* 2, 185; *Physics*, 187; on certainty being proper only to certain subjects, 212–13; *Organon* and Bacon, 235; order of demonstration, 239–40; teleological astronomy, 242–43; difference from Bacon, 251

Aristotelianism: bad, 71–75; Duhem's, 73–78
Armstrong, David, on use of dispositional concepts, 14
Aronson, Jerrold L., on bivalence, 11–12
articulations, in contrast to names, 37–39
assertions, in contrast to explanations, 40–45
astronomy, theoretical treatment by Carbone and Galileo, 186; teleological, 242–43
atomic: names, 37–39; propositions, 37–39; objects, 39; states of affairs, 39
Atomists, Greek, 29
Augustine: cited by Carbone, 184; on interpretation and truth of scripture, 202–3, 207, 219–23, 229
Averroes: commentary on *Physics* VII.1, 121–39; on subject matter of *De caelo*, 181–83
Averroism: at Padua, 26; two-truth view, 213–15
Avicenna on composition of heavens, 187

Bacon, Francis: new beginning, 26; critique of ancient philosophy, 235–51; interpretations and principal purpose of his critique, 237–38; limits of critique, 238–39; reform of order of demonstration, 239–43; starting points, ancient and correct, 243–49; anticipations, (experimental) interpretation, and laws of nature, 243–49; materialism, 246; heat as "simple nature," 245–46; question of the end, 249–51; *Advancement of Learning*, 237, 242, 251; *De Augmentis*, 241–42; *de Principiis atque Originibus*, 248; *New Organon*, 235–51
baffling phenomena, 81–93
Bailly, Jean Sylvain, 87
Barrow, Isaac, 264

323

324   INDEX

basic research, value-free and morally neutral, 102–3
Bellarmine: his *De controversiis*, 208; reply to Foscarini, 208–9, 220, 230; on interpretation, 227, 229
Berkeleyan idealism, 14
bivalence, 6, 13
Black, Max, on models, 10
Bodin, 236
Boethius of Dacia's Averroism, 213, 215
Bohr, Niels, 15–17, 51, 53, 55, 59, 74
Boyle, Robert, and policy realism, 7–9, 17, 20
Boscovich, 305
Brittan, Gordon, 275
Bruno, Giordano, 29
Buridan, Jean, on epistemological status of natural philosophy, 215–18; views shared by Galileo, 231–33
Byrne, Edmund, on probable arguments in Aquinas, 233

Cajetan on composition of heavens, 187
Campanella's *Apologia pro Galilaeo*, 210
Campbell, Alexander, 291
Capreolus on composition of heavens, 187
Carbone, Ludovico: in Wallace's "corpus," 28; commentaries on *De caelo* and *De generatione*, 179–92; summary of contents of commentaries, 192–98
Castelli, Benedetto, and letter from Galileo, 219
causal neutrality, 154
causality: weak and strong, 3–5; in terms of conditions, 3–4; David Hume on, 52; Reid and Reidian tradition, 291–307
Ceffons, Pierre, on probable and false propositions, 214–15
CERN, 11, 21
Cesi, 209
Chisholm, Roderick, 291
Clavius, 6, 177
Cohen, I. Bernard, on Newton's use of "analysis" and "synthesis," 254, 262, 264–66
Collegio Romano, 25–26, 175, 192
concept-displacement, 10
conceptual idealization, 34
conditions: necessary and sufficient, 3–4; circumambient, 4, 15
contemplation, Bacon's two ways, 237–39, 249–51
continuum, physical, according to Aristotle, 109–56

Copernican heliocentrism: condemnation by the Church, 199–200; probability and compatibility with Scripture according to Foscarini, 202–7; viewed by Bellarmine, 208–9; held by Kepler and Galileo, 225
Copernicus: regarded by Galileo and Carbone, 190–91; on truth of his physical theory, 218, 225–26, 234; book placed on Index, 223; hypothetical astronomy and relation to Bacon, 243
Copernican revolution, 26
Cosentino, 28
Cotes, Roger, 265–66
Cousin, Victor, 291
Crombie, 28
Cusa, Nicholas of, 29

De anima III, 53, 56–58
de Broglie, Louis, 74
De caelo: as treated by Carbone and Galileo, 179–92
definite descriptions, 10
De generatione, 178–80
Descartes: new beginning, 26; failure to discuss the view of Aristotle, 236; indebtedness to Bacon, 235–36; criticized by Newton, 266
demiurgic principle, 24, 31, 35
Democritus on the plurality of worlds, 185
differentiation of the sciences by Newton, 255–56
Dirac, 77
disclosure, 8–10, 11–14
dispositions, 4, 14–17
Duhem, Pierre: interpretation of Aristotle on mathematics in science, 63–79; on quantification in science, 67; on scientific development, 69; on history of Aristotelianism, 71–73; his critics, 72, 74; philosophy and physics, 75–79

ecological disaster and technology, 103–5
eidetic intuition, 49
Einstein, Albert, 74, 76–78
electrons, 18–19
Empedocles on composition of heavens, 187
energy, 6, 20
energetics, Duhem's science of, 70
Enlightenment, 26
entropy, 6
Epicurean thought and Bacon, 250–51
Euclid, 256, 269

experiments: significance of, 15–21; and Baconian "starting point," 243–45, 248
explanation: facts and, 38; in contrast to assertions, 40; forms of, 40–45; causes and, 40–44; clarification and, 40–44; stories and, 44; natural kinds and, 44

Fermi, Enrico, 54
Feynman diagrams, 18–21
form, in Aristotelian understanding of nature, 126–30
final causes: anthropomorphism according to Bacon, 241; in contrast to real causes, 242; defect of ancient contemplation, 250–51
Finocchiaro, Maurice, 28; on Galileo's *Dialogue*, 218–19
fission, 53–54
Foscarini, Paolo Antonio, 201
Foscarini's *Defense*, 206–9
Foscarini's *Letter*: condemnation by Sacred Congregation, 200; Latin translation by David Lotaeus, 201; English translation by Thomas Salusbury, 202; intentions, 202–3; substantive content and principles of interpretation, 203–5; Neoplatonic description of the sun, 205; controversy, 206–9; historical importance, 209–10
foundationalism and Bacon, 236
Franklin, Benjamin, 87
Fredette, Raymond, 28
Frisch, Otto, discovery of fission, 53–56

Gadamer, Hans Georg, 25
Galen, 114
Galileo: Wallace's work on, 23–28; the Collegio Romano and parallels with Carbone, 175–92; reaction to Foscarini's *Letter*, 201, 206; letters to Castelli and Grand Duchess Christina and notes on Bellarmine's letter, 209, 231; speaking at his trial, 211; on truth of Copernicanism (but not as matter of faith), 218, 225, 231–32; *Letter to Grand Duchess Christina*, 218–23; *Dialogue on the Two Chief World Systems*, 223–25, 228–29; on probable arguments, 225–34; on probable arguments as source of problem with Church, 229; and Buridan on reliability of science, 231–33
Garrison, James, 260–62, 269
Gibson, J. J., 8, 15
Gilbert, 235

Giles of Rome on composition of heavens, 187
Gilson, Etienne, 60
Gloy, Karen, 283–86, 288
Göttingen science and Husserl, 33
gravitation, 154–56
Gregory, James, 291, 295–96
Guerlac, Henry, on Newton's method of analysis and synthesis, 254
Guillotin, Joseph Ignace, 87

Hacking, Ian, and policy realism, 7–9
Hahn, Otto, 53
Hamilton, Sir William, 291
Hanson, N. R., 152
Hartley, 305
Heidegger, Martin, and existential hermeneutics, 23, 32–34
Heisenberg, 77
hermeneutical circle, 24–31, 32–34
hermeneutical method, whether scientific, 31–32
hermeneutical phenomenology, 24
hermeneutics: methodological, 24–31; existential, 32–34; and science, 31–32
Hesse, Mary, on models, 10
Hilbert space representation of quantum mechanics, 18
Hintikka, Jaako, on analysis, 258
historical method and narrative, 34–35
history of science, 23
home language of a community, 29
Hooke, Robert, 254, 263–64
Hobbes, 236
Hoppe, Hansgeorg, 280–81, 284, 288
Hume: on causality, 3, 52, 292–94; skepticism, 13; Reid, 292–93
Husserl: affordances and, 15; Göttingen school and, 26, 29; Heidegger and, 33; on historical method, 34–36; on eidetic intuition, 49
hypnotism, 86–87

Iamblichus, 182
Idola mentis, 235, 240–41, 250
imagination: role in science, 51–62; and models, 52
Incofer, Melchior, on Galileo's belief in truth of Copernicanism, 232
induction: economy of, 84–85; argument, 9–10; realism and, 13
inertia, 146–54
intermediate vector principle (IVP), 18–21
interpretation, process of, 29–31

Irenaeus, condemnation of view that heavens informed by rational soul, 189–90

Jean of Mirecourt's probabilism, 214–15
Jerome, condemnation of view that heavens informed by rational soul, 189–90
Jouffroy, Théodore, 291

Kant, Immanuel: Bohr and, 16–17; on psychology and physics, 271; Newton and, 272; philosophy and physics, 272–89; *Kritik der reinen Vernunft* (KrV), 273–76; *Prolegomena*, 274–75, 278, 285; *Metaphysische Anfangsgründe der Naturwissenschaften* (MAN), 277–89; outline of sciences in Architectonic, 276, 282; outline of sciences in MAN, 276–79, 282
Kepler: break with medievals, 29; on truth of Copernicanism, 218, 225–26, 234
Koertge, Noretta, on role of analysis and synthesis in scientific revolution, 260
Koyré, Alexandre, and origins of contemporary science, 26, 29

Laudan, Larry: "problem-solving," 13; positivism, 52; Reid's inductivism, 304
Lavoisier, Antoine Laurent, 87
Le Systeme du Monde, 71, 73
Leibniz: concern for method, 236; criticized by Newton, 266
light: Aristotle's theory, 158
Locke, John, 26, 236, 292–93
Lohr, 28

Mach, Ernst, 52
Mackie, J. L., 3
macrostructure, 4–5
Mahan, Asa, 291
manipulation, 9–21
Margolis, Joseph, and policy realism, 7
mastery of nature, 236–37, 251
mathematics, rooted in philosophical and geometrical traditions, 269
matter, Kant's concept of, 283, 287
Maxwell, 78
McCosh, James: Reidian tradition, 291–92; in contrast to Wayland, 296–99, 302–3; powerful particulars and causation, 300–302; Reid, 302–3; departure from rigid inductivism, 304–7
Meitner, Lise, discovery of fission, 53
Menu, Antonius, 179–80
Mesmer, Anton, 87

metaphysics, in contrast to physics according to Bacon, 242
microstructure, 4–5
mixed sciences and their subject matters, 165
Mill, J. S., 295, 302
mobile as continuum, 109
Models: iconic and sentential, 52–53; use in science, 54–55, 61–62
momentum, 20
Moore, G. E., 291
Moore, Ruth, 54
Moss, Jean Dietz, 28; on Galileo's *Letter to the Grand Duchess Christina*, 218–19
motion: Aristotelian theory of the divisibility of, 139–46; Aristotelian concept in contrast with concepts of momentum and velocity, 143–46; natural and violent, 149–51; in an imaginary one-body universe, 151–52; Kant's concept of, 285–86
motor causality principle: motion and causality of parts, 117–30; natural form, 128; soul, 130–34; stopping thesis, 134–39; fluids, 137–39; divisibility of the movable, 139–46; classical mechanics, 146; relation to Newtonian inertia and gravitation, 146–56

names and articulations, 37, 48–50
natural form, 128
natural kinds, 10, 45–47; contrasted with laws of nature, 244–46
Nature, British journal, 53
Newton: laws of inertia and gravitation compared to motor causality principle, 146–56; three laws of motion and their causal neutrality, 147–54; controversy over methodology, 253–56; on analysis and synthesis in natural philosophy; on empirical character of geometry, 269–70; *Opticks*, 253–70; *Principia*, 254–70; Kant, 271–72; Reidian tradition, 292–93; hypotheses, 305
Nicholaus of Autrecourt's probabilism, 214–15, 230, 233
Nifo cited by Galileo and Carbone, 182
nuclear disaster and technology, 103–5

Ockham, William of, 213
ontology: category, 10; common, 12; transcendental philosophy, 279–81
optics: in late antiquity, 157–58; philosophical theories of light and vision and geometrical optics, 157–58; Philo-

ponus' reconciliation of geometrical optics with an intromission theory of vision, 159–61
Oresme, Nicole, on natural philosophy and certainty, 216–18, 230
Osiander on the Copernican system as mathematical hypothesis, 225–26, 234

packing fraction, 53
Pappus of Alexandria on geometrical analysis and synthesis, 256–61
parapsychology, 86
particles, virtual and real, 18–21
perception, realist theory of, 7–8
Perpinian, Petrus, 177
phenomenology of life-world, 33
Philoponus: separating the three dimensional in optics, 157–74; commentary on *De anima* II.7, 158–61; commentary on *Physics* II.2, 161–68; *Corollarium de Loco*, 168–69; on space, 170–71
philosophy, task of, 37
philosophy of nature: perennial character, 64–65
photon propagator, 18
photons, 18–21
phronesis, 30
physical continuum and self-motion, 109
physical forms, separability in thought from the three-dimensional according to Philoponus, 161
physical theory: primary aim according to Duhem, 69; method and limitations according to Duhem, 76–80
physics: contemporary, 5, 16; classical, 16; high-energy, 19; Göttingen school, 26; as a probablistic endeavor for Duhem, 75; pre-modern, 109; Newton's, 146–56; post-Newtonian, 109–10, 146, 151; Descartes's, 152–53; in contrast to metaphysics according to Bacon, 242; and philosophy in Kant, 271–90
Pierce, Charles Sanders, 91
Pines, S., on motor causality principle, 114–15
Plaas, Peter, 279–81, 283, 285–86
place, as three-dimensional measure of a body, 170–71
Planck, Max, 69, 74
Plato: Koyré and, 29; *Timaeus*, 65; cited by Carbone and Galileo, 183, 187; on order of demonstration, 239; school corrupted by natural theology, 241; difference from Bacon, 250–51; on formal mathematics, 256
Poincaré, Henri, 52

Polanyi, Michael, 90
positivism, 51–52
Posterior Analytics, 26
powerful particulars, 300–301
prejudice structure of interpretation, 25–27
Priestly, 305
probabilism, in late Middle Ages, 214–18
probable arguments, 225–34; source of Galileo's problems with the Church, 229; conflict between Jesuits and Dominicans, 233
progress, 11
properties: constitutive and dispositional, 4, 6; pseudo-occurent, 6
protocol statements, 38
psychoanalysis, 86, 88–89
Putnam, Hilary, 52, 59
Ptolemy, 243
Pythagoras: cited by Carbone and Galileo, 183; superstition, 241
Pythagorean astronomy, 199–200

quantification, Duhem on, 75
quantity, independence and three-dimensionality, 166
quantum physics: beginnings and Max Planck, 69
Quine, W. V. O., 59

Ramus, Peter, 236
Randall, J. H., on role of analysis and synthesis in scientific revolution, 260
realism: scientific, 6; policy, 7–21; truth and, 7; positivism, 51–52
reduction, 11, 38
reductionism, 118, 153
reference corpus, 27–31, 35
Reid, Thomas: influence, 291–92; critique of Hume's skepticism, 292–94; analysis of causality no great improvement over Hume, 294–96; rigid inductivism, 304
Remes, Otto, 258
Rescher, Nicholas, 59
revisability, indefinite, 10–11
Riccardi, Niccolo, on probable but false conclusions, 230–31; view repeated in Galileo's *Dialogue*, 232
Royer-Collard, Pierre Paul, 291
Rugerius, Ludovicus, 179–80
Rutherford, E., 68
Ryle, Gilbert, 14

Schäfer, Lothar, 283, 285

Schon, 10
Schrodinger, 77
science: and technological progress, 85; basic, 95–97; applied, 97–98; in contrast to technology, 100–105; and scripture according to Foscarini, 202–3
scientific research and exploration metaphor, 84
self-evidence, kinds of, 42
semiotic field, 35
Shea, 28
Simplicius on subject matter of *De caelo*, 181–82
skepticism, 13–14
Soarez, Cypriano, 177
Socrates, 240
Sommervogel, 28
Soncinas on composition of heavens, 187
spatial extension and three-dimensionality, 169–70
species neutrality, 111
Spinoza, 236
standpoints, first and third person, 32–34
Stefani, Giacinto, 230
Stewart, Dugald: on Newton, 254; on analysis and synthesis among the ancients, 258–59; on analysis and synthesis, 267; Reidian tradition, 291–92; inductivism and hypotheses, 304–6
Stoic thought and Bacon, 250–51
Strassman, Fritz, 53
Strawson, P. F., and Aristotelian realism, 60
"summary law of nature" in Bacon, 246
Syrianus Magnus, 182

Tappan, Henry, 291
Telesius, 235, 242
technology, 98–101
theory: plausibility, 10–11; in contrast to phenomena, 92–93
Toulmin, Stephen, 10
tracks and clicks, 19–21
Trismegistus, 185
truth: policy realism, 10–11; poietic, 31, 35–36; *aletheia* and, 32

universe: causes, perfection, and unity in Carbone and Galileo, 183–86; eternity, 186
Ur-stuff, 16–21

Vallius, Paulus, 28, 175–79; 182
value judgments, in science and technology, 102–5
van Fraasen, 13
Villoslada, 28
virus theory of disease, 11
vision, theory in late antiquity, 157–61
Vitelleschi, Mutius, 179–80

Walker, R. C., 284, 287
Wallace, W. A.: contemporary physics, 3; work on Galileo's early Latin manuscripts, 25–28; on motor causality principle, 116–17; on Galileo and the Collegio Romano, 175–78; Reidian tradition, 292; on Reid, 304
Wayland, Francis: Reidian tradition, 291–92; analysis of concept of power, 296–99; knowledge of biological science, 304
Weisheipl, J. A., on motor causality principle, 114–16
Werkmeister, W. H., 283

yoga, 86

Zimara on subject matter of *De caelo*, 181–82
Zuñiga, Diego de, and Copernican heliocentrism, 199–200